ALL MY
PAIN
A N D
SUFFERING

Michael Milo Faff

BALBOA.
PRESS

A DIVISION OF HAY HOUSE

Balboa Press books may be ordered through booksellers or by contacting:

Balboa Press
A Division of Hay House
1663 Liberty Drive
Bloomington, IN 47403
www.balboapress.com
1 (877) 407-4847

Print information available on the last page.

ISBN: 978-1-9822-2360-1 (sc)
ISBN: 978-1-9822-2359-5 (hc)
ISBN: 978-1-9822-2363-2 (e)

Library of Congress Control Number: 2019902886

Balboa Press rev. date: 05/15/2019

CONTENTS

PROLOGUE

HABITS

Suspend your habits of beliefs around what you believe is the cause of your pain and suffering. This read will be a new and different journey for most who have stumbled upon this book. Since about 95 percent of the thoughts we have every day are habits of yesterday and our past, suspending them may be difficult. This is because we believe we are rational and independent thinkers, and we believe we can and do make up our own minds about what we believe and don't believe, what we see and what we don't.

However, the fact is, we have been programmed through family, culture, and society as well as other factors to automatically respond to life and our pain and suffering in habitual ways. And maybe, just maybe, there is another way of understanding that pain and suffering, an off-the-wall shift in our understanding, a shift in awareness. Sometimes when we become so accustomed to a behavior or understanding in a certain way and have carried it in our belief system from a very early age, we just accept it as the only way of being.

Because of our investment in our belief system and our past experiences, it becomes impossible to imagine any other way of understanding how life unfolds. However, we will approach our pain and suffering completely differently and present an interesting alterative; but we will have to set aside our current, habitual selves for a while.

In truth, it's not all that different, but it's far from the mainstream understanding by a long way. It's an old idea in new clothes, and it may look different at first. There is an old saying: "There is nothing new under the sun." And that's true, you know.

A Point of Interest

I am dyslexic. While it's challenging for me, reading this book may be an interesting experience for you. Throughout my life I have kept the fact of my dyslexia very secret right up to quite recently, because of the pain and suffering I felt from friends, lovers, and strangers who glimpsed this malady. If others caught me in a dyslexic moment, I felt judged as being less than them and not quite good enough, but I am too old now to care as much as I did when I was younger. However, on occasions I must admit that I still have the old fears come up inside me of shame, embarrassment, and anxiety when I'm caught.

While this book has gone through the hands of proofreaders, you may still encounter sentences that seem to have a missing word. If that happens, be creative and come up with a word or two that fills the space for you.

This piece of work can be challenging or fun. It may seem like a game of Where's Waldo? at times. But I can assure you that in my mind's eye, it's so clear and flows so smoothly; it is a beautiful and exciting endeavor, at least inside me. At times there may be a slight disconnect between what I see in my mind's eye and the way it ends up on the page. See how clever you can be at clarifying it in your mind's eye so it works for you.

Words are only metaphors for what lies beyond. You may even be stimulated to see life differently, and that can be a good thing and a lot of fun.

Science

Science isn't the driving force of this read. Science is referenced only occasionally. Our science is an ever-changing stream of ever-changing understandings of how things seem to work. What we hold to be true today doesn't mean it will be true tomorrow, even though it may seem to be scientifically true at this moment. To understand that science is an ever-changing commodity may be frightening to some, and that may be part of their habits of beliefs we will need to set aside for a while.

We may be stuck in the old paradigm of "I'll believe it when I see it." The truth is, when you believe it, you are more likely to see it. Why? Because where your mind goes, awareness will flow. The processes of believing and seeing happen together, and they have you believe it; its proof will rise with the belief. It is a dance between two energy systems, with the first being inside you in the mind and the second being outside you. The belief, the thought, happens first; then later, science or imagination uncovers the outer physical proof. Which one is more important—science or imagination? Imagination. You know that, right? Nothing happens without first imagining it is happening inside you. It's a game of "Let's pretend." Or a thought experiment of "What if?" Once you form the question of "What if?" the creative mind will move heaven and earth to answer your question.

BITS AND PIECES

Every day we pick up something for our minds to chew on. A little here, something there, and we just go on with our days and lives. After a while we have a lot of bits and pieces of things but no idea exactly where they all came from. This read is a way for me to put my bits and pieces into some reasonable order. In a real sense, this is what this book is for me, and I hope you will like it too.

Growing up, I had an Erector Set that came in a metal box. It was full of metal bits and pieces, little screws and nuts, small tools, and an instruction book for making models and ideas of how to use all the parts. I didn't play with it much. However, my head is a little like that metal box of bits and pieces, because inside of my head are all these models and ideas. The parts come from all kinds of sources, and I will never remember where I got most of them.

So there are a few references, but know that I got all these parts and ideas in this read from someone or something else, because there is nothing new under the sun; I said that before. The only thing that may be somewhat new is the way I put them together for me and now for you.

LITTLE BOOKLETS

I am a clinical psychotherapist at the masters level. I started late in my career as a clinical psychotherapist, receiving my graduate degree in humanistic and clinical psychology at age sixty-four after retiring from my day job. My clients thought I knew a lot more than I did, because I carried the mantle of years, which is another way of saying I'm on the mature side. They would ask questions, for which I had no idea how to answer. To not blow my cover, I would say, "We'll talk about that next session." Then I would go home, research the question, and write a page or two to answer their question and give it to them in our next session. I kept copies in case someone else asked the same question.

Some questions required more the than a few pages, and I ended up putting little booklets together. Sometimes clients brought the booklets back, all marked up in red and underscored to show me all the quirky things dyslexics do when they write things down on paper; and of course, I couldn't see them when I was writing them down. Dyslexics don't read what is on the paper; they read what is in their heads and project it onto the paper.

Over the years I have put together dozens of these papers and little booklets, and I gave them to clients. It is out of these booklets that this book has sprung. There is an interesting side to this approach. Since each separate booklet was a stand-alone endeavor, when I combined them in this book, certain topics and ideas came up more than once, but because they were applicable to different questions, they weren't always quite the same answers, even though it was the same idea and about the same topic. So you may notice the same topic or idea handled in slightly different ways in different chapters.

It is like looking through the different facets of a diamond. Looking through one facet, you see part of what is inside from that angle; and when looking at it through another facet, you see a different part of the stone from a slightly different angle. As you move through the book, you may have the feeling you are rereading some things over again, and you may be. However, it will be, in most cases, like looking from a new or slightly different understanding of that topic because it's an underpinning of a deeper process.

GLOSSARY OF TERMS

There is a glossary in the back of the book. I have defined some terms anew and make up others because I couldn't find a term that fit what I wanted to say or the way I wanted to use it. The first time I use a term that is in the glossary I put a "G" in superscript next to it.

Don't take this all so seriously. If you don't like the term I used, figure out how I'm using it and come up with your own definition for the term. I am developing models of how things work for me. Maybe you will get excited, look deeply into your life, and see things differently for you. Maybe you'll even see things a lot differently.

NOT MANY

Because your ego, your self-created identity, is always on guard to maintain its control of your life, I don't think there will be many who are ready to see their pain and suffering differently. The ego has a way of asking questions that completely blunt or stop communication; and of course, anything new or different is dangerous to the ego. Even so, there may be a few brave souls who are ready to step outside the illusion; move off the grid; disconnect from the norm; and become abnormal in new, different, and exciting ways.

Changing your habitual way of looking at things may cause you to look at things completely differently, and that could be a good thing. Because there's nothing new under the sun, there is nothing new in this read; so don't get confused and think this is so strange and ambiguous that it doesn't make sense. The only thing that may seem strange is the way I put the bits and pieces together, the ones I have been carrying around.

You Are What You Eat

Throughout this read, I keep mentioning the connection between the mind and body, and the fact that to have a healthy body, you must change your mind. What you put in your body and how the body feels are decisions of the mind. The choices you make in your mind determine what you will put in the body. For the most part, it is driven by family and cultural experiences. And it's also driven by the food industry, which knows how to manipulate the mind's filtering systems by increasing doubt in our food choices of what we put in our bodies i.e. "Are your tired? Studies show if you are not getting enough protein you can get tired. So eat more red meat." Their goal is to sell product, not to promote health. If what they sell also is healthy, that's good. If it isn't so healthy, well then, "Buyer beware." The more doubt we have about our food choices, the easier it is to manipulate those choices through our logical, rational, lying minds.

The food choices with little doubt attached to them are fresh plant-based foods. Even in selecting plant-based foods, each grower will add some doubt into our choices. Why would growers do that? They want to sell their product more than someone else's. They are in the food industry, and they need to sell produce. However, fresh plant-based foods will always be a better choice for the body.

So as far as our food choices go, I know you think you are making up your own mind. Unfortunately, you have no idea how contaminated your mind is because of the manipulative advertising you are constantly exposed to, starting in childhood. Cut through all that and stop listening to and watching advertising; start eating plant-based foods. It will be a good foundation for healing the body and changing the mind.

Self-Talk

As part of my process, I will be talking to myself. Well, I really know it is you I am talking to, but this helps me to reframe my thoughts as if I am talking to myself. I will be putting those thoughts in *italics*.

Have fun.

CHAPTER 1

Energy, Energy Everywhere, and Not an Electron Do I See

THE DANCE OF CAUSE AND EFFECT

When we have pain and suffering, we look to the body for answers to our problems, because all pain and suffering appear to be a reflection of feelings within the physical body. Even if we have emotional stress and discomfort, we know that only because of how they feel in the body, as our conscious minds reported them. There will always be a physical component in the body that needs to be relieved for the mind^G to become calm and stress free. When the body is at ease and comfortable, we feel at peace, calm, and normal in both mind and body.

To understand our current pain and suffering, we may need to journey through our past experiences with pain and suffering. We have memories of what they are. We have memories of how we dealt with our pain and suffering that go back to when Mommy kissed our boo-boos and made them better. This subject may excite our prejudices, beliefs, and memories—and also our hopes and fears. What has worked for us in the past and what hasn't are what we now accept and believe about our pain and suffering and are now a deep part of our total belief system, which includes who we think we are. Thinking of our pain and suffering differently may challenge our understanding of who we

1

think we are—our identities. And because our identities so firmly fit into our belief systems, resistance to change may cloud the very thing we need most: a new understanding of pain and suffering and where they come from.

To imagine our pain and suffering differently will take courage because it means letting go of a lot of truths we have held for a long time and accepting the possibility of forming new truths that aren't true yet. We may arrive at a new truth we never imagined before but one that has always been there in the shadowy recesses of our minds, and within the ancient roots of our mystic and cultural past. It may take some time to bring into the light of today the flowers of ancient yesterdays. Creating a new truth and getting rid of an old one may be the only ways to heal our pain and suffering.

To start, a new appreciation of the mind and body is needed, and a new understanding of the relationship between the mind and the body will be required.

EVERYTHING IS ENERGY

"Everything is only energy." You may have heard that statement before, maybe many times before, but you may have given it only a passing thought as if to say, *Right, but that's not the real world!* However, in a very real, scientific, provable, and factual way, everything is really energy and only energy. This statement is the foundation of everything. What we think of as "the real world" is a special case or a certain range of energy vibration that is slow enough for our senses^G to pick up information about it, much the same way classic Newtonian physics is a special range within quantum physics. We will treat the statement that "everything is only energy" as the fact it is and the world of our five senses as a special part of our overall energy universe.

I said in the introduction, "There is nothing new under the sun," which is another way of saying, "Everything is already here." All we are doing in this book is uncovering what is already here in the fabric of the world and the universe around us. If we can't uncover it, that doesn't mean it's not here. It means only that we haven't uncovered it yet, because everything is already here in some form or another.

THE BODY

When we look inside our bodies, we might come to the conclusion that the body is made up of just a whole bunch of separate systems, including the circulatory system, respiratory system, immune system, digestive system, heart stimulation systems, elimination system, and many other systems. There are systems on top of systems. There are systems watching other systems. There are systems waiting on other systems. There are systems triggering other systems into operating. The whole thing is one big, magnificent, interdependent system. When we try to understand one system apart from its interconnection with the whole, we lose its purpose.

While it is interesting to take a system apart and reduce it to its smallest components to understand its inner workings, we can appreciate its function only when observing it holistically as it operates within the complete magnificent system that is the body. Each of those separate systems has its own energy needs, frequency, method of operating, and function within the body; it also has its own methods of communicating with, and responding to, all the other systems. They turn on and off, and modulate depending on the needs of the whole body system. Each system is interrelated, interconnected, and interdependent on every other system in the body in some way, or it wouldn't be in the body; and in this whole magnificent body, not a word is spoken. Yet the most complex and magnificent system of communication is at work, using electromagnetic and chemical messages.

From outside the body, we view this whole matrix as an independent, moving, living human being. However, inside it is very much a dependent community of parts and systems; when healthy, the body's systems operate harmoniously with each other. When the systems aren't in harmony, the body is in trouble, and so is the mind.

The operating system for each of the dependent systems in the body is at root energy. Since each system oscillates somewhat differently, based on the changing energy needs of the body's systems, each system creates noise in the body. Oscillation of energy is the definition of noise. The energy fluctuations that create the different frequencies or oscillations may be in the form of electrical, magnetic, and chemical energies or combinations of these energy forms.

As each operating system radiates a unique and changing noise or pattern, it produces an energy signature. As long as we are alive, the interplay of all these operating systems together will create, generate, and radiate "noise," and that is the "energy signature" or "energy field" of the body. When the body is operating as a healthy and energetic whole within the total matrix of the mind and body, we will have a healthy energy signature. If one or more systems aren't operating normally or are diseased, the energy signature will be different. Many of these unique radiating energies can be viewed with modern equipment such as EKGs, MRIs, or a plain old stethoscope the family doctor carries around his or her neck.

The radiating energy doesn't and cannot stay within the skin of the body. It moves out into the surrounding environment, and depending on the operating energies that produced its energy signature, that radiating energy can be analyzed. The stronger the producing energy, the stronger and more penetrating will be its radiated energy within the body and into the surrounding environment. The strongest signature in the body is that of the heart. We can think of the heart as the carrier wave on which rides the whole energy signature.

We might think of a symphony orchestra. Its beautifully harmonized sound illustrates a healthy state of the body, while a lack of harmony between its sections represents a state of disease or disharmony. Each system operating in the matrix of the body affects the structure and energy signature of the total radiated energy field. The radiant energy of any one system will cancel, reinforce, neutralize, or balance the total system based on its interconnections and resonance within the body matrix. This consistently changing dance between the internal systems of the body will develop interference patterns, and when things inside the body are normal, the radiant energy field surrounding the body is normal. Of course, when one or more systems in the body are diseased, the radiant energy field will be different. *(You get the idea, right?)*

This resultant energy field is much more complex than any one individual system within the matrix. A funny thing about energy fields: most of the time, they operate in frequencies outside our ability to interpret them. Since this radiant energy field of the body isn't recognized within our normal sensory transmission, we find it difficult to accept that it exists at all, but there it is. There are modern electronic instruments that can detect some elements of this energy field.

Throughout human history, not knowing or having verification with our senses has always been problematic for us. "I'll believe it when I see it" has been our standard of acceptance. When the periodic table of elements was established, only a few elements were known. Spaces were left in the table for the undiscovered elements that were believed to exist but hadn't yet been found or known at the time. As modern instrumentation and creative insight have improved, more and more of those unknown blank spaces on the chart have been filled in with more added. There was a knowing long before there was proof that there were elements to fill those spaces.

There has always been knowledge that the body is energy and an energy system that has an energy field around it. But because of our poor sensory instrumentation and filtering of the input data by the subconscious mind, some have found it difficult to believe the energy field of the body is there or was real.

Humankind has always developed tools to expand our five senses and their limited abilities. Using tools is the hallmark of human beings. We now have instruments that can measure the energy radiation around and inside this matrix, which is the body. So now just because we can't detect the body's energy field with our unaided senses' abilities, we know there is an energy field around the body. We now have enough scientific data to know it exists for sure.

The human sensory system is quite limited compared to other animals as we know, and because of that fact, we develop distorted ways of looking at our reality and our bodies. There was a time when everyone believed the world was flat. Now, if people believe the world is flat, society may put them into treatment and give them wonderful medications to help them cope with the new reality of a round world.

Beliefs are very strong and potent defenders of our currently held reality paradigm. A paradigm is our individual and personal belief and understanding of how our current world operates. Our paradigm is our world. Paradigms can also be global, national, social, familial, and individual or a combination of all these; however, the most important paradigm is the one we have and believe to be true for ourselves. To change our paradigm, which is our belief system, we need overwhelming evidence that our beliefs are no longer true for us. Our ability to change is related to our insight and openness to the information around us. If we are a closed system for information, where new information cannot enter easily, it will be difficult to change. Some people enjoy this kind of security, and this may work for them. However, change will always happen.

For a global belief to change, a paradigm shift is needed. For a paradigm shift to occur, a "critical mass" of believers in the new paradigm must be reached. As the mass of consciousness begins to take on the new paradigm, a tipping point is reached, and at that point a paradigm shift will occur, and a new understanding of our world will be put in place.

The critical mass needed for a paradigm shift depends on many factors—in other words, which institutions or authorities support the old paradigm; which social, cultural, and religious histories support the old paradigm; and which family loyalties support the old paradigm and so on. New ideas have a hard time moving into consciousness, and this is appropriate given that they change the way our world operates. However, critical mass doesn't have to be very big to reach the tipping point for a new paradigm to be put in place. History has shown that, depending on the paradigm involved, the critical mass for a paradigm shift to occur and a new paradigm to be put in place generally varies between 5 and 12 percent. The critical mass needed to shift our paradigm around, understanding and acknowledging that the mind or body is an energy system and has an energy field or aura, is fast approaching. And when it happens, it won't be a big deal. It will seem quite natural, and we will say, "Well, of course, I knew that."

If you are a *Star Trek* fan, you may be able to picture Dr. McCoy, "Bones," scanning the body of an injured person using a handheld, little, black box device, about the size of a cell phone, to determine what is wrong with the person and what action is needed to save and heal him or her. The scanner apparently gathers information about what was injured, where the injury was in the body, and what was required to heal him or her, all from the radiating energy from the injured body. Does that seem much different from having a doctor perform an EKG or listen to your heart with a stethoscope before taking action to support the patient? So, to understand that the radiant energy field or aura of the body can give off information about the health, disease, and well-being of a person doesn't seem to be that foreign of a concept. If you talk to a physicist about this energy field around the body, he or she is more likely to tell you that "all we are is just energy" and quote Einstein's famous formula, $E=MC^2$.

Do you think we have wandered far from our goal of understanding our pain and suffering? No, we are right on target.

CHAPTER 2

Two Minds

THE MIND

In view of the fact that the body's energy field can give us information about the health of the body, the field is also able to give us information about the health of the mind—our mental and emotional health. Since in this life the body and mind are entangled, entwined, interconnected, and locked together, the mind is also an energy source and as such also affects and influences the radiated energy field. We might even think of changing the name "body energy system" to something more appropriate to this interconnectedness of the mind and body, because it isn't just a body energy field. It is a mind/body aura.

If we look at someone who is depressed, that emotional state will be reflected in his or her physical body; facial and vocal expressions as well as gestures of behavior are indicators of their emotional state and effect. We may see a person looking sad or lonely or showing some other physical trait we interpret as depression. Since our outside physical expressions are a reflection of our inside emotional energy, it would seem reasonable and obvious that the aura around the body would also reflect the inside mental condition.

Because of social conditioning, outside physical expression may not always reflect the inside emotional energy state moving through the body. We may hide our feelings. However, the energy field of the mind/

8

body hasn't been so conditioned and will therefore reflect our true inside emotional state. Some people have consciously lost awareness of their mind's or body's emotional state by consistently hiding their feelings because of fear or earlier family programming. Showing feelings or emotions may have proved to be too dangerous or unacceptable behavior in their family or social environment; therefore, they have learned to hide the physical expression of their feelings, even from their conscious awareness. Yet the energy is still trapped there in the body, affecting their lives, health, and energy fields.

We may hide the outer expression of our inner feelings, but the body will struggle to express its true self and will push out into the physical world in some way, asking for healing. When the pain of struggle in hiding our feelings becomes too intense to keep hidden inside, it will find a way of expressing itself through the body, both mentally and physically, consciously or unconsciously. There will be an inner discomfort or disease in the body until it is healed and released. If we don't release that inner stress, the body will continue to send us messages that change is needed; and they will become more intense.

So what is this part of us we call "the mind"? Is it the brain or something more? Like so many things we will stumble across in our quest to understand pain and suffering, we don't know; and there is little agreement between our fellow travelers on this quest to understand what the mind is. Though there has been a long investigation throughout history by philosophers, religious leaders, psychologists, and cognitive science, the mind is still an undefined, mysterious part of us. (Wikipedia—Mind: 3rd paragraph)

For our purpose, we need a working definition of "the mind"; and since there is no agreement, if the definition or model we use seems to fit most cases, then it will suit our purposes right now. We will be working with the relationship between the body and something else I have called "the mind." That something else appears to be a combination of the functions of the mind, brain, and central nervous system. The brain and central nervous system are components we can explore with our senses; however, the mind is more elusive. Our senses aren't developed enough to detect the mind. It's like the energy field of the mind/body; it's there, and we know it is, but we can't sense it, at least not directly.

(Since you may not agree with the model I am using, you may select another model. Just know I am using this one. If a better model comes along, we can change it. I don't want to get hung up in details here. It is what's behind the details of what the mind is that I am interested in.)

When we talk about the "active mind,^{G}" we will be talking about the combination of mind, brain, and the central nervous system. If there is a specific attribute of one of the components we want to highlight, we will specifically call it out. This may not be the perfect model, but it does leave the door open for us to change our minds and come up with a better definition for the mind if one occurs to us.

Since we aren't exactly sure of what the mind is, we can talk about a conventional understanding. We have two basic parts, types, or separate realms of the mind, which by convention we call the "conscious mind"^{G} and the "subconscious mind"^{G} or "unconscious mind.^{G}" Some theories separate the subconscious and unconscious realms, but in realizing we don't know what they really are anyway, we will use only "subconscious mind" for that realm, but in this model, subconscious and unconscious are the same. Each realm of the conscious mind and subconscious mind has its own part to play in how we experience our environment, world, universe, and lives.

We know a lot about how the conscious mind works, because we are consciously aware of its activities and how it functions. As for the other part, the subconscious mind, we have little knowledge or understanding of how it operates. The main reason for this lack of knowledge about the subconscious mind is because it is out of our conscious awareness, and we are unconscious of its workings; however, we can see its effects within the environmental milieu of our behaviors. We know some of the subconscious mind's inputs and outputs but little about what happens inside this black box of the subconscious mind.

THE TWO SEPARATE MINDS

The conscious and subconscious minds are like two separate countries. They may or may not have a common border; however, each appears to have its own language, laws, and methods of operating. Since we are aware of only the conscious mind, it's easy to conclude that the conscious mind is the most important part of the mind, and we may even think it's the only part of the mind because it fills our awareness so completely.

In truth, the conscious mind is quite small compared to the subconscious mind based on their operating functions, at least by a factor of a billion to one or maybe more. Any statistics mentioned about size and processing speed of the subconscious mind should be taken with a grain of salt because they vary wildly from one study to the next. There is a much closer agreement in the scientific community for the size and processing speed of the conscious mind. Also, there is closer agreement for the working and data transmission speed of our senses that delivers data to the mind.

Processing speeds are given in bits of data per second, where a "bit" is the smallest unit of data; and this will be our reference unit for our comparing processing and transmission speeds of senses as well as the conscious and subconscious mind. Searching for the processing speed of subconscious mind on the Internet has revealed a range of between forty billion bits per second to four hundred billion bits per second. We are looking for a relative comparison between the conscious and subconscious minds, and exact numbers aren't that important for our purposes, nor are they available.

The conscious mind processes data within a range from forty bits per second to one hundred bits per second. To arrive at this processing speed for the conscious mind, many different models were used and types of people where tested. While scientific research will continue to determine with more accurate ranges of operating speeds for the conscious and subconscious minds, for our purposes we need only recognize that the subconscious mind processes tremendously faster than the conscious mind; and to acknowledge the conscious mind is puny compared to the subconscious mind. This will be enough for now for our purpose. (Posted on 26/08/2009 by Speed Reader Conscious vs subconscious processing power; http://spdrdng.com/posts/conscious-vs-subconscious-processing)

The speed in which sensory data is delivered to the mind is important to know so we can gain a different understanding of our pain and suffering. The processing speed of our senses is pretty well agreed on. Again, this is because our senses are physical instruments and easier to test, which means we have a better scientific understanding of them. The combined sensory input data transmitted to the mind from all the senses is at a rate of eleven million bits per second. Of that, about ten million bits per second come from the eyes as visual data, and about 40 percent of the brain is used to process visual information.

The following gives a clear picture of all the actions going on inside us at every given second:

- Consciousmindprocessingspeed—fortytoonehundredbitspersecond (http://spdrdng.com/posts/conscious-vs-subconscious-processing)
- Subconscious mind processing speed—forty billion to four hundred billion bits per second (http://spdrdng.com/posts/conscious-vs-subconscious-processing)
- Sensory data transmission speed—eleven million bits per second (https://www.britannica.com/topic/information-theory/Physiology)

BACKUP INFORMATION ON TRANSMISSION AND PROCESSING SPEEDS

There is a lot of information on the Internet on different studies. The following are just a few to whet your appetite. They are so counter our beliefs about how the physical world operates that we may find it hard to work them into our paradigm of beliefs and may try to ignore or negate them. Why would we do that? Because they are outside our belief system, and they hurt the egoic self to have to change beliefs. Again, the conscious mind operates in the very slow lane and out of contact with what is happening on the superhighway of information between sensory input and the subconscious mind's processing of the information. The conscious mind isn't aware that the information it sees has been processed before it sees it, and it believes it is seeing the whole truth and nothing but the truth; but of course it's not.

Transmission Speed of the Senses

In other words, the human body sends eleven million bits per second to the brain for processing, yet the conscious mind seems to be able to process only fifty bits per second.

(https://www.britannica.com/topic/information-theory/Physiology)

Processing Speed of the Conscious Mind

Many researchers (being human) expected that the human brain would show a tremendous information processing capability. Interestingly enough, when researchers sought to measure information processing capabilities during "intelligent" or "conscious" activities, such as reading or piano playing, they came up with a maximum capability of less than fifty bits per second.

(https://www.britannica.com/topic/information-theory/Physiology)

Processing Speed of the Subconscious Mind by Asking Google, "How Fast Is the Subconscious Mind?"

Answer: "Another study suggests that the subconscious mind processes about 400 billion bits of information per second, and the impulses travel at a speed of up to one hundred thousand miles per hour!" (August 26, 2009).

THE ACTIVE MIND[G]

All that transmitting and processing of information is done without a word spoken. It's all by unique electromagnetic and chemical signals and messages happening at lightning speeds. It is much like Morse code; it all must be decoded in real time to be used, and that's the job of what we call the "active mind." The active mind appears to be a combination of the mind, which we know little about; the brain, which we know something about but not nearly as much as there is to know; and the central nervous system, which we know more about. We will use the term "active mind" for that unique interface between mind, brain, and central nervous system, where interpretations, perceptions, and the holographic picture in our heads are made.

The holographic depiction in our heads will have varying degrees of filtered sensory information, depending on the individual. Some people make more use of one sensory input than others, being more auditory (sound) or kinesthetic (touch) as the predominant orientation of their world. Therefore, while most people may be visual, our individual internal hologram of our world is uniquely ours.

All we know consciously is the decoded information after the active mind has created an interpretation and signaled the mind and body on how to respond, which is to say the end of a very long process of all our lightning-fast internal-processing systems. The conscious mind knows and reports to us only what has happened after it has already happened because of its slow processing speed. The conscious mind just cannot keep up with the rapid internal action. What is really out there in the outside energy system, on the edge of our awareness where all there is energy, is really unknown to us. However, that doesn't stop us from believing we know what is really happening out there in the outside energy world by the stories our conscious minds report to us. And the conscious mind is really the least informed and the last to know about anything happening in the mind or body, but don't we believe it knows everything?

The Subconscious Mind's Filtering System^G

We will be talking about and the term "subconscious mind's filtering system" a lot, and it will help us to understand the function of the subconscious mind better. Because we are concerned about our pain and suffering, we will be concerned now about negative and unhealthy beliefs, experiences, and references attached to negative memories and making up a great part of the subconscious mind's filtering system. Later, we will introduce a holographic model.

We need to clear something up before we can understand why the subconscious mind has a filtering system. We will go into more detail later, but for now know that all the information and input data from the senses go directly to the subconscious mind; and the subconscious mind filters through the data, looking for information that is important and familiar for us in the moment. *(You see, the subconscious mind isn't concerned about the event that is happening. It is concerned only about what is familiar within a relationship to protecting you and keeping you safe based on the past. Therefore, most of the information you get from your conscious mind is about keeping you safe; and you have no idea what's really happening inside you or in the outside energy system. But again, you believe you know all. It happens so very fast; your conscious mind just can't keep up.)*

The subconscious mind has a hierarchy of priorities of all our memories as to their importance to our survival. What has been accepted as true in the mind first has greater value and importance than what followed; and today's memories aren't as important as childhood memories, notwithstanding "significant emotional events." Memories that have been in storage in the subconscious mind the longest are more familiar and therefore are more important to the mind than current ones; consequently our beliefs, experiences, and references, accepted as true from early childhood, are more familiar and carry more weight in the mind's filtering process. As new information is received from the senses, the subconscious mind reviews the data for what is familiar to it; and what's oldest is more familiar and therefore relatively more important. If the subconscious mind is familiar with the data, it will be selected and sent to the active mind. Data the subconscious mind isn't familiar with, or for which it has no reference, will be filtered out, unused, or quarantined for later investigation.

Why would the subconscious mind not use all the data it receives? The answer is, if it has no reference to compare the new information with for relevance, it is meaningless to the mind and therefore meaningless for the process of creating interpretations or perceptions. Or it may be just too low on the mind's priority list, which would make it irrelevant and also meaningless to the process.

Data that is acceptable to the subconscious mind will be selected and sent to the active mind. From that data sent to the active mind, the active mind creates an "interpreted universe." The subconscious mind has more than enough processing speed to filter and pick through all the input data, selecting familiar data and getting it to the active mind without any gaps in transition. The subconscious mind operates at least four thousand times faster than the input data it receives from the senses.

This concept that the subconscious mind filters all incoming data is an interesting understanding because it's so counter to our currently accepted belief about how sensory data is used and processed; and since the concept is perhaps strange to us, it's important to look closely at it to understand it. Everything is first in the mind and then in the body. Once the data and information are in the mind, internal processes and systems are used to interpret the information. *(I call this function of interpreting the information the "active mind," which is a combination of mind, brain, and central nervous system. If the information isn't in your mind, you have no connection to it and therefore no knowledge about the information; and it's nonexistent to you.)*

A METAPHOR FOR THE BLACK BOX

We are presenting a metaphor here of how memories from the past determine our present-moment perceptions and also how and why the world we think we live in is the way it is. In this model, incoming data from the senses is filtered through the subconscious mind. The subconscious mind looks through all the input data to find data and information it is familiar with; that matching data from our past experiences is then selected for processing. Through the filtering system process, data is selected and sent to the active mind, and there interpretations are made. This is the ultimate streaming process, operating at billions of bits of data per second. The interpretations create holograms in our minds or brains; and like all thought forms we think into being, they produce chemical messages and electromagnetic signals to inform the mind or body of what is happening in the outside environment currently based on our past experiences. This in turn responds as is appropriate based on those past experiences. And then after that, the conscious mind comes along to tell us what has happened.

There are other models of how the subconscious mind works. They are all theoretical, and none have an absolute or complete answer as to what happens in the subconscious mind. All the models recognize the senses, presenting information to the mind in massive amounts of data; and that much data isn't used in the hologram we create inside our mind's eye. The resultant interpretations produce signals and messages that are sent to the mind or body. So for now, this model we laid out here seems to meet our needs and matches most other models out there in the scientific community.

It is like this; we have what I call a "black box." We know what is going in the box, and we know what is coming out of the box, but we aren't sure what is going on inside it. We know that what is happening in the box has something to do with our past experiences, which is to say our memories. The black box represents the subconscious mind because the subconscious is something we know little or nothing about; therefore, it is a black box. Since no one knows for sure what is going on in there, we can pretend that part of what the subconscious mind does is filter incoming data because that's the empirical information we have. Also, we know that what goes into the black box isn't what comes out of it; therefore, some kind of processing and manipulating of the data is taking place.

We need a way to work with the black box, and we will use the model set forth here. If a better one presents itself, we can change it. This is a simple approach; it isn't set in stone, and if it doesn't fit our needs, we can modify it. And it fits the criteria of Occam's razor as being the simplest explanation with the fewest variables of those theories that are around of how the subconscious mind works.

BETWEEN THE CONSCIOUS AND SUBCONSCIOUS MIND

In our inside inner-space, the conscious and subconscious realms of the mind don't appear to be closely connected at all. They each have different functions; and while they communicate for the good of the whole system, their functions are quite different. The model we will present here is far from the conventionally held understanding.

When new information and data enter the mind through the senses, they are presented to the subconscious mind, because that is where our memories are stored. The new information will be picked through, sorted, and filtered for relevance, as was explained above. The subconscious mind-set of filters is called "perceptual filters." In other models these functions may be called the "critical factor."[G]

Before age three, there is no filtering of incoming data, because there are no beliefs, experiences, and references to use to match the incoming information with. This means no meaning is given to the information, and it just flows directly into the mind, into the black box. It just pours into the mind and on to its hard drive of the subconscious mind. It may take a long time and more experience before all that childhood input can be put into proper prospective, maybe a lifetime, if the childhood was chaotic. However, by age six, we have a formidable set of perceptual filters, which could be called the "guard at the gate" of the "active mind."

The conscious mind sends data to the active mind, usually in the form of questions to clarify its reporting process. Most of the time it asks, "Have we seen anything like this before?" And of course, the active mind will make an interpretation of the data and send out signals to the subconscious mind, because that is where all our past is stored, and it gets information from the subconscious mind. It makes yet another interpretation and sends out new signals, which the conscious mind responds to, and then it reports to us what has happened. Is this starting to look like an ongoing operating system in the mind? *(Beware of how fast everything is happening in your mind and body, and of how slow your conscious mind is in reporting it to you. Yet it's only the conscious mind you listen to. All that internal communication at billions of bits per second is all out of your conscious awareness.)*

The critical factor, the guard at the gate, the subconscious mind filtering system, and the perceptual filters are all names for the process of filtering incoming information. Different disciplines and different modalities call this processing of filtering by different names. However, they are all around the process of filtering incoming information before it is used in the active mind because that is what the black box does; that is what the subconscious mind does. This filtering system is active and in place by the time we are about six years old. After the filter is in place, new information received will have a more difficult and tougher time getting into the mind; however, what we are familiar with will slip right through the filters as easy as pie.

Our habits of behavior operate out of the programming in the subconscious mind. For every behavior we express, there are beliefs in the subconscious mind that support it. Those beliefs, which are now programs, are in place to protect, support, and help us. Why? Because they are based on our truth of how we believe the world operates. They were put in place earlier in childhood before age six, and they will stay the way they are until we change them. They are the grounding place from which much of our pain and suffering originate.

Since those childhood beliefs were put in place first, they have a higher priority in the filtering system. We know they are true based on our experiences and proof from our past. Each experience we have will be filtered and manipulated before it is sent to the active mind. Therefore, our interpreted experience of the event will be different from the event and based on our past.

We may think we consciously know exactly what we need, want, and would like our world to be; and we may have set a course of action to achieve those goals. However, even if the conscious mind wants to change very badly, unless the subconscious mind agrees to the changes, putting those new behaviors into place and keeping them there may take a very long time, if ever. This is because the subconscious mind is the habitual mind. It has programs for each and every behavior we have. If the programs in the subconscious mind aren't changed and we force outside behavioral changes only by willpower, without changing the internal programming, we are only a keystroke away from the old program starting back up because the subconscious has an elephant's memory; and when willpower runs out of energy and gets tired, the inside program starts up again. We might say about our failed behavioral change, "Why does this always happen to me? Why do I keep ending up the same old way?" The answer is, that's the way we've been programed.

The programming isn't in the conscious mind. It is in that other part of the mind that is out of conscious awareness and out of view in the black box of the subconscious mind. How to get agreement between the two realms of the mind is a discussion for another time. For now, become familiar with how the two realms of the mind appear to work. Be aware of the function of each and how they might agree to work together, understanding how the critical factor, perceptual filters, and the filtering system in the subconscious mind operate. This understanding will give us a working knowledge of how the mind appears to function. This will help in comprehending where our pain and suffering comes from and how to change them.

The Conscious Mind

Scientists pretty well agree by observation on the things that go on inside the conscious mind and how it functions, because we are conscious of them. There may be some disagreement in selected areas, but in general the following is what the conscious mind does by observation and studies. The conscious mind analyzers, rationalizes, and judges. Willpower is a conscious mind activity that reports to us. *(When your conscious mind reports to you, whom is it talking to? What a question!)*

"Temporary memory" is a concern because we assume something goes on in the conscious mind first, and then the mind or body responds. This isn't the case; nothing goes on in the conscious mind first. The active mind's interpretation is the starting point of what the conscious mind is aware of. Then signals sent out by the active mind to the mind and body based on its interpretation start an internal dance between mind and body. There is a whirling dervish of internal processing, and the mind and body changes. The conscious mind basically sits on the sidelines and reports on the action. The conscious mind may have temporary or working memory; however, what the conscious mind holds and reports on is after the action has already taken place. *(I know it seems like the conscious mind is on top of everything, but it isn't and can't be because it's so slow in its operating speed when compared to everything else going on inside.)*

It appears that what is stored in permanent memory in the subconscious mind are the interpretations of the active mind, and they have nothing to do with the conscious mind at all, because interpretations are created first from selective information the subconscious mind sends. There is constant communication within the mind and body through the active mind. The conscious mind has no access, interaction, or input to anything going on in the subconscious mind, body, or active mind. It is just too slow. The subconscious mind, sensory input, active mind, and body responses operate at millions to billions of bits of data per second, and the conscious mind is nowhere near that fast. The conscious mind gives us stories and reasons for why we do what we do but only after everything has happened and we've done what we did.

What the conscious mind is analyzing, rationalizing, and judging will be brought into focus later. A different model will be developed later, out of which a new understanding of the conscious mind function will emerge.

THE SUBCONSCIOUS MIND

What goes on in the black box of the subconscious mind is unknown directly. Most of what we think we know about the subconscious mind is secondhand knowledge or empirical data, and there is a lot more disagreement as to what is happening in that unknown realm of the mind than there is agreement. Traits or attributes in the subconscious mind appear to be as follows: imagination comes from there, permanent memory is stored there, habits and ingrained behaviors operate out of there, our internal programming function from there, protective and survival responses are activated from there, and our currently held beliefs of reality, our paradigm, are stored in that part of the mind.

That realm appears to be nonjudgmental and just accepts and works with what manages to get in there. It also appears to be lazy. Well, *lazy* may not be the right word, but once a pattern or habit is set in the subconscious, it is very difficult to change. The subconscious is the habitual mind, and it follows its programming to the letter. Patterns and habits are habitual programs that rest in the subconscious mind.

If the conscious mind steps in and tries to influence outcome or activities, we feel an angst in the body, an uneasiness, because we are pushing against our natural, ingrained programming. We will notice that when we decide to go on a diet, lose weight, go back to school, stop smoking, or do anything else consciously without changing the internal subconscious programming, the change becomes more difficult. However, if programming is changed first, the newly desired behavior flows almost effortlessly into our lives. The secret is to understand and appreciate the fact that the body always responds to what is in the active mind, and it is the subconscious mind that determines what is in the active mind.

When and how were those programs instilled in the subconscious mind? Ah now, that's a good question. Our core programming will have been put in place before we were six or maybe seven years of age. What are the programs? Basically, programs are our beliefs. What are our beliefs? They are basically what we have taken to be true for us based on our proofs, which is to say our experiences mainly through repeated experiences within our family of origin. Beliefs become our self-identity, our egoic self; and those beliefs are who we think we are. And who we think we are determines what we believe our world is and must be, given our experiences of being in our world. Our experiences give us proof as to why we believe what we do about our world.

This is the key to why beliefs are difficult to change. To change a belief is to change, at least to some degree, who we think we are, our ego identity; and once it is in place, our egoic self will resist our changing our identity because if we change our identity, the current ego must die. We create a new identity of who we think we are, which will incorporate the new changes we now believe and want. While the new identity may be an improvement, the old ego self will be no more, and a new ego will be installed and integrated into our belief system. Ah, but know the old ego will fight hard to stay alive until the change is incorporated into our belief system. But don't worry, we will create another ego to take its place; as one fades away, another is born.

Real change happens on many levels, and change on the conscious level is the least important. The conscious mind is always the least informed and the last to know anything about what is happening in the mind and body. Change is a process, a dance between what is and what could be. To change is to overthrow the current truth we hold about ourselves and embrace the birth of a belief that isn't true for us yet; and the newly created identity will change who we think we are. It is a drama between death and birth. The change is complete when the subconscious mind has changed its programming and accepted the new self, and then new behavior will just flow automatically and naturally out of the new programming like magic.

CHAPTER 3

Sensing Differently

SENSES AND THE ENVIRONMENT

Our senses are needed for us to move around in our environment. However, they don't operate the way most of us have come to believe they do. The senses are instruments that gather information, and that is all they do. That may not be news, but what they gather may be, because what they gather is only data. The senses make no judgments as to what is good or bad about what they gather and transmit. They just gather data, and that's it; and the data and information they gather is presented to the mind in the form of electromagnetic and chemical signals that must be decoded.

While all the sensory organs rest in the body, their transmitted data goes straight to the subconscious mind and doesn't interact with or touch the body in any way. The body has no idea what the data is. If we hear something to our left and turn our heads to the left, it isn't the body that heard anything; it is the active mind's interpretation of the data received from the senses through the subconscious mind. Then signals are sent to the body that causes the head to move to the left. Everything goes through the mind first. The body knows only what the active mind tells it. The body moves only because the active mind has signaled it to move. The senses don't cause the body to do anything because they can't. They are just instruments, and their output goes to the mind, not the body.

Whether something is ugly or beautiful has nothing to do with our eyes or other senses. All subjective judgments are created in the mind. The senses just gather data, and the data is coded in electromagnetic and chemical signals; and then the data is transmitted to the mind. The mind decodes it, and it's the mind that makes judgments and gives meaning to what the data is. Nothing outside us has any meaning until the mind gives it meaning based on our beliefs, experiences, and references—which is to say our past memories.

We have a tendency to make the body and senses suffer because of the interpretations and judgments the mind puts on the data the innocent senses transmit; the poor body is just reacting in response to the active mind's interpretation and trying to survive. Remember that old ancient saying from the good book? "If thine eye offend thee, pluck it out." That's just a cop-out for what the mind is doing. The eye doesn't and can't offend anyone because it's just hardware. But then, what would be easier—to pluck an eyeball out or to pluck out one's mind. Everything is in the mind first, and it's all about what the mind interprets. Sometimes the body pays a high price for what the mind does as it responds to the interpretations of the mind.

In some religion paths, they took this idea that "it is the body's fault for the behavior we express" to extremes. Flogging and self-mutilation were ways to punish the body for its behavior. If the behavior was against the community, putting the body in stocks in the village square or in prison was always an option. None of these approaches came close to changing the cause of the problem, which is the mind. But they do change current behavior immediately, and maybe that is good enough for who it's for. Extreme physical pain and restriction can change external behavior very quickly, but they may not have any effect on the causal mind. *(You see how the body becomes the scapegoat for the mind? The sad thing is that your conscious mind is convinced that it is the body's fault and tells you so, and it never seems to catch on to the fact that it's the active mind's interpretation that is the cause of why we do what we do. This is because of how slow the conscious mind operates. By the time the conscious mind gets around to reporting what has happened, it looks like the body is doing the behavior all on its own; and the egoic self laughs at its deception.)*

It is in changing the mind that will pluck out what is offensive. Plucking the eyes out will definitely stop the incoming data, but it won't change the internal programming, which is the causal problem. It's all in the mind first, and we need to get this understanding. *(This is it, and you need to get it. Everything is first in the mind. Can you begin to accept or appreciate the possibility of this idea? Don't hold back now. If you think your body is the cause of all your problems, including your pain and suffering, that is okay. Your ego will agree with you. In fact, your ego wants you to blame the body. Why would that be? So you don't blame the mind, which is where the ego lives.)*

Everything outside us is neutral and meaningless until the mind gives it meaning through its interpretations. The meaning of any object isn't in the object outside us but in our minds' judgment and interpretation of the object inside. The meaning of any situation isn't in the situation but in our minds' judgment and interpretation of the situation. What an interesting concept this is, is it not? Think about it and begin to open to the concept that what we do in the mind is the causation of everything we experience, including our pain and suffering in the body; it is also the source of our happiness and joy. Here again we will confine ourselves to our pain and suffering, but the same concept holds true for the positive objects and situations in our lives.

Since the meaning of everything outside us is determined by our individual inside interpretations, and since each of us has different beliefs, experiences, and memories that determine that meaning, the meaning we give to each and every outside object and situation will be different for each of us. Yes, that's it. The outside is meaningless until we create the meaning in our heads, and that meaning will be unique and different for each of us. So what are the senses doing and sensing? What they are doing is collecting and transmitting data to the mind. So what is in this neutral and meaningless data from the outside? Whatever the mind wants to make of it is based on our individual, cultural, national, and religious beliefs, experiences, and references in our memories.

We will discuss how the senses function, but we won't get involved in the nitty-gritty details of how each sense operates. Our senses are very complex, and our discussion here will be only superficial. We are basically concerned with the input and output. The details of how each sense functions are beyond our discussion here. Our sensory instruments are magnificent structures in and of themselves, and it's easy to get mesmerized and lost in their details. We intend to stay at only the superficial level of understanding. *(I don't know how the senses operate in detail. However, I do know their purpose is to give data and information to the mind. They do that so fast that we consciously believe our senses are telling us the truth as to what is outside us and that they are showing and giving to us the good and bad of what is outside us, but they aren't. Through our inside interpretation, we tell ourselves what is happening outside us; and of course, it isn't what's happening outside us. What we think is outside us is always a reflection of what we hold within us, and it has little to do with what is outside. We know we live in an illusion, and that illusion is very complex and more complex than our senses.)*

WHAT THE EYE SEES

The eye can be likened to a camera. It takes in energy through its lens, converts the energy to electromagnetic data, and sends that data to the mind; it's a pretty straightforward process, right? Notice that the data doesn't go to the body. No data goes directly to the body. Here's the thing: the eye collects only energy in certain bandwidths of frequencies in the light spectrum, and that width is from 400 billionth of a meter to 700 billionth of a meter. The eyes don't see any objects as objects; they see only energy frequencies reflected from objects.

The visible light spectrum of energy the human eye can capture is quite small compared to what is out there in the total electromagnetic light spectrum. Now, if we look really closely, we will see that the eye doesn't capture color as color; the eye captures wavelengths of energy. It isn't color the eye sends to the mind; the eye sends energy data in the form of wavelengths of coded data. There is no color in the external environment, only wavelengths of energy. How wild is that?

It is the active mind, by its interpretation of the wavelength data it receives from the eyes, that creates all the color we think we see out there. The eye only collects energy data. *(Are you getting this?)* The eye doesn't interpret what it collects, and it makes no judgment as to what the data means; it just sends the data to the mind so the subconscious mind can select through its filtering system what data will go to the active mind. It is our active minds that do all that judging, creating of color, and giving of meaning to our external world. The eyes just gather data. The eyes are innocent of how the mind perceives the data. This fact is so counterintuitive to our belief; it is difficult to grasp at first, but that's the way it is. It's all in the mind first.

Yes, it's all in the mind. We need to say that a lot because we want so badly to have our problems be outside us so we can point a bony finger out there and blame something or someone outside us. And why would we want to do that? So we don't have to change our minds, identities, or beliefs—so we don't need to reframe our experiences and memories, so we don't need to kill our current created egos, so we can remain our habitual egoic selves. What we see, we see with the mind and not the eyes. It's a hard fact to believe because of our programming, but there it is.

What the Ear Hears

When a tree falls in the forest, does it make a sound if there is no one there? The ear is a fantastic organ. It takes fluctuations of energy in the external environment as pressure against the eardrum and on the bones around the ear and behind the eardrum, and it converts that energy into frequencies, which the active mind interprets into all the sounds we hear. The human ear can only pick up frequencies, pulses between 20 hertz (cycles per second) and 20,000 hertz, and from intensities over a wide range of pressures expressed in decibels from 0 decibels to 130 decibels (the edge of ear pain).

Recognize that there is no sound in the external environment, only energy pulsations that push against a membrane in the ear. The only sound that exists is created in our minds by our active minds' interpretations of all the data, which is first sent to the mind by the ear's auditory system. The ear doesn't hear sounds; it only collects patterns of energies. All sound is a construction in the mind by the active mind's interpretation of the data received.

What we think of as music is an internal construct. Music can be only good or bad based on the interpretation of the external energy by the internal mind, and it has nothing to do with what is outside in the energy field, because what is outside is neutral until we think about it. There is no music anywhere outside us, only energy vibrations. There is no sound outside our active mind's interpretation of the energy.

When a tree falls in the forest, does it make a sound if there is no one there? No. Sound is a creation, an interpretation in the head. If no one is there, no head, there is no sound, only energy. What we hear, we don't hear with the ear. We hear with the mind. *(It's all in your mind first.)*

WHAT IN THE WORLD DO I SMELL?

The sense of smell is a complex system starting with our nose hairs and ending in our brains. Basically, nose hairs are just hairs for filtering dust to prevent big particles from entering the nasal cavity. Deeper in the cavity are very small, specialized, microscopic, biological hair like sensory cell structures, called "cilia," and there are a lot of them. These cilia are designed to be stimulated by different smell molecules, and each is connected to receptors.

These receptors are used to detect the presence of smell or the molecules of smell; they are attached to nerve endings. At the other end of the nerve is a structure called the "olfactory glomerulus," which is inside the "olfactory bulb" but not connected to the brain. The olfactory bulbs (there are two) are connected to the brain through another nerve bundle, leaving an olfactory bulb, called the "olfactory tract." This serves different regions of the brain, and finally, the brain receives the data from the external environment in the form of electromagnetic signals. There is no smell or smell molecules in the electromagnetic information sent to the brain. The brain receives just coded data. There are no smell molecules in the brain, only electromagnetic signals.

For our discussion, we don't need to know all the details of smelling. However, we should recognize that the smell sense system sends data (and only data) to the brain, and the active mind interprets the data to create our external environment of smell the way it does from our internal interpretations. What we think of as the external smell is created inside by the active mind and not from the outside molecules floating around.

Some people hate a certain smell, and other people love the same smell. Each will have a different interpretation and view of the external environment, and it's not the external environment that causes it; it's the inside interpretation of the external data by our individual active minds. What we smell we don't smell with the nose; we smell with the mind. *(Everything is first in your mind.)*

Taste That!

Oh, what a tool the tongue is. It is used in so many different ways and is a great metaphor for clarifying our communication, as in "I have it right on the tip of my tongue," "Bite your tongue when you say that," or "Are you speaking to me tongue in cheek?" How clear is the impression, and how completely understood is the communication gesture of "sticking your tongue out"? It also is the body's first line of defense against any kind of foreign invaders trying to enter the body. The tongue organizes and manages the passage of all our food—solid or liquid—entering the body, and from this very sensitive organ comes our sense of taste.

Taste is the sensation produced when a substance in the mouth reacts chemically with receptors in the taste buds found mainly on the tongue. The taste buds are located around the small structures on the upper surface of the tongue, soft palate, the upper esophagus, and the epiglottis, which are called papillae. *(Notice that flavor isn't taste. Flavor is determined by a combination of several other nerve stimulants, such as smell, touch for texture, temperature, and other inputs. You don't need to know all this for our purposes. If you want to know more, go play on the Internet.)*

Taste buds contain the receptors of taste. Taste starts with a chemical reaction in the mouth that gets detected by a taste bud receptor. We have on average of three to ten thousand taste buds. They are divided into different areas, largely on the tongue, of salty, sour, sweet, and umami. (*Umami* is a Japanese word that can be translated "pleasant savory taste.")

Each taste bud is attached to a nerve (afferent axons) that carries nerve impulses to the brain. The active mind interprets the data from the taste buds along with other data from smell, texture, temperature, and so on to determine whether we like what we are chewing on. Some people like salty stuff, others like it sweet or a combination of other flavors, and "Some Like It Hot".

However, it's not what the data is that is important but how our unique active mind interprets it that creates the sensation of taste and ultimately flavor. Here again we see that what we think of as an external reality is, in fact, a creation of the mind's internal interpretation of outside data. It is never the outside data that creates our world but our interpretation of the outside data from inside us. What we taste we don't taste with the tongue; we taste with the mind. *(Everything is first in your mind.)*

TOUCHY FEELY

What we think of as touch is really a combination of several different systems throughout the body. The brain has an internal map of the body surfaces called a "homunculus" or "very small human," and it plays a fundamental role in the creation of our body's image of touch. All those different systems gather data about external pressures against the body and sometimes internal pressure and surface irritations we end up scratching. The body doesn't feel any pressure; it is the nervous system and nerve endings that get excited. They send data to the small human, which the active mind interprets and then sends signals to the body on how to respond.

Each nerve-collecting receptor is connected to a nerve ending, and the other end of the nerve is connected to the internal map of the body in the brain. The nerve endings on the surface are attached to their exact corresponding location on the internal brain map at the other end of the nerve. What a piece of hardware is the touch system.

Again, we must state that it isn't the data the brain receives that tells us anything about what we are feeling of the outside world but the active mind's interpretation of that data. It is from the active mind's interpretation and the signals sent out to the body that the body is responding to, not the outside tactile pressure against the body. The body doesn't know or care what is happening in the outside world because it knows and cares only about what the mind tells it through active mind signals. What we touch we don't touch with the body; we touch with the mind. *(Everything is first in your mind. How fast is this happening? Millions to billions of bits of data per second. How fast is the conscious mind working? At a snail's pace; it is so slow that it believes the body is feeling the outside world and tells us that. It has no idea the data has been filtered, manipulated, and changed thousands of times before the conscious mind becomes aware of it.)*

EMBEDDED SENSES

Senses are embedded in the body but operate from the mind. They are tools of the mind, not of the body. The body monitors the active mind's interpretation of the sensory input and the signals and messages the active mind sends out. It is the interpretation in the active mind the body responds to. The body is only connected to the active mind. It is the mind that determines whether the eye looks left or right. It is the mind that tells the head to turn to hear the direction of the noise energy. It is the mind that tells the hand to move away from the fire. The data-collecting senses have nothing to do with telling the body anything. The data passes straight through the body and directly to the mind, where it is filtered and sent to the active mind for processing and interpretation based on our beliefs, experiences, and references, which is to say our memories. *(Why am I continuing to beat this dead horse over and over again when I say, "It's all in the mind first"? Because the life you have now is lived out of your past from your memories. Your present moment isn't experienced the way it is but through our lenses of past memories. Therefore, your future will look much like our past unless we change our past, which is only memories. If you believe memories are absolutely real and unchangeable, you are doomed to live your present and future life out of your unchangeable past. This is simply not true. All you are is what you hold in your mind, which are your memories and that can be changed. You are only your mind.)*

If at times it seems that the body responds quicker than we think, this is because we are thinking that with our conscious minds. Behind the slow conscious mind's reporting to us its awareness, so much is happening at lightning speeds of billions to millions of bits of data per second that the slow, conscious mind can't keep up and will never understand all that is happening out of its awareness. But here again we believe the conscious mind knows all and tells all, but it doesn't.

While the senses are in the body, the body is like a puppet, and the mind pulls its strings behind the curtain of conscious awareness. The mind sends electric signals to muscles and releases chemical messages into the body, and bodily systems respond as is appropriate to those signals. It is the mind that is the master puppeteer, and the body only response to it. We can hit the puppet, yell at the puppet, pass gas in front of the puppet, expose anything to the puppet; but until the master puppeteer reacts and interprets the information, the puppet cannot and won't respond. What the mind perceives the body responds to; and it cannot not respond.

The body can be imagined as a thin membrane that surrounds and protects the inside workings of the mind or brain. This isn't unlike the membrane that is around each of the cells that make up the body. Since the body always and only responds to the mind, I wonder, where do all our pain and suffering come from? The body is the scapegoat for the mind's interpretations in many ways. Did we say something like that before? If not, we should have.

So if the body is in pain and suffering, where must that pain and suffering start from—the body or the mind? Oh, yes, we know we feel it in the body only because the conscious mind tells us that. However, the conscious mind is the slowest, the least informed, and the last to know anything; it is always behind the action of what's happening. But because it speaks in language and not in electrical, magnetic, and chemical signals, we believe what it tells us. All we know in words is what the conscious mind tells us. But what is going on in the whole matrix of the mind, brain, and body before the slow part of the mind, the conscious mind, catches up and tells us? Now that's another good question.

REALITY IS ONLY AN INTERPRETATION

The sensory input data isn't good or bad until the active mind interprets it, because all the data is neutral and has no meaning as received. The information received through the senses is meaningless until sorted by the subconscious mind and interpreted by the active mind, and then meaning is given to it. Again, we can see that it isn't what is outside us that is important but how our active mind interprets the data about what is outside us. The meaning of our external world isn't in the external world; it's in our internal interpretation of the external data, and each of us has his or her own variation of what that reality is. So many people, so many realities.

Thank goodness, our brains have evolved to process data somewhat the same, or we would be a lot more separated and isolated species than we are. We agree on much of the energy around us, because we process it about the same. We collectively agree on things like what is blue or yellow and what is hard or soft. However, we are never completely in agreement on everything. Since we never experience the outside energy the way it is, we need to acknowledge that what we think the external world is, is a reflection only of our internally created interpretation of the external data after the subconscious mind has filtered and manipulated it; as a result, each of us has our own unique world we live in. Is that surprising, or do we at some level already know that? *(Maybe you heard it here for the first time that you and I each live in different worlds. However, it's time you begin acknowledging and accepting that this has always been the reality of your life, and no one lives in your reality but you.)*

The eye doesn't see, the ear doesn't hear, the hand doesn't touch, the nose doesn't smell, and the tongue doesn't taste. The mind does all the seeing, hearing, touching, smelling, and tasting. All the senses do is transmit data to the mind. It's our unique interpretation of the data that determines the world we live in. Since the mind's interpretations determine everything else in the body, might the mind also have a lot to do with our pain and suffering?

There is an expression that states, "Perception is reality." This is a fallacy, of course, because we each have a different perception of everything, even though we seem to have developed certain cultural agreements that keep some of our perceptions close to each other. Perceptions are ever moving, ever changing, and dependent on what state of mind we are in at any given moment of time. Under all our perceptions rests the reality of the never moving and never changing, which is the grounding place of the infinite and eternal.

We may question what infinite and eternal are, however, since we can have different perceptions of what seems to be the same input data from outside us, and each of us has developed a different reality from that input data. How can that really be reality? That's an oxymoron. Now think. What do we call something that appears to be real but isn't? An illusion. And that is what we are doing, creating illusions and believing they are real and are our reality.

Everything outside us is neutral and without meaning. It is the raw material out of which we each create meaning, and each meaning will be slightly different. It's all meaningless until we think about it inside. We have said that before, have we not? But because it's so counterintuitive to our experience and programming, we need to say it a lot. The senses don't bring reality to the mind; they only bring data, just raw material. It is the mind that takes that raw material and builds and creates whatever it wants based on its beliefs, experiences, and references from its past, which are only memories; therefore, they are different for each of us.

Isn't that interesting? Our perception of this present moment is a construction from what happened to us in the past; therefore what we perceive as happening now can be seen only through our individual lens of the past. So, what is really happening now? We don't know, but we think we know, and we think it is real. What would we call something we think and believe is real but isn't? An illusion. And again, we see the sleight of hand by the great trickster, our egoic selves. However, it does seem so real to us, doesn't it? And it's scary to think it isn't real. It may be so scary that we will fight hard both intellectually and physically to keep our belief that the world is still flat.

The senses don't care what the data is that they transmit. They don't think. They just transmit the raw material from the outside environment to the inside mind, because they are just instruments. The mind is the artist, the creator, who uses the medium the senses bring to it. It is as if the senses offer a big sandbox filled with sand to the mind, and the mind makes sandcastles, houses, relationships, or whatever it likes from the raw material; and then it breaks them down as more sand is dumped into the sandbox from the senses, and then the mind creates anew. What and how the mind creates are based on its beliefs, experiences, and references from the past stored in the subconscious mind. We can build only from what we know, and what we know is from our beliefs, experiences, and references from older memories; and those past memories are the filters of the present moment. *(Can you begin to understand why you can see your present moment only through the lens of your past?)*

Where are our beliefs, experiences, memories, and references from the past kept? In the subconscious mind. Are we consciously aware of what is in that black box? No. Whatever that realm of the mind is that we call the subconscious or unconscious mind, no one knows for sure where it is or what is in it. There are many ideas about what and where the subconscious mind is, but no one can put his or her finger on it mentally or physically. Some guesses are in the brain, others think it's in the energy field the body rests in, and others theorize it's in the body or a combination of these. Still others believe it's in the synapses between the neurons' axons in the brain or maybe something else. So now we are in a pickle. We know little about this subconscious black box directly or indirectly, and yet it is where all our memories are kept and our programming of how our lives operate.

Wherever that mysterious black box part of our minds is, we need to make friends with it, because it holds the secret to creating a new and better world for us.

CHAPTER 4

The Importance of Being Inside

TWO SOURCES OF INFORMATION

Begin to appreciate that there are two sources of information the active mind uses to create our "interpreted universe," the world we live in. They are the subconscious mind and the body. The conscious mind isn't actively involved as an input source, not really, because it's just too slow.

The subconscious mind supplies information to the active mind in two ways: first, it filters and manipulates incoming data, then sends it to the active mind; and second, when triggered, it sends stored data of memories to the active mind. The body first supplies feedback information as to its response to the active mind's signals and messages; and second, when the body systems need attention (in other words, are thirsty, hungry, tired, and so forth).

These two sources interact and influence each other. While the subconscious mind is working with the incoming data and sending filtered and manipulated data to the active mind, the body sends feedback to the active mind as to its status. The active mind is the cauldron in which all this data is mixed and out of which come our interpretations and perceptions. Our "interpreted universe," which is to say the world we live in, flows from this process. The two sources of information dance together, and from their interactions the active mind creates and imagines into being the interpreted universe inside us.

Because the conscious mind's processing ability is so slow, it appears the conscious mind, which is all we are consciously aware of, actually has little to do with the interpreted universe except to rationalize into words what it knows after the resulting creations have been put in place. One of the important functions of the conscious mind is to give us a story as to why we did what we did so we won't think we're crazy. It's what the conscious mind does, and it's what we are aware of but not what is happening; it grabs the fast-moving action of mind and body as best it can, given its slow processing speed, and it reports to us so we feel we know what is happening, but of course we really don't.

Behind the picture the conscious mind paints in words is the whirlwind functioning and processing of the subconscious mind, body, and active mind. As the subconscious mind mines the information coming from the senses, generalizing, deleting, manipulating, and selecting data, it is operating at least at forty billion bits of data per second; then the selected data is moved in a constant stream and presented to the active mind. The active mind creates an "internal universe" from the stream of filtered data. From the perceptions in the active mind, signals and messages are sent throughout the mind and body. This is a continuous, dynamic process, in which universes are created and collapse in a millionth of a second.

It is at is point that the conscious mind moves into the process to report and describe in words what has happened in the active mind and how the body has responded. By the time the conscious mind starts describing what is happening, it has changed. So the conscious mind, to keep up because of its slow processing speed of only one hundred bits per second, generalizes, deletes, and manipulates the data of the picture it is describing again. *(Look closely here, and you will notice. The conscious mind is doing what the subconscious mind is doing to the input data. It manipulates the data. So what you are aware of has been drastically manipulated through two filtering systems. You see why you live in an illusion? But, of course, you believe it is reality.)*

We don't see what's going on. We experience what the conscious mind tells us, and we believe it's so. It adds to the illusion, but we believe what the conscious mind tells us is the truth, the whole truth, and that it is real. Or at least real enough for us to function in our world.

Since the body is always monitoring the moment-by-moment-created interpreted universe and its signals and from those signals, it is changing its systems and sending feedback to the mind. The pain and suffering we think we feel in our bodies are the effect of the interpretation of the body's feedback by the mind, which is the body's response to the created and constructed interpreted universe.

The effect of the pain and suffering we think we are feeling in the body at any moment resides in the causal interpreted universe we created in our minds. It is the effect of the interpreted universe we think is felt in the body but is really in the causal mind, brain, and central nervous system. *(When you take a tranquilizer or pain-killing medications, it goes to the brain, not to the body. Pain and suffering are interpretations in the mind. As such, pain and suffering can be moderated in the mind; and that is what most medications do. Might there be other ways of changing the mind or brain that don't have side effects and can also heal the body?)*

It is the feedback effect we think we feel in the body. There is no feeling in the body of our pain and suffering. All pain and suffering are interpretations in the mind; therefore, because of our conscious mind's slow processing and reporting, we believe the indicators of our pain and suffering are in the body. While moderating our bodies will change the body's feedback system to the mind, our pain and suffering are an interpretation in the causal mind's created interpreted universe. *(Can you see why, if the causal mind isn't addressed, you will spend all your time and effort trying to heal your pain and suffering by manipulating the body? Now you may be able to change the body's response by medication and other interventions; however, you won't heal the cause and may develop other symptoms of your pain and suffering until the causal issue in the mind is addressed. It's all a dance within you, and in that dance, you will believe the conscious mind because you cannot get inside the causal part of the mind, the black box, through the conscious mind.)*

Pain and suffering are symptoms we think are in the body but are really of what is going on in the mind. They are the feelings we think are in the body, which the conscious mind reports to us; and the conscious mind has no idea that the pain it is reporting on is an interpretation in the mind. The body's pain and suffering signals are fed back to the active mind that something needs to change how the

39

Interpreted Universe is created, which is to say the mind. When we first have negative symptoms in the body, medication may be appropriate to moderate the symptoms and effects in the body. However, it won't resolve the cause of our problem, which is the interpretation by the active mind, and that is created by the data sent to it by the subconscious mind, which is determined by our memories. But maybe to moderate the symptoms is good enough for right now.

If we have a headache once a month and an aspirin or two works fine in getting rid of it, that may be good enough. However, if we have a headache every day or one that lasts days, the body asks us to heal the causal condition in our minds. The headache is only an effect. Our causal interpreted universe needs to change. Pain and suffering are an effect; they aren't a cause. When the cause is resolved, healed, and cleared, the effect, which is our pain and suffering, will be no more.

> *Disclaimer: If the body has had a chronic, negative, long-lasting painful condition for which the body's systems have had to change to compensate for, even after the cause is resolved and healed, a residue of those body changes may still affect how the body functions (in other words, chronic alcoholism and drug use or diabetes). However, they will be better.*

Many times the cause of the pain and suffering is hidden from the conscious mind, or we may have lost our connection between the effects, the pain and suffering in the body and their cause, the constructed interpreted universe in the mind. In this dance between the cause and effect, the symptoms or effects don't need to consciously occur right after the problem event happens. When the problem event is over and gone, all the residue of the information and data of the interpretation of the event, along with its negatively attached emotional energy, are moved into permanent memory in the subconscious mind, adding to its filtering system of sensory input data. Many times the memory has to fester in the mind and body for a long time before the body develops symptoms of pain and suffering the conscious mind can recognize. Years can go by before the body expresses symptoms that are extreme enough for the conscious mind to recognize; there is no time frame between the cause and when its effects are expressed to the point that the conscious mind reports them to us.

There is a hidden secret about the cause; the cause isn't in the past. It is with us in the present moment. The event is over, but the emotional, hot memory of the event is in the subconscious mind 24-7. It is out of conscious awareness, but the memory is still alive in the subconscious mind, which means it is still radiating negative energy. Cause and its effects are always connected and never separated; they are entangled. The subconscious mind can easily do all the things it needs to do and still keep cause and effects connected because it's that fast. As for the conscious mind and its slow processing, it rationalizes that our pain and suffering condition is a body problem; it will report on the body's effects but may not have any idea what the cause is. In so doing, the conscious mind sees the effects or symptoms in the body as the real and only problem we have, and that is where it puts its attention. Therefore, changing the effect in the body becomes our goal of healing. And what about the causal condition in the mind? Well, that's a problem to be solved at another time when different effects show up in the body. *(Do you see how it works? Everything is first in the mind; and if it isn't healed, the cause remains in the mind. You will blame your body for all your pain and suffering, and manipulate the body, thinking you are working on the problem, but you aren't. Interesting, isn't it? Here again you can see how the ego keeps you off balance and away from what is really happening. Everything is first in the mind.)*

It's impossible to have an effect without a cause. Working with the body to modify the intensity of our pain and suffering, symptoms, and effects with medication or other modalities may be appropriate at the time; however, to medicate or use other modalities such as physical therapy for a long time, maybe a lifetime, without finding, resolving, and healing the cause may not be the solution the body is asking for or wants. All medications have negative effects on the body at some level; some we are aware of consciously, and some we aren't aware of yet. While medication may be needed in the short term, using it as an ongoing lifestyle process without resolving the causal condition may not be the best option.

While it may take some time for symptoms to be expressed consciously, when they do, the cause is right there with them. Since we

41

can't have symptoms without a cause, if we have a pain and suffering effect, the cause is there too. The cause will be a memory or memories of an event or events that are over and gone; it is the memories we keep right here in the present moment that are causing the ongoing responses the body is expressing. Cause and effect are connected and inseparable. When we have an effect, the cause is there, holding its hand. It is a system; the cause of chronic pain and suffering will always be found inside in our perceived and created interpreted universe. *(Now, don't let your ego start driving your thinking with, "What if … or what about this …?" situational statements. We are developing a general model. Hold off on your special situations.)*

To heal negative effects in the body, the cause, our created interpreted universe, needs to change. To change our interpreted universe, the data and information sent to the active mind must change. To change the data sent to the active mind, the subconsciously stored negative memories must be reframed and healed. It is a straightforward process, although it may not seem that way or always that easy. It's an interactive system where all the components interact and dance together.

THE OUTSIDE UNIVERSE

All there is outside us in the outside universe is energy. There is no color, form, or object to see; no sound to hear; no fragrance to smell; no object to touch; and nothing to taste. All the information from the outside universe comes into the subconscious mind from the sensory input in the form of electrical, magnetic, and chemical energy signals and messages. Each moment the senses transmit their coded data as visual, auditory, kinesthetic, olfactory, and gustatory (V, A, K, O, G) signals into the mind. The mind needs to decode and filter that information and move it into the active mind before we have any color, objects, music, smell, taste, or anything to touch. The senses just send data and nothing else. The universe we think we live in is created inside by the active mind's interpretations of the filtered data. *(Now don't get stuck in the ego's thinking that the "real world" is outside you, that the past is real, and that the present moment is so thin that it can be smeared over by the past and future and isn't important. This is the ego's thought system. The ego wants you to believe the present is just an annoyance you must get through to move into the future, where everything is happening. No. The present moment is infinite and eternal, and it's always* now. *It is never in the past or future.)*

But before the active mind receives any data, the subconscious mind tests all that incoming data, filters it, and if needs be manipulates it against our stored beliefs, experiences, references, and past memories to fit the current paradigm of our world. If we can't find any references in our stored history to the new input data, it is dropped out of the process. The data and information that make it through the filtering and testing process move to the active mind and are used to create our inside interpreted universe, and that inside created universe is the only environment the body is aware of. The body doesn't experience the outside world directly in any way. It can experience it only through our interpreted universe inside. This isn't the conventional view.

Again, we must stop for a moment and take a deep breath. This model is far from our conventional understanding. We may need to think about the next statement for a while. Nothing we think is in the outside universe is in the outside universe the way we think it is. This is because all we think is out there in the outside universe is an inside construction of our active mind that creates our interpreted universe; and then the conscious mind projects it into the outside energy system through its very slow processing speed. But really, the projection of what we think is out there is still and always inside us.

To understand this concept a little better, we need to look closer and notice that what we think we know about what we think we know we don't know.

THE FILTERING SYSTEM OF THE OUTSIDE UNIVERSE

Everything is energy, and that's all there is to it; and that's our starting point. The outside universe comprises only patterns of energies. Our senses all together can transmit about eleven million bits of data per second of that outside energy, which is only a small amount of what's out there to be gathered. As the information enters the interspace of the mind, the subconscious mind, operating at least forty billion bits of data per second or at least forty thousand times faster than the incoming input data from the senses, grabs the data. *(You probably heard before, maybe in this read, that everything is energy; but you may not have fully considered the broader implications of that statement. Think about this for a moment. Everything created, manifested, and brought into this three-dimensional space/time universe must be created or manifested twice. First, it must be created within the energy of your mind as a perception, a concept, and an idea; and then you can build it in the physical universe. A question: if that is so, where is the physical world?)*

Remember Einstein's formula, $E = MC^2$, where E = energy, M = matter, and C = the speed of light? The formula can be written $M = E/C^2$. Notice in that way of formulating the formula that inside, around, and through all matter is energy; and the energy must be there first. No energy, no matter. Energy is the matrix on which the physical matter is hung and grown. As Einstein put it, "It followed from the special theory of relativity that mass and energy are both but different manifestations of the same thing, [and] a somewhat unfamiliar conception for the average mind ... The mass and energy were in fact equivalent, according to the formula mentioned above" (From the soundtrack of the film, Atomic Physics. Copyright © J. Arthur Rank Organization, Ltd., 1948. Image © Brown Brothers, Sterling, PA. https://history.aip.org/exhibits/einstein/voice1.htm).

There is a saying in the ancient Upanishads of India: "First the thought and then the act." In Western culture, you might have heard the saying "In the beginning was the word." A word is the oscillation of energy, and sound is the interpretation of that energy in the mind. Without the mind, it is just meaningless energy noise. The two sayings can be combined to say, "First the energy and then the physical creation." There is another quote of Einstein. "Nothing happens until something moves."

Energy needs to be there first, or nothing can move, and nothing can happen. We are first energy and then matter; we are first energy beings and then physical beings. Everything is first energy. Energy is the matrix on which the physical is hung and grown. When the energy, sometimes called "life source," leaves the body, the matter returns to its lowest grounded energy state of separate molecules or particles.

Now the subconscious mind grabs the input data and mines it, looking for matches to see what it is familiar with. In the filtering process, while the conscious mind is poking along, the subconscious mind is whizzing around, selecting information from its data banks and comparing the new incoming data with our beliefs, experiences, and references from past memories, looking for matches. There is a whirlwind of activity streaming data to the active mind. When a match is found, based on how we handled similar situations in the past, information is selected or manipulated to fit our paradigm of reality. The incoming information is filtered and manipulated to meet our past understanding and actions. If we have no reference to the incoming data, the incoming information is meaningless to us and cannot be used, at least not yet.

We see what we want to see and are familiar with, we hear what we want to hear based on what we are familiar with, and we feel what we want to feel based on our past. Therefore, the present moment can be seen and experienced only through our lens of the past. We never consciously experience the present moment the way it is; it has to be seen, and it must be experienced through the smaller lens of our past.

There is judgment in this process. If the incoming information meets our belief system and expectation, we will wholeheartedly accept it and work with it, even if we don't like it or it causes us pain and suffering; and even though we may have a lousy and terrible belief system and experiences in our past, they will seem normal, familiar, and therefore acceptable. If the incoming information isn't familiar, we will question it and argue against it; we will generalize it, delete it, deny it, manipulate it, or not even consciously see it because it doesn't match anything in our paradigm of our worldview. Consciously and physically the information transmitted from the senses, for which we find no references, won't be there after the filtering process, even though there was something there from the sensory input information.

What we think we physically see, hear, and touch is a creation of the interpreted universe and isn't what is outside us. This is done so quickly that at the active mind level the conscious mind has no idea the sensory input data has been changed. *(I know, you are unquestionably sure that what your interpretive universe is telling you is the truth and the whole truth in regard to what is outside you. However, I am suggesting that you don't consciously know what is available for you to know and that you can know only what your lens, which is a filter of the past, allows you to know. Again, you can know only the present through the past. Look closely, and you may begin to question your own paradigm of the world. It could be scary.)*

Since as a species we humans process information in our brains about the same, and our senses collect and transmit data about the same way, much of our individual interpreted universe will be much the same as those around us, but not all of it will be the same; and that slight difference creates worlds of differences. We can agree on colors of blue and red, that 2 x 2=4, on what is up and what is down, but what is hot or cold may be problematic because that is subjective and based on individual experiences and preferences.

We use only a small amount of the information available from the outside to create our interpreted universe inside. What data we do use is highly selected and manipulated because of our filtering system. Ah now, the filtering system we each use, as you may have guessed, is another subjective part. It is dependent on many subtle factors, including our individual personal likes and dislikes.

What happens to all the incoming data that isn't used? It enters the mind as coded energy. Then what? Do all those impulses, nonverbal energies, and information just fall on the floor? We think some of them will end up in the subconscious mind for later processing and use, but there is no way of knowing how much or what it would be used for. It's an interesting question, isn't it?

What would be our best guess as to the cause of our pain and suffering? Is it the outside universe of everything, the body, or the inside-created interpreted universe of the active mind that causes our problems of pain and suffering?

It may be easier to metaphorically view the body as a membrane rather than the physicalness of the body we love and know so well. View the senses' data as going straight through the membrane of the body and into the subconscious mind. If we did, the body would be much like the membrane of cells that make up the body where the membrane separates the internal environment from the external environment. With that vision or model in mind, we may be reminded of an ancient saying. "As above, so below." As the body feels, so the cells respond; as the outside environment is filtered, so the inside environment is interpreted. The health of the cells determines the health of the body, and the health of the body determines the health of the cell. We can also extend this to say, "The health of the mind determines the health of the body." The mind and body are dancing so very close, cheek to cheek and holding hands in an endless internal feedback loop. They are internally locked together as one system, and it is so fast that the conscious mind has no idea which is which.

If we look closely, we may be able to appreciate that when the mind is healthy, all the other systems in the body are healthy. It's the mind that causes everything in the body to start moving. The mind is first cause for the body. This, by default, would mean the seeds of our pain and suffering must first be in the mind. By correcting the misperceptions in the mind, which are our memories, we will experience our pain and suffering differently, or maybe they will disappear altogether. Maybe it's only the mind that needs to be healed, and then maybe the body will just follow along with the mind, which is, in fact, what it does.

When the body heals for no known physical reason, it's called an "anomaly," a deviation from the common rule. However, the body is designed to self-heal if given healing signals from the active mind. *(Here again, it is the mind that determines the state of the body. Your ego may jump up now and shout, "Accidents! It is accidents, all kinds of dangerous pathogens and genetics that cause your pain and suffering." But notice again that your state of mind determines which signals are sent to the body, and those signals determine how the body will respond, both before the event and after it occurs. Can you begin to understand that the body never responds to what is outside? As for genetics, less than 5 percent of diseases are caused by genetics-related factors, and they can be changed through the process of epigenetics.)*

WHEN THE BODY ISN'T OPERATING "NORMALLY"

The body consistently monitors the signals of the interpreted universe because that is how it is wired and therefore all it's aware of. When everything is normal in the interpreted universe or is as expected, the body operates and feels normal. All the body systems just hum along in a normal way. All the body's internal communication systems are normal, and the conscious mind doesn't pay much attention to normal and is off doing more interesting things to report on.

However, when the interpreted universe perceives a threat or danger, the body quickly changes to defense, protection, and survival mode. All the communication systems change to high alert, and the body vibrates differently. Notice that threat or danger is signaled from an interpretation in the active mind, either from filtered input data from the outside or inside or from a vividly recalled memory.

When the body perceives from the signals that it is under an attack or in danger, that perception can come only from one place, the interpreted universe, because that's all the body experiences. It doesn't even need to be a real threat from outside the body; it can be a memory that drives the body to go into survival mode. It's the signals from the active mind that drive the body into survival. Watching a scary movie will turn the body's fight-or-flight systems on and make us jump because of the signals the body gets from the active mind's interpretation of the movie. Or it could be a vivid memory that has nothing to do with what is happening outside us.

When the body isn't operating "normally," the conscious mind is awakened and becomes aware; and it begins analyzing what is going on in the body. Up to this point, no word language has been used. All communication within the mind or body and the active mind has been nonverbal and just electric, magnetic, and chemical signaling, but now the conscious mind is involved. The conscious mind uses language to tell us and, through us, others what the energy in the body seems to be expressing. The words will be emotional words that will try to define the vibrational energy moving throughout the body.

If the body is vibrating in a way the conscious mind defines as depressed, anxious, or fearful, it is the conscious mind's description of what vibrations are already being expressed in the body. The body itself is just responding to signals from the interpreted universe, and they aren't in spoken words. The body is changing its internal systems to appropriately match the signals it's receiving. The active mind's interpreted universe is creating the signals the body is responding to;

then the conscious mind describes what has happen in emotional words (in other words, depression, anxiety, or fear).

The filter system is the way it is and can be the way it is only because of our beliefs, experiences, and references from our past memories. Our memories are just stored, unreal, untrue, and incomplete interpretations of events that are over and gone. Therefore, we can say without a doubt, "It is our past that is creating our present moment." The mind may be reprocessing an old vividly remembered memory, which was created the way it was because of the past or from a new event filtered through the subconscious mind. Either way, the body is responding to the created interpreted universe's signals, and the conscious mind is reporting on how the body responded to those signals.

EMOTIONS

Look closely and notice that our emotional words don't cause the body to do anything. Emotions are just words that describe what energy is already moving in the body. If we say, "I am anxious," the word *anxious* doesn't affect the body in any way. The word *anxiety* describes how the body is already responding to the active mind's signaling, as the conscious mind reported; and because the conscious mind has references to that vibrational expression of the body from past experiences, it reports it. Emotions are descriptions of how the body is responding to the interpreted universe inside.

We must clear something up here. Emotions are verbal descriptions. They are word symbols of feelings in the body. In and of themselves, emotional words have no effect on the body. Emotions aren't things that are physical and can be touch. Emotions aren't things; they are only descriptions of how the body is vibrating. Emotions don't do anything *to* the body. They describe only what is happening *in* the body.

There are a lot of references to emotional effects in our bodies, as if emotions are causing the body to do something. Pay attention here because this will seem like I'm making a mountain out of a mole hill. The body vibrates with energy all the time. That vibration is caused by the body's response to the active mind's interpretation. When that vibration isn't normal, our conscious mind wakes up and tells us in words what the body is already doing. However, because of the conscious mind's slow processing speed, we have come to believe that the emotional word is the cause of the condition. The word *anxiety* is a description of an effect in the body; it isn't the cause. Why is this important? Because we will try to heal our anxiety in our bodies, which is only a description of an effect and doesn't address the cause, which is in the mind. This can be put into a kind of step-by-step cause-and-effect understanding.

- "Emotions" are descriptions of vibrations in the body
- Vibrations in the body are the effects of signals from the active mind's interpretation of selective data.
- The active mind's interpretation is the result of the selective data it gets from the subconscious mind. It has no idea the information is filtered and isn't all the data from the senses, and it doesn't care.
- The subconscious mind filters the data the way it does to send it to the active mind, because of past beliefs, experiences, and references, which are memories.
- Therefore, emotional descriptions we get from the conscious mind are because of our past memories. The past determines the present moment. Amazing, is it not?

How fast are the subconscious mind and active mind working? At billions of bits of data per second. If we could just get over our obsession of listening to the conscious mind and believing everything it tells us, we might heal quicker. *(You do know this would take a paradigm shift, don't you? You may get the idea that shifting may be a good thing but don't look for any shift around in the conscious mind anytime soon.)*

Emotions don't cause anything; they just describe in words the vibrations felt in the body. What is the cause? The mind. First cause is always in the mind. Is the mind the first place we look to heal our pain and suffering? Well, probably not. It's to the body where we go to relieve our pain and suffering. However, if an aspirin solves our problem, we probably wouldn't need to do anything else; but if we are taking a handful of aspirins a week, maybe we should look for a better solution.

We have confused cause and effect. The cause is the mind. It's the mind, the central nervous system and brain, that sends out signals to the body. Then the body responds. We have a tendency to believe the emotions do something, but they don't. We need to change the mind, and then the body will receive different signals and respond differently; then we will describe how the body is vibrating differently. We will have changed our conscious mind's emotional descriptors.

Again, the interpretation in the active mind is the way it is because of the information it receives from the filtering system in the black box; and the filtering system is the way it is because of our beliefs, experiences, and references from past memories being the way they are. We on the inside are the cause as to why the body vibrates the way it does. Whether our interpreted universe comes from our filtering system or from a vividly remembered memory, it doesn't matter to the active mind, because either way it's just data; and it's always us doing it to us.

We may need to rethink the way we think of emotions. Consider the fact that emotions aren't an action in the body but only a description of what energy is active in the body and therefore what behavior is being expressed by the body. Emotions describe how we feel, which is to say how we describe what is already happening in the body. Here is a brave statement, "Emotions don't cause anything or do anything." Because we know our emotions only through the conscious mind and because the conscious mind is so slow, it can tell us only what has already happened; therefore, emotions don't cause anything and can only describe the history of what did happen.

This brave statement is at odds with our current understandings of emotions. Most serious research on emotions states, emotions are complex. The theories vary, but most agree that emotions are what cause physical and psychological alterations affecting our bodies and their behavior; and they are connected to the central nervous system and therefore to the brain. *(I am stating here, "Emotions are just descriptions that you use to communicate with yourself and others about what is already happening in the body." What is happening in the body is determined, not by our verbal emotional description, but by the active mind's interpretations and the signals it sends to the mind/body, which are not in words. This happens long before our conscious mind describes it. Emotions have no effect on the body. Here again we need to get the connection; our bodies respond the way they do because of the mind. This again, is counterintuitive to your training. When you say, "It's snowing." You are describing what is already happening. You saying, "It's snowing," didn't cause it to snow. Saying, "I'm depressed," does not create depression. There is something in the mind that needs to be addressed and not in the body.)*

Emotions, being linked to behavioral tendency and resulting in physical and psychological changes that influence our behavior, seem to be saying, "Emotions affect and influence behavior" and that emotions are part or the cause of our behavior. Therefore, we act and behave the way we do because of our emotions. We are culturally programmed to believe emotions are some kind of physical things that are the cause of our physical feelings and behavior, but as I have stated here, they don't cause anything. They are a description, and that's it. *(Can you see the difference here? It's important because if you focus your healing on your emotions, you will be focused on the body and may not believe or understand that the cause of your pain and suffering is in the mind. Why don't you want to look at your mind and seek to heal it? Because it is scary in there and unknown; and for the most part, you don't know how to heal and change memories. Why? Because you are too materialistic and believe memories are real and can't be changed.)*

Why is it important to change this understanding of emotions? Because by trying to change emotions by moderating their effects in the body, we are confusing cause and effect. What we call "emotions" are just descriptions. They aren't anything but words; therefore, they aren't the cause of anything. Emotional words are ways of explaining what is going on in the body and aren't the cause of what is going on in the body. What is going on in the body is determined by the signals it receives from the active mind. The active mind sends out the signals it does because of the data it gets from the subconscious mind. The subconscious mind sends the data it does because of our past memories. Therefore, emotional, descriptive words are the result of our past memories; thus emotional descriptions don't cause anything, nor do they affect anything. *(I know I have said this several times before, but each time I say it, we will cover more ground, and you will hear it somewhat differently.)*

If we want to change our emotions, which are only descriptions, we need to change our past memories. We need to change our minds.

BACK TO THE BODY NOT OPERATING "NORMALLY"

Be aware and remember that a vivid memory can excite the active mind by sending it data to create an interpreted universe just like filtered data from the outside inputs, but in this case, the data comes fully formed from its storage location in the subconscious mind. When a memory, which is data, comes back into the active mind, the active mind creates an interpretation of the data of the memory, which will be much the same as the original interpretation of the event that is gone, because it is created with the same data saved in the subconscious mind from the original interpretation of the event.

Remember, there is no language until the conscious mind becomes involved. Therefore, the body is already vibrating abnormally by the time the conscious mind gets around to describing it. The conscious mind is always behind the action, but it's all we know, so it's what we use and what we believe to be true, complete, and real. *(I know this is an off-the-wall understanding of what you believe is currently going on inside you, but for a moment, let go of your beliefs. This may be difficult at first because your cultural programming is so ingrained. Begin to recognize that you are much more than you think you are and much more than your body.)*

CHAPTER 5

Ancient Wisdom

ONE SOURCE

Every wisdom and spiritual path has its own approach for reaching a deeper understanding of who we are. At root, most wisdom and spiritual paths acknowledge that everything comes from one source, expands, fragments into many, coalesces, and returns to one source again. Each path has its own story to tell, and those who find a particular path interesting (and it seems to be helpful for them as they move through their lives) will develop beliefs around it. Their beliefs are part of the fragmenting and breaking apart from the one source into the many, because at the root level they are all the same. *(Now don't let your ego get all bent out of shape with thoughts that you know the path you are on is the only "true path" of whatever your ego and belief system are telling you. You are on the edge of a rapidly expanding system that at root is oneness and at its edge is fractured into the many.)*

In physics this type of design is called a "fractal." It is a never-ending pattern. Fractals are infinitely complex patterns that are self-similar across different dimensional scales. They are created by repeating a simple process over and over in an ongoing feedback loop. It is driven by its self-similar process, where the future is much like the past; yet it is never exactly like the past. And the pattern is constantly expanding.

What does the fractal pattern expand into? It expands into another energy system. We may think of the two systems, the expanding edge of the fractal and the contracting void around it, as a yin and yang relationship. In this relationship the active edge of the fractal is the yang energy, of the expansion; and what it expands into, the other energy system, as the yin energy. This yin energy is mysterious since it yields to the advancing edge of the fractal. The yin energy retreats, moving back into the oneness from which it starts over again. It is like a dog chasing its tail. This is a dance between the energies of expansion and contraction, of yang and yin. How long will this dance go on? We don't know, but at root all is oneness. *(You won't normally see the oneness from the active edge of the fractal because you are too involved in being "in" your little created world and being "of" your little world. This I call "surface structure," which so fragmented that it is impossible to tell where one system starts and the other ends. Oneness is beyond surface structure in the "deep structure" of the never changing.)*

We as a species are fractal in design, which means we are self-similar across different dimensional scales of time and space. Our future will be much like the past yet never exactly like it. Things change, but we are still dualistic in our expansion. We come from oneness, expand into many, and will coalesce back into oneness. So even though the future will be much like the past, on a day-to-day, year-to-year basis, we will experience it as if it were brand new. The following quote is from T. S. Eliot, who put this adventure of life this way. "We shall not cease from exploration, and the end of all our exploring will be to arrive where we started and know the place for the first time."

THE UPANISHADS

One of the ancient paths of wisdom is that of the Upanishads. It is the foundation for Hinduism and is over five thousand years old. Upanishads mean something like "sitting at the foot/feet of" some spiritual teacher. In that wisdom path is a saying that goes something like this: "There is no outside universe. The only universe there is, is the one you create inside you."

The perceptions we create are ever changing and come and go at lightning-fast speeds. Our conscious minds report as best they can about those fleeting perceptions, and what our conscious minds report becomes our reality; yet perceptions can never be reality because they aren't real. They are perceived from filtered and manipulated data. They are unique, individually created fantasies of what we expect them to be, based on our past experiences, and aren't reality. So, if our perceptions aren't our reality, what are they? Perceptions are constructions of the active mind and become our interpreted universe. And what is our interpreted universe constructed from? Filtered and manipulated data sent by the subconscious mind. *(That data sent to the active mind is highly filtered and manipulated, and those constructed perceptions made from it are only in your head. The Upanishads had a name for these constructs; they called them "illusions." However, because of the slow way your conscious mind reports them to you, you absolutely believe they are your outside real world and that there is an outside universe of real things. Do you see what a perfect illusion you have created and live in? The active mind creates an interpreted universe inside, and the conscious mind projects it outside.)*

Since we live in an illusion and believe it is reality, we have great influence over the world we have, if we but recognize it, because our belief system determines what our created perceptions will be and what worlds we will bring into focus. If we don't like the world we have, we can bring a different world into focus. All we need to do to bring a different world into focus is to change our belief system, which we have fashioned from our past experiences and memories.

Changing our beliefs may not be easy because we have so much proof and investment in our current beliefs being true that changing them may seem like madness. We have created our whole life and the world we live in around our beliefs, and so has everyone else. Changing beliefs will change the world we believe we live in, which is our identity, because the world we currently have is brought into focus by the lens of who we think we are. Even if we don't like the world we have created, at least we know it's real, true, and familiar for us, right? Well, it's not.

Here is the point. The past and who we think we are, which is to say our memories, are all created from within our internal interpreted universe. It is an illusion; and as such, it is fluid and can be changed. Why is our past an illusion? Because our memories, which are our past, aren't true and are incomplete. Our beliefs are fabrications, most of which are given to us by others before our filtering system was in place from the time of our birth until about age six. They are an inside construct that determines the world we have brought into being. Different beliefs will bring different worlds into being. If we want a different world, all we have to do is have different beliefs. We have accepted our beliefs, either because of our family of origin or in spite of them. In either case, it is because of our family of origin that we have the beliefs we do. *(If you aren't happy with the life you have now, why not create another one, a better one? I did say that all you had to do is change your belief system, didn't I? Oh, there's the problem. You don't know what your beliefs are. And that is true. You may know some, but most of your beliefs were poured into your ear and onto your mind's hard drive before age three, and the rest of your core beliefs were in place by about age six. The only way you can know what they are is by observing the current world you have. If it's a happy world, great. If it's an unhappy world, change it.)*

What makes it so difficult to change beliefs? The reason is that each belief we have will also have tons of proof supporting that belief. All our proofs, which are experiences from the past, are all the evidence we need to convince us that our beliefs are real and true; and since we believe they are true, how or why would we ever want to change the truth we have? With all that proof the egoic self will provide to convince us, it would be stupid to try to change the truth. *(You need to understand that beliefs are believed because of all those unreal past memories and proof you think you have due to unreal memories. What are your memories? Constructions you have made from manipulated and filtered data, and they aren't the events. They are interpretations of the events; and whatever the events were, they are now gone. You can't even compare your constructed memory to the event because the event is gone and will never come back, and remember that your memories are only your memories. No one has your memories, so if your memories are unpleasant, why not change them? They are all yours, and you are the only person in them.)*

Do you see how convoluted this is? Others give us our core beliefs, they are not ours; and from those core beliefs, we construct the world we think we have. And we will not know or believe it's our construction. We will believe, it's the reality of our life; and that template is in place by age six. We don't know exactly what they are because they are deep in the subconscious mind, and way beyond what our conscious minds can remember or know; and yet, they are the bedrock of our basic programming of how our current world is. We may struggle trying to remember and understand why our lives are the way they are from our childhood. It doesn't matter whether we remember a happy childhood or a not-so-happy one. That's not the question because that's all conscious remembering. If we have negative effects in our lives, this is because we have negative causes. Now we need to change, because at this point in our lives, it doesn't matter how the programming got in there; it's there, and that's what we have. It is now we who need to change and heal. *(Blaming your past on others won't change or heal you here in the present. It is you who must change. Forgive yourself and heal and let go of the past; and through that process bring a new world into focus. You do know the past doesn't exist, don't you? The past is only a construction inside you. To let it go is to experience relief and release of a heavy burden.)*

There is another point to understand here. In the outside energy system is everything under the sun, which is to say everything. And that everything is in an unmanifested form of "the everything." No matter what our beliefs are, we will always find proof that they are true. Why would that be? Because our beliefs are the filters we use to sort through the everything, looking for what matches our beliefs. As we look through "the everything" outside us, we will find proof that our beliefs are true. Why would that be? Because everything is there in an unmanifested form. *(Begin to appreciate that everything is already here. It is streaming to you all the time. But what you receive must be like you are, because you will sort through that stream of everything and only select what matches who you think you are. You radiate a frequency of what you want, and the "everything" sends you what matches that frequency you are radiating. To get something different from what you have now, all you have to do is change your frequency to match the frequency of what is there, waiting for you. How do you change your frequency? Heal your past. What is your past? Your memories. Think of a radio station sending a signal. To hear a different station, all you need to do is change the tuner, the frequency, to that new radio frequency. See how straightforward this is?)*

State any belief we have, and no matter what it is, someone will have a complete opposite belief; and both beliefs, yours and his or hers, will have proof that his or her belief is the truth. How could both opposite beliefs have proof that they are true? Because everything is in the outside energy field, which means the proof of both is out there. Our subconscious mind will filter for the proof of our belief and throw out all the data contrary to our belief, and it happens so quickly, billions of bits per second; we don't even consciously know the data was filtered, and the proof that the other believer's belief is true will be there also, but we won't see it either. Why? Because we are looking for our proof. And the other person's filtering system is filtering for proof that his or her beliefs are real and is throwing out proof that supports your position.

Since we know our belief is the true belief, because of all our proof we have that the other person's belief is wrong, the difference between the two true beliefs could cause bad feelings between you two people. Maybe we stop talking to him or her, maybe we avoid each other, and maybe we start a war with him or her. We can do the craziest things when we believe we are absolutely right and the other person is completely wrong. *(When you are looking for your proof, consciously you have no idea that you have filtered and how the data was manipulated because it was happening so fast at the subconscious level. Does your conscious mind know all that "hocus pocus," filtering and manipulating, is going on behind the scenes? No. You absolutely believe you are right and that only you have all the truth and only the truth.)*

We did say we live in an illusion, didn't we? It's easy to forget when the egoic self distracts us.

THERE IS NOTHING GOOD OR BAD

> "For there is nothing either good or bad, but thinking
> makes it so … Since nothing is really good or bad in
> itself—it's all what a person thinks about it."
> —Shakespeare, *Hamlet*, Act 2, Scene 2

When we experience anything in the outside energy system with our senses, what we sense is neutral, which is to say it has no meaning and is meaningless as observed. It isn't good, and it isn't bad; it's just data. As encountered by the senses, the outside is just information. What gives meaning to what our senses encounter around us? All the meaning of anything in our lives comes from our inside interpretation of data based on our beliefs, experiences, and references from our past. Our past determines whether the present moment is good or bad based on our thinking about everything we encounter. The meaning of any object or situation doesn't come from the object or situation outside us. All the meaning of anything we have in our lives comes from our inside processing of the data and our inside interpretations, which is to say what we think about the object or situation, both consciously and subconsciously. *(You do remember the conscious mind is puny compared to the subconscious mind, don't you? You've got to keep that in mind, or you will start believing what the conscious mind tells you is the truth.)*

Different people with different belief systems will interpret the same objects or situations differently. The information and data received from the senses of each person aren't much different. What is different is how each person filters the data and interprets the information with his or her different belief systems and past. In so doing, different worlds are created for each of them to live in. While the active mind creates the interpretation, it's the subconscious mind that feeds the raw material to it; and we may not know consciously why we have placed the meaning we have on the objects and situations that populate our internal world. Not to worry; the conscious mind, the puny mind, will come to our rescue. Being the least informed and the last to know what is happening, it will rationalize, generalize, or delete enough so we can justify a logical response to prove to ourselves we have the right interpretation so we don't feel crazy. It's all smoke and mirrors, but we think it's really real; and that is good enough for us. *(Imagine sitting in a room at a friend's house. As you look around, you automatically get an impression or feeling about the space and what is in it. You experience the space based on your experiences of being in similar spaces with similar objects; it's not a conscious act, and it's based on your past; and for better or worse, you give meaning to the objects and space. It isn't the space or the objects that have any meaning in and of themselves. It is you. You give meaning to the space and the objects. Your friend will have a completely different meaning for the space and for each object in the space. The space and objects are meaningless until you give them your unique meaning based on your interpretation. All the meanings of everything in your world are given to them by your inside interpretation. Get this: the outside world is meaningless, is meaningless, until you think about it.)*

When we begin to appreciate that each of us gives meaning to the world we have, we begin to recognize we are creating the world we live in. Our world isn't outside us. The only world we have is the one we create inside, in our minds. What creates our current world the way it is? Our past. To change what we have, what must change? What we hold on the inside, which is to say our memories. Are they real, true, and complete? We have gone over that already but just to be clear—no, they aren't real, true, or complete.

How Do We Determine What Is Good or Bad?

Our sense organs don't tell us whether something is good or bad because the data they transmit is neutral and has no meaning. Sensory data enters the mind in an endless stream. The subconscious mind grabs the data and compares it to its vast data banks of stored memories. It mines and picks over the data, looking for things it is familiar with and that match our past experiences and memories; it looks for something it has reference to. If there is no reference or experience to the incoming data in our data banks that compares to it, or if the information is contrary to our belief system, the new incoming data is useless and can't be used. The subconscious mind is trying to find something in the new data it is familiar with. If no reference to the data is found, out it goes. *(Notice that consciously you don't even know there was any unselected data transmitted by the senses, because the conscious mind reports only on the perceptions in the active mind; and perceptions are created after the data has gone through the subconscious filtering system, with the data modified and manipulated. So when the conscious mind reports to you, you have no idea you aren't getting the whole truth. There is so much going on behind your back that it boggles the mind, at least the conscious mind.)*

The speed of the filtering process, from which the subconscious selected, manipulated, and high-graded data and information, and then sent it to the active mind, is amazing. With this purer information, the active mind interprets and creates our perceptions; and from this process, meaning is given to the data but of course only using the data that got through the filtering process and into the interpreted universe. Can we begin to appreciate that we aren't interpreting from what the senses captured from the outside information but only from the filtered data. The subconscious mind can process data at least four thousand times faster than the incoming data from the senses can flow into the mind. The active mind for its part is producing an ever-changing stream of internal interpretations from the subconscious mind's filtering process of high-graded data.

From this stream of inside perceptions, can we tell what the outside events really are? No, we can't. Do we believe our inside perceptions are the real outside event? Yes, we do. Why? Because of the conscious mind. We know only what the conscious mind tells us. What is the conscious mind observing? The perceptions in the mind and the responses in the body have already happened. The conscious mind is reporting, not on the outside events but only on the inside perceptions of the outside events as filtered by the subconscious mind; and we believe it is telling us what is really happening outside us.

The conscious mind has no connection to the outside energy system whatsoever, and the subconscious mind isn't connected to the outside energy system whatsoever either. All we know about the outside is from the data from the senses, and that information is filtered and manipulated immediately by the subconscious mind. The only connection the conscious mind has is to the perceptions it is observing inside from the active mind and the body. It is a reporter of the inside news and not of the outside news. The conscious mind is a reporter of the news and not a maker of the news. The conscious mind knows nothing about what is happening outside or in the subconscious mind. The subconscious mind is the only part of the mind that gets information from the sensory input, and it immediately changes it based on our past. Look closely and notice; the subconscious mind isn't connected to the outside energy system either. Only the senses have information about the outside energy system. Again, we need to be aware; outside us is only neutral, meaningless energy until we think about it. *(Do you see that on a conscious level, you are never connected to what is happening outside you? Do you see that on a conscious level, you are never aware of the speed and actions going on between the subconscious mind, the brain, the central nervous system, and the body? And yet you believe the conscious mind knows all.)*

So what we believe is true of the outside universe is because of what the conscious mind is telling us. And what the conscious mind tells us can come only from an inside perception created by the active mind's interpreted universe. What did the ancients tell us? "There is no 'outside universe.' The only universe there is, is the one you create inside you." Maybe they were onto something there and were far ahead of us.

It is by putting all that neutral data, neither good nor bad, from the senses through our subconscious mind's big filter system that we individually determine from inside what we think of as good, bad, beautiful, and ugly in the outside environment, what is really from our inside interpretational environment. We are the ones inside who determine the goodness or badness of everything and not the outside world and surely not from our senses. The outside world is always neutral; and even after we have given meaning to the filtered data inside through our interpretation, the outside world is still neutral. Nothing changes in the outside world because of our inside interpretations and the meaning we give them. Nothing changes in the outside world because it is the infinite, unmanifested everything. How can we ever change that?

It is our interpretation of the data, based on our beliefs or filtering system, that determines what is good or bad, beautiful or ugly, right or wrong, true or false for us; and that determination isn't based on the good or bad nor the neutral data outside us, but it is our inside interpretation of the filtered data that determines what we take to be true of the outside energy system.

What we take to be true is our reality. However, what we take to be true is real and true only for us individually, because of the big filtering system we use to process the data from the outside. If someone else or another group from a different family, culture, religion, country, social media structure, and more were to filter the same neutral data through his or her big filter system, he or she would determine a different truth and therefore a different reality from the same data. Isn't that interesting? *(You might begin to wonder,* What is really real in our created world, and what can we change? *You see why it is okay to change your painful memories; they aren't real anyway.)*

Since the truth we and others have is different, our truth isn't the real, true reality, and neither is theirs. We are both blind to the really true reality. The sad thing is that we each believe we have the real, true reality and will fight, suffer, and maybe die to maintain our not-so-real reality.

HOW DO WE KNOW WHEN THE REAL, TRUE REALITY IS REACHED?

What is reality, and how do we know when we have reached it? When we all have the same truth, we will all have the real reality. To have the real reality, we must all have the same big filtering system. To have the same big filtering system, we must all have the same belief system. To have the same belief system, we must all be of the same family, culture, religion, country, and social media structure; and have the same experiences. To have the same experiences, we would all have to be the same person. To be the same person, we would all have to be an integrated whole of one thing. This concept of One Thing or Oneness is what all wisdom paths and religious traditions have always claimed we are. We have danced around and around this mulberry bush a long time. It's kind of funny, don't you think? We end up where all ancient wisdom paths have said we were all the time; and that is in an illusion of separation; and behind the illusion, beyond the illusion, is what has always been there, the oneness. We come from oneness, we fragment into the many, and we must return to oneness to find reality. *(Do you see the illusion here? You are never not in oneness. You are the one dreaming so magnificently of the fragmented many in your illusional dream. How cool is that?)*

Some radical groups in the gross energy system have tried to force their members into an outward show of oneness by bullying and intimidating them, both psychologically and physically, into compliance. While this may ensure compliance of the body, all that it manages to do is to move the minds into more fractal expansions and thus away from oneness.

When we are standing in the separateness of our adopted belief systems as we are now, it is so difficult to see the oneness. Now, if you look really close, you will see there is only one of us in the room at any time. This oneness is tough to get, given our current way of seeing and experiencing our world; and of course, our egos at all levels will in every possible way convince us that we are and must be separate beings. No way in this egoic world can we be one because if we were in oneness, there is no ego of any kind because we would be the oneness.

If we can't or won't see the oneness, the only other way to reach the almost-true reality is through individual oneness of understanding, compassion, forgiveness, and very deep self-love; and the greatest of these is love. Currently we make our own reality anyway, and our individual realities are real for each of us. How well our reality is working for us may be questionable. If we aren't happy, content, and peaceful, we may want to change our world; if we want to change our reality, which isn't the real reality, we must do something differently, and that will require us to change our belief system.

Oh brother, there's the rub. We will need to do some work. We will need to think differently, and the work of thinking differently has to be about changing ourselves on the inside. If our external behaviors haven't changed, that means we didn't do the right work on the inside of us, because if nothing changes, then nothing changes! Behavioral changes will happen automatically when our internal programming has changed.

If we haven't changed internally, we really haven't done anything, because using willpower to change external behavior without changing the inside programming won't last. The changes that are needed must be in our belief system, not some kind of external behavior change. External behaviors are always supported by internal beliefs and programming. If we use our willpower as our only method of changing external behavior, it will work only for a short time until we stop using our willpower or get tired of using it. However, with no internal program changes, we will snap back to the way we were. The energy of willpower won't last forever, and to really change and be different, we must change our internal stuff.

Can changing external behavior change internal programming? Yes. Our core beliefs were put in place by repetition. Repeating a new behavior over and over many times a day for a long time can create a new habit and new internal programming. The process of doing this is normally called "affirmations." While there are techniques to speed up the process of imprinting and reprogramming the subconscious mind through the use of affirmations, the success rate is low, not because it doesn't work but because it does, because we run out of willpower long before we have completely integrated the program changes into the subconscious mind. If we stop before the complete change is in place, the subconscious mind will snap back to its old programming in a short time. There is no partial change; it is either complete, or over time the old behavior will begin to re-express itself. It is inside change that must take place. *(Again, you can see a cause-and-effect relationship—the effect being your behavior and the cause being your inside programming, which is your beliefs; and at root are your memories.)*

The subconscious mind doesn't forget. What was there in the mind first has the greater influence than what follows. The subconscious mind operates on what it is most familiar with. It is the habitual mind. There is a priority in the filtering system, and the oldest negative beliefs have the highest priority.

CHAPTER 6

Making Friends with the Subconscious Mind

SUBCONSCIOUS MIND AND CONSCIOUS MIND

We will go back over some things about the mind again so we are on the same page. We appear to have two minds: the conscious mind and the subconscious mind (or unconscious mind). Each realm has its own part to play in how we experience our lives, environment, world, and universe.

We know a lot about how the conscious mind works, because we are consciously aware of its activities and much of its functioning. However, for the most part, we have little knowledge or understanding about the subconscious mind and how it operates. The main reason for this lack of knowledge about the subconscious mind is because it operates outside our conscious awareness, so we are unconscious about what it is doing; and it is viewed for the most part as a black box to our understanding.

BETWEEN THE TWO MINDS

The conscious and subconscious minds are like two separate countries that have little in common. Each country has its own language, laws, and methods of operating; yet because of the common goals and the survival needs of both, they must cooperate. Since we are aware only of the conscious mind, it is easy to conclude that the conscious mind is the most important part of this two-mind system; and maybe the only mind because it fills our awareness so completely. Within the mind or body, the two countries are also divided by their responsibilities.

In truth, the conscious mind is extremely small compared to the subconscious mind, at least by a facture of a million to one. *(Don't hold me to that million to one. I really don't know about their sizes. But the subconscious mind operates a billion times faster.)* The subconscious mind holds all our permanent memory, our habits of behavior and the paradigm of our world; and it is where all our programming is and much more that is just unknown to us, at least consciously. What a fantastic piece of gear it must be. The conscious mind, not so fantastic in its moment-to-moment operations, is all we know. The conscious mind rationalizes and analyzes what has happened after it has happen. The conscious mind is the reporter of the news, as to what has happened in the mind or body, but it's not the maker of the news; it is like a Monday-morning quarterback. The conscious mind is always the least informed and the last to know about anything going on in the mind or body. *(I said this before, but it seems so off the wall and counterintuitive to what we have been taught to believe that it needs to be repeated many times so it sinks in.)*

As stated before, when the mind or body is operating normally and just humming along, the conscious mind is off doing other things. Maybe it goes daydreaming, maybe it is imagining other worlds of possibilities, or maybe it pictures different outcomes of current issues. The habitual subconscious mind doesn't do that stuff because it's busy running "The Good Ship—Mind/Body" based on its habitual programming. So while the conscious mind can't keep up with the inner working of the mind or body, it is the spirit of new possibilities and change. The subconscious mind is 95 percent of our habitual day's activities, and the conscious mind is 5 percent of the new possibilities of the day.

So while the conscious mind is the least informed about what is going on in the mind or body, it is the first to present to the active mind information of new possibilities; and that data creates new possibilities of perceptions and questions as signals are sent to the mind or body, for which a response must be made. There is dialogue between all the stakeholders in the mind and body. When all the stakeholders agree on a common goal, including the conscious mind, the results seem almost magical. However, at times it seems like the conscious mind may be out for lunch or sleeping. If they cannot agree on the goal, in the long run, the subconscious mind will win every time. *(You may be thinking, why should that be? Why yield to the subconscious mind? It's because the subconscious mind has all the weight in the interaction between the conscious and subconscious minds, and it is the habitual mind. Even though it's the biggest, the subconscious part of the mind or body can be changed; and the secret of its change is your memories.)*

The programming is the answer. The subconscious mind is where our programming is for all our habits of behavior, which are locked into combinations of our past experiences, our memories. Each of our habits of behavior and the beliefs that go with them are backed up by specific programs that are in place in the subconscious mind. One behavior may have many memories that play and dance together to form our programming for the outside-responding behavior. We may think consciously that we know exactly the changes we need to make or would like to make to create different behaviors and a better life for us; and maybe we have set a course and put a plan in place to achieve those goals through using willpower. Even if the conscious mind wants to change very badly, unless the subconscious mind agrees to the change, putting those new behaviors in place to stay may take a very long time indeed, if ever. Why? Because the programming of the old behavior is still active in the subconscious mind. It's only a keystroke away from starting up again; with only a slight lapse of willpower, it is back. The programming must change before the desired behavior can be permanently put in place.

To change the programming, we need to work within the context of the subconscious mind. To do that, we need to get past the mind's defenses and enter that subconscious country. And what are the mind's defenses? They are screens of different perceptional filters around our beliefs, experiences, and references. If information is coming to the mind, for which the mind has matching information and experiences, something we already believe and have references for, it easily gains access to the subconscious mind; and it passes right through the filtering process. However, if we have no match, reference, or history with the information and data presented by the senses, it will have a difficult time getting in.

The new information won't easily get in, at least, not until it has been put through a rigorous interrogation process. It may seem like a trial by fire that new data has to go through. The information is questioned, criticized, and rationalized to see whether the subconscious mind can use it. It is appropriate that the mind uses caution in what it lets in because the information will have an effect on the matrix of its programming and could change how we create and operate in our world. This system of perceptional filters and feedback looping together is called the "critical factor." It is the guard at the gate of the subconscious mind.

In infancy and early childhood, there is no guard at the gate, critical factor, or filtering of information. The information just flows directly into the child's mind. This is how family patterns, beliefs, and behaviors get passed from one generation to the next. It happens so effortlessly and without our knowledge, understanding, or permission; and we are likely to blame our genetics for what are just learned traits and behaviors in childhood. While 5 to10 percent of our genetics may affect how the mind or body operates to some degree, 90 to 95 percent of how we operate will be learned and ingrained patterns of beliefs and behaviors from our family of origin.

That's a difficult fact to get, is it not? Why? Because we would like genetics to cause all our poor patterns of behavior so we can blame them on our genes, which we don't believe we can control and therefore cannot change. Why would we do that? So we don't need to change ourselves and can say, "Don't blame me. Blame my genes. I'm just a victim of my genes." What a neat egoic defense against having to work on ourselves to create change. The good news is, since they are habitually learned behavior, they can be unlearned. *(It is my hope that you will slowly come to the understanding that you aren't stuck in the world you have and can begin to explore as you move forward in this read, that you aren't stuck with the genes you think you are currently expressing.)*

We are products of our environment, and this started in the womb. Genes are changed throughout the gestation period in the womb. In the womb, the cell's intelligence changes its structure to match the environment the child is growing in and will be born into. The cells change their genes for their own survival but not for the survival of the child. Once we are born, the cells continue to change genetically to match the environment the child is now living in, and this is true throughout our lives. The cells change genes throughout their lives for the same reason they did in the womb, for their survival. Cells aren't stupid and mindless. The signal they use to determine what genes get expressed comes from the environment the cells are living in, which is to say the purity or toxicity of our blood. The toxicity of our blood is determined by the chemical signals produced by the active mind's interpretation of the current moment, which is determined by our inside beliefs, experiences, references, and memories in our minds; and also by the chemicals the body uses to change its systems in response to the mind's interpretation. Those factors determine the chemical makeup of our blood, and that is the environment the cells need to survive in. If the blood is toxic to the cell, the cell will do whatever it takes to survive, including expressing genes that might be dangerous to the rest of the body. *(The process of how your cells respond to their environment and call for certain selected genes to be unwrapped and expressed from the DNA is called epigenetics. A gene is a blueprint for a protein. If the cell feels it needs a certain protein to try to survive in its current environment or for a cell's normal maintenance, it tells the DNA what it needs. When your cell asks the DNA for a particular blueprint of a protein, the DNA provides a copy so your cell can produce the needed protein.)*

I need to add a factor here that is part of the blood toxicity. Diet and other lifestyle factors and behaviors also affect the blood's toxicity. We knew that, right? I didn't mention this before because I didn't want to get lost in the pros and cons of which causes the most toxicity, and that isn't the point. The idea that "what we think affects the blood's toxicity" may be a new understanding for some, and that is the point I am making. When we are depressed or anxious or suffering any other negative feeling, that feeling goes right down to the cellular level; and it affects how the cell reacts individually and interacts in its community.

Also, family history can install programming in the child's mind before the critical factor and perceptional filtering system is in place, with specified instructions and requirements of time and situations to activate the program. The program for certain genetic expressions can be already set in place to turn on and off as needed to meet the earlier-installed programming of childhood in the subconscious mind. As mention before, the child is in a trance state most of the time and just absorbs information and turns that information directly into his or her belief system in the subconscious mind. Everything the child absorbs is absolutely true to the child's subconscious mind, and that programming determines what must happen in his or her life, unless the installed programming is changed or uninstalled. *(You might think of your earlier family of origin programming as a "posthypnotic suggestion." Once you have deeply installed the suggestions before your perceptional filters are in place, they just wait for the conditions given in the suggestion to be met, and when they are all in place, the suggestion will be activated. They are like little ticking time bombs.)*

Where are all the child's early programming of beliefs, experiences, references, and memories stored? In the subconscious mind. By about age six, the guard is in place at the gate, and the critical factor, the filtering system, is now operational and will determine what new information will be allowed into the subconscious mind. However, what is already in the mind isn't easily changed or corrected because we have no idea at a conscious level what is in there; nevertheless, that programming is basic for determining how and what our world will be. Our beliefs translate into our biology as the interpreted universe determines what signals will be sent to the body. The signals are chemical and electromagnetic, which means they change the way the organism, our bodies, responds, and that is biology. Also notice that the signals affect how toxic the blood is to the cells.

Now, if the child absorbs family history before the age of six, stating that all men die of heart attacks before age sixty or women get breast cancer in their fifties, the program is installed, the timetable is set, and the subconscious mind has started the clock ticking. The child belongs to a family and is loyal to that system; to belong to that family, the child must do what the family does. At the right time, genes will be expressed as instructed by that earlier programming. We need to understand that we can change our programming; however, if we don't understand that or don't believe internal programs in the mind are running our lives from the inside and pushing the effects out into the body and onto our world, how would we know to change them? Our conscious minds may think, *That's silliness to think something heard and believed in childhood would have any effect on me later in my fifties or sixties.* But the conscious and subconscious minds are two different minds, two different countries and worlds apart. Our programming is out of our conscious awareness. Our conscious mind, knowledge, and understanding aren't involved in the programming of the subconscious mind; and it has no idea what programming is active or which timetables are set for the program's activation. *(Everything is in the mind first. You know that, right? Your conscious mind has no idea that the trap is set; and when heart disease or cancer arrives, you will say, "It's genetic, and it runs in my family." And of course you will be right and will never think to add, "It is related to lifestyle and beliefs generated in childhood, and I have been holding this program inside, waiting for the right time to activate it." Welcome to the active world of the "nocebo effect," which is the opposite of the placebo effect.)*

Since all our beliefs and programming are in the subconscious mind, we need to make peace with that part of us. We don't need to follow the family scripting until death. It isn't the body that decides to develop any pain or suffering. It is the mind that is the causal agent for all the effects in the body.

It is the mind that determines everything. It is the body's response to the causal mind that produces all effects that happen in the body. By far and away, the biggest part of the mind is the subconscious part. Therefore, it is the subconscious mind that causes the body to respond the way it does; and what does it use to do that? Our memories. The body always suffers for the mind. First, the thoughts, beliefs, and references in the mind, and then the responses to them in the body. The body is so often the scapegoat for the mind. Understand the body is responding and can be responding only to the inside interpreted universe.

Whatever the subconscious mind does, it always does for the protection of the whole mind or body system based on our beliefs, experiences, references, and past memories. It habitually follows the programming the past set in place until it is changed. The subconscious mind sits behind its defenses of the critical factor and all its filters with all its habitual programs; and that operating system determines what data is used to create our interpreted universe of the present moment. By default the body responds, and the subconscious mind can't and won't change easily. *(Your subconscious mind absolutely knows that what gets into the subconscious is absolutely true; and since it's absolutely true, it won't easily change it. Even if your body is experiencing great pain and suffering, and in some cases even death, the subconscious mind won't change. And why is that? Because it absolutely knows its programming is helping all concerned.)*

However, if it had different information, new information, then different programs could be put in place, and old programs might be able to be reframed into a different understanding. But to get different information into the subconscious mind, we must get by the guard at the gate to get new information in there. How can we do that? We know repetition can work, but its success rate is low. How else can we get inside the subconscious and make changes? *(Maybe the same method used in early childhood that put the programming in place before age six could be used.)*

THE GAME'S AFOOT

We can think of getting into the subconscious mind as an adventure, a "spy thriller," with the subconscious mind as a foreign country. And that subconscious country is known to have many secrets and treasures hidden within it. It holds the secrets of a whole new, happy, and healthy life for us; it holds the key to changing our lives for the better, and it holds the key to our obtaining abundance. There will be much intrigue in our quest to get into that country and get its secrets of creating a new life for us and getting what we want.

The subconscious mind's boundaries are well guarded by the guard at the gate and its systems of filters and defenses. How can we get by the guards? Ah! There are ways; there are always ways. Ways that go back to the dawn of time. But once inside, what do we do? What do we look for? We are looking for ways to change current negative programming. We are looking to reframe negative and painful memories. What happens if we are caught inside? We disappear like a ghost. A spy doesn't reveal all his or her secrets, but maybe a few would be helpful here so we can understand that it can be done and that it's all right to do this work for the good of all. *(Again, you may be thinking,* You can't change memories. You can't change the truth. *You must begin to realize and question your belief that memories are real, true, and complete. You are at the crossroads between truth and illusion. You are right; you can't change "the truth," but you are wrong to assume your memories are true, real, and complete. And your subconscious mind can't tell you because everything it holds is true for it; and your egoic self won't tell you because that would spell death to the ego. As long as your ego is integrated into the belief system, to get a straight answer from the ego would be difficult.)*

SHOCK AND AWE

Shock and awe is one way of getting past the critical factor, the guard at the gate, and filters we might not have thought about. It can be a way of getting past the guard and into the subconscious mind. We shock the guard into freezing in place or running away. When the guard is in shock, the mind has no reference information on which to form a response to the situation. The gate to the subconscious mind is wide open, and new information can flow in; and so, too, new programs can be installed quickly. And in that moment, old programming can be reframed.

This is sometimes called "a significant emotional event." What constitutes a significant emotional event is different for each of us. For one person, an event for which he or she has no references or understanding will put him or her into shock. For another person the same event will have threads reaching back into old experiences in the past. The past references don't have to be about the exact same event but threads that are similar and close enough memories that the subconscious and active minds can piece together and form a meaning out of them so the body can respond.

Military boot camp and war are good metaphors for this approach to help us understand how the mind and the guard at the gate are trained. In boot camp, the new, green recruits are given references as to what may be experienced in combat and how to respond; and by repeating those experiences as exercises over and over, they program the mind in how to filter and form perceptions and body responses. These new programs aren't isolated but are integrated into what is already stored in the subconscious mind.

Now if we are in combat, we have references as to how to respond. However, those references are still associated and integrated into what's already there in the subconscious mind; therefore, each person will still respond differently. Even so, they all have more references. This is why one person may have PTSD because of an event and another person won't, even though they both experienced roughly the same outside event. It isn't the event that makes the difference but the unique interpretation each gives to the event and how it is integrated into their memories; and that is determined by past stored beliefs, experiences, and references as older memories in the subconscious mind going all the way back to birth and maybe beyond.

We have significant emotional events throughout our lives. However, the ones that have the greatest impact are those we experienced first, those of childhood and adolescence, because our reference material was so small, and they were the first inputs. Experiencing family physical, emotional, and sexual abuse; being bullied in grade school; suffering date rape; or enjoying one's first sexual experiences and many others all quickly move past the guard at the gate and change our internal programming in profound ways. We will understand our world differently from that moment of the significant emotional event and on. Some are rites of passage, and others may be traumatic events. In either case, we are changed from that moment on.

A good spy doesn't use these heavy-handed methods to move past the guard at the gate. Oh no! What he or she uses is much subtler. A handshake, an arm drop, a sudden physical movement, a word or two, and all is very peaceful and quiet. Yet the guard is distracted for a moment, the gate is open, and access is gained. The guard will never know what hit him or her. The attack is quick and effective. These are ancient methods of the mind ninjas.

Boredom

Boredom is a great method to use to get by the guard at the gate, past the filter systems of protection, and into the subconscious mind. We do it to ourselves all the time but don't recognize that's what we are doing. When we are reading a book or watching television and fall asleep with the book on our chest or the clicker in our hand, at that moment when we are hung between awareness and sleep, in that small gap, the guard is gone, and a good spy can slip right through the gate.

Here is a little-known fact. Anytime the mind moves away from the current moment of awareness and into the past or the future, into a book or movie, the guard isn't at his or her post on the gate. To understand this fact may take some reprogramming because it's counterintuitive to what we have been taught. There is only one place we can ever be, and that place is right here, right now, in the present moment. *(You do know mind and body are always connected, don't you?)* When mind and body are here and now, we are present. If the mind moves either into the past or into the future, we aren't here; and we aren't present. We have slipped into an altered state of consciousness, into a trance state, into an imaginary place that is only in our heads. If we are engrossed in this read, as you are now, we are in a trance state and don't know it. See how easily we slip seamlessly from the present into a trance state of the past or future and back again? This isn't a bad thing; it is just what happens to us.

Our egos might say, "That's not right. I'm still here, even if I'm thinking of something in the past. I'm still sitting here. That's just crazy talk." Whatever is going on in the mind is what the body is responding to, and it cannot not respond to the mind because that's the way the body is wired; mind and body are always connected. When the mind moves into a past memory, the body must respond and follow the active mind's interpretation of that remembered memory and change its systems in response based on how vivid the memory and how intense the signals are from the active mind to the body. The body never responds to outside events; it can't. It can respond only to what is inside in the active mind. *(This is a hidden truth of how your mind and body works. You are in a trancelike state a lot of the time. You move in and out, back and forth, between past, future, and present so naturally, so seamlessly; and it is such a normal process. You aren't aware of this mystical time traveling you are doing of moving in and out of reality any longer. You are in a trance from birth through adolescence, as stated before, and throughout your life. There is nothing wrong with this. It's just the way you and all of us are wired. Oh, but your ego will tell you differently because it's the master hypnotist, and who do you think your ego is hypnotizing? You, of course.)*

We have all experienced the phenomenon of being on a date, in a meeting, or in school and letting our minds wander back into past memories or into plans for the upcoming weekend; and then we realize time has slipped by. Maybe our date or someone in the meeting kicks us back into the present moment. Our eyes are open or maybe not. We are sitting there. We are breathing and maybe holding a pen or a cup of tea, but where are we? We are definitely not there, and this becomes obvious to those around us. The body's internal systems are where they should be based on where the mind goes, even though the physical body is still just sitting there. We have all done this, and we have seen others do it. Wherever we go, it's an altered state of awareness. Why is it called "an altered state"? Because the mind has moved to a place that doesn't exist anywhere except in our heads.

Wherever the mind is, it will form interpretations of the memories it has move into, and from those created perceptions, the body must respond because all it is connected to is the inside interpreted universe. So even though the outside physical body may appear to be here, how it is operating, functioning, responding, and reacting inside is in response to what the mind has created through its remembering and interpreting of the created memory; and that's the crazy part. The person's eyes are open, looking at you, coffee or teacup in hand, but we sense he or she is gone. What part isn't there, and what part is? And where did he or she go? Ah now, he or she moved into a space that isn't here; the person moved into a space that is only in his or her head and into an altered state of awareness. *(You might think of a person in a coma, except you can't kick him or her back into the here and now.)*

Think about this for a moment. If on the outside a person looks all smiles but inside is seething with hate and anger, what is the poor body having to deal with? What chemical messages are flooding the body and preparing it to attack and survive, and yet the person looks physically happy? That dichotomy of mixed purposes might be confusing to the cells of the body, and it may cause him or her to order strange genes; maybe the body gets sick for no apparent conscious reason. If we have no apparent reason for our illness, whom do we blame? The body. We always blame the body and its reactions, genes, age, weaknesses, or anything else except why the body responds the way it does. And why does the body respond the way it does? Because of the active mind's interpretation, which is caused by the data the subconscious mind sends to it. And why does the subconscious mind send the data it does? Because of stored past memories it holds within. Therefore, the negative past is the causal condition of our current body response, and we can say the unhealed past is the cause of our current pain and suffering.

We can't go there. We can't look in those old, dark corners of our minds because of family loyalties, old guilt, and shame or old traumas or other issues that cause us to experience our pain and suffering. And since we can't or won't deal with those unhealed issues, maybe we don't or cannot recognize them consciously; we can't heal, and the body must remain sick. However, to help feel better, we blame the body or someone or something outside us. Sometimes we push those old issues so far down the rabbit hole into the subconscious mind that they aren't remembered consciously, and we lose the connection between the cause and effect of our pain and suffering; and we don't understand or don't want to remember what the cause of our discomfort is.

Everything starts in the mind. The body is the scapegoat for the mind most of the time. Why? So we don't need to look inside us and at our stuff and so we don't need to change our stuff. However, if we don't change ourselves and heal our minds, which are our past memories, maybe our pain and suffering will be our bedfellows for a long time indeed. *(Did you recognize that I equated the body as being outside you? You need to start recognizing that you aren't your body. Your ego will tell you that you are your body, and you have got to stop listening to that little rascal. He'll lead you down the primrose path into more pain and suffering.)*

The past is over and gone, and that is true; however, we hang onto our old interpretations of the past through our memories, which aren't real, complete, or true. They keep us stuck and unable to heal because the energy they created is trapped in our bodies. We already say that the egoic self will defend itself by projecting negative emotional energies out into the body or anyone or anything outside us.

How is the mind healed? By changing its programming. How do we change our programming? By reframing our beliefs, experiences, and references, which are in the subconscious mind, and those are our memories. Again, we must make friends with our subconscious minds. We need to work with and get inside the subconscious mind. When all is said and done, what is the first tool of healing the mind? This shouldn't be too big of a surprise. It is self-forgiveness, and that process starts with self-love.

When all else fails, we need to get into the subconscious mind and reframe unsupportive and unloving memories. A good spy knows how to use the mind and the guard at the gate to gain access to the subconscious mind. When we engage the guard in a long, boring conversation, at some point the guard just leaves or falls asleep, and the gate is accessible; and in we go. As we think about it, we may come to realize we are in a trance state most of the time, but then we knew that, didn't we? *(95 percent of the time you aren't present, but you consciously think you are. It is the subconscious mind that is driving your bus, and you are just going along for the ride. Ah, but don't you believe you are consciously in control? See how the ego keeps you distracted?)*

WHAT'S THE PLAN?

We have discussed only two ways to gain access to the subconscious mind—shock and awe, and boredom—and to acknowledge and recognize we are in a trance state most of the time. There are other ways of gaining access to the subconscious mind, but this will be enough for now because it's not techniques we are concerned about but the purpose for using them. Again, the purpose is to reframe our negative beliefs, experiences, and references stored in the subconscious mind. They determine its programming and give us the life we are living, and that life is all about our memories.

Now again, why would we want to get into the subconscious mind anyway? To change our programming. What creates our programming? Our beliefs, experiences, and references, which are our memories from the past we have taken to be true for us, and they determine our programming. Therefore, what we really need to do is change our negative beliefs, experiences, and references; they are only memories, but they are high on the priority of the subconscious mind's filtering system. They have created the programs causing our behaviors and our world to be the way it is, including our pain and suffering; and also to acknowledge what has been alluded to up until now. But now stated directly, we need to change our unreal, negative past memories to heal our current pain and suffering.

Before we start on a program to change our memories and beliefs, we need to know what isn't working in our lives. The life we have is a reflection of what we hold to be true inside us, which are our memories. If we have a less-than-positive life, at root its cause will be negative memories. Whatever the unhealed condition or unwanted behavior is, it will have a program in the subconscious mind that supports its expression; and that is what needs to be changed.

CHAPTER 7

The Subconscious Mind

PROGRAMMING THE SUBCONSCIOUS MIND

Since all programming that controls our behavioral responses to our world is in the subconscious mind, it might be a good idea to get to know this part of us better. As was pointed out before, the subconscious mind is tremendously big compared to the conscious mind, and the subconscious mind processes information extremely fast compared to the conscious mind and input from the senses. The subconscious mind does things the conscious mind could never understand and will never know because of the conscious mind's slow processing speed. However, there is a problem with the subconscious mind, and it is this: it is habitual. It operates based on its programming. If it doesn't have a program for a situation it encounters, it defaults to its most common denominator, which is protection and defense; and the body is signaled to turn on its fight-or-flight survival systems. Being habitual, it would be interesting to know where all that subconscious habitual programming came from.

When we came into this world of the five senses and three-dimensional space/time, we came with little programming in place. While there are some memories acquired in the womb after the brain was electrically turned on, most of our programming is acquired once we are here.

To form a program of physical behavior, we need to do something over and over many times. First, we mentally do the behavior in our heads by making interpretations and holograms in our heads. The interpretations signal the body regarding what muscles need to respond to perform the intended behavior or action. The body moves its muscles and feeds back results to the active mind, and then another interpretation is made, and new signals are sent back to the body with different signals for muscle movements. If body movements don't match the desired behavior based on the feedback, new signals are sent back to the body by the active mind to adjust its movements, and the body tweaks its response until there is an agreement between the input signals from the active mind and the output feedback data from the body. At the speed they are operating, this agreement based on thousands of interpretations and types of feedback is accomplished in nanoseconds. Each of those interpretations and feedback interactions between mind and body creates a memory. For the child to learn how to move his or her center of gravity and take one step, hundreds of thousands of memories are made. *(How you move and walk today is because of all those thousands of memories and hundreds of times you practiced those movements; and you are still using those memories to move through your world today. If you were to lose or forget those memories, you would stop moving. You might think of an Alzheimer's patient here, who begins to lose his or her memory.)*

Practice makes perfect. The more we practice any behavior, the better we get at it; and the better we get at it, the faster and straighter the neural pathways in the mind or brain get, and the easier it is for the body to perform the behavior. Whether it's learning to walk, improving our golf swing, or driving a car, it is all muscle memory to our conscious minds as they observe the behavior; however, there are no memories in the muscles. They are our minds' memories. Look again because what we call "muscle memory" for a given behavior isn't muscle memory. It's a program in the subconscious mind, and it follows the process we have been describing. It looks like the muscles have memory only because of the slow processing speed of the conscious mind and how the behavior is reported. The mind or body is operating billions of bits of data per second. *(Everything is in your mind first. Everything. If it isn't in the mind, there is no way for you to interact with it. The body is always, and can only be, a reflection of the mind.)*

This interaction includes both the physical and mental. We must be taught and then practice what we have been taught we must do over and over again to make it a skill, a behavior. But this isn't a straightforward process; our programs are based on our beliefs, experiences, references, and past memories. Watch how a child learns to feed himself or herself and manipulates his or her spoon over and over; watch the parents' feedback information, which causes changes in the child's neural pathways and how his or her muscles respond. When the child becomes our age, he or she won't need to consciously think about how to use a spoon, because a subconscious program beyond our conscious awareness is still operating every time he or she picks up a spoon. *(Everything is in the mind; you need to get this.)*

When we were infants, we had little reference information or internal programming. Everything an infant experiences is being downloaded for later reference. In infancy, the mind is one open hard drive, and it hasn't yet separated into the two realms of conscious and subconscious minds, which happens at about age six. We discussed this earlier and will now expand on this idea.

TRANCE STATE

Let's start at the very beginning. The starting point of who and what we are starts before birth. However, when we are born, we are more or less like a blank slate. As a newborn and a blank slate, we end up in some form of family system we are raised in; and that blank slate gets written on with all the good and bad prejudices and beliefs of our family of origin.

For the first three years of life, the brain of a child, for the most part, operates in a deep trance state of awareness; this puts the child's brain wave frequency roughly between 0.4 hertz (cycles per second) and 4 hertz. This is a brain wave frequency called "delta." It's a deep, dreamless sleep and meditative state or yogic sleep, and it is very peaceful. The inner mind or brain/body, whether awake or asleep, is just absorbing information from its environment and downloading all that information into the mind and to its hard drive in the subconscious mind.

This process actually starts in the womb during the last half of the gestation period in the middle of the second trimester. The child's genes are being modified during this period by his or her internal environment, as expressed through the mother's physical and emotional state. Whatever the mother is experiencing stress or comfort, happiness or sadness, the child as an energy system is experiencing the same thing, and that inner experience of the child modifies his or her internal environment, which causes the cells to modify their gene expressions in response as the cells of that little body adapt to their environment to survive. This prepares the child genetically to match the environment he or she will have to survive in after birth, which is to say the environment the mother experiences inside during the child's gestation.

At that time in the womb, the brain is also electrically turned on; and primitive memories are being recorded. From this internal activity, a primal personality is being developed. This may give us some insight into the problems and concerns of adopting a child as well as the primal personality that may come with the child. While personalities can change because personalities are only responses to memories, and memories can be reframed, it may help to know the starting point so a change process can be adapted. No matter. In all cases, the happier the mother is in her pregnancy, the happier the child will be in life; and of course the opposite is true. Again, the good news is that it can be changed.

In the first three years of life, the child's brain operates, for the most part at 4 hertz called "Delta." This is a very deep hypnotic state. The child is just absorbing information. It doesn't question the information. It just absorbs it and comes to believe that it is the truth for them in their world and their reality.

During the period from three to six years old, the child's brain operates for the most part at a brain frequency between 4 and 8 hertz, called "theta," which is another trance state but not quite as deep trance as Delta. At this period, the information gathered during the first three years or so is used as reference for new input information and data; and the new data received by the mind will be compared with what has already been accepted into the child's mind as true. It is at this time that the child's core beliefs or programming, about how the child is to operate within his or her world is put in place in the mind. This will be the ground on which life will be experienced until or unless it's changed. Change can always occur, but it does take awareness to know it is needed and that it is possible.

After age six, change becomes more difficult because the critical factor is in place and the guard is at the gate. To change, we must set aside what we know as truth for us and do something counter to our now-inside programming. *(Do you think this is a conscious process and something your conscious mind is aware is taking place? No. It just believes that's the way you were born and that it's genetics and can't be changed or altered. You see how we get stuck in the same beliefs generation after generation. It isn't genetics; it is learned behavior.)*

When we sleep at night, we move into trance states automatically. This is part of our natural sleep cycle. Now if we were to play a CD or a recording of some good affirmations of changes that we would like to have in our lives, we could influence our subconscious programming because our internal filtering system and protection systems of the mind are turned down at that time. The reason why this may not work for us is because we aren't able to move into restful sleep and may not reach the automatic trance state required.

However, an infant has no such problem. Everything he or she experiences with his or her infant senses goes directly into his or her subconscious mind and onto his or her hard drive as memories, where they will be used as reference material for his or her reality. We have the personality we do because of our pre-birth experiences in the womb and our experiences in the first six years in our family of origin. Now the good news, if we don't like what we have become through this process, we can change it. Here is the difficult part. We must recognize change is needed and that we want to change. Usually we just want to blame others or our bodies for our condition so we don't need to change; and we get really good at blaming others and can get really upset at them for their not changing to meet our needs so we don't need to change.

From six to twelve years old, the child operates more or less in brain frequencies from 8 to 15 hertz. This is the state of consciousness we are in just before we fall asleep, called "alpha." It's a peaceful and relaxed state, a state of high suggestibility. It's the time of life the child is still absorbing, but he or she now interprets the world around him or her through the lens of his or her beliefs, experiences, and references from the past. The neural pathways in the brain are strengthened around the core of his or her belief system, and the child spends more time in the next frequency. *(You might be thinking,* That wasn't a peaceful time for me. A lot of crazy things happened to me while growing up. *However, your mind was in a trance state, which means whatever you experienced will have a deeper and longer influence on your internal programming, whether good or not so good.)*

From this point on, the adolescent will spend more and more of his or her waking time in the brain frequency from 15 to around 40-plus hertz. This state is called "beta" and is considered waking consciousness, where we all spend much of our awake time unless we fall back into a trance. It isn't important to know exactly what trance state a child is in at any given moment; however, what is important is to recognize that all children are in a trance state and are downloading the experiences and information they are being given from their environment, which is to say from their family of origin and later from their peer environment. *(You now operate in combinations of these trance states. You can be in beta and then slide in delta. It's just that as a child you are more likely to be in delta, and now you are more likely to be in beta. Unless you train yourself to experience a deeper state of relaxation and become as a little child, you won't recognize what state you are in. It might be interesting to be more open like a little child.)*

The child creates beliefs through repetition of processing the same movements, thoughts, and experiences, resulting in learned behaviors over time by experiencing the same information or movements over and over again. Beliefs can be changed, but they are more difficult to change after age six because of the developed filtering system of incoming information in the subconscious mind. This filtering system takes any sensory input data and compares it with what has already been accepted as truth in his or her belief system. If the information matches or appears acceptable to the child's belief system, it is allowed in and is used to create perceptions of his or her reality, which is to say the world he or she lives in. However, if the incoming information is something he or she has no reference for and/or is counter to his or her belief system, he or she won't allow it in so easily. It won't make it through his or her filtering system, and therefore it won't be part of his or her perceived reality, at least not until he or she gets more information and data.

So we, as children, start out as a clean slate and in a trance state. In that state, we develop an internal world based on those very critical first beliefs, experiences, and references absorbed mainly from our family of origin. And what we absorb and manipulate becomes the basis for our interpreted universe and the world we live in. This is all done largely from the closed environment, surroundings, and teachers in the family of origin. In essence, our families give us much of our core beliefs; and it isn't a conscious thing. *(What you believe is your uniquely well-thought-out and created beliefs about your world isn't yours. Your core beliefs were forced down your throat and through your ears while you were in trance. And you now just live with them and believe they are "God's honest truth" of who you are, and they can't be changed, or you will die and go to the bad place.)*

How does the child get out of operating in this trance state of the core belief system? Basically, he or she doesn't. Our brain wave frequency will increase into the beta range, but we operate our lives on the basic foundation of our core beliefs of childhood. We build our world around our childhood trance-state mentality; even though we are now fully grown, fully cognitive, and appear to be awake and making adult decisions, we're not. When push comes to shove, we default to our childhood defense systems unless we change those internal beliefs, which is to say changed programming we are operating under.

We have been in this trance state for a long time, as has everyone else. In some cultures, philosophies, and religions, it is recognized that we are in a trance state or dream state throughout our lives; and they offer different practices to awaken from this state. In the east, the practice of meditation is used to pierce through this state and find "enlightenment," and some say they have found it. In Western cultures, they normally use prayer to move out of this state and to pierce through this state, and some say they have found it. But throughout history there has been only a handful of people who have awakened from this trance state. The rest of us keep dreaming our dreams from inside the dream state and call it "life."

Oh, by the way, many of those who found their way out of the dream were silenced by those who wanted to stay asleep in the dream of illusions. You may have read about them. Enlightenment can be a bitch.

SEEING THINGS DIFFERENTLY

We have so much invested in our dreams and have no references for life outside the dream state; it might be uncomfortable at first, or at least it would feel different to move beyond the dream because we would need to leave so much behind if we left the dream. Thus it doesn't seem to be an option many of us are willing to take, given what little we know of being beyond the dream state. *(Maybe if you saw an advantage to awakening, you might try it. Yes, no, probably not. Can you see why dreaming is your chosen way of living your life, at least for most of us?)*

We learned from our experiences, and our experiences led us to our personal beliefs, which are the truth for us. Our truth, our belief system, is the lens, the filter, through which we perceive the outside world. Our lens will let us see and experience only a world that fits within our lens, which is to say the world we have and are living in right now, because it is the only world that fits through the lens of our currently held beliefs, experiences, and references from the past. It gets a little convoluted as we justify our beliefs, most of which others gave to us as family, culture, religion, country. *(You do understand that if you were raised in another family, culture, religion, or country, you would have a different belief system, don't you? Belief systems are like anuses; everybody has one. So what makes yours the best one? Basically, it is your consensus with family, culture, and your religious training around you. Change your beliefs, and you live in a new world. Notice closely, and you will see that it has nothing to do with the outside energy system. It is all determined by what is going on inside you. Amazing, right?)*

To justify our beliefs, we need to manipulate the information we receive from our senses just a little to get it through our filters and our lens. We may from time to time rationalized the information in extreme ways, maybe generalized it a little too much, or accept parts and disregard other parts or lose or forget parts, because what we perceive must fit into our lens to create our perceived and interpreted world the way it is for us. But not to worry; this is all done in the subconscious mind. Consciously we will experience only the end result of a very long and fast process, and it is all done behind the screen of our conscious awareness; it becomes our lives automatically. See how easy it is to stay in our dream state?

If we like the world we have and think it's great, we are in the right place. If our world isn't so great and we would like a different one, we will need to change our lens. Since our lens is our truth, we will need to change our truth; and our truth is built from our beliefs. Because we have so much proof that our beliefs are real and true, it may seem like an impossible task to reject what we believe to be true and move to a new belief that isn't true, and for which we have no proof as yet. *(It's an interesting idea though, don't you think? I mean, throwing out your truth to put an untruth in place. But then the truth you now have really isn't your truth; it just happened because of those who wrote on your blank slate while you were in a trance state growing up.)*

All beliefs are true for the believer, and the believer will need proofs that his or beliefs are true. That's not the point. The point is, how are our truths working for us? If we aren't happy in our world, we can change the beliefs that aren't working and generate different ones; and when we do so, we will create a new world. We made up our current truths or just absorbed those truths from others around us. *(You do know that you absorb other people's truths, their beliefs, don't you? You do that particularly in childhood. But since you are in a trance state a lot, you can pick them up from many other people and places throughout your life. I'll bet you thought your beliefs are real because of your proof. Don't be silly! Whatever beliefs you have, with all your proofs that seem so real, someone else will have the complete opposite belief than you, and he or she will have bunches of proofs that he or she is right. It's all one big game. Nothing is really all real, and nothing is as you think it is. Why? Because it's all an* illusion. *I said that before, didn't I? It's hard to remember, given your egoic mind-set, isn't it? And of course, your ego will keep you believing your beliefs are the real and only true beliefs there are. See how much help you have in being stuck where you are, in your dream state and in the illusion?)*

However, if we look very closely at our experiences, we will see it's not the outside event that creates our truth but our inside interpretation of the event and not the event at all. And an interpretation of an event isn't the event itself; we know that, right? It is a distortion of the event; it is a new creation inside us, and it isn't the event because the event never happened the way we interpreted it happening. At least it never happened the way we think it happened, although our conscious mind and ego tell us it did, but then the conscious mind has no idea of all the things that are going on behind the scenes and out of its awareness.

Let's stop right here for a moment and take a deep breath. What is the difference between the event and our interpretation of the event? The event is the complete energy system released from an occurrence or event. From the complete energy of the event, we can experience only what our lens will allow us to receive; therefore, we will never experience the whole event but only the portion that fits through our lens. From that small portion of information, we interpret the whole event for us; and we rationalize, generalize, and delete stuff. We never see the event the way it is but only from the way we are, which is to say that we experience the event through our beliefs, experiences, and references from the past.

Since we never experience anything the way it is, what we do experience isn't complete, real, or true; therefore, it is an illusion. We know it's real for us because it feels real based on how the body responds, but it's not complete; it's shifting haft-truths, generalizations, rationalizations, and sometimes out-and-out lies we tell ourselves. Sorry. But it does seem real at the time, doesn't it?

The following diagram may give us an idea of how events are filtered through our lens of the past and why we end up with the perceptions and interpretations we do.

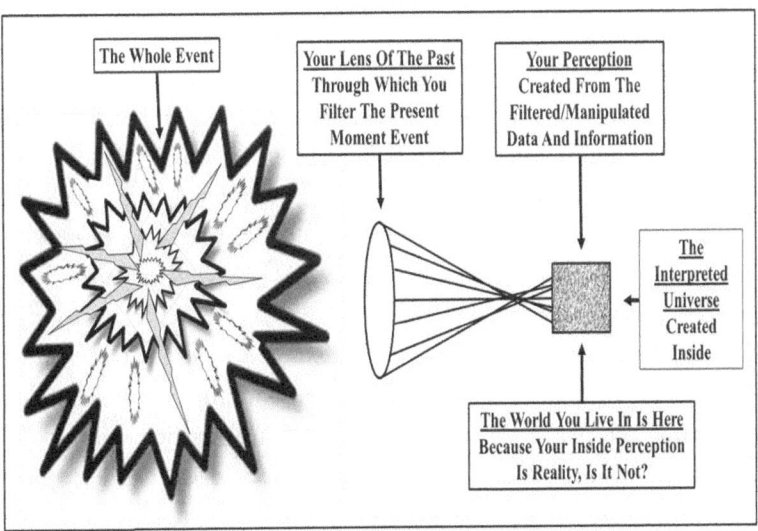

Diagram 01 - Perception Isn't Reality

Since we alone are making up our truth by our interpretation of bits and pieces of each event we experience, we create the perception of the event that never happened. At least it never happened the way we think it did. Therefore, what we experience is our creation of the event, and we believe our created perception is the reality of what really happened. When the event is over and gone, our perception along with all its emotional energy is turned into a memory of something that never happened the way we think it did. Isn't that weird? And yet we believe it really happened the way we created it. And of course, we find it difficult to believe that what we created is only an interpretation and isn't the exact event itself and that our memory of the event is, therefore, not real, true, or complete. But because we are so sure with great conviction, belief, and intensity that our memories are all complete and real, and we believe the truth of the events they depict, our ego will fight hard and long to keep the unreal real. *(Can you begin to appreciate that your memories aren't events? Events happen, and then they are gone. Memories of events stay forever until you change them, but they aren't the events. Memories are your inside constructions made from your interpretations of what didn't happen the way you thought it did. Why? Because the data you used to construct your interpretation was filtered and manipulated data made to fit the lens of your unique past, you consciously don't know or believe that all your memories have been made from filtered and manipulated data.)*

When we recall a memory of an event that is long gone and over, we remember a creation. It isn't a memory of the event. It is a memory of our interpretation of something that exists only in our minds and never existed in its completeness in any place, especially not in our heads. *(I know, your memories seem real. I know, you are absolutely sure your memories are complete, real, and true. But up to this moment, you may never have known you have created them from filtered and manipulated data. You may have always believed consciously that your interpretations of events are real, true, and complete. See how your egoic self has kept you deep in the illusion.)*

All our memories aren't quite real. Some memories may be close to representing the original event, and others are farther away from the reality of the event, but in either case they are never real, complete, or true. And the sad thing is, we can't tell the difference between which ones are close to the event and which ones are far out there. Yet they are all used as an integral part of our belief system, which is to say our filtering system of the outside world. There is an old saying. "We see what we want to see and hear what we want to hear." *(There is more there in the input data from your senses to be seen and heard, but you filter it out because it doesn't fit through your lens. There is truth in that saying from within the dream. You do see what you want to see and hear what you want to hear. Can you see how your beliefs can keep you in the illusion? It is very subtle, isn't it? And you just don't see it and therefore can't believe it. What a great illusion you have created and are in.)*

We are very creative beings; what we create has to fit our lens of interpretations and perceptions because for us perception is our reality. Why? Because it's all we know. As the diagram above shows, perception isn't real and therefore cannot be reality; however, it can be an illusion we believe is reality. Beliefs are very powerful creators of our illusions.

The lens through which we bring our world into focus is easily changed. All we need to do is change our lens, and that will bring a different world into focus. What is our lens? Our memories of the past. To have a new or different world, all we need to do is reframe our memories because they are all the past we have; and as we have stated many times, they aren't real. The following statement by Dr. Wayne Dyer makes sense when we begin to realize we are making it all up anyway; therefore we can change it. "When you change the way you look at things, the things you look at change!"

When we change our lenses, we will cause a different world to be brought into focus. That different world we see after we have changed our lens has been there all the time in an unmanifested form. What we think of as the outside energy system doesn't need to change or be different in anyway at all for us to have a different world. In fact, the outside energy system cannot change because it's already everything. As we change our lenses, a different world will be there, created from the same external input data. It is through our lens, a lens we have created, that brings into focus the world we are experiencing right now. By changing our lens, our filtering system, we bring a different physical world into being. We can create a new world by changing something inside us. Isn't that crazy? *(You need to notice something carefully here. By changing your lens, you will bring a different "physical world" into focus.*

This isn't magic. Photographers have always known that if they change the lens of their camera, they will get a different physical picture. Fishermen have known that if they change their fishing lure or fishing net, which is a filter, they will catch different fish. Since everything is in the outside energy system, does it seem so strange that if you change your hook, you'll catch different stuff? Or that if you change your lens, you will see different things? Does it seem so strange that if you change the lens on your camera, you will see a different world? It's not magic. "When you change the way you look at things, the things you look at change." And that change will be physical.)

Can we change what is outside us? And just what is outside us anyway? Only energy is there outside us in an unmanifested form, and what is inside us? Only memories. Now, a question or two might come to mind about how our lenses can be restructured and reformed and what reality is anyway? We will try to second-guess those answers later on.

If we try to understand that the physical world can changed through using Newtonian physics, we may have a problem. However, if we look through the lens of quantum physics, the problem will become clearer. The link between reality and its observation in quantum physics is based on what has been called the "Copenhagen Interpretation of Quantum Mechanics." In part of that Copenhagen interpretation is the following statement: "The observer affects the observed!" *(I am not going into quantum physics here. It's not my field, but I am interested in the statement that has come out of quantum physics, "The Observer Affects the Observed!")* (Wikipedia, Observer effect (physics))

What a simple statement for all the problems it originally caused science, philosophy, and religion when it was first proposed, because this didn't match our old paradigm of the world, and we had a lot invested in the old paradigm. What was the old paradigm? Basically it was, "The observer has no effect on what was being observed."

The observer was just observing, like watching a movie. The observer couldn't change the movie. The cause of our lives and our world, which was outside us, was also outside our control and was separate from us in the old paradigm. We were somehow just pawns of the outside universe, which was constantly pushing against us and determining our lives, over which we had little control.

Now, after some time has passed since the Copenhagen interpretation, it makes more sense to more people, although it is still scary to many. "How can what I do or think inside effect what is going on in the outside universe?" The short answer is, you can't; the outside universe is just energy and is everything. Begin to explore the possibility that the outside universe isn't the universe we live in. In the above diagram, our interpreted universe is where we live. *(Slowly I have been bringing this idea into focus for you to appreciate that you live in your created interpreted universe and that what you experience is the way you experience it because of your unique memories of the past.)*

On one level, consciousness basically means what we are consciously aware of. What our conscious mind is aware of isn't that much, and it is the least informed and the last to know, but it is all we know consciously, so we tend to think it is all there is to know. The greatest contributor to our state of health is our subconscious mind, which is our memories or our created beliefs, experiences, and references from our past. Therefore, our past determines our current state of health. To change our current state of health, the past needs to be reframed and changed. *(Now this is a different understanding of your responsibility for your health. Since your body is a direct reflection of your mind, whatever your health is in the body can be moderated by the mind. Change your mind, your memories, and you change your life. I said that before, right?)*

However, we must look deeper into consciousness here, for the state of consciousness suggested here is far from the conscious mind. I relate it to a field of awareness we are embedded in. I will expand on this subtle field[G] throughout the read.

We are the most complicated organisms we know of in the whole cosmos, and we as a species have been around for eons of time, evolving and changing; and some of the old ways of thinking may be coming back into vogue. The following statement is from ancient wisdom and has followed us around on our long journey. It's like a perennial flower because it comes up on a regular basis wherever we find ourselves on our evolutionary path, and it is this: "At root, all problems are spiritual!"

The question of what is spirit and where it comes from is well beyond the scope of our little discussion here. Besides, we each have our own lens we look through to bring those answers into focus for us. So we will leave that to our individual determination.

This in a nutshell is the essence of our journey. Keep in mind in our discussion here that we will be trying to look through a different lens at our universe. And hopefully for a while we can suspend our current understandings, beliefs, and prejudices. It might be interesting and fun to fantasize a brave new world into being for a little while.

THE ULTIMATE ASTRONAUT

We come into this three-dimensional, space/time environment with a body. We can think of the energy that keeps our bodies working as a life force energy within the body. Metaphorically, the body is the spaceship that holds our life force, and that life force is the ultimate astronaut; with a good spaceship, the ultimate astronaut is able to move through this outer environment with ease.

We will say this several times: "We aren't our bodies." It's difficult to think of us not being our bodies because our whole culture operates on the premise that our bodies are who we are. Even if at some level we may know we aren't our bodies, that belief is difficult to maintain for long periods of time because of the overwhelming evidence the egoic self uses to support the statement "We are our bodies." Because so much is invested in our culture and society about us being our bodies, it's difficult to resist that thought. Being the body not only puts us in our world of objects but also integrates us deeply in the illusion of the gross energy system.[G] This energy system is the playground of our senses and what we can experience through our interpretation of our sensory input. *(Your ego is created from within the gross energy system, and its existence depends on your staying in that system; it does that with guile and persistence, keeping you believing you are your body. But understand now that you aren't your body. You at root are far beyond your body.)*

So we need to be clear on this point. "You aren't your body." We need a body, or we couldn't be in this environment. The purpose of the body is to be a vehicle, a spaceship, for who we really are, the life force, the ultimate astronaut. So the body is the means by which life force can be in this environment. When life force leaves the body, the body is no longer needed and dissolves back into this three-dimensional universe from which it came, and the ego will be no more. And life force returns to its source also.

All information, data, and experiences from the outside world must come to us through the spaceship's instrumentation, the body's senses, to the spaceman inside for analyzing, interpreting, and being acted on. *(This is what I have called the active mind.)* But this process isn't all that simple or straightforward inside us. Basically, the spaceman just sits inside the spaceship, monitoring the outside through the ship's instrumentation. Notice the spaceman isn't directly connected to the outside environment in any way, and he gets all his information secondhand through the spaceship's instrumentation. Our relationship to our bodies, our spaceship, is close but not perfect. Much of what is going on in the subconscious mind, body, and brain goes on without our conscious mind's awareness, understanding, or consent; and that's a good thing because we consciously could never keep up with all the things that need to be taken care of in the body on a moment-by-moment basis. It's necessary for the body to operate independently from conscious awareness. However, notice it's always connected and responding to the active mind. This is a very complex dance between the body and what we are aware of consciously. *(You are now aware of how slowly your conscious mind is compared to how fast the body/mind has to work to keep us going. But somehow your conscious mind convinces you that it is in charge and running the ship. And the sad thing is, you believe it.)*

When the body responds to the interpretation of the active mind, it sends feedback data to the active mind in the form of a feedback loop of information as to what systems have been changed. The active mind then interprets the feedback data. It is at this point that the conscious mind reports pain and suffering. Why is that? Because our pain and suffering are always an interpretation in the mind and not in the body. The body communicates only through the mind. Minds communicate, not bodies. Everything happens in the mind first.

It is at the point of the mind's interpretation of the feedback information from the body that the mind becomes aware that we have pain and suffering. When we have pain and suffering, look to the mind for the cause. The mind has signaled the body on how to respond, and feedback from the body is its response to those causal signals. If it looks like the cause is something other than the mind, this is a misperception.

There is wisdom in the body. It operates quite well without conscious awareness and interference. In most cases, when the conscious mind tries to take over the controls and run the ship, chaos follows. The conscious mind operates at a much-too-slow processing speed compared to what the body needs to function normally, let alone operate in a crisis.

When the body and mind are balanced and operating "normally," we feel nothing unusual consciously, even though much is going on and happening in the body, in the subconscious mind, brain, and central nervous system. When operating normally, there are no alarms or whistles going off in our heads. We become accustomed to that normal feeling and disregard the body's aliveness. In fact, when things are normal, the conscious mind doesn't stick around. It's like watching clothes dry; the conscious mind finds something more exciting to do, and off it goes. So the body has to be able to function on its own and without help. However, it's always connected and responsive to the active mind's signals.

When our bodies are just humming along and vibrating in their normal way, we are healthy and normal, and we are unaware of the body consciously, and normally we don't care on a conscious level. We are unaware of our bodies' aliveness, energy, vibration, functioning, and wisdom. What a magnificent instrument the body is.

THE POWER OF THINKING POSITIVELY

There are those who believe that if they think positive thoughts, the universe is more likely to give them their hearts' desires, and this is true. This approach is called the "law of attraction" or using "positive affirmations." The law states that what we attract into our lives is determined by what our most dominant thoughts are. Therefore, happy thoughts should bring us things to make us happy. However, the effectiveness of the law of attraction depends on the energy system of the whole body and not just a few positive conscious thoughts in the conscious mind. It is the whole energy system, the whole body and mind, that produces the energy signature the universe is responding to.

In theory when energy, like radio waves, are generated, they go on forever. They can be deflected and change form, but they are still there. In fact, even now with the right instruments, we can pick up microwave noise from the big bang when the universe started. Now the radiant energy of the body isn't the big bang; however, in theory it too goes on forever, and that's a long time. So, what energy from the mind or body is radiated out into the universe? And what is carried on that energy wave? It is the energy signal of our most dominant thoughts. What are we asking for within that energy signal?

If we think positive thoughts, they will affect the radiated energy field of the body, and that's for sure. Thoughts in the mind do generate energy. However, there are two minds: conscious and subconscious (or unconscious). If we are aware of the thoughts we are thinking, they are coming from the conscious mind. On the other hand, thoughts in the subconscious mind aren't known and are out of conscious awareness. The conscious mind is very small compared to the subconscious mind, as we stated before. The subconscious mind is big and is functioning outside our conscious awareness. It doesn't sleep, and it operates 24-7 and is fast; it far overshadows the little conscious mind and the small intermittent energy it generates.

Recall in Chapter 1, "Energy, Energy Everywhere, and Not an Electron Do I See," that we pictured the heart as the carrier wave on which rides the whole energy signature because we can detect it the farthest away from the body. The information riding on the wave is determined by the body's responds to the interpretation in the active mind, the constant programming in the subconscious mind, and the reporting of the conscious mind. While the heart is the strongest radiator of energy, what it carries with it is the mind's message; and the overwhelming embedded message in that energy is the subconscious mind's information.

Since it is the whole energy signature of the mind or body we are sending out into the universe to get our heart's desire, it can be quite confusing as to what we will receive back. What we get back may not be what we consciously thought we were asking for. We might say, "Hey!

I didn't ask for this stuff! Why in the world is the universe sending me this stuff? I don't want this."

However, for some crazy reason, what we get back from the universe and in our lives always matches the request of the total energy signal we have sent out; and that is what the universe is giving us back. Why would the universe do that? Is the universe stupid? No. We are getting exactly what we are asking for. We always get what we are asking for from the universe. What we get back is the effect of our causal, most dominant thoughts. If we get what we consciously want, great. That means the conscious and subconscious minds are in harmony. If we aren't getting what we consciously want, we need to change the way we are asking. The two minds aren't together. *(Guess which of your minds is the most dominant and has the most overriding powerful energy signature? That is the one determining how your life is and what you get from the universe, and it is the subconscious mind, but then you knew that, didn't you? Or do you still think it is your little conscious mind running the show?)*

In the subconscious mind are all our beliefs, experiences, memories, references, and programming. This subconscious part of us drives and determines the life we have, and as such, it determines the greater part of what we are asking for from the universe. Since it's out of conscious awareness, it shouldn't be surprising that the conscious mind has no idea what we are asking for or why we keep getting things the conscious mind may not want.

Again, if we know what kind of positive thoughts we are thinking, they will be coming from our small, conscious minds. What are we creating in our subconscious minds? Ah, now that's the question. How do we know what those thoughts might be asking for, because those thoughts are dominant and will determine the energy signature we are sending to the universe on our hearts? What is returned to us is our life experience.

Again, what is going on in the subconscious mind is out of conscious awareness because it's a black box. So how can we know what energy signature we are sending out? The answer is, we don't consciously and can't know directly.

To find out what kind of energy is being generated and radiated from the subconscious mind, we only need to look for clues. The clues are all around us. A smart detective should be able to figure them out. For example, are you angry a lot? Do you play the victim role? Are you always trying to get even for some perceived slights against you? Are you abusive? Do you always agree with others because you are afraid they won't like you if you don't? Are you addicted to substances or behaviors? What role, what family script, have we taken on from our family of origin or in the life we are living now? These answers will create an energy signature that will give us specific returns from the universe, and those returns might not be what we would consciously like to have, but they will match what signature we are sending out to the universe.

The subconscious mind is where all our learned, ingrained behaviors, beliefs, and habitual programming are stored; and they all operate from there. What kind of energetic thoughts are going on in that deeper part of us? That is the energy we are radiating. What have we attracted into our lives? The law of attraction doesn't start working when we start thinking a few positive, happy, little thoughts from our conscious minds. They're always operating day in, day out, year in, and year out. Whatever we have in our lives right now is what we have been asking for and working hard to get from the universe. What we have now in our lives has to match the energy we have been radiating, because that's the way the law of attraction works. *(Oh, by the way, the thoughts your subconscious mind is sending aren't in words. The language the subconscious mind uses isn't the same as that of the conscious mind. They don't operate in the same language. I said that before, didn't I? So do you see why the conscious mind has no idea what you are asking for?)*

If we don't like what we have received, we will need to change our total energy signature. Just thinking happy positive thoughts now and then won't do it. Healing at a much deeper level may be indicated. Maybe changes are needed that go clear down to the marrow of the bones and clear back to our family of origin. Do we really think that thinking a few happy, positive thoughts now and then, without changing anything else in our lives and reframing our past, will really excite the universe to give us our hearts' desires?

Rather than sending out requests for the stuff we want from our conscious minds, it might be more helpful to ask the universe, "What am I doing currently in my life that's preventing my desires from manifesting?" As we heal and change from our old paradigm, our old programming, and our old negative memories, our desires must begin flowing into our lives. We, not the universe, need to change. So what needs to change in us? It always gets back to us, doesn't it?

Remember, outside our skin and maybe also inside is the universe of everything in its unmanifested form. It is ready to give us what we are asking for. It doesn't need to change. Why doesn't it need to change? Because it is already everything there is and all we could want or ask for. We are touching hands with the universe. We are dancing with the universe; and based on our feedback, it is responding to us perfectly in its own way.

Energy and the Body

"Everything is energy," as we have said before. First things first, before anything can happen, anything can move, anything can be manifested into physical existence, there must be an energy system and pattern. The mind or body would seem to be a good place for us to start manifesting energy patterns of what we want; and of course, that starts in the subconscious mind. *(I know, you want the conscious mind to be involved in the process because that's what you know and are aware of; and it does have its part to play because it thinks outside the habitual self, the black box. However, getting those new insights into the subconscious mind to change programming may take some time and a lot of repetition. Your subconscious mind carries the big stick here. You will need to get around the guard at the gate first.)*

Think about this: everything that is created or manifested into this three-dimensional, space/time universe must be created or manifested twice. First, it must be created within the energy of the mind. Here again think of the subconscious mind because our imagination is more active when the conscious mind is distracted or asleep. Those eureka moments in the mind happen when the conscious mind is preoccupied, and then the information flows into the active mind; then as it is interpreted, a hologram is manifested in our heads. The conscious mind now becomes aware of it and tells us about it. And we absolutely believe the conscious mind came up with the idea. From there we manifest them into the physical universe. Thomas Edison used this method. The story goes that when Tom was stuck on a problem and couldn't figure something out, he would take a catnap for half an hour or so and wake up with the answer. He even had a cot put in his workshop just for that purpose.

We might reverse our thinking about the energy field or aura around the body. Maybe the energy field isn't radiated from the body. Maybe the body is hung inside that field, and we see the body through that field. Maybe the body is a manifestation of the energy field, and maybe the body is only an interpretation of the active mind. Maybe that old, ancient saying is true. "We are spiritual, energy, beings having a physical experience." But then maybe not.

Energy needs to be there first, or nothing can move, and nothing can happen. We are first energy and then matter; we are first energy beings and then physical beings. Everything is first energy. Energy is the matrix on which physical matter is hung and grown. When the energy field releases the body, the matter returns to its lowest grounded energy state of separate bits and pieces of separate molecules.

Energy, Disease, and the Body

Since the energy must be there first, all discomfort and disease in the physical body must first be in the energy matrix before it can be experienced in physical matter in the body. The interface or border between energy and matter is our minds. What our minds think becomes our bodies' state of health.

Let us look again at our minds and its two realms, the conscious mind and the subconscious mind. What we are aware of right now is what the conscious mind is reporting to us; and because of its slow processing, it doesn't have all the information there is to know, but it's all the conscious mind is aware of. It has only screenshots of what is going on in the active mind and the body, not the whole story. From those screenshots, it pieces together a story of what has happened, and it is that make-believe story we are aware of. Behind the screen and out of sight of the conscious mind is the subconscious mind. The subconscious mind is filtering incoming data of the senses, sending data to the active mind, answering inquiries for information, and sending responses back and forth; this is all done in fractions of a second. *(You may recall this was said before. Things are happening so fast in that hidden realm of mind, body, and central nervous system that it's difficult to really understand or appreciate it.)*

The conscious mind is easily distracted and jumps from one thing to another, a process often called "monkey mind." It has the least information and is the last to know anything, yet it is all we know. We heard that before, and it will be said again.

In the hidden realm of the subconscious is where most of our energy is moving. It is the space where all our beliefs and experiences are stored. It is where our learned and ingrained programming operates out of. It is where what we think of as muscle memory is stored, which is just memories, and where our automatic behaviors are, along with their automatic responses and reactions to external and internal triggers in our environment. It is also where our ego identity of who we think we are is stored. This hidden realm never sleeps and is always active. *(Can you begin to understand why what goes on in your subconscious mind is what determines what you receive from the universe and why you consciously may not agree with what the universe is giving you?)*

Remember, the subconscious part of our minds is bigger, is more active, and operates billions of times faster than the conscious mind. The secret of getting what we want in our lives is to make friends with that deeper part of us. We said that before, too, right?

Recognizing the Energy Systems of the Body

Many ancient cultures have recognized and acknowledged that the body is an energy system and that it responds only to the mind, and that our bodies aren't who we are. Western cultures struggle with the concept more than Eastern cultures, but that's another story. The statement "We aren't our bodies" is true. There are two major understandings or recognitions that the body is an energy system, and they come from China and India. We will touch on only a few points of interest of these two very expansive systems of understanding and healing; and to understand their healing and energy potential for the mind and body.

In China the body's energy system is understood to be around meridians, which are seen as energy conduits or rivers of energy that flow in the body and are seen as channels, through which life force or chi moves. In this system of understanding, when chi is in balance, we are in health. When chi is out of balance, we are in discomfort and disease. To move from disease to health in the body and mind, different forms of traditional Chinese medicine are used to bring chi back into balance. One of those forms is acupuncture, in which needles are put into specific combinations of points in the meridian energy system, depending on the discomfort experienced in the body. By stimulating the meridian system through needles, pressure, and other means, balance is restored to the body, and health returns.

Since mind and body are always connected, ultimately the mind will decide to heal. As the communication from mind to body and from body to mind, signals, and feedback dance together, it is only the mind that tells the body how to respond. External agents work only as the mind accepts and expects them to work. *(You may have heard the saying "If you believe it will work, it is more likely to work." Who must believe it, the mind or the body? It is the mind, and you knew that, didn't you? Your body doesn't believe anything. All beliefs are in the mind. Changing your mind can heal you. Changing your mind can make you sick. Changing your mind can keep you sick. Everything is in your mind.)*

In India the body's energy system is around chakras, which are seen as vortices of whirling energy or wheels. These vortices of energy are throughout the body. However, depending on the practitioner, there are seven major chakras; in some systems, twelve or more major chakras are used. They are mainly on the center line of the body along the spinal column and go through the body from the front and out the back. The energy that moves through the chakras is life force or prana. Emanating from the chakras are energy pathways throughout the body called "nadis." When the chakras are open and clear prana is balanced, moving freely through the chakra system, we are in health. When any of the chakras are blocked or not completely open and clear, we are out of balance and in discomfort or disease. To move from disease to health in the body and mind, the chakras need to be open and clear; and when they are, the body's energy is balanced, and we are in health. Some of the forms for balancing the chakras are yoga; meditation; sound, light, and diet therapies; and Ayurvedic medicine.

There are many systems of healing that use the body's energy systems to release and dissipate physical and emotional pain, suffering, and discomfort. At root these two systems use the ancient pathways in slightly different ways. One of the more recent methods used for releasing and balancing energy in the body is called "tapping." Tapping is a form of acupressure that uses acupoints in the meridian energy system and the chakras energy system because the two systems interrelate. There are different forms of "tapping" to release negative and trapped emotional energy and energy imbalances in the body. One of the tapping systems shown to be quick and affective is Faster EFT (Faster Emotion Focused Transition), which uses the energy systems of the meridian system to release negatively trapped emotional energy attached to or within our negative memories. Notice what I said, "ancient pathways" of healing. They are ancient only from the standpoint that this energy system was recognized in ancient times; however, this is the way the body has always functioned, and it will always function this way. Every animal, including humans, has this energy system. Both acupuncture, chakras, and different forms of tapping or trigger point healing therapy are used on all domestic animals, such as horses, dogs, and cats as well as people today. *(This isn't new information I am giving you. It is ancient wisdom in new clothes.)*

There are several different methods for releasing negative energies trapped within memories and within the body. They can be found under the general headings of "energy psychology," which includes tapping, hypnosis, neuro-linguistic programming (NLP), and many other methods. There is more than enough empirical and scientific data to know they are effective. However, for some people, because of their deep investment in their belief system, which is to say who they think they are, these approaches aren't available to them; and they will fight hard to maintain their egoic self-identity of who they think they are. We always see what we want to see, and what we see is determined by the filter system of our unique belief system. *(Your filter system is unique all right, and only you have it; and only you have the one you have. Therefore, only you have the output you do, which is to say the world you have. It is your mind's decision to have the world you have with the pain and suffering you have.)*

To embrace a different understanding of healing may challenge our belief system of who we think we are, which would be viewed as a direct attack on our identity; and this might be too overwhelming for some. Therefore, holding on to their current belief identity may cause change and healing to happen much more slowly.

When our identity is under attack, we quickly move into defensive and survival mode. When we are in that state, we aren't open to experience any different approaches to healing. What the mind believes, the body must respond to. What is in the mind? Our past memories. What do we use those memories for? To create our interpreted universe, the world we have. And what is the body responding to? It responds only to the created interpreted universe. And what is causing the interpreted universe to be the way it is? Our beliefs. See how convoluted our thought processes are and how responsive the body is to them? To experience a different approach to healing, we need to set ourselves aside, which is to say setting our beliefs aside for a little while, and become much more wondrous, curious, and childlike to the process of healing; that may open us to a brave new world of understanding.

CHAPTER 8

The Untrue Past

WHAT ARE WE REFRAMING?

We need to be clear on what is being reframed and reprogrammed when we change memories. What we are changing are our unique beliefs, experiences, and references, which are our past memories. And now here's an important question: "Are our beliefs, experiences, and references, which are now our memories from the past, real, complete, and true?" We are now aware that it is our past that determines what our current present moment will be, but do those beliefs, experiences, and references determine the present moment as real? Is the past real? Don't answer too quickly because we are going to look at this topic in a little different way for a while.

We have said earlier that we never see the whole event that unfolds before us. We can see and experience only what will fit through our lens or the filter of our past. The lens has two side, a primary side and a secondary side. The primary side of the lens is the side the event information enters from the senses. The secondary side of the lens is the distorted, selected, and manipulated output information after going through the lens. The lens represents the filtering systems and defenses of the mind, our perceptional filters, and our guard at the gate of the subconscious mind. The lens isn't pure. It has interference patterns of old memories in it, and what comes out of our lens is different from what went into it.

Each belief, experience, and reference builds on, and is determined by, older memories experienced before. The matrix structure of memories is the subconscious mind's filtering system, and older memories determine newer memories. To understand the distortion of our belief system, we need to go back to our very first experiences. How can we do that? We can't, at least not consciously. However, we can use a technique that has proved useful in science, "a thought experiment." Thought experiments have proved to be helpful in science, and maybe they will be helpful here for us.

A thought experiment considers some hypothesis, theory, or principle around a theme, concern, or problem for the purpose of thinking through all its consequences; and experimenting in our mind's eye, our imagination, of going through the process. It gives structure to our thought process, and we move into the experience in our imagination. It is like playing "Let's pretend" to understand more clearly what would happen. We may never be able to go back to our first memory and experience it consciously; however, we know we had a first memory, even though we may not remember what it was with our conscious minds now. By using a thought experiment, we may be able to shed some light on this process. We will be in good company in using this process, for many scientists have used thought experiments, including Maxwell, Schrödinger, and Einstein. Besides, it may be interesting and fun to play with this for a while.

Information begins entering the mind or brain after the brain is electrically turned on in the womb in about the middle of the second trimester. But what kind of information or memories can be experienced in the womb? Our first memories, of course. Even though consciously we can't remember them, are they meaningful and accurate? It doesn't matter whether they are or aren't meaningful or accurate, because they are what we have, and they are the starting point and foundation of our belief system.

What we have experienced in early childhood in the womb is now understood to be an important stage in our developmental process and very much involved in determining the genetic expression of the newly emerging child. However, are memories formed in the womb real, true, or complete? Not so much, but again it doesn't matter because they are what the child has, and they are the oldest memories he or she will have; therefore, they will be high on the priority of the belief system of the child. Whatever those experiences were, they will have an effect on our genes' expression at the cellular level and the developing belief system.

Once more is the question. What do you think? Are memories real, complete, and true? And again, it doesn't matter because they are there, and they will be used. They determine our genetic changes and our early personality as an expression of our developing time in the womb. If our experience in the womb was pleasant and happy, we will come into the world with the beginnings of one kind of personality. If it was less than pleasant and an unhappy experience, a different personality will emerge; and the experiences will affect our lives because they are the foundation on which we build our beliefs.

Good or bad, complete or not so complete, those early memories will affect us. New experiences will moderate them, but they never completely go away. (*Changing your early belief system and memories isn't impossible, but it will take much patience and self-love. Since you aren't aware of what those early memories are, not just those in the womb but in early childhood as well, you can look up the body of works by Erik Erikson, PhD, and his book* Childhood and Society. *In the book he lays out the developed eight psychosocial stages in which humans develop throughout their entire life spans. The first stage is from birth up to one year old, called "Trust vs. Mistrust." It determines the grounding place on which all your future development will rest. Your belief of how much you trust the world you are in right now was in place before you were one year old, and it will stay that way until you change it. It becomes the cornerstone of your developing personality. Again, here is the question: "Are the memories of those early events real, true, and complete?" Well, no, they're not.*)

The first experiences after birth—are they real, true, and complete? No. That little immature child's mind can't make heads or tails out of all the information it is being bombarded with. But, again, it doesn't matter because that's all the child has got to work with, and he or she will use what he or she has been given to begin understanding and creating his or her world. There is no guard at the gate of the mind, no filtering system of the incoming information as of yet in the mind of the child; and everything just flows right into the child's mind and onto the hard drive of the mind or brain. Memories are formed the best way they can. And for better or worse, slowly a primitive filter system begins to get installed based on the unfiltered information now in the mind. The child has some things in his or her world that he or she now has come to believe are true for him or her, based on the child's small experiences that create his or her world. Again, are the memories really real, true, and complete? *(You do recall the discussion earlier that you were in a trance state during those early experiences, don't you? And you consciously can't remember them. However, you are responding to those internal interpretations of those experiences and the memories created with the child's mind. They may not be appropriate for you now, but how can you change them? Ah, now another mystery. You've got to stop thinking you know how things really work.)*

The dust settles a little for the child around age three. There is enough foundation at that time for his or her small belief system to now install a little immature filtering system of his or her world. Also at this time the child's basic programming and operating system are being put in place. This basic programming is deep in the subconscious mind beyond what the conscious mind will ever know, understand, or be aware of.

Earlier we mentioned that a child is in a trance state to some degree from birth through adolescence. The younger the child, the deeper in trance he or she will be. So how real, true, and complete can beliefs, experiences, and references be that are used to create his or her primitive belief system, which will be with him or her throughout his or her life? This is the start of the child's core belief system, which will be with him or her until he or she dies or until it is changed. This core belief system is in place by about age six, and the guard will be at the gate at that time, because the filtering system is now mature enough to be operational. At this point, all new information coming to the mind from the senses will be filtered for relevance and for what the child's mind is familiar with from past experience and family history, and the information will be accepted or denied based on what matches and is found in that small subconscious mind. The subconscious mind always filters for the earliest most familiar information first. If the information isn't familiar to the child, it cannot and won't be used. *(You know major caregivers can force physical behaviors on the child because they are big, and they can also pour their beliefs into the child, causing him or her to develop a personality with fears, anxieties, depressions, and other traits expressed by their caregivers, sometimes consciously but mostly unconsciously. How did you do by getting through your first year of life? Is everything working for you now? If not, what needs to change? Do you realize your conscious mind can't tell you? Children see their childhood as normal and okay because that is all they know. Later, you may realize it was screwed up, but by then you are already programmed.)*

How is the thought experiment going? Those early beliefs, experiences, and references that determine how we see our world are they real, complete, and true? Can they be depended on to provide a solid foundation for the universe the child will create and live in? And what about the beliefs, experiences, and references that will be formed in future experiences? Can they be any better than the foundation they rest on? The child doesn't create early childhood beliefs that form the core of the child's belief system; his or her parents and caregivers from the family of origin give and sometimes force them on the child.

It is our core belief system that is the basis on which we will develop our universe, lives, and reality. The core belief system is all about the past, and the past is only memories. Maybe we need to understand memories a little more. Let us follow one memory to see how it develops and what happens to it. It may be helpful to ask, What is a memory?

FORMING A MEMORY

We will go into memories in detail later, but for now some insight may be helpful as we expand our understanding. When an event happens in the outside energy system, our senses capture some but not all the information. The senses transmit what information they have captured to the mind. As the information enters the mind, the subconscious mind grabs it and sifts through the information, looking for matches to familiar things for which it already has experiences and references. The data for which a match is found is selected and moved to the active mind; there it is used to piece together a perception of the event as best it can, based on the filtered data received. We must be very clear here; a perception of an event isn't the event, and it is less than the event, which is to say perceptions aren't real, complete, or true because the subconscious mind in selecting matching data will generalize, rationalize, manipulate, and delete some or a whole lot of the data before sending the selected remaining data on to the active mind. *(When you are experiencing anything, you aren't looking for "the truth." You are looking for your truth, and your truth is found in your past memories. Here again you see that it is your lens of the past that determined your present moment, and it isn't what is happening. It isn't the event.)*

From the filtered and manipulated data, the active mind creates an unreal, incomplete, and untrue perception of the event; and why would it be unreal? Because it is using filtered and manipulated data. Because the subconscious mind has high-graded the information and selected only part of the data. *(What is your subconscious selecting? Only what is important to you at that moment in time that you have references to. It doesn't care about the event; it cares only about what is important to you and your survival. So is your interpretation of the event the real event? Absolutely no. But do you believe it's the real event? Absolutely yes. Keep in mind how fast the subconscious mind is doing this filtering. The active mind and later the conscious mind have no idea that the information they received was filtered and not the real event.)*

From the interpretation in the active mind, signals are sent out as electromagnetic and chemical messages to the mind and body; and the body decides how it must respond to the signals received. If the perception indicates danger, the body will move into survival mode, battening down the hatches and preparing for combat or leaving the scene. If the perception in the active mind indicates a friend, much different signals will be sent out, and the body's response will be much different, and different systems will be engaged in the body. In this little scenario, we may have noticed that the body responds not to the outside event but only to the active mind's perception of the event, which isn't real, complete, or true. It isn't the event.

At this point in memory development, when the body is acting out in response to the perception, the conscious mind is awakened to the body's response as it moves from normal to survival. The conscious mind rationalizes, analyzes, and generalizes what has happened in the body, and then it reports to us in emotional words about what has happened. Up to this point, no language has been used. All communications between the active mind and the mind and body have been in the form of electric, magnetic, and chemical nonverbal signals. Now the conscious mind is reporting in words, and what is the conscious mind reporting anyway? It's reporting on what has already happened in the active mind and the body.

I sometimes think of the conscious mind as a radio announcer of a horse race describing the action in the body. "And they're off. The *heart* is out in front, pumping hard, followed by *blood pressure*, which keeps gaining. Way in the rear is *digestion*, which looks sluggish and won't finish in the money. Now *muscles* twitch on the inside. *Eyes* are wide open, looking for an opening. *Elimination* is running wild and out of control."

No doubt about it, folks. The only way to describe this race is anxiety.

The names the conscious mind comes up with are only a description of what has already happened in the body, and what is the cause of what has happened in the body? You guessed it: our perception, the interpreted universe. What is happening in our bodies when we are stressed is called "symptoms" or "effects." The cause of the symptoms is always our perceptions, our interpreted universe. Emotions don't do anything but describe what the body has already done to survive.

If we hide our symptoms through external protocols such as medications, physical therapy, rest, and so forth, do we resolve the cause? Rarely! If we stop the external protocols, do the symptoms come back? If they do, the cause was never addressed and is still active, and healing is still required. *(Are you starting to get the idea that everything, including your pain and suffering, comes from your created interpreted universe? Why haven't you seen that before? We'll look at that next.)*

While the event is happening, we have no memory because we are having an event. When the event is over and gone, we now have a memory of what our interpretation of the event was. Notice that we don't have a memory of the event; the memory is our interpretation of the event. Keep that in mind. All the data used in forming our perception of the event is now in permanent memory in the subconscious mind, and that stored data is called a "memory." *(Notice again that the memory isn't of the event. It's a memory of your interpretation of the event. I'm not splitting words here. The event and the interpretation of the event are two completely different things.)*

We can't have a memory without an event of some kind happening and then ending. Once the event is over and gone, now we have a memory of our created perception of the event but not of the event itself. Do we believe our memories are real, complete, and true? Yes. It may be that parts of our memory are real, because they are what was important to us at the time. But the parts of the event that were important to us aren't the whole event. Therefore, our memory of our interpretation of the event cannot be the memory of the event, and our memory must be something less than the event. Since our memory isn't the whole event, is our memory real and true? Is it the complete event? No. *(How is your thought experiment coming? Are memories real? Are your memories the whole and complete event? If they are partially real and true, why are you keeping the unreal and untrue parts? And how do you know which parts of your memories are real and true, since you don't have the whole and complete memories of the events since the events are gone and cannot be used as references? The answer? You don't know. So you hold onto what you aren't sure of and make believe it is true, real, and complete.)*

HALF-TRUTH AND THE TRUTH

If something is half true, is it true? No. Parts of it may be true, but as a complete truth, it's not true. That is what our memories are, incomplete half-truths. We may be able to rationalize them into the truth or say something is mostly true or partially true or close enough to the truth, but it's not "the truth." Therefore, if it's half true or almost true, it's not true. To say it is true, we would need to manipulate the data to make it fit our needs, and if it is manipulated to fit our needs, is it, or is it not, true? Our interpreted universe is never the whole truth because it's always created from filtered and manipulated information. However, we can sure convince ourselves that it's true, can't we?

Is the past real, complete, and true? No, the past isn't real or true, because it is created from memories that aren't real, complete, or true. Memories aren't real or true or complete because they are the residue of the interpretations of events created from highly selected and manipulated data.

However, when we remember events, memories feel so real and true in our bodies, don't they? It is how they feel in the body that makes them seem real and true and complete to us, but the event is over and gone. None of the event is here. So what is driving the body to feel the way it does now that there is no event? It is the remembered bits and pieces of memories, which aren't true, real, or complete. Illusions will do that, you know. They are ghosts and shadows of what never was the way we thought it was.

To heal our pain and suffering, we will need to unravel what we think we know about our reality. It's all in our heads. In the past when someone would say to us, "It's just in your head," we would get offended and reply, "No, it's not just in my head. It's real!" Here is the new scientific understanding. It's all in your head. Everything we have is first there in our heads. Nothing has any meaning at all for us in the outside world until we create its meaning in our heads, and what is in our heads isn't truly real either. It's all an illusion, and that's all we have; and that's all anyone has. It is what we have created from the uniqueness of our beliefs, experiences, and references from our past; and it's called our "interpreted universe." It's an illusion, and the illusion is what the body is responding to. Since all our pain and suffering are feedback data from the body to the mind, the feelings we think are in the body are really interpretations in the mind. Where then must our pain and suffering come from? Take a guess. The mind or the body? *(It is always your interpretation in your head that is the subtle cause of your pain and suffering. Your body can respond only to the signals your mind sends by the active mind. So if your body is responding with feedback data your active mind is interpreting as pain and suffering, the pain and suffering are felt in the mind and not in the body. Your pain and suffering start in the mind and are a reflection of the mind. Look to the mind and your memories before you start blaming your poor body for your pain and suffering.)*

What the Body Responds To

Earlier, using a very large brush, we discussed the different senses and how they operated. The sense of touch moves into the body through the nervous system, then into the mind or brain, then into the active mind; and from the active mind's interpretation, signals are finally sent to the body. The body doesn't know it has been touched or that something has touched it until the active mind interprets the information sent to it through the nervous system as filtered by the subconscious mind. The body doesn't respond to the outside world in any way; the body responds only to the active mind's perceptional signals because that is all it is connected to. The body doesn't experience the outside world directly. Just to say that may cause the conscious mind and ego to freak out. This doesn't seem to be right at all to our conscious minds; therefore, we don't think it is right because all we know is what the conscious mind tells us. Pay attention here because this may get a little dicey and convoluted.

We may need to review our sense of touch. What we think of as touch is really a combination of several different nervous systems throughout the body. The brain has an internal map of the body surfaces called a "homunculus" or "small human," and it plays a fundamental role in the creation of our body image and what we think of as the body's reaction to the outside environment. All those different nerve systems gather data about external pressures against the body and sometimes internal pressure and surface irritations we end up scratching.

These touch receptors channel data into the central nervous system in such a way that a map is created in the brain. The receptors aren't uniformly distributed over the body surface. Different parts of the body have more receptors based on the body's need to survive, protect itself, and reproduce. The face, lips, tongue, hands, feet, genitals, and a few other locations have the most receptors.

Each of those data collector receptors on the surface are connected to nerve endings. The other end of the nerve is connected to the internal map of the body in the brain. The nerve ending on the surface is attached to its exact corresponding location on the internal brain map at the other end of the nerve. What a piece of hardware is this touch system.

When there is pressure against the body, the body doesn't know it; however, the nerve endings on the surface of the body know it. Those nerve endings send an electromagnetic signal to the body map in the brain. The data is than sent to the mind and the active mind. Interpretations are created, and signals are sent out to the mind and body based on past experience; and the body, which continually monitors the inside perceptional signals, now knows it was touched and decides how to respond. All this happens in milliseconds; and of course, the conscious mind reports it is the body, which felt the touch. *(With the slow processing speed of the conscious mind, can you see why you believe the body is feeling and responding to the outside world? The body isn't, you know. It always responds and can respond only to the interpretative signals from your active mind.)*

Notwithstanding, the body needs rest and nutrition. However, if the body is tired, run down, overworked, sad, or disappointed, it will react differently to the perceptional signals it receives than when the body is well rested and healthy. This may seem quite obvious. What might not be so obvious is that the body is tired, run down, overworked, sad, and disappointed because of what is going on in the mind. The body's being tired, run down, overworked, sad, and disappointed is all in response to the active mind's perceptions. Create different perceptions, and the body will respond differently. It is all relative, you know.

> Put your hand on a hot stove for a minute, and it
> seems like an hour. Sit with a pretty girl for an hour,
> and it seems like a minute. That's relativity.
> —Albert Einstein

Any condition we think is in our bodies is in direct response to the active mind's perception. The body is the scapegoat for the mind a lot of the time; we said that before, didn't we? We blame the body for our pain and suffering, and we try to manipulate the body to end our pain and suffering, but rarely do we address the active mind's perception, which is the underlying cause. We look outside the mind to end our pain and suffering and into the body through medication and changing external behaviors or circumstances. They all may be good things to do;

however, they won't change the active mind's perception, which is the driving force behind the pain and suffering we think we feel in the body.

What causes our perceptions to be the way they are? Our beliefs, experiences, and references from the past, which are our memories, are the filter system we use to create our present moment experience. Are they real, complete, and true? They aren't, but we think they are because that is all we know consciously; beliefs, experiences, and references from the past drive our subconscious programming. Actually, we have no idea consciously what our subconscious programs are. We know only the results of our programming, and the results are our behaviors. Our behavior is always a reflection of what we hold within us, which is to say our past memories. We look outside us to other people, places, and things to blame so we don't need to change our inside egoic stuff of who we think we are, which is the cause.

Blaming is an ego-defense thing. It keeps our ego from feeling bad about itself and keeps us from having to change. Our great defense system tactic is to blame others, although it does keep us stuck in our pain and suffering; but then we don't need to change, which means we won't heal very quickly. Blaming others has always been a great ego-defense mechanism. However, it does keep us locked in our old maladaptive belief system and behaviors.

CHAPTER 9

Memories

THE PRESENT MOMENT

The present moment is happening now. It can only happen now. It is infinitely thin in duration and time. It is eternal because it is always now. We can't get away from it. There is nowhere we can go that isn't now. With that in mind, nothing can ever happen in the past. Everything must happen in the present moment, and then it's gone. All we have left of events, when they are gone, are incomplete and untrue memories, which aren't the events. We tend to believe our memories of the events are the events. We need to be clear here; memories aren't events. Memories are thought forms we created. They aren't physical things. They are stories we tell ourselves about what never was the way we think it was. *(I know I said this before, but you need to hear it a lot, because it is so counter to what our culture believes.)*

There are no memories in the present moment, because there is nothing to remember yet; everything is happening now, and that is what makes it the present moment. The active mind interprets the present moment, and it is that interpretation that becomes the memory of the momentary event. However, in our present moment we have memories because we bring them with us, pulling the past into the present. Notice the distinction here between "the present moment," which is happening now outside, and "our present moment," which is a created interpretation inside us and not the event happening outside. One is happening now, and the other is an interpretation of manipulated data of what has happened as viewed through our lens of the past. We always bring the past with us into the present moment. It is difficult for us to do anything, go anywhere, or be anywhere without pulling our memories with us into what is happening now. This learned habit causes us to limit how we interface and respond to the present moment.

So what can we say about the present moment? It is happening now. What can we say about memories? They are incomplete representations and artifacts of things that are long gone. They aren't here now and are never coming back, and they never were the way we think they were. We discussed earlier the need to prove the past is real, because the past is tied to our self-identity, our egoic identity, of who we think we are. By viewing the present moment through our lens of the past, we have made the present moment uniquely ours and not real, true, and complete. In so doing we have stepped out of the reality of now and into an illusory, nonexistent created space that is only in our heads. We did mention before that we live in an illusion, didn't we?

The closest we can come to being in reality in this three-dimensional space/time universe is to be completely in the present moment, and that moment, which is infinitely small in terms of our concept of time and eternity because it is always the present moment, is the gateway into reality. It is the crack or gap in the cosmic egg that gives us a hint of the underneath reality beyond this illusionary creation of the present moment. Only in this special place of now can the underlying grounding of reality be glimpsed.

Since it is always the present moment, we may begin to understand what keeps us from glimpsing reality. It is because of what we always bring with us into the eternal present moment; it is our memories. The lens of our past and its memories distorts that gap in the cosmic egg; they smear over the gap with the past and keep us in an illusory state, which we believe is real. Reality is never experienced; only a perception can be experienced, which is an untrue illusion. *(If you saw the movie* The Matrix, *you may recall the scene in which the decision was made to take the blue pill or the red pill. Which pill did you take? There is much scientific study and mathematical investigation into the possibility that you and I are living in a computer simulation. But that's just science fiction, right? However, recognize you are living in an illusion and believe it is real.)*

THE MEMORY

Some of what we have already discussed about memories will be recapped here but in a slightly different way. Memories are all that is in the subconscious mind. The conscious mind has no long-term memories. Any memories in the conscious mind are short term and temporary. Within seconds, the memories we are aware of in the conscious mind are being moved into permanent memory in the subconscious mind. If the conscious mind needs to know anything, it just asks the subconscious mind through the active mind, and the subconscious mind quickly gets the information. The conscious mind is too small and slow to hold or carry memories around; besides, its job is reporting on what happened in the interpreted universe and our bodies, and not holding onto memories.

The subconscious mind is where everything is happening, and it is out of conscious awareness. However, we must understand that what we know about the subconscious mind is secondhand knowledge; little is known directly about what is going on in the subconscious mind. We know things through experimentation, empirical data, or metaphors; and by analyzing behavior. Begin to appreciate all that might be in that black box. In the subconscious mind, there is no need for language, as we know it, because there is no one in there with ears to hear and respond to it. The subconscious mind appears to function in pictures, signs, sound, symbols, numbers, and sometimes words; and it responds to metaphors. Recall that earlier we stated the conscious and subconscious minds use different methods of communication? The created interpreted universe doesn't use word language either; and in the body, the heart doesn't talk to the brain in words. Nor does anything else inside us use words. Only the conscious mind uses word language, and sometimes the subconscious mind does too.

Whether we have completed the thought experiment around how real, complete, and true beliefs and memories are, we will state for the record that beliefs and memories aren't real, complete, and true;

therefore, we have memories of events that never happened the way we remember them, and they're just stories we tell ourselves. Again, what is the definition of *illusions*? "Something that deceives by producing a false or misleading impression of reality," http://www.dictionary.com.

Whether a memory is a little bit not true or a lot not true isn't important. What is important is understanding that memories aren't completely real, complete, and true. Even if we think, *Well, my memories are true enough for me*, we will never know which part of any of our memories is a little or a lot untrue, because we believe all our memories are true, or we wouldn't have them as memories. New incoming data and information from our senses will be accepted, changed, modified, or thrown out based on our memories, which aren't true and will result in more incomplete, untrue, and unreal memories. *(Can you see how dynamic your memories and the past can be? However, if you are a black-and-white rigid thinker, you will suffer a lot in relationships throughout your life and believe a lot of the lies you tell yourself about your past, which was never the way you believe it was.)*

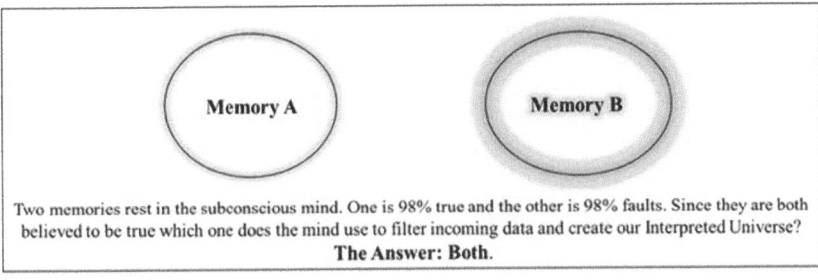

Two memories rest in the subconscious mind. One is 98% true and the other is 98% faults. Since they are both believed to be true which one does the mind use to filter incoming data and create our Interpreted Universe?
The Answer: Both.

Diagram 02 - Memories Not True a Little
and a Lot. Which Is Which?

The subconscious mind searches for and selects information and data by what it is familiar with. The most familiar beliefs, experiences, and references are the ones held for the longest time; therefore, they are the ones we are the most familiar with. These will be beliefs, experiences, and references from childhood. And of course, the conscious mind won't have any idea what they are because it doesn't have access to most of those early memories, which will be before age six or so. We will have effects in the body but won't be able to get in touch with the causes.

Remember this: you cannot have an effect without a cause. Effects we think are in the body, based on how the body feels, must come from the active mind's interpretations, because those are all the body responds to.

For the vast amount of our memories, it doesn't matter whether they are almost true, not so true, or completely false because they have no emotional energy attached to them. They are neutral and just drift into the background within the subconscious mind. An example might be to recall the memory of what you had for lunch seven weeks ago from today. If you didn't get food poisoning, you probably don't remember what you ate, and your life continued on normally. How the body responded to the interpretation of your lunch will determine whether you remember it and also how the subconscious mind will use that memory in the mining of new data. Our memories can be plotted on a chart based on their emotional intensity and shown on a bell-shaped curve of normal probability, which would look something like the following chart.

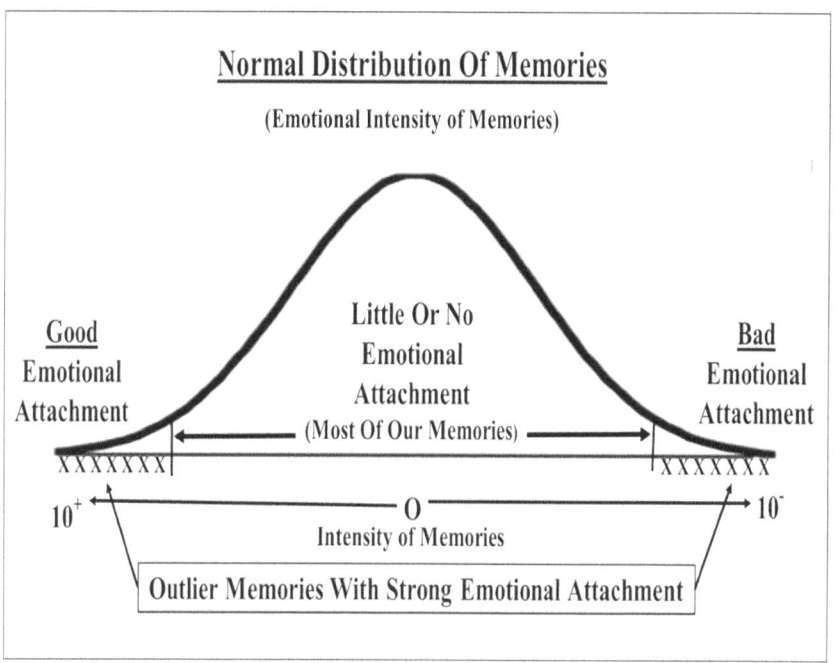

Diagram 03 - Normal Probability of Memories

Almost all our memories have no emotional attachment, and our lives operate just fine for most of us. It is the outliers, those extreme abnormal emotional attached memories that cause our problems. Good emotionally attached memories won't be a problem. However, outlying bad emotionally attached memories will cause the body to go into its survival mode; and when triggered or recalled, it will override anything else happening in the body as the body moves into fight-or-flight behavior to survive the created perception in the active mind. It is the bad memories we are concerned with here. *(I said that your active mind cannot tell the difference between data coming from an outside happening and data coming from a vivid inside memory, didn't I? If not, I will. The data from both comes from the subconscious mind and follows the same path into the active mind; therefore, the active mind cannot tell the difference between them.)*

Here is an interesting fact about how the active mind functions. The active mind cannot tell the difference between data coming through the subconscious mind's filtering system from an outside event or data coming from a vividly remembered memory or data coming from feedback information from the body; we said this before, but it needs repeating. To the active mind, it's all just data; and when data gets into the active mind, the active mind does what it does, which is to create interpretations and perceptions from the data received; and then it sends out signals. The body changes its systems in response to the signals from the internal-created perceptions, turning systems on and off in its response to those signals from the active mind. If the interpretation is dangerous and threatening, the body doesn't know or care whether it is because of an outside event or inside memories. If the signals are of danger, the body will move into survival mode. Those extremely negative outlying memories, when recalled, drive the body into action; and it will feel like the event is happening again. Even though we know intellectually the event isn't happening, it feels that way in the body, doesn't it? That is why we avoid certain thoughts, places, and situations because they trigger what we don't want to feel, even though we know the event is over and gone. *(You may think of PTSD, situations of extreme embarrassment, and sad losses in your life at this point. When you remember them, you will feel your body's response and wish you never thought of them. While I have said, "You will feel your body's response," you aren't feeling the body. What you are feeling is the active mind's interpretation of the feedback information sent to it by the body. Everything is in the mind first, even your pain and suffering.)*

Memories are only memories, and no event is happening now because the events they are imperfectly depicting, describing, and remembering are gone and over. And what are memories? They are the residue of the not-so-real interpretation of events that never happened the way we interpreted them as happening. Memories don't recall events; they recall interpretations of events we created, which aren't the same as the events. They are lies we tell ourselves and believe they are true.

Why are we spending so much time discussing why memories aren't real, complete, and true? So we can break through our cultural hypnosis that they are real, written in stone, and unchangeable. So we can wake up to the fact that they are untrue, incomplete, and unreal. So we can understand that they are just artifacts of events that never existed the way we think they did. So we can change our beliefs, reframe our memories, heal from our pain and suffering, and fully enjoy life. Aren't these terrific goals? Unfortunately, they are not our ego's goal.

Everything is energy, and everything starts in the mind. By healing negative memories and beliefs, we can release those dark emotionally attached energies we have trapped in the body and in our memories; and by so doing, we can bring into focus a different world for us. Healing from our past breaks no laws, forgiving ourselves breaks no laws, and forgiving others breaks no laws unless we believe they do. We can't wait for others to forgive us before we can forgive ourselves, feel better, and heal because in their world that may never happen and because in their world, their interpretation of the event won't be like yours anyway. We need to step out in front and heal ourselves, and maybe they will recognize they can heal themselves also. We don't need anyone's permission to heal ourselves. We only need to get our permission. *(You do see that if another person forgives you, he or she isn't forgiving you for the same thing you think you need to be forgiven for, don't you? His or her remembrance of what happened isn't your remembrance of what happened. You see that, right?)*

If we withhold forgiveness from ourselves, we are truly lost and doomed to live the life we have. It doesn't matter whether we are the offender or the offended. The event is over and gone, and it is never coming back. All we have is a memory, which isn't real, true, or complete. It is only the egoic world that needs to maintain a world of guilt to keep us imprisoned in the illusion; and to do that, our memories must be maintained as if they are real. And so we must always be in a state of guilt.

CHAPTER 10

Memory Coding System

CODING BY THE SENSES

Whatever comes into the mind from the outside must come through the senses and only through the senses. The senses are our only connection to the outside energy system. Any coding of memories will be around the senses, because they are where the information came from. Even though the senses don't see, hear, feel, smell, or taste anything, they transmit data that is interpreted into those modalities. However, we have been programmed to believe the senses really interpret and judge what they encounter in the outside energy system, but they don't. All interpretations of what is outside us are done in the realm of the active mind. It is the active mind that creates what we believe we see, hear, feel, smell, or taste with the senses. Refer to Chapter 3, "Sensing Differently."

Each memory appears to be stored in some form of filing system or matrix in the subconscious mind, which is a black box. The system has a retrieval mechanism, and as such, memories are moved out of storage into the active mind when triggered and returned to storage after use. The following table is normally used to code information from the senses. *(Remember, stored information in your subconscious has already been filtered and manipulated; therefore it isn't a memory of the event. It is a memory of your interpretation of the event. Since it isn't the event, it is the story you made up about the event.)*

Senses	Description	Code
Sight	Visual	V_x
Sound	Auditory	A_x
Touch	Kinesthetic	K_x
Smell	Olfactory	O_x
Taste	Gustatory	G_x

Diagram 04 - Coding the Sense Modalities

To get some idea of how this coding might be done, think of a computer code's color. In the computer, we can change the colors of fonts and objects. If we want to customize a color, we are taken to a color screen with a coding system of three colors—red, green, and blue. Each of the three colors combines to make up the custom colors we want. By moving the cursor around the color screen with the mouse, the numeric value of the three colors changes, indicting the location on the color screen. Therefore, once the numeric values of the three individual colors are known for the color we want, the location of the color on the screen is always known, and you will always get that same color based on its numeric location on the screen.

WHAT IS STORED IN THE SUBCONSCIOUS MIND?

The subconscious mind stores, retrieves, restores, and uses memories to filter incoming sensory data all the time and all at the same time, and memories can be reframed and edited. Memories are like Silly Putty. They can be manipulated into an endless variety of forms and combinations of forms to meet our belief system's need so we will always be who we think we are, and of course to meet our egoic goals. There are a lot of theories about how this is done, but there is no smoking gun, no real knowing. Again, no one knows how the subconscious mind does all the stuff it does. However it is done, it is felt that there is some kind of coding system used to manage all the information the subconscious mind has stored. Remember, the subconscious mind is processing billions of bits of data per second. It has more than enough processing power to do all things we think it does and more. We will need to come up with a model we can use to represent how the black box does its magic. The model may not be that accurate, but it will give us a starting point.

A Coding System, Maybe

The mind has a coding system for all our beliefs, experiences, and references that are now only memories. We can imagine they are located by the modalities of the following: visual—sight, auditory—sound, kinesthetic—touch, olfactory—smell, and gustatory—taste components. They are coded by V_X, A_X, K_X, O_X and G_X. X would indicate a location in the matrix where a specific memory is stored. We don't know exactly where or how the subconscious mind stores all the data and information it has. Some theories hold that memories are spread throughout the brain; other theories hold that memories are stored in the body, and other theories put the memories in the synapses between the axons and the neurons in the brain. Yet other theories hold that memories are kept in the energy matrix around the mind or body system. There may be other theories or ideas; however, no one knows for sure what the real method is.

Whatever the system is, we just don't know. The subconscious mind is a black box, and we can't find the edges of the box, let alone what is inside it and how it works. Wherever the data of the memories are stored, after the filtering process and the interpretation by the active mind, they are just unknown. What we do know is that the interpretation of the event is stored, not the event; the sensory data is part of its locational coding system because when we recall memories in the active mind, sensory data is there. Data before the filtering process won't be used because it is meaningless until the subconscious mind has found references for it and the active mind has given it meaning through its interpretation.

While there have been documented instances of probing the human brains with electric probes and exciting memories into being recalled, these cases are usually by accident during brain operations; the patient recalled memories when the probe touched certain spots. However, that doesn't mean the memory was stored there. That may only be the spot where the mechanism by which the mind recalled memory was excited. The probe may have accidentally touched a "memory trace," which is another theory of how the subconscious mind finds memories it has stored; besides, if the memory is scattered throughout the brain, touching one spot wouldn't excite the whole memory. There are so many theories and so little evidence that any are correct. The subconscious mind and its memories' storage system is still a black box and a very mysterious black box indeed.

We will uncover more of the mind's secrets over time, but for now we can use any theory that seems to work, within limits, of course. And even though we will continue uncovering and gaining more new scientific understanding, the infinite will always still be infinite, and the finite will always still be finite.

MEMORY STORAGE MODEL

The model that is most interesting to me is the theory that memories are stored in the energy matrix around the mind/body system because it is easy to visualize. Think of a three-dimensional, flexible spiderweb. Then picture the body at the center of the web; at each intersection of two strands of the web rests a memory, a little dot of energy, an icon of the total memory. Each memory is a small speck interconnected within the web with all the other specks within the matrix in an energy field around and within the body. Each memory is entangled with all the other memories through the web of the matrix. Imagine that kind of a structure. Let's just use this model until a better one comes along.

This model will be very dynamic, with the matrix constantly changing as memories are used in the filtering of new input data, new memories moving into storage and memories being recalled into the active mind when triggered. Notice that when a memory is recalled into the active mind, it is the whole memory that is pulled into the active mind. It isn't a copy of the memory that is sent to the active mind; it is the whole stored memory that is pulled into the active mind with all its data and energy. When the memory is in the active mind, nothing is left in storage. When the active mind is through with the memory, it is reconsolidated back into storage within the matrix; and it is stored back in a location based on the modalities coding of V_X, A_X, K_X, O_X, and G_X for easy access by the subconscious mind the next time it is needed. Remember, we are talking about billions of bits of data per second of processing power moving stuff around in the subconscious mind.

What is stored in the subconscious mind's data storage system anyway? Memories, only memories. All we can store inside us, in our minds, are memories of what we think happened in the past; and of course our memories are never the event. Therefore, memories can never be what really happened. *(Can you see that in a real sense nothing happened in the past? Everything must happen in the present moment, and then it's gone. What do we have left of the past? Only memories, which aren't accurate, complete, or true.)*

The future can be stored only as a past memory, because we can look at the future only through the lens of our past. What we store in the subconscious mind of the future is a memory of our interpretation of our imagination, created through the lens and memories from our past in the active mind. Here again, it isn't the future we are storing; it is only a perception, and when we stop thinking about it, the perception moves into permanent memory just like all the other created perceptions. We make memories out of all our perceptions, and it doesn't matter whether perceptions are made out of data from an outside event, a recalled memory stored inside the subconscious mind, data from the body, imaginary thoughts about the future, or dreams. They are all perceptions.

We can also make up stories and fantasies that never happened out of bits and pieces of stored memories and then store those fantasies as memories. In that process, we can be very creative in how we do that. These are actually "Faults Memories." But since we made them up and they are based on memories we believe to be true, we call them reality; and how real they seem when recalled. *(You may think of schizophrenia at this point. Schizophrenics believe their world is real, and for them it is. We do this all the time and don't realize it; and since our actions match other people's schizophrenia, we think they are normal and our normal reality. Think of* Playboy *magazine and the fantasies created. Anytime data is presented to the active mind, it creates interpretations and perceptions, and signals are sent to the body on how to respond; then memories follow, flowing into permanent memory in the subconscious mind. The eye can never be offended; only the mind can be so.)*

Events happen in the present moment, and then they are gone and can never come back. We never experience the complete event, and then it's gone forever. Since now we don't have the event to compare with the memory, we have no idea how close or far away, true or faulty, the memory is. *(Recognize your memories are never 100 percent true.)* How can we find the evidence to prove memories are real and true or how faulty they are? We use history. We have a lot of broken pottery, pieces of stone, old weapons, pieces of bone, clay tablets, pictures, YouTube videos, and school yearbooks; there is a lot of stuff like that, but we never have the complete event again. It's like Humpty Dumpty falling off the wall; once the fall is over, it's over, and the memory will never be the way it truly was. By using all the old stuff and "reverse engineering," we try to reconstruct the event. And again, we never get the event; we can get only an interpretation of the event, which isn't the event. But we will convince ourselves we have the whole event or close enough to declare it was real. However, nothing ever happens the way we think it does, no matter how much proof we have, but we can convince ourselves and believe it happened the way we think it did.

We may think, *Well, my memories are good enough for who they are for,* but this isn't our concern here. The concern is to begin to recognize and bring into our awareness the fact that memories aren't real. They aren't carved in stone; they aren't God's truth. They are our created truth; therefore, they can be changed. The reason they can be changed is that they aren't real. They are Silly Putty. *(Now don't let your ego get all bent out of shape here. It needs your memories to be real so it can stay alive. Your memories aren't real and can be changed. When you change your memories, what happens to your ego? What happens to your old identity? It dies, and another identity is put in its place, which means a new egoic identity is created; and the old ego is gone.)*

So now visualize again that three-dimensional spiderweb with the body sitting in the center; at each intersection of any two strands rests a memory. It's a little dot of energy that is our interpretation and perception of the event again; it isn't the event because all we can know of the event is what we were able to fit through our egoic lens of past at the time. When the event is over and gone, we put our perceptions of the event into permanent memory in the subconscious mind's matrix. It's like a compressed data file sitting there in the matrix, waiting to be recalled and used.

Memories are all that can be in the subconscious mind. Events happen in the present moment, and then they're gone—bang! Nothing ever happened in the past, and nothing ever will happen in the past. Everything must happen in the present moment, and then it's over and gone; and it doesn't exist anymore. We don't have events happen in the past. However, what we do have left over from the event are memories of something that never happened the way we think it did. It is the interpretation of the event that is stored in the subconscious mind. *(Pay attention here; this is the tricky part.)* I'll say it again. It is the interpretations of events in the active mind that are stored as memories in the subconscious mind.

What are interpretations? They are creations of the active mind. Since memories are stored as creations of the active mind, where does the data come from that is used to make those interpretations that get stored in the subconscious mind as memories? The data can come only from the subconscious mind or the body. If the data comes from the subconscious mind, it could be as filtered and manipulated data from input sensory information or from stored memories—or maybe it's a combination of both. If the data is from the body, it could be because of the needs of the body or as feedback about the body's response to signals the active mind sends. Does the active mind care where the data comes from? No. To the active mind, it is all just data, and it needs to be interpreted—which is the world we live in, the events outside us, or the interpreted universe inside. Which determines our pain and suffering?

Let's break it down into finer steps:

- An event is happening.
- We receive some (but not all) of the data and information about the event through our sensory inputs.
- The subconscious mind grabs that data and mines it, rummages through it, picks over it, and pulls apart that incoming data, looking for something it can relate to by using past memories, trying to find something it is familiar with, something it can use, something it has experience with. And it is doing it very fast, so fast that the active mind and the conscious mind don't even know the data was filtered
- Data found by the subconscious mind that it has some reference or relevance to is selected and/or manipulated to fit its current paradigm and then sent to the active mind.
- The active mind creates interpretations of the data. *(Notice, to the active mind there is no outside event; there is only data to be processed. It has no idea where the data came from and doesn't care. It is just data, and it processes it.)*
- The body, which monitors the interpreted universe, is sent signals based on the interpretations of the active mind. From those signals, the body responds because they are all the body is in contact with. Is it friend or foe? The signals tell the body. Does the body need to survive, or can it relax?
- The event ends, and the flow of sensory data of the event also ends.
- The interpretations created in the active mind are now stored in the subconscious mind as memories. *(Question: Are the memories you have stored, the event or a creation of the mind? Perhaps that black box and the memories it holds have more to do with the world you live in than you ever thought.)*
- Now we have more untrue, incomplete, and unreal memories sitting in the matrix of the subconscious mind's storage system, waiting to be used.

None of the memories in the subconscious mind are completely true;

therefore, they are all incomplete and unreal because they were created based on earlier memories, perceptions, and interpretations, which are also untrue, incomplete, and unreal; but that's all we have to work with. The subconscious mind will use each new incomplete memory, and it will be used to determine what data will be selected, manipulated, and sent to the active mind. Out of this data the next perceptions and interpretations of the next event will be created. They won't be true, complete, or real either; but we will believe they are.

Here is an interesting thought. Do we need the past? Imagine for a moment there was no past; the present moment would be all we had, and it would be the way life truly is. With no past, we would have no memories and no filtering system to distort the infinitely thin and eternal present moment. Since the present moment is the gap into true reality, we would always be in the underlying reality of everything within that subtle field of everything. No, no! Stop. That's crazy talk. Who would we be without a past? Everything. *(Without a past, you wouldn't have any enemies, prejudices, complaints, problems, pain, or suffering. Oh, but this would take all the fun out of the life we create and are living in right now in our heads.)*

We need to appreciate that everything that ever happens can happen only in the present moment. Once we move our thinking minds outside the present moment, which is to say into the past or the future, we aren't present. We are in a place the ancients called "illusions." Why is that? Because when we move the mind into the past, which appears true, complete, and real as viewed through our memories but isn't, we are in a place that is only in our heads; and if we move the mind into the future, we have stepped into a make-believe land where nothing is, except in our heads. *(Can you appreciate that nothing real is in the past? There are no events going on in the past. They are all gone. The past is the true land of "Let's pretend." So neither the past nor the future exists anywhere except in the uniqueness of our individual heads. But don't you believe the past is real? I'm telling you, nothing is there. It's a game being played in your head. It's an illusion, and isn't it fun sometimes and painful at other times? And isn't it great to know you can change that land of "Let's pretend"? Or not?)*

Even to question the reality of the past or to think our memories as not real will raise the hackles on the backs of some people's necks. It will cause angst and an uneasiness in their stomachs. This is because it brings into question their personal identity of who they believe themselves to be, which is their individually accumulated past and their identity. If we had no past, who would we be? A lot of us would be happier.

THE NEED TO PROVE THE PAST IS REAL

We have a vested interest in keeping the past real in our minds, because it is tied to who we think we are, our identity. However, the past we have as an individual past is something no one else has, and it is only in our heads. No one knows our past completely, not even us consciously, because it is only in our minds. And the greater part of the mind is a black box, and the important thing to keep in mind is that it's not real.

Without the past being real, how will we know who we are? What an interesting question to think about. Not to have a past can be scary. If we think of dementia, Alzheimer's, and amnesia, we can see why we want and need the past to be real, and why we want memories to be true. Even though the past we have is a creation and isn't true, complete, or real, it is all we have. If we believe it is real for us, then the past is real for us and only for the individual us. Again, no one has our individual past but us. Even people in our lives, whom we love and who were in many of the events of our lives, will have different memories of the same events than we do; and those memories won't be true, complete, or real either. But then perception is reality, isn't it? *(You do remember you are in an illusion, don't you?)*

Without a past we would be in a very interesting place. It would be a place we have never been in for a very long time, the present moment. We may think, *What are you talking about? I am always present. I know what the present moment is. And that is a dumb statement!* But we never have been in the present moment except as very young children. The reason we are never in the present moment is because of something we always bring with us, no matter where we go. It is something that always separates us from ever experiencing the present as it is. It is our past. We look through the unique lens of our individual past and see a distorted present moment, and it becomes for us what we think it is, not what it is;

yet we believe it is accurate and true, even though it can be distorted and untrue only by the way it is interpreted. Crazy, right? The best we can hope for is to be aware that our perceptions are flawed and untrue, and develop a sense of right-mindedness of not taking ourselves so seriously.

We all have our own unique and different past, which means we each experience a unique and different present moment because we each have a different lens with which to look through and observe that present moment. Since the present moment is different for everybody, which one is real—yours or mine? Since each of us has created a different interpreted universe of the present moment, where is reality? Ah, now we are back in the illusion.

How in the world do we manage to communicate with each other and survive as a nation, a society, a culture, and a family? We do it by making agreements with each other both consciously and unconsciously. Each of those areas of agreement is called a "consensual agreement of reality." Our spoken and unspoken agreements create our agreed-upon mutual reality, and it is a consensual reality we have until there is a paradigm shift. But of course we all know that "my reality" is the real reality, and yours—well, it is questionable at best.

ONE HAND WASHES THE OTHER

Since we believe the interpreted universe we create in our heads is real and therefore reality for us, we need proof. Most people believe the world they live in is real. It looks real. It feels real. It sounds like something is really there. So why wouldn't we believe the interpreted universe in our heads isn't real? What would be our poof that the world we live in is real? *(You might think of the interpreted universe as a movie. Movies are the creations of many different inputs from many different sources. The movie, which lasts only a short time, is the result of a lot of work, taking months or years to put together. Then you see it and hear it. And if the director has done his or her job, the editing is right, and the sound is good. For a short time, you may believe and feel in your body that the movie is real. Your interpreted universe is the same way, except rather than taking months or years to put together, it takes nanoseconds, and it is streaming at billions of bits per second. You believe the movie in your head is real.)*

Consensus! The proof we normally use for our proof that our world is real is consensus with other interpreted universes, and if all those other interpreted universes are the same or almost the same as ours, they would be our proof that our world is real. We may not think about it as looking for others like interpretive universes that match ours, but that is what we do. We look to others for poof that our world is real. We find friends, strangers, countrymen, and family members with similar filtering systems as ours; and then ask them, "Do you see, hear, touch, smell, and taste in your body and mind the same things as I do in mine?" And of course, they will because that is why we picked them for our proof. They have the same type of filtering systems we do or close enough that they will give us the proof we need. If they don't have our type of filtering systems, we won't pick them to be used for our poof, because they won't have similar beliefs, experiences, and references as we do. *(You see how you select the others you do to get the results you want? And most of the time, you will not know consciously you are doing it.)*

It's not the outside sameness we are looking for as proof; it's their inside similar filtering system that gives us the poof we are looking for, because they will create similar interpreted universes. Their bodies will respond in similar ways, and their worlds will be about the same as ours. Therefore, consensus is assured; and it is that proof we are looking for that will prove to us that our world, our reality, is real.

The more things we have in common with those whom we pick to find consensus with, the more consensus we will find. Since our interpreted universes are created from memories that aren't true, complete, and real, what we have consensus with are other illusions. This line of reasoning has led us to an old statement. "Perception is reality." But it is not. It's just another way to stay in our common illusions. In the following diagram, the more consensus or gray area we have with others, the more proof we have that their illusions must be real; therefore, so also must ours be real.

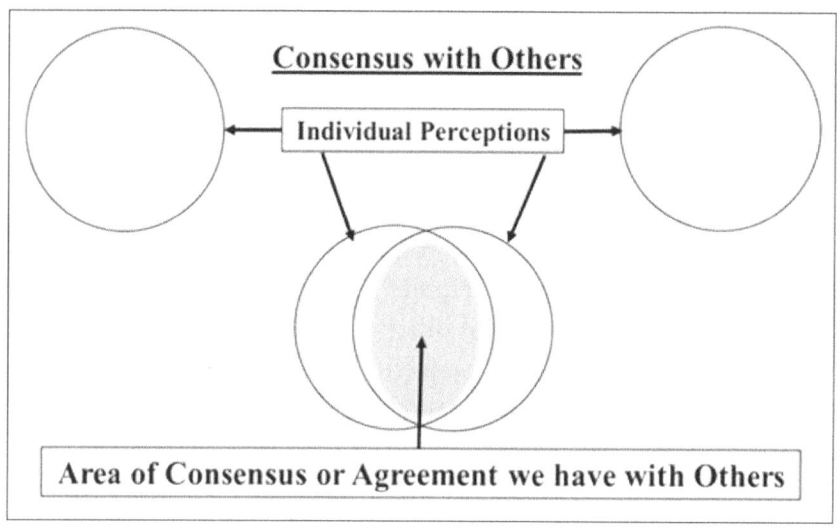

Diagram 05 - Consensus

We aren't together in everything. With some people, we will have more consensus or agreement than others, and then with others we will have less consensus or agreement. But never will we have complete agreement with any one person. Why? Because we each have different beliefs, experiences, and references, which means we have different memories that create different perceptual filtering systems of the outside incoming data and information. From that data we will create different interpreted universes, and they will separate us from complete consensus.

HOLOGRAPHIC STORAGE MATRIX FOR MEMORIES

We said earlier that the body is embedded within an energy system or field and that the energy must be there before the physical body. While this is so, we need to appreciate that the body itself is an energy system, because everything is energy. The memories we create are energy forms also. We are storing crystallized energy within energy, a wheel within a wheel. This isn't easy to visualize because we have little reference to this kind of concept or idea.

The closest metaphor for this may be a radio signal, where there is a carrier wave. Within the wave information transmitted by the radio transmitter, where either the amplitude is modulated (AM) or the frequency is modulated (FM), is the information or data; and on that moving wave, information rides or is stored. Think of that moving energy system or carrier wave as the energy in which the body is integrated and also the energy in which memories are stored and embedded. Our senses can't see, hear, or touch radio waves; and the energy radiating around the body is also difficult for the senses to capture. So just because the senses can't sense something, that doesn't mean something isn't there; our senses aren't all that acute, you know. There are radio waves and other wavy forms of energy all around us and going through us right now; how many can you sense? Make believe something is there, and it will be easier to experience. Make believe nothing is there, and it won't be there for you. *(It is impossible for you not to believe what you can see or sense. It is equally impossible to see or sense what you don't believe is there. It's all about you and what you believe. What are beliefs? Clusters of memories that aren't true, but here again, you believe they are true.)*

In our model, memories are stored in that subtle energy field around the body and which the body rests in. They have V_X, A_X, K_X, O_X, and G_X coordinates, by which the subconscious mind stores, locates, and retrieves them. Our beliefs, experiences, and references are all memories of past interpretations and perceptions, and those are what is stored. Everything in the mind is a memory, and those memories are interconnected.

We really don't need to define how the subconscious mind stores and retrieves information. Whatever definition we come up with won't matter anyway because the subconscious mind knows what it is doing and how to use its systems. It has been storing, locating, and retrieving what information it needs for a long time, at least since we came into this three-dimensional-plus space/time universe. If we knew exactly how the system operates, what would we do with that knowledge? Would we change it? Oh, now that's an egotistically based, arrogant thought question, isn't it? Would we really want to stick a wrench into the gears of such a beautiful running piece of equipment to help it work better? Right now it's a black box. Let's see how we can use what we already know about it.

Who is it who wants to know how our subconscious minds work?

Is it the conscious mind? If so, whom is the conscious mind going to talk to about it? Because all we know is what the conscious mind tells us. The subconscious mind operates at over forty billion bits of data per second and the conscious mind at one hundred bits per second. The conscious mind will never understand or know all there is to know about the subconscious mind. And we don't need to know everything about the subconscious mind to use it. In other words, I don't have to know how my car or my computer operates, but I can still use them, and I don't know how the large Hadron Collider in Europe works, yet I can use the information it provides. What we need is a good working model of our friend, the subconscious mind, so we can more efficiently and effectively understand ourselves. Now that's an oxymoron— understanding ourselves—because we have no idea who we really are.

Metaphorically, storing the memories of our perceptions and interpretations in a holographic matrix in the energy system the body is embedded in and using V_X, A_X, K_X, O_X, and G_X coordinates for storage, location, and retrieval is a great model for now. We know memories are stored somewhere because they can be retrieved; therefore, we know there is some way to locate them and restore them when we're through using and thinking about them.

We live in a metaphorical world. Everything is a metaphor; even our words and the language we use are metaphors. Words are symbols of something else; they are representations or models of other things. When we say a word aloud or to ourselves, we create a model or interpretation in our minds of the thing the word represents. The word *cow* isn't a cow. It's a symbol for something else. The word *anxiety* isn't anxiety. It's a symbol for something else.

Do the words we say completely describe the things they name? No. All of us will have our own model or perception of the thing named. If you say the word *dog*, will everyone have the same perception you do? No. Some people love dogs, some people hate dogs, and some people don't give a rip about dogs. Different perceptions come from the same word. We all have our own models of how things are. Usually we don't even think about them consciously. When we say a word or sentence, or give a lecture, we just assume others know what we are talking about and have the same meanings for the same words as we do. If others don't see things the way we do, we are more likely to believe they have a problem and not us.

So metaphorically and in general, the holographic matrix of memories as an energy sphere around and within the body is a good, usable representation of the subconscious-mind storage system. Will we all agree on this model? No. Does it matter? No. We are using what works for us because no one for sure knows how the subconscious mind really works anyway. Whatever model we use, all it needs to do is store, locate, retrieve, and restore memory information.

Again, are our memories true, complete, and real? And is the present moment we perceive true, complete, and real the way we perceive and experience it? No. Since the memories we use to filter the present moment aren't true, complete, and real, the present moment we are now perceiving and experiencing is distorted into something that isn't true, complete, and real. Therefore, we can change our present moment because what we perceive it to be isn't what is really happening anyway, except in our heads. It's like we have a camera with a certain lens setting, and we look through the camera lens and see a certain picture without changing what the camera is aimed at or the outside energy in any way. If we change the lens of the camera to a different one, we will see a different world, and a different picture will come into focus. Nothing has to change outside us to create a different world. All we need to do is change our filter, our lens, and like magic, a new and different world will come into being for us. It's all just smoke and mirrors anyway. We did mention that we live in an illusion, didn't we? *(You never need to change anything in the outside energy system to get what you want. To get what you want, you only need to change what you are doing inside. It's what you hold inside that will determine what you will get from the outside, and it has nothing to do with what is outside. It is all inside stuff that needs to change.)*

Some may be thinking, *How in the world can my changing something inside me, like my beliefs, change anything happening outside me in the physical world?* Because this idea is so counterintuitive to our current way of thinking, we need to say it again. "The observer affects the observed." Quantum physics is very clear on this point, and it has been mentioned several times in this read. The act of observing affects what we observe. This shouldn't be a surprise to us. Think of someone you love. Consider how loving he or she looks and how much you enjoy being with him or her. Now think of someone you don't like and get upset or mad with. Imagine how grumpy and unpleasant the person looks and how he or she makes you feel. As we think about these two people, many times they are the same person; the only difference is our attitude at any given moment in time. We are the causal force behind what we observe, and we give meaning to all the people and situations in our lives, based on how we feel at any given moment. *(Sooner or later, you will recognize that you don't live where you think you do. Do you live in the outside world or within your interpretation of the outside world, which is to say your inside created, interpreted universe? You don't need to be a rocket scientist to figure this out and get it.)*

"Nothing in the outside world around us has any meaning at all." What an unusual statement. Outside us everything is meaningless. The meaning of people, places, and things doesn't come from the people, places, and things. The meaning comes from our interpretation of the people, places, and things. The thought processes on the inside about those people, places, and things determine what the meaning is for every and all people, places, and things we observe and are in our lives from the inside out. The meaning we give to any person, place, and thing will change as we change; and the change will be both physical and emotional. If we are tired, sad, or depressed, we will experience things a certain way; and if we are energetic, happy, and excited, we will experience the same things differently. We give different meanings to the same things, not based on them changing but on us changing. Therefore, everything outside us is meaningless until we think about them; and each time we think of them as a memory, we may give them a different meaning because of where we are mentally and physically at that moment. Look again, and we will see that we are the ones who give meaning to our world from the inside. The outside world has no meaning at all. That energy system outside us is neutral until we give it meaning from the inside.

Quantum physics looks at this differently and can demonstrates at the quantum level that the act of observing does indeed affect the physical behavior of things. We don't need quantum mechanics to begin to understand that the way we are inside effects what we observe outside. The outside is always a reflection of what is happening inside.

Since we are made of quantum particles and the world is made of quantum particles, we are affecting what we observe.

At this point, we may get caught in what-if scenarios, recalling the worst of the worst things we ever experienced and trying to test and see whether the way we observe or interpret the outside really can affect it in any way, let alone in any physical way. We would like to believe the old paradigm that states, "When you change the way you look at things, *the things you look at can't change by the way you look at them, and they remain the same thing.*" It is the old programming belief that "what is outside us is real and is the cause of all our inside problems of pain and suffering," because if we could affect what we observe, we could change it. And if we could change it, we are responsible for what we have; and if we are responsible for what we have and don't like what we have and haven't changed it, because we can, we have no one to blame but ourselves. This will make our egos feel bad. *(When your ego feels bad, you feel bad because your ego is your creation. Think again. What is the world you live in? You live in your created, interpreted universe on the inside, which is to say you live in an illusion.)*

Now, if we look hard enough, we will find things in our world that don't seem to fit this model because we can always find situations that can't be changed right now. It's not that they couldn't change, but we, from within our belief system, can't change them now and will believe the whole idea is crazy talk. The secret is to start with small changes in our beliefs around little irritations. Don't start with the worst of the worst kind of stuff. Gain some success by changing small irritations and then move forward and on to medium and then larger changes. *(When you change the way you interpret things, the things will change physically. They will feel different. Colors will be brighter, sounds will be more melodious, and fragrances and how things taste will change. You might think,* Well, of course, yes, it is all subjective. All that stuff is in your head. *That's the point. Everything is in your head. It's not outside you. It's all inside you.)*

At this point I need to make a kind of disclaimer. I have said, "Everything is in your head." In some theories, the created interpretation or hologram isn't in the head. And indeed it may not be in the head. However, for our purposes, we will still use the phrase because we are creating a model. It isn't carved in stone, and we can change it as we expand our understanding.

CHAPTER 11

Gross and Subtle Energy Systems

THE TWO SYSTEMS

We will expand a little on the idea of the unmanifested everything, which is the energy field outside us. In quantum physics the unmanifested might be called a field of all possibilities or probability waves. We aren't going into quantum physics except to use the idea that we are surrounded by an unmanifested probability field or wave functions or what may be called a "subtle energy field." What I refer to as the subtle energy system^G others might call the "quantum field," and still others might call it the "dowsing field." This energy field is everywhere, and everything is unmanifested within it; therefore, it is infinite.

We appear to live in two different energy systems at the same time—the gross energy system and the subtle energy system. The word *subtle* is use here to denote an energy that isn't available to our subconscious minds and maybe not directly to our senses either. The gross energy system is what we are aware of as the world around us. The gross energy system is our active mind's interpreted universe from data and information it receives from the subconscious mind and the body. The active mind never directly receives the gross energy input data, nor is it complete when it receives the data, because the data the active mind receives has already been highly filtered and manipulated by the subconscious mind based on our belief system, experiences, and references from the past.

And what does the active mind do with this incomplete data? It creates our interpreted universe, which is the gross energy system we live in. We call it our world, and it is an inside creation of our active minds.

The subtle energy system isn't known directly. It is more mysterious, unknown, and much more interesting than the gross energy system. It appears to be connected to the subconscious realm of the mind, because the subconscious also cannot be experienced directly. There seems to be something there, but we're not sure what it is.

Since subtle energy cannot be experienced directly, at least by most people, it is difficult to get our heads and thoughts around this system in a conscious way. We haven't developed the awareness or instruments that can detect this strange system. It may be in the data the senses transmit, but the subconscious mind can't directly detect it; or maybe the subconscious mind detects it but doesn't know what to do with it, because we have no experiences or references to it. It's similar to what scientists call "dark energy." Again, they know something is there, and they keep poking at it, but as yet, they don't know what it is, and they can't detect it directly. Subtle energy is a lot like that dark energy; it has always been there since the beginning of time and maybe before the big bang, but only now have we reached its awareness because of its indirect effects on what we thought we knew about the cosmos and the mind.

The evidence of subtle energy may be all around us and in the data and information our senses send to our minds that we don't use. Without some kind of reference experience or model, the evidence just passes straight through our subconscious awareness like those small "neutrino particles" scientists have also been hunting for and trying to catch for such a long time. However, we will never see or use that evidence hidden in the unused information we receive because we aren't looking for it and don't belief it's there; at least, most of us aren't looking for it or believe it's there. *(Your beliefs and experiences are strong determinants of what you will experience. If you believe something is there, you are more likely to find it than if you don't believe it is there. If you believe the world is a dangerous place, you will see danger around every corner and within every interaction in your life. The opposite is also true, of course. If you believe your world is safe and friendly, you will experience safe and friendly things around every corner and within every interaction in your life. It's like a big game you play with yourself, within the subtle energy system and the gross energy system; and it is what is all created from the inside out.)*

Energy Model

We have a lot of information and good models around the gross energy system, which is our everyday world. The subtle energy system is another story. A model is needed for it so we can begin to add structure to this theoretical system that cannot be experienced directly. The model we develop and use may not be 100 percent correct, but it may start a meaningful discussion about this proposed energy system. But then probably not, because moving from our current belief system will take more than this little read, although it might be interesting and fun to play with for a while.

To begin the development of this model, we start with what we believe we know. There is a world—the gross energy system—we for sure know is there, right? It is our world, even though the world we have is our individually created world. We operate in a three-dimensional space/time universe, and this is what I refer to as the gross energy system. In this system we are individuals and see ourselves as different and separate from all others. We use our five senses to navigate through this universe and with our five senses send information as data back to our minds through our subconscious perceptual filtering process, and we do quite well for the most part.

From the data our subconscious mind has accepted, we each interpret the external world we think we are consciously in. Since our human brains have evolved as a species over eons of time, we more or less developed similar interpretations from the similar data we receive; and basically this is because our brains mechanically process data about the same way. For example, I see a blue-colored object, and you see the same object as blue. This is a good thing, or we wouldn't be able to get along and communicate with each other as well as we do. *(Recognize that you and I have consensual agreements upon which we base our common reality. However, your belief system and mine are different, and that is problematic.)*

Since our three-dimensional space/time environment is navigated by the use of our senses, we are conscious of what we believe the external environment is, not because of what is in the external world but by our interpretation of the data the subconscious mind sends us. As I have suggested, the created interpreted universe is the universe we live in, and the gross energy system is the result of our interpretation. *(Just so we are clear here, the gross energy system isn't outside you. It is your inside creation and constructed universe. It seems outside you only because of the slow conscious mind, which projects it out there. Strange, right? Your gross energy system is always inside you.)*

We know a lot about the gross system but little about the subtle energy system. It is like a yin and yang relationship. *(I used the yin and yang model earlier when discussing fractals, and it seems to work well as a metaphor here.)* The gross energy system is the manifested, open, and available energy as interpreted by our active minds, bodies, and conscious minds; it is the yang or active energy. The subtle energy system is mysterious, hidden, and unmanifested; it is the yin energy. Separating them is a gray area, where the two mingle and dance together at times. Which mind is bigger—conscious or subconscious? The subconscious mind. Which energy system is the biggest—gross or subtle? The subtle energy system because it is infinite, and the manifested gross energy system is finite.

The following diagram tries to show their relationship of gross and subtle energy systems.

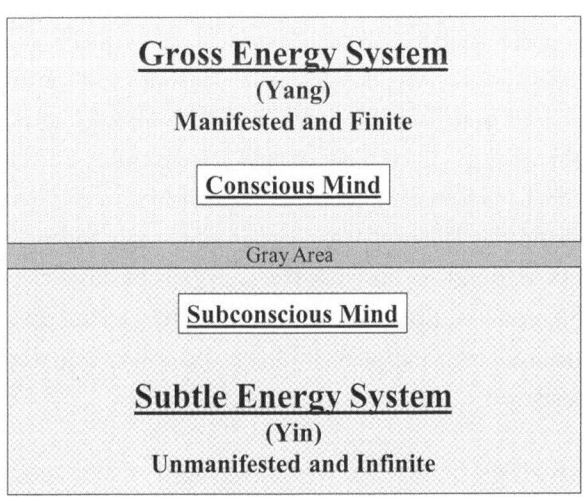

Diagram 06 - Gross and Subtle Energy Systems

Since the conscious mind doesn't directly know the subtle energy system, we consciously tend to believe it doesn't exist or that it has little or no consequences in our conscious lives. We do all our conscious living in the gross energy world. The conscious mind is the only realm of the mind we are concerned with or know about, even though it's the least informed and last to know anything. But because it is all we are aware of, we tend to think that's all there is to know. We said that before, right?

The two realms of the mind, conscious and subconscious, have very little in common. The subconscious mind operates and processes data billions of times faster than the conscious mind, as we have said. The conscious mind has no idea what the subconscious mind is doing, and it isn't connected to it except through the active mind. It can report only on what has already happened; and by the time we hear the news, it has already changed. The conscious mind can't keep up with what is going on in that black box; therefore, it must rationalize, generalize, truncate, and delete what it tells us because it's just too slow to keep up, and basically it doesn't know. But—and this is a big but—it's all we know, so we believe it is all there is to know.

Between the two realms is kind of a no-man's land, the "gray area" where a lot of interesting things go on. In the gray area are our precognitive thoughts. These are thoughts we are having, but they haven't as yet bubbled into our conscious awareness. Dreams that go on at night and are sometimes remembered by the conscious mind when we awaken are caught here for a while. Resentments and fears move into the gray area and then slip back into the subconscious, depending on how much energy they have at any given time; and at times the conscious mind reaches in and pulls them into its realm for a while. When that happens, the body may experience pain and suffering or joy and happiness, depending on what the energy is because they are all just memories. So, you see, the gray area is a very interesting and active area.

The conscious mind appears to have the following responsibilities and characteristics:

> **Analyzing**—It reviews the perceptions of the active mind and how the body is responding to those perceptions; and verbalizes

its analyses to us so we know what has happened. *(Have you ever wondered who is listening when your conscious mind is talking to you?)*

➢ **Rationalizing/Judging**—It comes up with reasonable and logical explanations for why we do what we do. The conscious mind makes up scenarios or rational stories that justify to us and to others why we are doing what we are doing. It keeps us from thinking we are crazy. Rationalizing is an important function of the conscious mind. *(Again, recognize the rational stories aren't what is happening. They are only stories and creations you tell yourself, based on haft-truths and partial information; but you do believe they are true, don't you?)*

➢ **Willpower**—Willpower is like a short burst of emotional adrenaline to get us over emotional and physical hard times and current issues. It is short-term help and not a long-term answer to our life problems. *(If you use willpower as your only solution to your problem, you will get tired, and at some point, you will stop using it. And then the problem issues will re-express themselves.)*

➢ **Temporary Memory** (Working Memory)—The conscious mind can report on the interpreted universe for a short time before the interpretations slip into permanent memory in the subconscious mind. Studies indicate temporary memory is available only for about twenty-five seconds. Then it slips into the subconscious mind as permanent memory, and if the conscious mind needs help from the subconscious mind, it just asks, but it does so through the active mind.

The subconscious mind does all the heavy lifting in the mind. The actual responsibilities and characteristics of the subconscious aren't 100 percent known; however, by observing what goes into that black box and what comes out through indirect methods, we can say that the following appear to be some of the functions and responsibilities the subconscious mind performs and handles for us:

➢ **Imagination**—Nothing new would ever happen in the gross energy system without this faculty. Everything is created twice.

The first time is in the imagination of the creative subconscious mind and the active mind. Note: the jury is still out on this one. There are some who believe imagination is a conscious mind activity, but because it is the active mind that creates the interpretation of everything and gets its data and information sent by the subconscious mind or the body, I have put imagination in the subconscious mind. In the long run, it doesn't matter unless you can tie it to some theory that requires it to be in the conscious mind.

➤ **Permanent Memory**—Every created interpreted universe and every perception we have ever made about any event, along with its emotional attached energy, is stored in the subconscious mind. Also, thoughts, fantasies, daydreams, nighttime dreams, and all that extra data from the senses that isn't used in our perceptions may be there somewhere, quarantined in permanent memory.

➤ **Control of Automatic Functions**—The brain has three basic brain forms that were developed in its evolutionary process. Notice that the functioning of the brain is also out of conscious awareness.

○ The first developed brain was the "reptilian brain." The term *reptilian* refers to our primitive, instinctive brain function, shared by all reptiles and mammals, including humans. It is the most powerful and oldest of our coping brain functions, since without it we wouldn't be alive. It is instinctive, programmed to survive, and it is that part of the brain that does most of the automatic physical functions of the body (http://www.copingskills4kids.net/Reptilian_Coping_Brain.html).

○ The second developed brain structure is the limbic system. The primary structures within the limbic system include the amygdala, hippocampus, thalamus, hypothalamus, basal ganglia, and cingulate gyrus. The amygdala is the emotion center of the brain, while the hippocampus plays an essential role in the formation of new memories about past experiences (https://www.boundless.com/psychology/textbooks/boundless).

o The neocortex is the last and newest developed part of the brain. The neocortex is part of the cerebral cortex (along with the archicortex and paleocortex, which are cortical parts of the limbic system). It is involved in higher functions such as sensory perception, generation of motor commands, spatial reasoning, conscious thought, and language in humans (https://www. sciencedaily.com/terms/neocortex.htm).

➤ **Habits and Ingrained Behavior**—All habits and repeated behaviors, good and bad, are programmed and function from the subconscious.

➤ **Protective Response**—This relates to the "reptilian brain." It will always respond to protect us against real or perceived, imaginary, and physical dangers. Here again the body is responding only to the interpreted universe, and that universe is determined by the subconscious mind's perceptual filtering system.

➤ **Our Current Picture of Reality**—Whatever our currently held picture or paradigm of our personal reality is, it is held and maintained in the subconscious mind. Our picture of reality is determined by our currently held beliefs, experiences, and references from the past. Changing our filtering system will change our reality.

➤ **Lazy**—Well, lazy may not be the right word; however, once patterns or habits are set in the subconscious, it is difficult to change them. Maybe it's not lazy; it just doesn't want to change because it believes what it is doing is right, needed, and the best and most helpful and supportive method of operating for the good of the whole mind and body based on our accepted beliefs, experiences, references, and memories.

Our two minds appear to straddle the two-energy systems of gross and subtle, with the conscious part of the mind in the gross energy system and the subconscious part in the subtle energy system. They are like two countries; and just like two countries, the conscious and subconscious minds don't speak the same language. Yet they need to communicate for the common good and health of all.

SEPARATION IN THE GROSS ENERGY SYSTEM

The gross energy system is also the realm of the manifested objective reality. In this realm, everything is an "object," and every object in our objective reality has a location because we are in the three-dimensional space/time universe. Each object in this universe is separate from every other object, or at least it appears to be separate; and it has a three-dimensional location.

However, the appearance of separation in the three-dimensional space/time universe may just be a trick of the minds or our egoic selves. Recall that earlier, we discussed the evolution of the brain in the human species over eons of time and that for the most part human brains process similar data in similar ways. With that in mind, recall that the sensory inputs are in the form of electric, magnetic, and chemical-coded signals that need to be decoded, reviewed, and filtered by the subconscious mind and then sent to the active mind. Each sensory organ is unique in how and what kind of data it collects. In the animal kingdom, human sensory organs aren't the best. It's a good thing we have such great brains, or we would have disappeared as a species long ago.

What we think we are seeing is only the interpretation the active mind created. As stated before, it's not good or bad until the active mind interprets it. The information received by the active mind, after being filtered, is meaningless until it is given meaning by the active mind's interpretation. Again, we see that it isn't what is outside us that is important but how it is interpreted inside. The meaning of our external world isn't in the external world; it's in our internal interpretation of the external filtered data, and all of us have our own variation about what is meaningful and what degree of intensity it has. We need to acknowledge, what we think of as our external world is only a reflection of our internal, created interpretation of external filtered data.

RELATING TO QUANTUM PHYSICS

If we relate the subtle energy system to quantum physics, it appears to be more like a field with wavy-like qualities than a system; and if we relate the gross energy system to quantum physics, it seems more like the realm of separate things or particles. The subtle energy system, the field, is the realm of the unmanifested or pure possibilities and the gross energy system, the realm of the manifested, physical real stuff or the land of finite separate things.

SUBTLE ENERGY SYSTEM OR THE SUBTLE FIELD

The "subtle field" is the starting point and the ending point of all physical things. In Eastern philosophy there is a branch of understanding called Taoism. In that philosophy (for some it is a religion) the Tao is the foundation and ground of everything. All things begin and end in the Tao. It moves everything into being, and it brings all things back to itself. The Tao is everything and is the beginning and end of everything (Wikipedia, Outline of Taoism).

This description seems to fit the model we are developing. Everything starts from the subtle field of the unmanifested, moves into the gross energy system, becomes separate things, and then dissolves back into the subtle field. It is like a lava lamp. In a lava lamp, when the blob at the bottom of the lamp becomes hot enough, usually with an electric light bulb, little blobs separate and move up to the upper part of the lamp, leaving the mass at the bottom. Then when the blobs have lost enough energy, they one by one move back to the source blob at the bottom. The little blobs are absorbed back into the mass. But they are always inside and part of the subtle fluid that holds both the mass at the bottom and the little blobs floating around at the top.

What is the subtle field? I don't know for sure. We mentioned that the subconscious mind seems to be in the subtle field in some way and is also the essence of who we are, which could be called "inner wisdom," "higher self," "life force," "soul," or what some spiritual and wisdom paths have called "your original self." Many different cultures, philosophies, and religions have added different names or aspects to this subtle field, and some of those are "collective unconscious," "source energy," "unity consciousness," and "god." This subtle field doesn't appear to be in time's realm, and information seems to be instantly entangled throughout the field; from that aspect, time and space collapse. There is a wholeness and completeness about the field and a sense of oneness of being.

The following diagram suggests a model for the subtle field. Recognize that we each may have our own model for this field. See if your model can fit into the suggested model presented here and try not to get hung up on all the names, because in the end, the name doesn't matter, because it's all just an illusion in the gross energy system anyway.

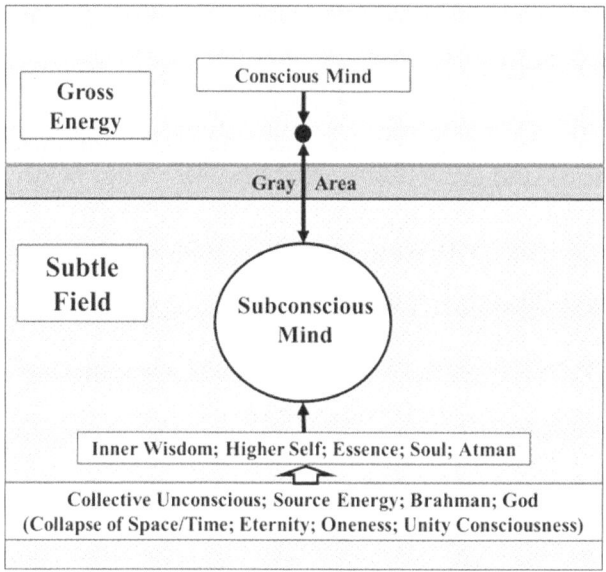

Diagram 07 - Gross Energy System and the Subtle Field

The model cannot be verified, of course; and it is an idea, a thought form. We clearly and currently don't have the tools in our conscious three-dimensional space/time universe to verify the subtle field. However, that never stopped us in the past from speculating and believing in this elusive field. Throughout history philosophies, spiritual paths, and religious beliefs have all centered around the idea that what we know of our physical reality is built on the foundation of the unknown, some form of subtle field; and this is true right up to today.

Even science at its core is the study and investigation of the unknown or unmanifested and the desire to bring pure thoughts and ideas of the unknown or unmanifested into the known and manifested. The scientific method starts in the gross energy system of the known and moves to the subtle field of the unmanifested and unknown, while on the other hand philosophical and spiritual paths and religions start in the subtle field and move into the gross energy system. If we sense a gap between these two approaches, it's because each one gets stuck in its own dogma, and it clouds its eyes to the underlying truth. And just what is the common ground of both? Quantum physics. Science is more likely to move to the quantum state because there is just too much dogma in philosophical, spiritual, and religious paths. But all in all there is too much dogma in both, and they have difficulty appreciating each other.

Each path and belief system has its own unique way of approaching this subtle field; we must embrace it, reject it, fight against it, or ignore it. However, it's part of everyone's life process, even yours. So let us view it a little differently.

REALITY

Reality isn't real. Well, yes, in a certain way it appears to be real. However, what aren't real or true are our collective and individual interpretations of the data sent to us by our senses and filtered by our individual and collective egoic lenses. Our interpretations are what aren't true, complete, or real. What the senses are transmitting to the mind is the energy they encounter of the unmanifested and unreal objects, because there are no objects until the active mind gives them life by its interpretations. We create the objects of our objective reality by the way we have chosen to interpret the data, and a lot of our creations appear to be the same or close enough between us that we can talk about shared experiences. The "sameness" of reality appears most likely to be the same reality for people in the same family, culture, country, society backgrounds, and so forth.

There is no real reality out there in the unmanifested everything, only energy; I know this is tough to get that at first or even think about because of our culturally learned programming. We literally create our reality the way it is because of our programming, which is to say our past beliefs, experiences, and references, which are now our memories. And this created reality basically changes from second to second and year to year because of us. So how can this ever-changing tapestry of life ever possibly be a real reality on which everything else rests? It may appear real and trustworthy today and tomorrow be something else. With that kind of smoke-and-mirrors reality, it may be more appropriate to call it an "illusion." Oh, isn't that what ancient wisdom has said it was? It's like a reality show, and the more we try to make it real, the more unreal and elusive it becomes. *(The closer you look at it, the deeper your questions become, and the answers are more speculative and slippery. It's almost like you are at the event horizon of a black hole and at the singularity. If you ask too many questions and get to close, you could be sucked in and not be able to find your way back to the gross world. To heal your pain and suffering, you may need to rest in the field for a while and allow your memories to reframe and also heal.)*

This unreal reality we think we are in is dualistic. It is the realm of opposites. For every belief someone has, someone else will have a completely opposite and different belief. Both believers will know their beliefs are true and real because of all the proof they have that they are true and real, and that the other person is wrong. With that kind of understanding, they will beat each other up over who is right. There is hardly anything believed a thousand years ago that hasn't changed and isn't believed now the way it was then; yet back then people fought and died for those beliefs. Crazy, right? I wonder whether in another thousand years from now other people will look back on us and say, "They fought and died over the dumbest and silliest things back then, and they weren't even real things." Our unreal reality is always shifting sands under our intellectual feet.

Oneness

When we move from the dualistic gross energy system into the subtle field, space and time have no meaning, and they collapse. When we enter the subtle field, we as separate individuals also collapse into oneness. Let us use the lava lamp as a metaphor again. When that big blob at the bottom of the lamp is heated up and smaller blobs break away, they rise to the upper part of the lamp and are separate things; they learn and experience separate things. When a little blob of separateness loses enough energy, it falls back into the substance at the bottom. Once back in oneness at the bottom, its separateness is lost, and it's all one substance again. Its separateness, knowledge, and experience is absorbed into the whole and shared by the whole; and in the whole, separateness and knowledge of the small blobs are integrated into the whole, and all is one again. Its knowledge, its information, is integrated into the whole as is the whole integrated into all. They are entangled into the oneness, and each part is a hologram of the whole. No matter how small a piece of the infinite subtle field we try to take, the whole is reflected in that small holographic piece. We can't take anything from the infinite because the infinite is always and everywhere, so when we believe we have a piece of oneness, think we understand the infinite, or think we can view the infinite as separate pieces, we can't because it all is already there. *(You are inseparable from the subtle field, because it is everywhere. If it is infinite, then you are the subtle field. Oh wait, that is a little too much for you at this time. Let's just say, "You are part of the infinite subtle field.")*

In the oneness of the whole, where neither time nor distance exists, where everything is one, knowing is instantaneous, and there is no distance, the oneness is "entangled," and there is only one integrated field.

REACHING DOWN, REACHING UP

The gross energy system and the subtle field are always connected. Following an ancient path, new little blobs come from the subtle field into the gross energy system, and older blobs lose energy and reenter the subtle field of oneness; there is a constant coming and going. Such is life in eternity.

While in the gross energy system, we can reach into the subtle field. There are many ways to do this. Prayer is one of the most acknowledged methods. But there is a long list of time-honored ways to connect with the subtle field: meditation, hypnosis, dowsing, healing touch, quantum healing, Reiki, emotionally focused transition, and other techniques. These are only a few of the methods. They aren't magic. They are natural approaches and ways of using the subtle field. Each method has its own protocol and techniques for moving from the gross energy system and entering the subtle field, normally through the subconscious mind. We all have this ability unless we choose to believe we don't.

Since time and space collapse into the oneness of the subtle field, distance is meaningless in the field, and communication is instantaneous. It is the feeling energy in the body and our intentions that open a path or wormhole from the gross energy system into the subtle field and back into the gross system. Intention is the key that allows the path to open so we can flow between the two systems, and it must be in the mind first. However, there is more evidence that it's more of a physiological process than we thought. Intentions and beliefs are thoughts, and energy flows where thoughts go. Intentions and beliefs in the active mind are thoughts that create perceptions, which stimulate the body into response.

The following diagram is a model for imagining moving from the gross energy system into the subtle field and back into the gross energy system.

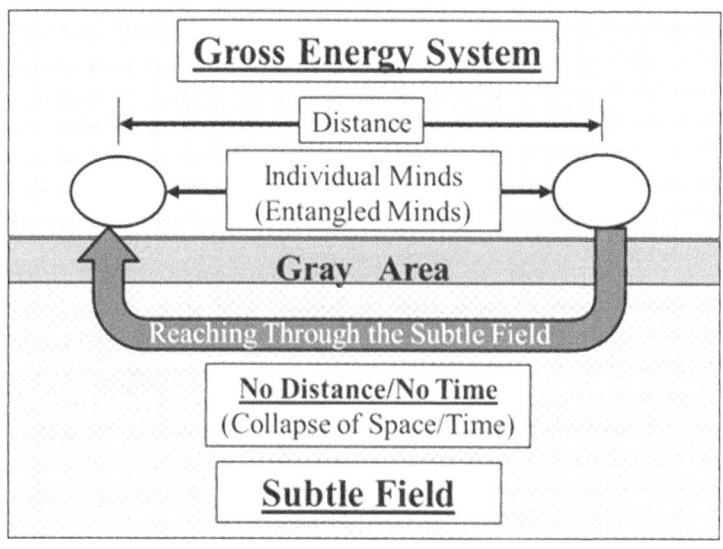

Diagram 08 - Reaching Down, Reaching Up

With this model, healing at a distance may be easier to understand as well as other so-called psychic phenomena, such as remote viewing or viewing at a distance, intuitive knowing, dowsing, telepathic communication, clairvoyance or second sight, and so forth.

Restructuring the Model

The model we have developed shows the gross energy system resting on top and the subtle field underneath, appearing to support it and hold it up. This is a convenient way to view the model to explain the different aspects of how it works; however, it isn't accurate. The subtle field is infinite; therefore, it is everywhere. The gross energy system, our world, is within the subtle field. We are like fish swimming in an infinite ocean; just as the fish is unaware of the water it is in, we are unaware that we are supported by an infinite subtle field.

We are so used to living within what we interpret as "the physical world" that we cannot imagine we're not. We tend to see our environment and world as reality and a fixed, solid, and dependable place to be; but it's not. It is an ever-changing, undulating mass of changes that seem to go on changing forever. As we look at our world moment to moment, it appears fixed, solid, and dependable. However, if we open our lens only a few hundred years, we come to realize nothing is ever the same and that everything is moving. It's like watching a magic show; as we figure out how one trick is done, there is always another mystery to solve or another trick being played on us and then another. It's so cool, and there are so many tricks; and they are all so interesting. We get distracted and forget it's all an illusion and that we are in our own created illusion.

Take the Higgs boson subatomic particle, nicknamed the "God Particle." What a long, drawn-out struggle scientists and physicists had to find this elusive piece of the cosmic puzzle, and what hype there was around its discovery. It's not that it wasn't an exciting find, because it was; and it will help science move forward onto bigger and more interesting discoveries. The point is to recognize that it's part of "the everything" in the infinite, unmanifested subtle field. Maybe if we were to approach the subtle field directly, we wouldn't need to struggle so much. *(Oh, by the way, it's over. What is your memory of the event of finding the God Particle? Is your interpretation of the discovery of the God Particle real, complete, and true? Has it changed your life? Did you even know about it? Don't worry about it; it's all part of the illusion anyway. Science has moved on now and has bigger fish to fry.)*

Since our perceptions are continually changing, what we interpret as reality cannot be the "true reality." There must be something underneath or around this ever-changing, observable reality; something that this ever-changing reality is embedded in—something that is constant, something that is never changing. What is this true reality? Science is all about measuring and comparing. To measure anything you need a yardstick, a constant to compare things to; and nothing is constant in the gross energy system, because everything decays. Nothing is constant in the illusion of the gross energy system. But then it may be good enough for whom it's for at this moment.

Could it be, might it be, that the universal unchanging constant is the "subtle field"? It is difficult to argue with an illusion of reality that has been around for such a long time and is supported by so many, who are inside the illusion with us. If we look closely, we may notice all those who have a stake in keeping us in the old paradigm and in the illusion we are living in. They are looking through the egoic veil, the lens of their own self-interests, a distorted lens; and we are seeing through something that isn't there. And what isn't there isn't real, complete, or true. It is their yardstick that defines their world. What is their yardstick? It is their past memories, of course; and their individual egos will be supported by all the other ego states of family, culture, country, and religion that will have to change if we begin to embrace the subtle field.

Ah, but don't we believe our illusions are true? Don't we have proof that our world is true and real? Well, yes. But as we have found in this read, they're not; and as we uncover more of "the subtle field of everything" we are embedded in, the more our paradigm will shift. *(I know it may be a stretch for you to notice how ingrained you are in your own illusion because of your egoic created identity. But perhaps you can appreciate and change that viewpoint. For a moment, can you imagine how freeing it would be to let go of the past with all its guilt, pain, and suffering? Your past is your creation. What would it feel like to heal and reframe it? You might be a lot happier.)*

Stepping out of our commonly shared illusions and viewing them from a new perspective are impossible to do in a physical sense. However, stepping outside by using our mind's eye, our imagination, is a very doable thing. We can perform another thought experiment or just use our imagination and fancy looking down on the game of life being played out from high above the fray, like being on Mount Olympus, where the Greek gods looked down into the arena of life.

What kind of reality would we see from that higher perspective and new vantage point? Would we see a fixed, constant, compassionate, and loving reality? Or would we view a chaotic, ever-changing panorama of perceptions? A play so apparently real that it might even fool the gods? However, if it is an ever-changing and chaotic view, how could that be the ground place of reality? It can be only another illusion, an egoic sleight of hand. We have no constant to compare it to.

The following diagram is an attempt to show the gross energy system is inside, ingrained, and part of the subtle field. When we are in the gross energy system, which we are, we are *separate* from each other and are like particles. When we are in the subtle field, which we are, we are in *oneness* with no separation, distance, space, or time, like a wave of energy. And in that understanding lies the paradox of life. This is quite close to the paradox of quantum physics, where energy can be a particle, a wave, or both at the same time. What determines whether it is a particle or a wave? We look at the event and measure it. If we look and measure the event, it will be a particle, and the results will prove it. If we don't observe it and look only at the results later, it will be a wave, and the results will prove it. It's the damnedest thing, but then there it is. *(You can look up the "double-slit experiment." It is part of the craziness that goes on in quantum physics, and yet quantum physics is the most complete and accurate approach to understanding our world.)*

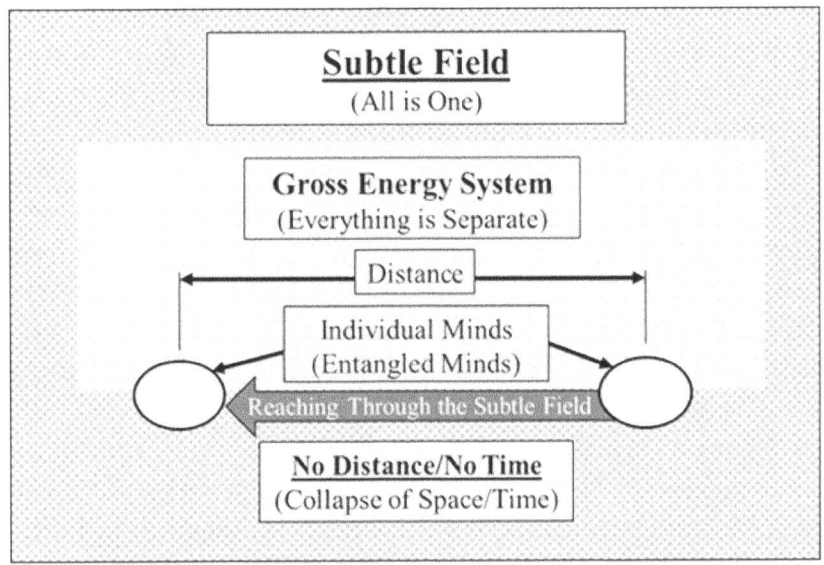

Diagram 09 - Gross Energy System inside the Subtle Field

At the beginning of *A Course of Miracles* is this statement: "Nothing real can be threatened. Nothing unreal exists. Herein lies the peace of God." This model calls the realness of the gross energy system into question. How can we verify the existence of the gross energy system? Our senses are poor, unreliable sources of verification, as was shown earlier, because they just transmit data and don't judge anything. The active mind is just a clever interpreter of data, and the data it uses is the filtered and manipulated data of the subconscious mind, where the input data from the senses has been generalized, manipulated, and deleted to fit our paradigm of beliefs before the active mind receives it. Therefore, how reliable and real can interpretations be from such a data source? And what is the filtering system made up of? Our memories of the past. The past again determines our present experience, and memories from the past aren't real, true, or complete. *(Can you see why healing the past will affect how your present moment is experienced? If you do, you are on the path of creating miracles. If you have pain and suffering in the present moment by healing the past, you change the present moment. When you change the present moment, you moderate your current pain and suffering to some degree.)*

Now, if we sit very still and close our eyes in a quiet, peaceful, and darkened place all by ourselves, it's very difficult to prove we exist at all or that what we think of as our reality is real; and to know that anything is really there. Only random firings in our brains would be going on, and those random thoughts would have no verification or reference point. As we quoted before from Einstein, "Nothing happens until something moves." When we move, the universe trembles and comes into being as we interpret it to be. What great creators we are.

Now, if we sit very still in a quiet place, we are basically practicing the art of meditation. Meditation is an ancient path to enlightenment, and enlightenment is seeing or visualizing the reality behind the illusion of the gross energy system. What do we find there? We find nothing and everything.

The Oneness in the Many

Now we have a real dilemma. To be able to see it more clearly, the model of gross and subtle must again be shown with the subtle field below and support the gross energy system. We can see the separation of individuals in the gross energy system and the oneness in the subtle field, but to see or touch them at the same time in the same space defies our imaginations.

However, keep in mind that the two systems aren't separate; the gross energy system is always within the subtle field. How to display oneness of the many in the three-dimensional space/time universe is a daunting task. It's like making a paradox seem real. This line of inquiry seems to lead back to the ancient concept, which is stated most clearly in the *Hindu Vedic and Upanishads* texts. The gross energy system—the physical world—is an illusion. Or another way of stating it is this: "We are the oneness dreaming of separateness," and in true reality, there is really only one of us here dreaming the many into a virtual existence. We are the dreamers experiencing the illusion as a virtual reality, and it's so very, very real, isn't it?

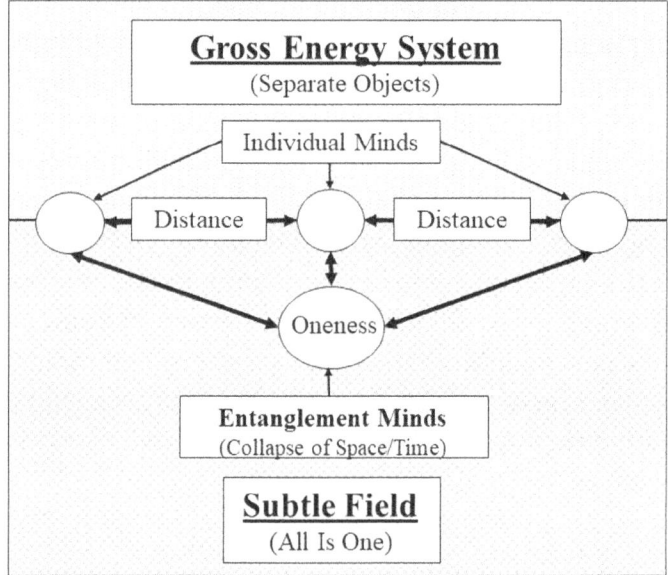

Diagram 10 - Entangled Minds

We, as entities within the dream, have created a virtual universe to support our dream state, and the oneness has been fragmented into the virtual many in the process. And our goal within the dream seems to be to find our way back to oneness.

We might be like Dorothy, who was lost in the land of OZ and trying to find her way back to Kansas and home; all she had to do was click the heels of her ruby-red slippers together and say, "There is no place like home! There is no place like home!" And she was home just that quickly. Only we must say, "There is no real place except oneness! There is no real place except oneness!" What a great and powerful illusion we are in, and what great and powerful wizards we are. We have fooled ourselves so completely.

SPEAKING OF THE BODY

The body is an instrument for our "true self," our "original self." What is our true self? we might ask. This is all speculative, of course, because words are only symbols that represent something else; some answers may be "life force," "soul," "Christ consciousness," "Buddha nature," or "our essence" *(you pick)*. It is the source that animates, gives energy and life to the body, and keeps it going. When that life force leaves, the body stops working and dissolves, moving back into the gross energy system, from whence it came; and the life force also moves back into the subtle field and oneness, from whence it came, back into the blob at the bottom of the lamp.

If we see the body as an instrument of life force, we are seeing our oneness. When we see the body as *who we are*, we are in the virtual world of separation and in the dream state. We have moved back into the illusion, into the gross energy system, and here we are. It seems so real and right to be in the illusion, doesn't it? And yet ...

We actually flow quite easily and seamlessly between the two energies of the gross energy system and the subtle field. When we are dealing with life events and concerns, we are particles and separate entities. When we are relaxed, with mind and body integrated into the nature around us with a pet, gardening, meditating, and such, we are a wave within the infinite ocean of the subtle field.

When we see ourselves as separate bodies, it is difficult to see or even imagine the oneness. Our separate egos will fight and try to support our remaining in the illusion because the ego can exist only in the illusion of separation. *(You do know your ego from within the illusion, don't you? It is a product of separateness or the dream state, and when the life force leaves the body and the body dissolves, then the ego is no more. The ego will struggle mightily to exist until the very last moment, and it is your belief that it is real that keeps it alive.)*

Bodies don't communicate. We may have thought our bodies do all the talking to other bodies or people, but they don't. Only minds can communicate. The body is just an instrument, a tool like a hammer, a computer, or a telephone. It is never the tool that does the communicating; it is the mind behind the tool that interacts with the minds of other people's minds from within their bodies. When we believe we are a body, we are in the illusion; and then we will think we see and believe bodies are communicating. If we like what another body says, we like that body. Our egoic self encourages us to see our bodies as who we are. When we do, we put the ego, our created identity, in control; and we move deeper into the illusion and away from oneness.

Now, don't get confused by thinking about body language as communicating. The body always must respond to the active mind's interpretative signals. The body is a puppet on a string. The body doesn't respond the way it does by accident. What we think of as body language is a reflection in the body of what is going on behind the body in the mind. No matter what the body is doing both consciously and unconsciously, it is because of the mind. It can be only minds that are communicating. Why? Because everything is neutral and meaningless until we interpret and think about it in our minds, because that's a mind's function. No matter how we want to consciously think about it, only minds can communicate.

INFINITE SOURCE AND THE LIFE OF THE BODY

We have no concept of what an infinite source might be. Maybe we would imagine that source to be a really big person with hands and feet, a tongue, and sex organs sitting on a cloud with its feet on a really big footstool. To think of an infinite source without humane traits and characteristics is almost impossible because that is all we can to imagine and picture. When we talk about an infinite source and the infinite subtle field, they are just way too much infinity for us to handle in our minds.

Let's think about the concept of infinite source of everything and the life of the body for a while. This creative infinite source is like the overseer of all that is because the infinite source is all there is; and since it is all so infinite, it is in the finite physical world as well. Why? Because it is infinite. *(If that isn't a convoluted statement, I don't know what is. However, when you are thinking about a really big number or a big thing, it isn't the same as your thinking about infinity. Being infinite and being eternal aren't the same thing. Again, words are just symbols for something else that lies beyond the symbols. Infinity is about collapsing size and space, and eternal is about collapsing time. Remember, in the subtle field, space and time collapse, and there is no time.)*

Here is an interesting thought; we can't give what we don't have. The infinite source can only give or create from what it has to give, which is infinite source of itself because that is all there is. Infinite source is the subtle field, and infinite source is also the gross energy system. Our life force or soul isn't a part of that infinite source or a piece broken off infinite source; it is the infinite source. A tree isn't made of wood; a tree is wood. Within all the fractal expansion and the creation of the cosmos, the infinite source is still all infinite source.

Notwithstanding everything is infinite source or the subtle field, which would include us. If we were to take a very little small piece of that infinite source, just enough for our essence or our original self, how much would we need for our essence, original self, or soul?

When we take anything from infinity, does it affect infinity? Have we diminished infinity in any way if we take a piece of it? No, it is still infinite. To say the infinite gets smaller and somehow less than infinite after a little piece is taken from it is meaningless. If we took the smallest or the biggest piece from infinity, separating it from infinity, how much would that be compared to infinity? Since infinity is everywhere, where could we put our piece of infinity that does not already have infinity there? Whether we have the smallest or biggest piece we can imagine from infinity, we have all infinity because we can't divide infinity. When we have a piece of infinity, we become like entangled particles and are forever connected to, part of, and inside infinity. We are infinite, but in this three-dimensional space/time universe, we see only our separateness; and since we see separate things, we believe what we see really exists. *(Don't be silly. You know the eyes don't see. The separateness you think you see is an interpretation of the active mind. You can't take a piece of infinity away from infinity. If infinity is everywhere, where could you put your piece of infinity where infinity isn't? You can't separate any part of infinity from infinity. When you are in the gross energy system of separateness, you are in an illusion, and that is it. Behind the illusion is the oneness of everything, which is to say infinity. Notice also that the illusion is within the infinity of the subtle field.)*

Our problem is that we are relating taking a piece of apple pie to taking a piece of infinity. When we take a piece of apple pie, the pie gets smaller. The pie gets smaller because it is finite. We need to see infinity differently. When we take a piece of infinity, the piece we take isn't really taken away from the infinite because infinity is everywhere, and as such, it can't be separated. If it's not everywhere, then it's not infinite. We are entangled within the infinite. We are infinity, pretending to be separate, and we do a really good job of pretending and acting out our separateness because you sure fooled me.

Again, think of oneness and what's infinite; the only way we can be a separate entity is to be in an illusion of separateness. While we are in the illusion, we are separate; and I kind of like that. If we were one, that might be too close for comfort. We don't know each other all that well, and I don't want you in my business. Being separate is just fine with me. *(Do keep in mind that you and I are in an illusion. When we move out of the illusion, we will be different; and when you and I move back into the glob at the bottom of the lamp, there will be a paradigm shift, and love will be all there is; and won't that be fun? Fun? I don't know about that.)*

Here is the point. We have and will always be entangled within the infinite because the infinite is all there is. We are on the fractal edge of the infinite *(if what's infinite can be said to have an edge)* that is expanding into itself. The how and why of our connection to infinity have caused us to create so many different approaches in philosophies, science, and spiritual paths for us to imagine life in this virtual illusion of separation. Of course, each approach is absolutely true to the believer of any particular approach. Once an approach has been accepted as our belief, our virtual illusion gets more separated because now we have us, the believing true believers; and then there are those who have a different, distorted, and wrong belief or approach to the infinite source, the true self, the original self, the essence of the individual and the soul.

This can get very confusing because our ego self so needs us to be right in our chosen approach. Why would that be? Because our eternal life is at stake; and as we fight so hard to be right, we give up much of our happiness. Being separate, even though the egoic self is very much alive, in the end, we aren't separate; and we will lose our sense of separateness as we flow into oneness that follows the end of days. Nothing is ever lost forever.

BRAHMAN AND ATMAN

We may be able to gain some insight into our understanding of infinity, reality, and our illusion by looking into different philosophies and spiritual paths other than just a Western approach. The concept of Brahman and atman is part of Hinduism.

> Brahman in the Upanishads (Indian sacred writings), the supreme existence or absolute reality ... thought a variety of views are expressed in the Upanishads, they concur in the definition of Brahman as eternal, conscious, irreducible, infinite, omnipresent, and the spiritual core of the universe of finiteness and change. (https://www.britannica.com/topic/brahman-Hindu-concept)

> Atman is the immortal aspect of our mortal existence, the individual Self [Life Force, Soul, Christ Consciousness, Buddha Nature or Our Essence], which is hidden in every object of creation including humans. It is the microcosm which represents the macrocosm in each of us, imparting to us divine qualities and possibilities and providing us with consciousness and the reason to exist and experience the pains and pleasures of earthly life. (http://www.hinduwebsite.com/atman.asp)

We may be able to relate but not measure for measure the subtle field to Brahman and the original self to atman.

> In Hinduism, Brahman is the over-soul and the "unchanging Absolute Reality amidst and beyond the world of constant change" and it can't be defined exactly. Brahman is infinite and as we take away any part of that infinity from the infinite, the infinite is still whole, infinite, unchanged, and the complete oneness of infinity.

> Brahman is what the universe is made of. All physical objects come from this infinite substance of the Brahman; and return to it is they dissolve at the end of days. (Wikipedia—Brahman)

> As stated above, Atman is a Sanskrit word that means basically "inner-self" or soul." In Hinduism Atman is the *"true self"* of the individual which is outside of their identity within the world of illusions, the Original-Self or Essential-Self. To attain liberation or "salvation" the individual must obtain "self-knowledge," which is to grasp and understand that the Self, the Atman, is the Brahman. This experience of liberation is also known as enlightenment. (Wikipedia—Atman [Hinduism])

As we can see from the above understanding, the infinite oversoul, Brahman, and the true self or soul, Atman, are the same. To see them as separate is to be deceived and be in the illusion. It is the true self or soul that struggles to become enlightened. The infinite is always infinite and doesn't struggle because it just is.

Earlier we mentioned Taoism, which is another philosophical understanding and religion of the infinity source and the subtle field. The philosophy comes from China. In its approach to the infinite, all separate things in the gross energy system come from the Tao, the subtle field, and return to and dissolve back into the Tao or the subtle field.

There seems to be a central pattern of understanding deep within all these different systems, a togetherness of thought not seen from inside any one approach. As we stand too close to our own particular belief system, the emerging pattern becomes obscure as we struggle to support our own beliefs. We tend to see what we want to see from inside our own belief system and not what is there to see.

The pattern that emerges appears to be this: "Everything comes from one infinite source, the subtle field; moves into the illusion of separate things, the gross energy system; and dissolves back into the infinite source, the subtle field." The problem we have from inside this virtual shared illusion of separation is that we cannot agree on the details of the how, why, and when of this inevitable underlying pattern. From outside the illusion, as we sit on Mount Olympus, looking down, it must look very silly indeed the way we treat each other and ourselves, knowing we are all one and that the separateness is only an illusion.

OCCAM'S RAZOR

William of Ockham (also known as Occam) was an English Franciscan friar and scholastic philosopher and theologian, who is believed to have been born in Ockham, a small village in Surrey (Wikipedia). We will look at three understandings of Occam's razor and its modernized equivalent: "The simplest answer is the best and most likely the right one."

> Occam's razor (also Ockham's razor; Latin: Lex parsimoniae "law of parsimony") is a principle used for looking at competing theories or concepts that states the simplest with the least added attributes and "the fewest assumptions should be selected" because it is more likely the correct solution. Another way of stating the principle, "Keep it simple." (Wikipedia—Occam's razor)

The Basics:

> Ockham's razor (also spelled Occam's razor, pronounced AHK-uhmz RAY-zuhr) is the idea that, in trying to understand something, getting unnecessary information out of the way is the fastest way to the truth or to the best explanation. (https://whatis.techtarget.com/definition/Ockhams-razor-Occams-razor)

Ockham's razor:

> This principle of simplicity in scientific models and theories is commonly called Ockham's razor, or Occham's razor. It is popularly attributed to the 1400s

English friar and philosopher William of Ockham, also known as William of Occham. The razor alludes to the shaving away of unneeded detail. A common paraphrase of Ockham's principle, originally written in Latin, is, "All things being equal, the simplest solution tends to be the best one." (http://www.cycleback.com/ockham.html)

In other words, we should avoid looking for excessively complex solutions to a problem and focus on what works, given the circumstances. Occam's razor is used in a wide range of situations as a means of making rapid decisions and establishing truths without endless empirical evidence. It works best as a mental model for making initial conclusions before adequate information can be obtained. "A further literary summary comes from one of the best-loved fictional characters, Arthur Conan Doyle's Sherlock Holmes. His classic aphorism is an expression of Occam's razor: 'If you eliminate the impossible, whatever remains, however improbable, must be the truth'" (https://www.fs.blog/2017/05/mental-model-occams-razor/).

The simplest explanation, which is to say the one with no assumptions or the fewest assumptions, is the one to be selected; and the one with the fewest assumptions of all the hypothesis competing is this: "We are the whole thing." Each of us is the center of our universe. You are your universe. You are the infinite source. There is only one of us here, and you are it, no matter what it appears like from within the illusion. You have fragmented the oneness into the many, and now your goal is to find the oneness again. *(Your universe emanates from you. Your universe is the way it is because of what you hold inside, which is your memories. You can bring a different universe into focus anytime you want just by healing your past memories. Ah now, there's the rub. You believe your memories are real and can't be healed and changed. Don't be silly. You change your memories all the time, some for the good and some for the bad.)*

CREATING THE ILLUSION OF REALITY

Creating the illusion of reality is a process that takes place from within the illusion. The major components of this created process from within the illusion is the ego in all its different forms of individual, family, culture, society, nation, and others. Every separate individual and grouping of individuals creates and develops an ego. The ego is their identity of who they think and believe themselves to be. And so each separate grouping of individuals has its own unique ego identity develop from within the group. This is an illusion of separation within the oneness. Since these egos are created from within the illusion, they aren't real. Why? Because the illusion isn't real; therefore, whatever is created from within the illusion cannot be real, no matter how real it appears to individuals from within the illusionary grouping.

Our ego and all ego identities have a life of their own. Once we have accepted our ego as who we think we are, it is alive and integrates itself into our belief system like a virus and disguises itself as us. It is our creation; it is our child. At times it will pander to us like a little bird in a nest; and at other times, it will yell at us and scold us like an angry parent. And we will keep it alive and healthy because it is who we think we are. This is why real change is difficult, because to change is to get rid of who we think we are and create a new identity of ourselves. We kill off the old ego and create a new identity when we change. If we don't kill the old ego and just use willpower to try to change, when we get tired and stop using willpower, the old identity will exert itself back into our lives. The old ego will just step out of the shadows of our belief system within the illusion, and there it is again. What gives life to the egoic self is this: We believe who we really are is our created identity, our egoic-self; and this is just a clever way to cause the virtual reality to appear real. The ego will fight hard and long to live and keep us from changing. Remember, real change means death to our old ego.

CHAPTER 12

The Egoic-Self

CONSTRUCTING THE EGO

We come into this three-dimensional space/time universe with a body. Without a body we wouldn't be here. So having a body with a brain is an important thing; however, we aren't the body or the brain, and that is also important to understand and realize. The "You" that came into this dimension is what we refer to as the "Life Force," and it has a purpose. The body/mind system is the means by which our purpose is accomplished. For without "You," the body/mind is without life, without purpose, and it will dissolve and be no more. "You" are the life and the purpose in the first place. And again, we have a symbolic relationship of interconnectedness and support between "You" and your body/mind system. The following diagrams depict that relationship metaphorically. *(Now, please don't get hung up on the words I use. Words are just symbols for something else. Look at the model I'm developing. Use your own words to describe the model. It is the metaphoric model that will help you gain insight into your pain and suffering. You probably already know many ways to express this model. Whether you think or believe there is a "life force" or not isn't important. Just use what you can of the model.)*

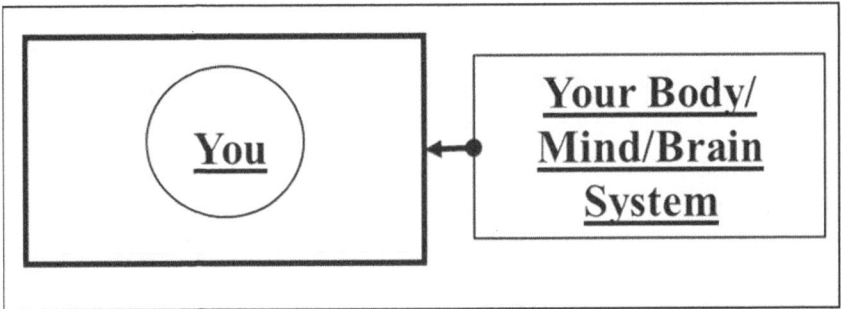

Diagram 11 - You and Your Body

All the physical elements of the physical body/mind or brain come from within the three-dimensional space/time universe, the gross energy system, or the illusion; and "You," on the other hand, come from the subtle field. The body/mind function and purpose is to support the "essential you" or the life force that came into this dimension. The body helps us move through the external environment of space/time by the use of the senses. These senses are designed to probe the outside environment and send information back to the mind. That is all they do; they just gather information and send it back to the mind. They don't analyze, judge, or determine the goodness or badness of anything. One of the problems with our senses is that they aren't designed to probe the inside environment where the "You" are. *(There are other models you may have seen, where "You" as life force, surrounds you as body/mind or brain. The larger "You" surrounds the smaller you.)*

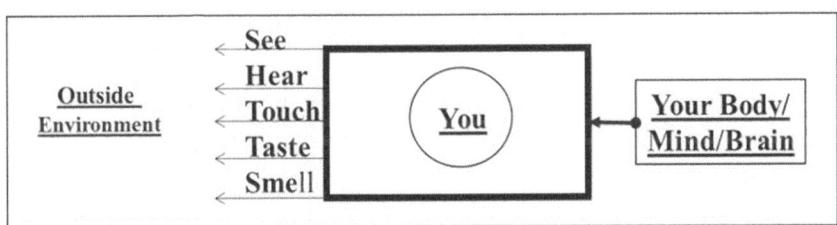

Diagram 12 - You and Your Senses

Since the senses probe only the outside, the body/mind or brain cannot experience the "You" inside that gives life to it and is its purpose. The body/mind or brain through the senses cannot know "You" directly.

As far as they are concerned, "You" don't exist; and the body/mind or brain, therefore, is unaware of its purpose. *(Can you see why it's easy for the ego to convince you that you are your body?)*

What's a body to do without a purpose? Well, the only thing left to do is to create its own purpose from inside the illusion, and that is what it does. It creates a self, based on what it can learn from probing the outside environment, because looking outside is the only way the senses can probe.

Where can the body/mind or brain system find information about itself? Since the senses are designed only to probe into the external environment, that seems like a good place to start to look for information. What or who is in the child's environment and can tell the body/mind or brain who it is? Now remember that we are oneness and have moved into the illusion of separateness. Who can tell us how to live in separateness? Since our bodies come into the world as infants, parents and major caregivers would be a first guess, and then others around them would be a second guess.

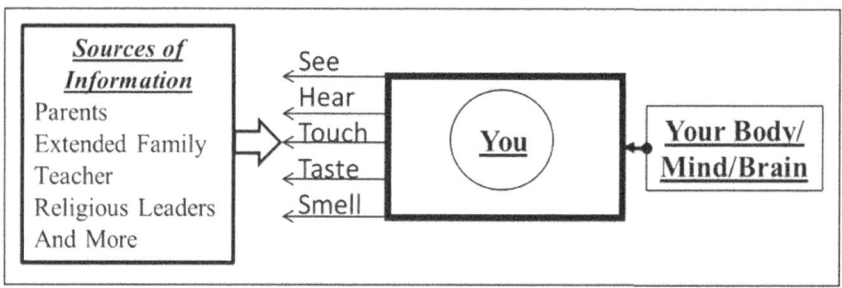

Diagram 13 - Sources of Information

The child's mind, which is receiving all the information through its senses, is just absorbing it all as raw data from around itself with no questioning, no analyzing, just absorbing. Recognize that the child's goal is to find out who it is. The child then interprets the information through its immature child's brain, trying to understand who it is; and what kind of world it has been thrust into. From the information and data received, the child begins to construct an image of who it thinks it is. Recall that the child comes into this environment having some memories from experiences in the womb; therefore, it has some small filtering system.

Also recall that earlier we described the trance state children are in from birth through adolescents. The data and information the child receives in infancy go straight into the depths of the child's open mind and onto its hard drive, and this is a time before the mind has divided into conscious and subconscious realms, which means it has little to no filtering system, and the information just gets accepted since it is received by an immature mind, which is in a deep trance state, as the truth.

The child, through the information and messages it gets from the external environment, creates what it believes is a real and true image of who it believes itself to really be. This is called our self-identity or ego-self, and this is who the child believes itself to be from its experiences from within its family of origin. This created image is deeply integrated into its whole being and belief system. It is a perception of who it believes itself to be, but it isn't who it really is, because who it is, is its essence or original self. In the deep inner part of us is the "essential you" that came into this dimension, now like a ghost in the inner workings of the mind, experiencing this three-dimensional space/time environment.

"You" are there *(big you)*, but you *(the small created you)* don't know it. What is known is the egoic self, your created self *(small self)*; and you now believe you are the self-identity. We look out into our environment, and all we see are other bodies with egos and egoic personalities; and those egoic personalities were formed and honed into beings of who they think they are from within their family of origin system. Our personality didn't come with us when we came into space/time at birth. Who we think we are was grown from within the illusion starting in the womb, and therefore it can be changed. Why can we change it? Because it isn't real. How can we change who we think we are? We can change who we think we are by changing what has convinced us we are who we think we are, which are our memories because they aren't the real "You." They are a creation made from within the illusion; and even though we have come to believe they are real, they aren't. But they feel so real, don't they? *(You see how you can be led away from the truth by how the body feels? What causes the body to feel the way it does? The mind. It is all in your mind first.)*

179

The following diagram shows the forming of the egoic self and the unimportance given to the "You" in the process. Maybe now we can see why the ego wants the body to be who we believe we are.

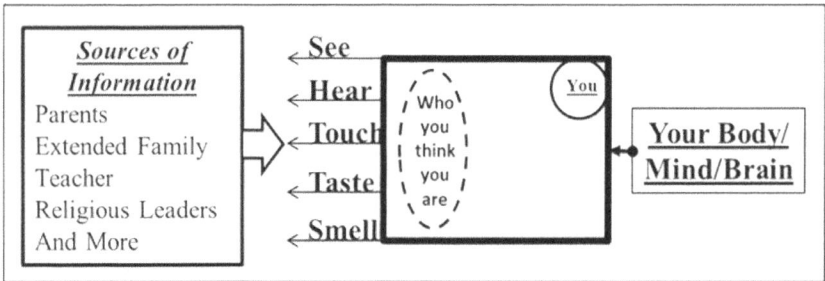

Diagram 14 - You and "Who You Think You Are"

As we gain conforming evidence and consensus from the external world that who we think we are is real, our egoic self becomes more dominant. Others tell us who we think we are, and the ego identity becomes more solid and more real to us. Once we fully believe and accept that the ego is our real self, the less of "You" can be felt and experienced by the body/mind or brain system; and "You," therefore becomes nonexistent to them. Even to mention the essential you or your essence self or life force will cause some egos to go ballistic.

The following diagram shows how the egoic self is empowered and how small and unimportant "You" have become in this process of living your life in the illusion.

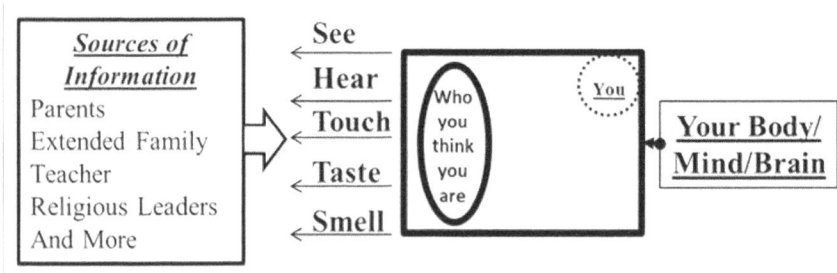

Diagram 15 - The Dominance of Who You Think You Are

At this juncture we should begin to appreciate that our ego identity is created, for the most part, by outside forces that act on us at a very young age from inside the illusion. And the majority of those influences, the ones that have the greatest influence on programming our minds and affect us the most in the creation of our egoic identity, are from our family of origin, particularly parents or those who took on the parental role of us when we were infants and children. It isn't that they forced us into being who we think we are but into recognizing that, whatever our ego identity is, it is because of their influence on the information given to us and our interpretation of that information. All in all, it is our interpretation of the information we receive from them that creates the ego identity we have, not the information received per se. Sometimes we are who we think we are because we just accept the information we are given, and at other times we fight against the model presented to us, or we have developed a combination of all that information and experience we receive. It always comes back to us as the cause of who we are, not them. *(Besides, what they did or didn't do doesn't matter now because now it's all your programming and your problem; and if you want a different life, it's you who has to change the programming you hold inside you. Blaming them won't help you change or give you the life you want. So stop it and start healing your wounds.)*

When the ego identity has been integrated into our belief system, dark magic can come into our lives. The ego becomes the lens through which we see and experience the world around us. It is the major part of the subconscious mind's filtering system. We have stated that before, but now we have some structure as to how it occurs. If we have created an ego that has a victim identity, we will experience a world through that lens. To be a victim, we will need persecutors in our lives; and that is what the subconscious mind will set its filtering system to find and bring into our life so we can continue to be a victim and match our belief system of who we think we are; and what the subconscious mind filters for is what it will find, or it will die trying to find it. Why will it help us be victimized? Because that is what it believes is our truth, based on our beliefs of who we think we are. Will it find what it needs? Yes, because everything is outside us, and so will be the means of us being victims. *(You see, it isn't what is outside you that is important because everything is there in the outside energy system. It is how you choose to filter and interpret the information to meet your inside beliefs about what is out there. You aren't trying to find "true reality" or the truth. You are trying to find homeostasis with your belief system, and that is what you are filtering for. Your ego wants to live, and the only way it can is to show you proof that you are who you think you are. And so your ego will filter through the outside data of everything until it finds proof it is right, or it will get really pissed off and start yelling at you; and you will yell or act out with anyone who is around. Why? Because you really don't want to change and kill off the ego, which you have created. Therefore, you must find evidence that you are a victim, or you can't be a victim, and the ego would be wrong. If you don't want to be a victim, you will need to change and kill off your current ego. Notice that if you kill your ego, you change the lens through which you have been finding all those persecutors and abusers you have been living with in your life now.)*

What is outside in that energy system? Everything. What are we filtering for? Whatever we are most familiar with. Proof that we are who we think we are. So if we believe we are victims, we must find and have persecutors and abusers in our lives. *(If you have no persecutors in your life, you cannot play the role of victim. Once you get that, change is pretty straightforward. It is all inside you. So don't blame the outside. When you change your beliefs, there won't be any persecutors or abuses in your life because you won't be sorting for them.)*

Now if we believe we are victims, we will do things to create situations that bring persecutors or victimizers into our lives. If we don't have them in our lives, we will self-sabotage events, relationships, and situations we have in such a way as to cause persecutors to rise up like mythical monsters out of thin air right in front of us. We can be very creative in this process; and for the most part, it will all happen out of conscious awareness. Why might that be? Because our programming is in the subconscious mind, and our ego is telling us we are victims. *(Why would you self-sabotage relations and situations? To stay who you think you are, which is your egoic self. If you believe you are a victim, you must feel that in your body. If you don't feel like a victim, you will do things to get that feeling back in your body, or you won't be who you think you are. You see how it works? This isn't crazy talk; this is how you operate out of conscious awareness.)*

Well, maybe others don't victimize us. However, whatever they do, you will interpret it as if they are victimizing us. We will create them through our interpretations of our lens of victims; therefore, they will look to us like victimizers, and we will do that outside our conscious awareness. We do it to save our egoic selves, which have convinced us we are "victims." *(Try to resist the thought that you are a victim when your ego is whispering in your ear all the proof it has that you are. And of course, the proof will be memories from past events that are long gone. But you will think they are true, even though throughout this read I have mentioned in many ways, "Memories aren't real, true, and complete.")*

To protect our egoic selves, we will blame the external world, not our internal egoic created selves, because it is our child, and we created it and will protect it. When our egoic self gets bruised, we rush to its defense and blame what is outside us or our bodies. Why do we do that? Again, it is because the ego is our created child of who we think we are. To attack our ego identity is to attack us. "All for one and one for all" is the banner that flies over the fortress of our egoic identity. "If you attack my ego, you attack who I think I am, and I will fight to the death to save my ego identity." Again, appreciate why change can be so difficult. It is us inside, behind the curtain, pulling the strings. We are the master puppeteers, and unfortunately the conscious mind is unaware of this; and because it's so slow in its thinking process, the outside energy system seems to be the cause. Come on now. We know it's always us, no matter what it looks like to the conscious mind, right? We just keep blaming others or our bodies so we don't need to deal with our own stuff.

Look closely, and again we will see. It isn't the external world that is the problem but our inside interpretation of information we are receiving about that external world. It is the egoic lens through which we are filtering our world. We might be thinking at this point, *You look again, smart ass. How else could you ever interpret what they did and said to me? I know what I know, and it's not me who has the problem. It's them!* And as we say that, we point in their general direction with a shaking, bony finger to emphasize our point.

All incoming information we receive is filtered through our subconscious mind's beliefs, experiences, and references, which are past memories stored in its warehouse. Think for a moment. Who is integrated in our belief system? The ego. And what determines the filtered data that creates our interpretations? The ego. It is the egoic lens that determines how and why we interpret our world the way we do. The only meanings we have of outside events and objects aren't the outside events and objects but our inside created perceptions of them. To create a different interpretation of the event, we must change the lens, the filter through which we have created the one we have. Again, what is outside us? Everything. Why do we take "the everything" outside us, which is all the good as well as all the bad, and end up only as a victim? Why don't we ever see the good as our lives? Because of the egoic lens, through which we are distorting everything.

In the following diagram, notice how far into the background the "essential you" has been pushed and how fully in control the egoic self is. Again, notice that the ego is a lens *(I drew it to look like a lens so you wouldn't miss it being a lens),* and it is that lens that determines our interpretations and perceptions, which are our lives and the world we live in.

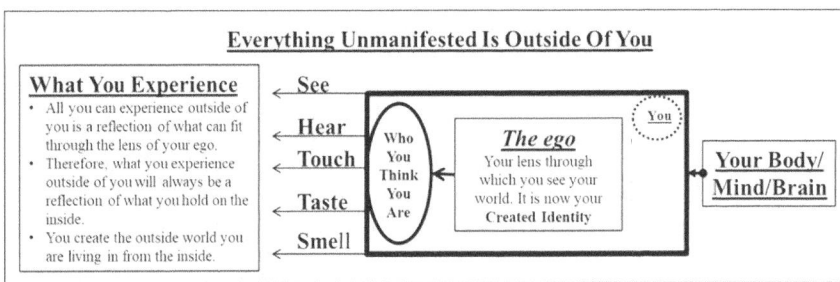

Diagram 16 - Your Ego Is Your Lens of Your World

If we have created an ego identity, a personality of a people pleaser, martyr, codependent, dependent, abuser, or a bully, we must experience the world and our lives through those lenses; and we must find proof that our identity is real. It's easy to find the proof that ego identity is true and real, is it not? Yes, because we use our egoic lens to sort through the "everything" we encounter. In this filtering process, what do we find, pull out, and keep from all the data encountered? What we want to find and what we are looking for. What do we filter out and throw away? What we don't want to find. Does the conscious mind know we are doing that? No. The conscious mind has no idea what is going on inside the black box of the subconscious mind. And yet we believe the conscious mind knows all. Amazing, is it not?

We mine the incoming data from the "outside everything" through our subconscious minds, looking for proof that we are who we think we are. Will we find it? Well, of course we will. We just said that above. Look now. The same is true if we have created an identity around caring, loving, happiness, abundance, or joyfulness. That will also be the lens we will use to experience our world. Our life experience is determined by what is going on inside us, not by what is going on in the outside world. The external world we have and live in is only a reflection of our inside state of being. Oh, how we fight against recognizing that we are doing it to ourselves. "No! No!" we say. "It's really them out there. They are doing it to me." See how interconnected we are within our common illusion? We support each other so we can all have the life we believe we should have based on our created ego identity. *(Whose ego do you have? Your ego. And who created your ego? You did. It's all your creation. What a great creator you are. If you want a different life, you need to change, because the outside everything isn't going to change.)*

There is a book I read. I call it a "reference book." It's titled *The Prophet* by Kahlil Gibran. I liked it, but there were parts at the time I didn't quite understand. One such part in the book was called "On Crime and Punishment." The following is an excerpt:

> The murdered is not unaccountable for his own murder,
> and the robbed is not blameless in being robbed.

> The righteous is not innocent of the deeds of the wicked,
> and the white-handed is not clean in the doings of the felon.

> Yea, the guilty is oftentimes the victim of the injured,
> and still more often the condemned is the burden bearer
> for the guiltless and unblamed.

You cannot separate the just from the unjust and the good from the wicked.

For they stand together before the face of the sun.

(http://www.katsandogz.com/oncrime.html)

Who we believe ourselves to be is always in balance within our environment. It is the law of attraction. We must get what we have been asking for; and at some level, we are always asking for what we get. If we consciously aren't in agreement with what we are receiving in our lives, it means the conscious and subconscious aren't asking for the same thing. The universe responds to our most dominant energy signature. If we are consciously in disagreement with what we are receiving, the requests being filled are being sent out by the subconscious mind. Why would the universe answer the subconscious mind and not the conscious mind's request? Because its energy signature is tremendously bigger than the small conscious mind.

Look again. Those who have learned to be a "bully" are looking for someone to bully, maybe not consciously but at some level. A victim is looking for someone to victimize them, maybe not on the conscious level but at some level. This, for the most part, is outside conscious awareness; and almost like magic, these players in this game of life within this illusion find each other. And they blame each other for why they are the way they are. It's amazing how balanced the illusion is, don't you think?

The world we experience is an illusion. *(Are you getting this?)* Whether we create a chaotic and sad world or a loving, kind, and caring world, it's all created from within the illusion and isn't the real reality. It's all an illusion. Again, the goodness or badness of our world is determined by the meaning we give to it from inside us; and how we do that comes from our past memories. We are what we hold inside us. *(You see why changing, forgiving, and healing old negative memories will change your life?)*

In whatever we have created as our ego identity, we will experience an outside reality that will complement that identity. Our created ego is deeply integrated into our whole being, including our belief system. We will see and experience an external reality the way it must be to support the created ego identity we have created inside us. Why? Because we will focus our world through that lens.

If we don't like the external reality we are experiencing now, we must change our ego identity, which is to say our ego-soaked belief system. We never see the external present moment the way it really is. We can only experience it the way we are because we don't have the lenses or the tools to experience it any differently. We can only see the external the way our internal belief system is. To experience a different world, we must change our beliefs and internal programming.

If our world is happy and content, there is nothing we need to change. If, however, we are unhappy or parts of our lives are unhappy, and we want to be happy and content, we must change our belief system. Why is that? Because the outside world we think we live in is only an effect of our causal belief system. Changing the outside effect won't change the cause. Since we created our beliefs and "who we think we are" in the first place, we can change them. The first step to change is to become *aware* that change in us is needed and to recognize that *change is possible.*

We are so much more than we think we are. If we aren't happy, then we need to change. We may be thinking, *Yeah, right, change. How do I do that? You keep saying change, and it is getting old. How do I change who I am?* We created the world we have, and we can create a different one. *(Oh! I forgot. You may have forgotten that you are the creator of the world you have. That is easy to do in the illusion.)* Actually, we are really good at creating, and we have created the world we have now; and we didn't know we were doing it. Now that we know we are the creators of our worlds and how we did that, we can do a much better job this time.

At root we are energy beings. We are subtle energy beings, and as such we aren't our bodies. With just a slight shift in our understanding, we can bring into focus new and different worlds, maybe one that has always been there just beyond our ego and waiting in the unmanifested everything. We can change our lens, our filtering system, and see the universe as it truly is or at least differently. And wouldn't that be a nice thing?

CHAPTER 13

Everything Is in the Mind

NOTHING IS NEW UNDER THE SUN

We stated before that there is nothing new under the sun, and we related that fact to the saying "Everything is already here." However, as we scan the environment around us with our senses and then filter that data through our subconscious minds, we aren't experiencing all that "everything" consciously. We also said, "Everything is energy," and we can't experience that either. So, where is all this "everything stuff"? It is unmanifested. It is here but isn't expressed in a form we can capture and experience, and that makes it difficult for us to approach the unmanifested everything directly.

Manifest and *unmanifested* are terms used in the shipping industry. The manifest is a detailed list of what is there on the shipping pallet. It is a symbolic list of what is here now. *Unmanifested* is something hidden and not available to see; it cannot be counted or weighed. There is no list to refer to and nothing to hold in your hand. In the way it is being used here, the unmanifested is the ground from which the manifested comes forth.

The unmanifested everything is complete in itself and is infinite. Being complete and infinite, it is therefore eternal. Since in the eternal there is no time, there is no rush to manifest anything. It doesn't change because it is already everything. It is the infinite at rest, quiet and still;

it is inactive and motionless, waiting for something to move. And like the whole concept of the infinite everything, it isn't explainable or comprehensible to those residing in the manifested finite realm in most cases.

The unmanifested is an energy state beyond our current awareness. It waits for the right filtering system to bring it into a manifested state in someone's mind and then in the world. Everything is created twice; we said this before. The first is created in the mind and then in the physical world. We might think metaphorically here; imagine a piece of the unmanifested energy as a marble block, which a sculptor might select to carve a statue. The block has the possibility of everything being inside it. What is inside that block of possibilities is restricted only by the artist's imagination and artistic abilities that are also in his or her mind.

> The marble not yet carved can hold the form of
> every thought the greatest artist has.
> —Michelangelo

The interface between the outside energy system of the unmanifested everything and the body is the mind. The body doesn't directly experience the world outside; all the body knows and is aware of is the mind's interpretation of the incoming filtered information. To appreciate this statement, we may need to look again at our touchy-feely sense of touch, which was grossly outlined in Chapter 3. When anything touches the body, that pressure is picked up first by the nervous system inside, not by the body. Those nerves that were touched are coded into electromagnetic signals and sent to the subconscious mind's filtering system; then they are screened for matches and sent on to the active mind. Whatever gets through that filtering process goes to the active mind, and a perception is created. It is at the point of perception that signals are created and sent to the mind/body; and the body, which is always monitoring the interpreted universe of the active mind, is now aware that something has touched it through nonverbal signaling sent to it. Then it knows how to respond to what's happening, not because of what is happening outside but because of what is happening inside the mind. We need to restate, "Everything happening in the black box of the subconscious mind, active mind, and body is at billions of bits of data per second," because to the conscious mind, it looks like the body is responding to the outside pressure, but it's not. *(You can see by this model that everything you think you are experiencing in the outside energy system is actually coming from your created interpretations, can't you?)*

All our sensory inputs go straight to the subconscious mind's filtering system. The body isn't involved at all with the passing of the information, except to provide a space to hold the sense organs. What gets through the filter process system goes directly to the active mind; and like magic, we have an internal universe created. It is this internal universe the body and conscious mind are responding to. It is also the internal universe we live in consciously. What we believe is outside us in the energy system is a reflection of our mind's perception, and then our conscious mind projects the inside into the outside. This gave rise to the saying "Perception is reality"; but as we know now, perception is nothing like reality.

Everything we know is in our minds first. If it's not in our minds, it is meaningless to us because we have no reference to the information. Inside us is the manifested world we live in. What is outside us in the energy system is the unmanifested everything. If we want to manifest a different internal universe for us to live in, we need to change the data the active mind uses to create the universe we now have, which is to say we must change our filtering system. And again, to change the filtering system, we must heal our past by forgiving ourselves for past errors and letting go of the negative memories from the past that still haunt us on a subconscious level and sometimes consciously.

We have millions and maybe trillions of memories in our subconscious mind, depending on how old we are and how much we have experienced, and only a few of these memories will cause us any problems. Almost all our memories are neutral and have no emotional attachment, and they won't cause us any problems; and for the most part, we get through life just fine. However, when one of those negative memories we buried in permanent memory with negative emotional energy still attached gets awakened, the mind and therefore the body will have problems.

The following diagram depicts two individuals experiencing the same input data and information; from the same source of information, two different interpreted universes will develop. The bodies don't experience the outside directly because they respond only to their individual interpreted universes created in the active mind. The conscious minds of the individuals aren't aware of anything until there is a perception in their active minds, which is to say the creation inside the two interpreted universes. The two individual conscious minds analyze their individual interpreted universes, and their bodies response to the interpreted universes; and then the conscious mind reports to us in words so we know what has happened inside, even though we believe it's happening outside. Look closely and notice that by the time we get the report from the conscious mind, another interpreted universe has already been created, and the body has responded to it. Again, we see the conscious mind is the least informed and the last to know, but don't we believe it knows all?

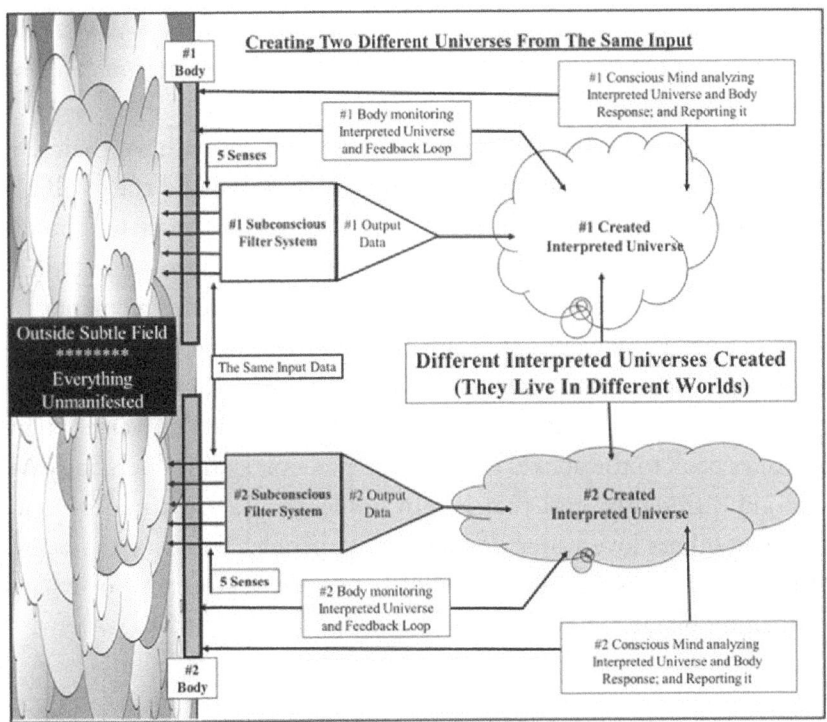

Diagram 17 - Creating Different Universes from the "Everything"

We have said, "Everything is in the mind," which is to say, "Everything we know is in our minds." If we don't know it, it doesn't exist for us. Since they are our minds, everything that is in our minds can only be us. Nobody else but us can be in our minds. Every character that populates our memories and dreams can only be us; those characters in our memories and dreams are us as we have interpreted them, and then we disguise ourselves as those other people. They aren't inside us; we alone are inside us. The event is over and gone. All we have left of the event is our untrue, incomplete, and unreal interpretations of every person who was in the event and is now in our memories. Memories aren't about other people; they are about us and our interpretation of those other people, because those other people just won't fit in our heads; so we alone are in there with us. We are the playwright, director, and all the actors and actresses in our untrue memories; and there we are, struggling with us. But doesn't it feel like others are there? *(I'm telling you—and you need to get this—that you live in the greatest magic show, the greatest illusion, there is; and it feels so real. You are so good at your job of creating plays from your memories. You even fool yourself and me. And who is the audience you are playing to? It is you.)*

Those people who experienced the event with us have their own interpreted memories, and those won't be like ours; and they will also be untrue, incomplete, and unreal. However, like us, they will believe they are real. When we talk to them, we will both believe we are talking about the same event because of our consensual reality agreements, but we won't be. Why would they not be the same? Because we will both have different filtering systems, beliefs, experiences, and references of the event data—and therefore, a different interpreted universe we live in. Refer back to the above diagram again. Look again. Each body will respond differently, and that is why some people are afraid of water and why others love water. It's why some people like spicy foods, and others don't. This isn't due to what is outside; it's because of what is happening inside.

CAUSE AND EFFECT

There is a cause-and-effect process going on here. There can be no effects without a cause. This may seem obvious, but what may not seem so obvious is that "without effects there is no cause." Cause and effect are locked together, in another one of those symbiotic relationships. There is an interdependence between them, and we can't have one without the other. If we have one, the effect, we must have the other, the cause. Our pain and suffering are the symptoms or effects felt in the body. *(I said that wrong. The pain and suffering are felt in the mind first and then projected into the body by our slow conscious minds, and then we believe and think we feel them in the body.)*

Why does the body respond the way it does? Because of the underlying causal interpretation in the mind. Depression and anxiety are names of groupings of symptoms; just saying *depression* doesn't "cause" the symptoms of depression. Therefore, our problem isn't the name *depression*. Depression is just a name for a cluster of effects felt in the mind or body. Saying *depression* or *anxiety* is just a shorthand way of referencing the effects felt in the mind or body. However, there is a direction to this cause-and-effect relationship. When we modify, change, or mask the symptoms in the body, we may feel better; however, we don't heal the cause. When we heal the cause, we will eliminate its effects, and symptoms, which are in the mind first, will be no more.

Symptoms and effects are signals that something needs to change. If we stop the effects or symptoms by modifying them, we may stop the warning signals of the pain and suffering in the body; however, this won't heal the cause. The body may develop different warning signals with escalating signals of different symptoms and effects to get our attention. Defining depression by its symptoms is like saying depression is causing depression because its symptoms define depression. Depression is a list of symptoms; that's it. We can state it as an algebraic formula: things equal to the same thing are equal to each other; and a list of symptoms equals depression, and depression equals a list of symptoms, which equals depression. Therefore, depression equals depression, and symptoms equal symptoms. A little convoluted logic, isn't it? If there is an effect, there must be a cause; and the body responds only to the active mind's interpretation and its signals.

Oh, now wait. If we know we have symptoms of depression, can we modify those symptoms so we won't feel so much pain and suffering in our bodies? Yes, that may be true. However, the body is responding the way it is because of the systems it is changing. The body is changing its systems the way it is because of what is going on in the mind. Therefore, maybe it's the mind we should be modifying, changing, and healing, and not the body. But then the body is the scapegoat for the mind. And why is that so? Because everything is in the mind first.

If a person says he or she has depression, that next question should be, "What is your problem? What is causing your depressed symptoms?" If the person says, "Well, I'm depressed! Didn't you hear me?" we will know the person doesn't understand the symbiotic relationship between cause and its effects. The name given to groups of symptoms is never the problem or the cause, and moderating the symptoms may help the body feel better but won't identify or heal the cause. That may be why so many folks are on antidepressants and have been on them for so long and maybe forever, because if they stop, their pain and suffering return. This also indicates the cause was never addressed. Fear is a strong driver of behavior. Notice that since everything is in the mind first, then only the mind needs to be healed. When the causal mind is healed, the symptoms disappear.

The effects or symptoms are what we experience in our minds or bodies. The cause will be an express perception in the active mind because the body responds only to the interpreted universe, which is to say the creative and interpretive mind. What we think we are experiencing in the body is what the conscious mind tells us about the body's response to the mind's interpretations and perceptions. It's all in the mind first before we feel it in the mind or body, and then the slow conscious mind reports it to us, pointing to something outside or to the body as the cause as it sees it; but it's not true.

We won't be concerned in our discussions here with positive and loving effects, which follow the same path. Our concern is with the path of our pain and suffering. When we have pain and suffering, they will always have a strong physical component in the body, which the conscious mind will inform us of in due course but not always. In some cases, the body will need to suffer for some time before the conscious mind is awakened and becomes aware of its symptoms and effects. *(I must be clear here. When I say, "Pain and suffering will always have a strong physical component in the body," know that the affects you think are coming from the body are coming always from the mind. It happens so fast; the conscious mind just projects the results onto the body; and you believe the pain and suffering is in the body.)*

When we have physical concerns, we seek medical help; and medical support is in the form of doctors and other medical professionals. This is appropriate because the focus of our pain and suffering is the physical body's reaction, and moderating the symptoms becomes our first concern. However, the symptoms aren't the cause of our pain and suffering; they are its effects. It is counterintuitive in our culture to look to the mind as the cause of our pain and suffering, but there it is.

The cause will be our interpretations of events accumulated over time in the past, and of course all the events are over and gone. What is left of the event now is our remembered memories of our interpretations of those events, which as stated before aren't true, complete, or real memories of the events; nor are our interpretations of the events the events. If we have pain and suffering, they will be connected to symptoms expressed in the mind or body. The causal memories may be lost to our conscious awareness. However, the conscious mind will report on what has happened in the body, not on what is happening. The conscious mind isn't directly connected to past memories, and it is connected to the past only through the active mind. If a memory isn't triggered in the active mind, the conscious mind is unaware of it. However, the conscious mind will be aware of our pain and suffering, and will project it into the body, and that is what it reports; it may have no idea where the effect is coming from. Not to worry because the job of the conscious mind is to come up with a logical story of why we are the way we are and why we react the way we do. And for the most part, we will believe what the conscious mind tells us, because we have been programmed to do so, and we will want to. If we don't, our ego will beat us up and make us feel we are wrong; and that will make us feel worse.

If the cause isn't addressed and only the effects or symptoms are moderated, new and different effects or symptoms may occur. There is a cultural belief that we are our bodies; we said that before, and said that the body is somehow separate and independent from the mind. We have missed the understanding that the body responds only to the active mind and that they are in partnership and directly affect each other. As mention before, if we have a headache once a month, and an aspirin or two works and removes the headache, there is no need to spend much time or energy looking for the cause; however, if we get a headache two or three times a week or have migraine headaches, we need to look for the cause.

"Memories buried alive, never die they just show up in another uglier pair of shoes in the present moment."
—Robert Smith, founder of Faster EFT

Causal Interpretation of an Event and the Cause of Our Pain and Suffering

When an event happens outside us, it isn't good or bad until we process it through our filtering system inside and create an interpretation in our active mind of the event. Then through our beliefs, experiences, references, and memories from the past, we determine whether it is good, bad, or a little bit of both for us. We and not the event are what makes it good or bad. The event is neutral in all its aspects until we think about it. We have said this several times, but it is so counter to our understanding of our world that it is easily forgotten. We determine the meaning for everything in our world from the inside out, and it all changes as we change.

The reason we don't think things outside are neutral is because of how the slow conscious mind reports the interpretation of the event to us. *(Notice that the conscious mind never experiences the outside event. It can experience only the inside interpretation of your active mind.)* Behind the slow-moving conscious mind is a whirlwind of activity operating at billions of bits per second. By the time the conscious mind gets around to reporting on the interpretation of the event, the active mind has determined whether it is good, bad, or a little bit of both and moved on. The conscious mind projects its latest findings into the outside energy system of the event, which is no longer there because it is gone. *(Notice here that the event doesn't move on. It is gone, gone, gone; and it is no more. Once over, it is nowhere. It's like a cluster of different energies that came together and then dissipated. It is like a little bomb going off, and then it is over.)*

Therefore, the conscious mind believes the meaning of the event, object, or situation is in the event, the object, or the situation. It has no idea the meaning was created in the active mind. When we get the report and are made aware of the event, we believe the event outside has meaning. To realize all meanings for everything in our lives come from inside us may take a paradigm shift inside our belief system.

So when a neutral event is happening now, we interpret the event from our filtered and manipulated data and determine whether it is good or not so good from inside. The body, monitoring the created interpreted universe and responding only to the perception, will respond to the signal of the created interpreted universe and change systems and behavior as is appropriate. When the event is over and gone, all the data, information, and energy of our perception is moved into permanent memory in the subconscious mind. *(You can, can you not, appreciate that the meaning of everything in your life is inside you and can never be outside you?)*

All we have left after the event is gone is a memory. Again, is the memory true, complete, and real? No. If we are bothered at any time because of what we think happened in the past, it isn't the event. It is our memory of the event. Understand that it isn't the event that is bothering us because the event is gone, and it's not here. It is our interpreted memory of the event that is bothering us. All we have inside us about the event is an untrue, incomplete, and unreal memory. What is the cause of our pain, suffering, and discomfort? Don't say the event because the event is over and doesn't exist anymore. The only thing left of the event is the untrue memory. If we are bothered, we are bothered only by the memory, which is an internal creation we made. *(Are you starting to get the idea that all you have is you inside you with no events or people? Everything is first in the mind and then projected onto the outside by your conscious mind, and your projection and my projection have to be different because you and I have different belief systems and experiences;*

197

therefore, there are different worlds we live in, but we believe they are the same. When you think about it, one doesn't need to be a rocket scientist to get this understanding, because it's pretty straightforward, isn't it? But your ego will tell you, "This isn't right.")

All our pain and suffering are in the mind or body; and they are due to the body's response to the interpreted universe created from the filtered information about the event or a memory from the past. As stated before, the body is the scapegoat of the mind; and all the body is trying to do is protect itself from the dangers reflected in the interpreted universe, which is the only world the body lives in. When recalled or triggered, memories move into the active mind. The memory needs no filtering because the data was already filtered before by the interpretation of the original event before it became our memory. When the memory moves into the active mind, the interpretation and perception of the recalled memory will be much the same as was created from the event, because it's the same data that was stored in the subconscious mind's permanent memory banks from the original interpretation of the event.

Communication between the active mind and the body isn't in words. They communicate in nonverbal electromagnetic and chemical signals, and it's a two-way system. The body also communicates with the active mind. When the body is low on water or food, it sends signals to the active mind, which creates a perception that causes the subconscious mind to change its filtering system and start looking for matches for water and food. This mind/body is a community; for it to live a long, peaceful, and happy life, they both need to support the community because they are interconnected and need each other.

There is a feedback system or loop that goes both ways. And so again, when the body needs water, it signals the active mind. When the active mind gets information about water from the subconscious, it signals the body, and the body responds appropriately to the signals and moves to the water. When the body is satisfied, it signals the active mind, and communication is changed to a new goal. There is always a nonverbal dialogue going on between all of them. They affect each other, and again we see a symbiotic relationship that is mutually supportive.

The conscious mind also sends data to the active mind, usually in the form of questions to clarify its reporting process. "Have we seen anything like this before?" And of course, the active mind makes an interpretation of the data received, sends out signals, and will get information from the subconscious mind; it makes yet another interpretation and sends out new signals, which the conscious mind responds to. Is this starting to look like an ongoing system or method of operating? It should. Just remember how fast everything works except for the conscious mind. *(You may find it difficult to appreciate how fast everything is happening, because your conscious mind can't just report or tell you.)*

The following diagram depicts the process of recalling a memory, and it gives us insight into why we feel so bad when we remember memories that still have strong negative emotional energy attached to them. Notice the two-way arrows between interpreted universe in the active mind, the subconscious mind, the body, and the conscious mind. Those two-way feedback loops can get quite complicated at times. The active mind is the cauldron where our world is being created and forged into a manifested reality for us. Also notice that the conscious and subconscious minds don't communicate directly in this model; everything goes through the active mind. At some point the memory will be reconsolidated back into the subconscious mind and move out of conscious awareness and back into the nowhere of the "black box." However, just because we aren't consciously aware of it doesn't mean it isn't active in the subconscious mind's filtering system.

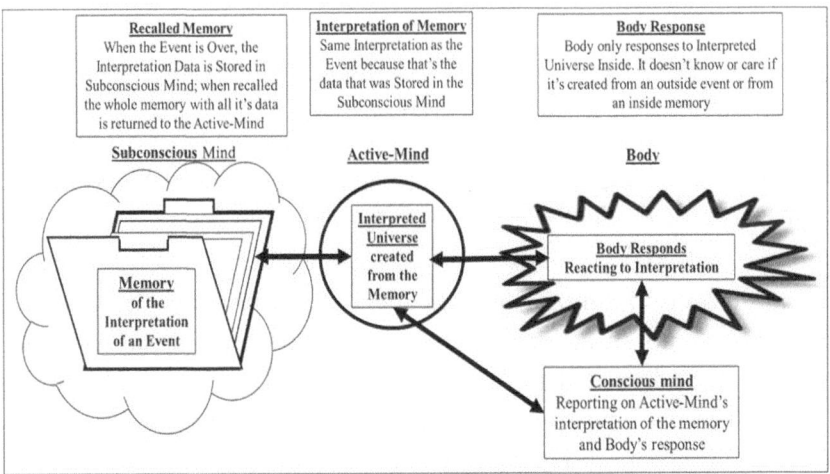

Diagram 18 - Recalling a Memory from the Subconscious Mind

The active mind for its part is just processing data and information because that's what it does; and again, it doesn't care where it comes from. If data gets into the active mind, it will be processed, and an interpreted universe will be created; the body that continuously monitors the signals from the active mind will respond to those signals because that's what it does. If the active mind sends friendly signals, the body will react appropriately; and if the active mind signals indicate a foe or danger, the body will also react appropriately for that condition and armor itself for survival. Since the body is in connection only with the active mind, it can respond only to the created world within the active mind. No matter what the conscious mind tells us, the body can respond only to the world created inside the active mind; and that's it—period.

> Disclaimer: The body has its own wisdom and many automatic functions and systems. Some are free floating, which means they operate without active mind signaling and without the body's consent. Growing fingernails, blinking eyes, dividing cells, digesting food, strengthening the immune system, and much more are going on behind the scenes. The inner workings of the body are too important and too complicated to depend on something else telling it what to do. There are signals, but they are between the inner systems within the body. This is a magnificent instrument we are walking around in. However, even these functions can be overridden for survival needs.

The body's responses and reactions are appropriate based on the signals sent by the active mind, and the active mind's interpretation is appropriate based on the data in the memory it receives from storage in the subconscious mind. And the memory is the result of the untrue, incomplete, and unreal perception of an event that is gone. Therefore, the causal condition for the body's response and how our bodies feel is the result of the interpreted memory. The cause of the body's response and how we feel, as reported by the conscious mind, is due to the memory because there is no event. Notice the body isn't responding to the event because there is no event; it is responding to the memory of the event, which reflects the active mind's interpretation of the original event. And of course, it isn't true.

We cannot have effects without a cause, and the cause must be there before any effects are felt in the body. *(Recall this was said before.)* Since the cause of our pain and suffering is a memory, our pain and suffering aren't restricted to time and place because we are always carrying our memories with us in our subconscious minds; therefore, at any time and in anyplace we can have effects come up in the body just by thinking about a selected memory, or by being triggered from new or different outside events, including talking to ourselves in our inner mind and by secondary gains associated with the effects in the body. We can be very creative in how we use the effects of the body. We did say, "The body is the scapegoat of the mind," didn't we?

There is a time between the causal condition and before the effects are felt consciously in the body. Since the causal condition is a memory and the memory is the interpretation of an event that is gone, the memory is always there and available to restimulate the body into a painful response. The event is gone, but the memory lives on in the subconscious mind. It's right here, right now, waiting for the right signal or trigger; and while the effects or symptoms may not be full blown yet, cause and effect are always connected, like a hand in a glove, which is another symbiotic relationship as discussed before. Whenever the memory is triggered in the active mind, the body responds; however, the response may not be severe enough for the conscious mind to take notice. Each time the memory moves back into perception, the body's response gets more and more pronounced until the conscious mind is awakened and makes us aware that we have a problem. "Memories buried alive never die; they just show up in our present moment in another pair of shoes." That was said before too, wasn't it? It's all interconnected mind, body, and active mind; and then of course the conscious mind tells us about it, kind of.

Just because we consciously can't remember the event from the distant past, which the active mind is using to create the causal memory, that doesn't mean it's not there. The conscious mind is the least informed and the last to know anything about what is happening in the mind or body. If we have an effect in the body, there is a cause in the mind. The senses, the subconscious mind, the active mind, and the body responses all operate at lightning speeds; and the conscious mind operates at a snail's pace in comparison; yet it's the conscious mind we believe and think knows all. If we have effects or symptoms in the body, we also must have a causal memory that keeps poking its head into the active mind, because if we have an effect, we must have a cause, and that cause must be in the mind first—period.

If we have experienced incidences or happenings, they are now memories; and it makes no difference whether they happened five minutes ago or twenty years ago; and if we have pain and suffering, the memory needs to be reframed. This will affect how easily and quickly we will recover from the incident. Pain and suffering are an interpretation in the mind first and then a response in the body. To change it, we must look inside for answers, which means looking deep into our past memories of beliefs, experiences, and references. *(I am aware that this is far from your normal understanding of pain and suffering. Even writing this brings angst up in my stomach as I am caught in my own old programming, but nevertheless everything is first in the mind and then in the body. The secret to the art of healing in the present moment is to reframe the past. Think about small irritations and not the worst of the worst to start reframing incidents.)*

When the cause is healed and gone, what happens to its effects and symptoms? They dissolve, disappear, and are gone also. For that to happen, the past needs to be reframed and healed, and memories are changed in some way. What happens if the effects or symptoms are moderated, lessened, or removed through interventions without addressing the causal memory? If the signals from the active mind are still in danger, the body will express other responses to the perceived threat, which will cause other effects and symptoms to be expressed in the body. Why? The effects and symptoms are feedback signals from the body that healing is required in the mind. The body is only a reflection of what is happening in the mind. Disease in the body is always a sign that something isn't right in the mind. Effects spring from their cause, and cause must develop before effects and symptoms occur; and the cause must happen before we can have any effect.

We have within us all the time-negative bacteria, viruses, and cancerous molecules of many different types of pathogens; and we aren't aware of them because the wisdom of the body is constantly removing them. It is a thankless and unrecognized job until the body gets distracted from its job by signals from the active mind; and the body changes its systems to accommodate the active mind's interpretation. Then we could be in trouble as the body gets distracted to fight or flight by actual and perceived threats from the outside or inside that are first in the mind.

As mention in Chapter 6, "Making Friends with the Subconscious Mind," the subconscious mind can be programmed to respond to beliefs that are put into the subconscious mind before the age of six, which is before the subconscious filtering system is in place. *(Notice that with the right stimulation, programming can be put in place in the subconscious mind at any time.)* The conscious mind more than likely won't remember when or how the programs were installed. They may be beliefs around family history or matter-of-fact comments by parents or other family authority figures, and the child just absorbs them as absolute truths of how he or she is expected to respond to life as a member of their family of origin. So strong are beliefs of early programming that there are several documented cases of adopted children getting genetic diseases from their adopted families (for example, breast cancer or early heart attacks based on specific family time frames). *(Can you see how early programming can lie dormant in the subconscious mind until the time the embedded program is supposed to operate based on earlier programming? The elephant never forgets, and neither does the subconscious mind. However, now that you are aware, you can change your programming. The expression of genes is determined by the environment your cells are living in, that is to say your internal chemical environment or your blood. Every thought you have creates chemistry that signals the body into some action. If you think the thoughts that change programming are your conscious thoughts, you haven't been paying attention. Your dominant thoughts are in the subconscious mind, and those are what run the programming.)*

We have heard this before: The surgical operation, the intervention, the physical therapy, the psychotherapy, or the weight-loss program was successful; but the patient died anyway, has reoccurring symptoms, went back to self-medicating, or gained the weight back. This may be because the underlying cause was never addressed. The law of cause and effect is operating 24-7. The cause needs to be addressed, or things may go south after a while as the body responds to the mind, which still has the old programming installed.

Again, if we have a headache once a month and an aspirin or two removes the headache, great! If, however, we have a headache three or four times a week or migraine headaches, something needs to be healed in the mind. Taking more aspirin won't heal and revolve the cause.

Everything that happens to us is first in the mind; then it is reflected in the body and then out into the energy system beyond. Once in the energy system, we will see our beliefs reflected back to us, and we will believe it is all happening out there in the outside energy system. Believing all our pain and suffering is caused by the body will cause us to moderate the body's symptoms; and all that will distract us from healing the internal causal problems in the mind. It's an ego-defense technique to blame others for what's outside us or our bodies so we don't need to change our stuff inside. *(Can you see what a good ego defense it is? You do recall that the body is the scapegoat for the mind, don't you? And of course, if you blame others or your body, you don't have to do a damn thing to change and heal, because now it's a SEP—Someone Else's Problem. You give control back to the ego. Your ego isn't your friend, although it will convince you it is. However, one could, you know, see things differently. You could, you know, change your vision.)*

CHAPTER 14

Switching of Purpose and Means

PURPOSE AND MEANS

If we want to accomplish a task or make anything, we need to have a plan, tools, and materials to complete the task, or we won't be able to complete it. The things we need to accomplish the task are called "means." Means are the action or system by which a result is brought about. We may have heard the saying "Means to an end." The means are what is needed to get from start to finish and to get to the end result we want.

The end result is our purpose. It is the reason why we need the means. The means aren't the purpose; means are what is needed to get to the end result. If we have all kinds of tools stored in nice-looking tool boxes and a lot of material lying around, but we have no purpose, goal, or end result in mind, they are meaningless and useless. With no end result in mind, all that stuff is useless; it's just stuff, no matter how pretty it looks. It's just stuff without something to use it on.

Purpose is the driving force that causes us to act. We live in a purpose-driven universe. From our human standpoint, knowing the universe's purpose may be beyond us; however, our purpose in being here seems to be to experience this dimension as it expands and to survive as best we can, because that is what we do every day.

Purpose determines what means will be required to obtain our goal or the end result we want. The means, tools, materials, and maybe plans are all physical; and at this point the end product is only an inside vision, an idea, and isn't physical as yet. Since the end result isn't seen physically, we many times have come to identify the means, which we can see as the purpose, because purpose cannot be seen until it is manifested. Since the end result doesn't exist yet and is only a thought, it is a mind creation in our imagination. When purpose is accomplished, there is no need for any means, because we will be where we want to be, and we can put our tools away. *(I did say everything is created twice, didn't I? First in the mind and then in the physical world, right?)*

If our goal is to reach the top of Mount Everest, we will need plans and certain tools, materials, and financing. The means to achieve the goal isn't the goal. If our goal is to sail around the world, we will need different plans, tools, and materials; and again, having the means to achieve the goal isn't the same as achieving it.

CAN MEANS BE MORE IMPORTANT THAN PURPOSE

An example may be helpful here. If we want to display a picture, we need something to hold the picture so it can be displayed. We may decide to make a frame (the plan), and that will require some wood (material), maybe a saw, a nail or two, and a hammer (tools). The frame is the means by which the picture will be displayed. To make or create a frame for our end result, plans, tools, and raw materials are needed. The purpose or end result is to display and show the picture; and the only function the frame has is to hold the picture so the picture can be displayed, and the frame is the means that will meet our purpose of displaying the picture. Therefore, the frame is the means to satisfy our purpose.

The purpose must be understood before work can begin on the frame. Let us be clear as to what our purpose is in our example; the purpose is to display the picture. What is most important in our project? The displaying and showing off of the picture.

Losing Purpose

If the frame becomes more important than displaying the picture, the purpose can get lost, and the means won't satisfy the purpose. How might this happen? If the picture is hidden by a massive frame, if the picture is lost inside a very beautiful and ornate frame that outshines the picture, or if the frame won't hold the picture, then the purpose isn't met. How could that happen? If the frame overpowers the picture, purpose isn't met. Another way of saying that is, "The means is without purpose," and means without a purpose is meaningless and useless as was said.

The frame may be a beautiful work of art; it may be highly praised and of great value in and of itself, but if it doesn't meet the purpose for which it was intended, which was to display the picture, then it is meaningless of purpose. So with a beautiful, overpowering frame, means and purpose are now confused. The end result is upside down, and purpose is lost. The means are meaningless because they don't meet its purpose. In hanging the picture, the picture becomes the means for displaying the frame. This upside-down confusion of purpose and means is what happens in the illusion we live in.

The Original Self and the Body

Each of us is the life force that energizes our bodies. The body is the means by which the life force is here. This life force may have different names, depending on our cultural and religious prejudices, such as soul or essence. When the life force leaves the body, the body dissolves back into the environment from whence it came. Without life force there is no need for a body, and there won't be one.

The life force is the "original self" or "essential you," and the body is the vehicle for this original self. However, in this egoic, illusionary world, we have turned means and purpose around; and means have become purpose, and purpose has become means. If life force is acknowledged at all, it is viewed as the means for the body being here. Life in the illusion is turned upside down. The body has become the purpose of our existence, and life force is viewed as the means to support the body.

When the body stops functioning and dies, we mourn the loss of the body and have little concept that it was only a vehicle and is no longer needed. We don't mourn so much for the original self or life force. Either we don't believe it exists, or if we believe it does exist, we know it's off experiencing new realms of possibilities, and there is no sense in mourning that. While there is an adjustment period, long periods of mourning seem like an overreaction to the loss of a vehicle, unless of course there was an overdependence on the other body and a loss of our connection with our own "essential you." *(Does this upset you? Death, grieving, and mourning go together in our society, do they not? They hold hands and dance with each other; and if you don't dance for a long time, society will lay its judgment on you. The wife throwing herself on the funeral pyre or being thrown onto the pyre to satisfy ancient customs of society seems like a misunderstanding or misconception of the natural process of dying. The body dies for sure, and there is no question there. Either the life force doesn't exist, and there is no sense in mourning it, or life force does exist, and there is no sense in mourning it, because it doesn't die. After the adjustment period, continued mourning has more to do with secondary individual gains than with honoring the deceased.)*

Without an understanding of life force, the body is viewed as self-created from biological processes from within the illusion. In that case, means and purpose of the body are the same, which is an interesting concept, is it not?

THE BODY AS A FRAME

The body is the point of entry for the life force into this world and is also the means that allows life force to be here. Since life force is subtle energy, it is outside the ability of the mind or body to interact with it directly; and it appears that here in this dimension, we can interact only with bodies. However, bodies cannot communicate, as was pointed out before, and only minds communicate. Bodies can respond only to our active mind's interpretations. No matter what it may look like from outside, it's always what is happening inside that determines what is perceived as happening outside; and again, the body is responding only to inside signals from the mind.

Recognize again that when we communicate with others, we send out energy. That energy is neutral and has no meaning to the other person at that point, because it's just energy and neutral. It's important to understand that we send out energy to the other person, and it's meaningless to them. The other person must bring the energy we release inside them through their senses, which go directly into their subconscious mind; and their subconscious mind will filter it, looking for what is familiar and send that selected data to their active mind. It's at this point that meaning is given to energy that is coming from us. Again, we need to be aware that this is all happening at nanoseconds of time; and the conscious mind will tell them, "It is our bodies that are communicating to them." But of course, this isn't true.

Others will send out signals to their minds or bodies based on their interpretations, and their bodies will respond as is appropriate based on them. What is an appropriate response for the other person will depend on their beliefs, experiences, references, and memories? The other person may have a completely different response than we expect. We need to get this and realize that bodies don't communicate; they can't. Only minds can and do communicate. *(I know it looks like bodies are communicating as you view them through the lens of your ego, but can you begin to grasp the idea that bodies don't communicate? Look closely and appreciate that only minds communicate, not the bodies. You aren't your body, as I have said. Your body is an instrument, an apparatus, a vehicle for "you" to move around in. It is your spaceship. Every movement of your body must be activated by signals from the active mind. The body is an instrument like a phone. When you call someone, the phone just relays what the other person is saying. The phone goes dead if the mind behind the phone stops talking or hangs up and stops communicating.)*

Metaphorically in our example, the body is the frame that holds the picture or life force. The body is the means by which life force is here. Again, we must be clear. The body doesn't care because it knows only what the mind tells it, and then it responds. All our obsessions with the body are because of the mind. The body unfortunately has lost its purpose in this egoic world, because the body doesn't know it is only a means to an end result. Look again and remember the body is a puppet in the hands of the master puppeteer, which is the mind.

The body per se doesn't have a belief system or a purpose, and it is always responding to the mind. Everything is in the mind; we have said that before, right? So purpose is lost. Not to worry. Our created ego will continue convincing us that our bodies are the most important purpose in our lives, and life force is the means for our bodies to be here; we will believe it because we created our ego and are in an illusion. We have made the first last and the last first. We have turned means and purpose upside down. And we like it that way. How crazy is that?

I wonder whether we are really aware of how extremely persuasive our ego is. Since it's integrated into our belief system, it knows all our logical arguments before we consciously do; and it knows where all our buttons are. It can outthink the conscious mind with ease and convince the conscious mind to follow it anywhere within the illusion. The conscious mind is the least informed and the last to know what is happening, and it's so slow too. *(I need to keep repeating, "The conscious mind is slow and the last to know." Or you will fall back into the arms of the egoic self.)*

THROUGH THE EYES OF THE EGO

As stated before, the ego is our self-created identity and is integrated into our belief system. It moves in like a virus; and once we accept it as "who we think we are" and is in place, we interpret our lives and the world we live in through the created lens of our ego. This egoic self isn't our original self; however, it has become the filter system of beliefs and prejudices, through which we create the world we think is outside us but is really inside; and the ego determines the life we have and the world we live in. If we don't like the life we have, we need to change our beliefs, which in turn will change our self-identity. This will, in turn, change our filter system, which will, in turn, change what we perceive. And this will, in turn, create a new world for us to live in because our perceptions will be different. It's our created perceptions that force the world we experience into focus and also into existence. It's all very simple in concept, right?

If we ever recognize the ego and can catch it, we should kill it because it isn't who we are. If we kill it, we move closer to our original self. There is a saying in Zen Buddhism. "If you meet the Buddha on the road, kill him!" Why? Because he isn't the real Buddha. He is your interpretation of the Buddha, and an interpretation of an event isn't the event and isn't the Buddha. Our ego isn't the real self; in fact, it is nothing until we believe it's something. When we kill the ego, behind that illusion is a new path, which is straighter and easier to walk. It leads more directly to the original self; however, it is still an illusion.

We can see now that our perceptions are self-created from data filtered through our unique individual beliefs, experiences, prejudices, and references from the past, which is the say our egoic identity. Our perceptions have little to do with any kind of reality outside us and a lot to do with the world we create and live in inside us.

As stated before, to change our beliefs is to kill our currently held ego or self-identity; however, the created and integrated egoic self won't go easily, and it has a warehouse of tools and old memories it uses to convince us that its view of life is correct. And that change isn't needed and is even dangerous; we naïvely and ignorantly agree with our ego self because of how the ego can make us feel about ourselves in our bodies based on old, guilty memories. The frame, the body, has hidden the picture, and purpose is lost; we are slaves to our own created ego identity, to our own created habitual self.

LIFE CAN FEEL BAD OR GOOD

The thing that convinces us the egoic self must be right is how we feel, which is to say how our bodies respond from our perceptions, which is to say the interpretation of the information we receive from our sensory input after it has been filtered and manipulated. Then signals are sent out to the mind or body. From those electromagnetic and chemical messages, energy or vibrations are created in our bodies that are appropriate based on the perception and our belief system, experiences, and references from the past. From this vibrational energy in the body, the conscious mind describes what has happened in our bodies, using language in the form of emotional words.

Again, the conscious mind is describing what has already happened in the body. The emotional descriptions of the conscious mind don't cause anything. The words *depressed* and *happy* don't cause us to be depressed or happy; they describe only what has already happened. The conscious mind is just describing to us what has occurred, not what is occurring. The conscious mind isn't an active player in what goes on in the mind or body. It is only a reporter of what has happened. *(I know this is counterintuitive to what is the conventional understanding of the conscious mind. Suspend your current understanding for a while and begin to appreciate how slow the conscious mind processes and responds. It just can't do all the things we have traditionally appointed as its duties. This is basically because all we know is what the conscious mind tells us. By the way, did you ever find out who the conscious mind is talking to when it is talking to you?)*

Since everything is energy, the energy we feel in our bodies is created by the internal dialogue and communication between all the different systems within the body as it responds to the perceptions and signaling of the active mind. It is an ongoing communication process in our bodies, and it isn't in language but in electromagnetic and chemical messages. The inner communication in the body is determined by the type and intensity of the signals it receives from the active mind; and that energy moves throughout the body. If the current perception of the interpreted universe is that we are under attack or in danger, certain signals between mind and body are initiated, and energy is felt in the body. As the body turns on its survival responses, the conscious mind becomes aware of the change in the body's energy systems. At that point we can consciously talk about what has happened in words to ourselves and others through the conscious mind.

If the current perception is that all is well, different energy responses are felt in the body, and different words will be used to describe that energy in the body. Again, become aware that the body doesn't respond to the outside environment but only to the inside interpretations of the active mind.

The systems of the body and active mind are always communicating.

However, we are never aware of this consciously because the dialogue is so complex and moves so fast, and it isn't in words. The conscious mind just cannot keep up. So when the conscious mind does report on what has happened, we get the headlines and not the whole story. Most of the time, things just feel "normal" in the body, and there is nothing to report, although there is always much happening. When things are normal in the body, the conscious mind amuses itself with other things and zones out. *(You know this isn't a conventional way of recognizing how the conscious mind operates. What would happen if you began to recognize the complexity and speed of what is happening within the mind and body? You might uncover an amazing, new universe.)*

As mentioned before, by changing our perception of a situation in the active mind, we change the internal communication systems of signaling between the body and the active mind, which will produce a different response in the body. By creating different feelings in the body from those new perceptions, a different world will come into focus and with it different experiences; and the conscious mind will report to us how the body feels and projects that new world onto the external energy system. See how our creative ability brings into focus the world we have; and it also can bring into focus the world we want. It's all done through changes in perception. *(Do you have any idea who the conscious mind is talking to when it talks to you?)*

The Feelings in the Body Are Primary

The body vibrates the way it does because of the signals sent out by the active mind's interpretations and perceptions. The signals inform the body of what environment it has to deal with, not from outside data but from inside interpretations. Is it a friend or foe? Are we at peace or under attack or something in between? As the body responds, its vibration will change; and the conscious mind will describe the change, starting with the phrase, "I feel _____," and it adds descriptive words, which are communicated to us and others through language. Language is a secondary learned skill; however, word language isn't the communication medium used in the body/mind. The stories the conscious mind tells us are secondary to the body's response; first is the thought or perception in the active mind, then the reaction as the body responds, and then the reporting by the conscious mind. The stories we tell ourselves consciously of what happened in the body that describe the active mind's interpretation of the event or memory are all after the fact. The conscious mind is the reporter of what has happened, and like all reporters of the news, it is reporting after the fact, after the event.

The story the conscious mind tells us is an incomplete, untrue creation of the conscious mind, and it isn't even the interpretation in the active mind. Look at it this way: the subconscious mind, the active mind, and the body are operating and processing at the rate of millions and billions of bits of data per second, and the conscious mind is reporting at only bits per second. The subconscious mind and active mind are streaming data, creating interpretations and universes, and sending out signals many times per second. We may be able to appreciate that what the conscious mind reports to us is just the tip of a very large iceberg; however, we believe we are getting the whole truth and nothing but the truth, which of course we are not.

The body responds and reacts to the internally created perceptions in the active mind; and then afterward, we tell ourselves the story in words. All our memories are like fairy tales we tell ourselves. Some are scary, and some are happy; but they are just stories, and they start, "Once upon a time in a land far away," because they are far way in the past. It makes no difference if they happened yesterday or ten years ago, because they are over and gone, and it doesn't matter whether it was yesterday or ten years ago. We can't live one second in the past. The only place we can live in and the only place you can be in is right here, right now, in the present moment.

The more we tell the stories, which are only memories, and the more we take them in and out of permanent memory, the more we add, subtract, rationalize, and generalize the stories; and the more the stories change. They become different memories and experiences, and they will move farther away from the interpretation of the original event. This happens in such a way that we are consciously unaware that we are changing memories. Why would that happen and the memories slowly change over time? It happens so that the memories match our belief system more completely. *(You do recall that "you see what you want to see and hear what you want to hear," don't you? You remember what you want to remember; and if your memories aren't what you want to remember, you slowly change them over time to what you do want to remember. Here is the thing. You consciously won't know you're changing them because they happen in such a way that the supporting memories around will also shift and change to support all the subtle changes; and they will seem very natural to the conscious mind as if they are the way events have always been. I will get deeper into this issue later. But for now, know you are changing your memories.)*

If we are now upset and angry at a lover or friend, and we recall happy memories we experienced with them in the past, we will recall the event differently now, while we are upset with them. We will interpret the memory at this point in time differently than we would if we weren't upset and angry with them. The memory has the same data, but now the mind has a different attitude; therefore, a different perception and response in the body will be felt. When we consolidate the memory back into the subconscious mind, a different memory will be stored than the one we took out. Consciously, we won't know anything has changed. If in the future we recall that memory that used to be a happy one, it won't be quite has happy. This happens a lot when relationships end. *(Do you see how flexible and changeable the past is; and the past is only your memories, don't forget. Look closely and notice. You will see that it isn't the event that changes because it is over and gone. It is your memory of your past interpretation of the event that has changed, and now you will remember the past differently. Isn't that cool? Are you beginning to come to grips with how your ego and the illusion subtly operate on you and hold you captive to the past?)*

After we tell a scary story enough times, it can get converted into a higher cognitive-level memory and be scarier than the original happening. As the experience in the mind is repeated over and over, being pulled in and out of permanent memory, it changes. If we have a hidden agenda to protect our ego, the memory will be changed to tell a story that fits the lens of our ego; and it becomes a "meta-level memory," which means it is now above and beyond the original experience. We have so creatively changed and manipulated the memory by retelling it

215

that we have made black into white and white into black, and we believe it is all so very true. These creative changes in the memory, of course, won't be known to the conscious mind, and we will believe consciously that the now meta memory is what really happened. This is how the history of our past is now remembered; and it will affect our filtering system, which will distort our present moment even more. *(Do you know consciously this is happening? No, not for the most part. Again, you need to take note that your past is so flexible and will change with or without your conscious mind ever being aware or involved. But now, will you believe it is true? Sure!)*

Now the meta-level story will take on a life of its own. When the meta memory is recalled in the active mind, it creates higher emotional-intensity perceptions than the original event; and with that higher intensity, the higher will be the energy produced in the body. Think of chronic conditions such as chronic pain, depression, anxiety, panic, grief, and PTSD as related to becoming meta memories.

What can we do about meta memories? The same thing we can do about all memories that negatively affect us. Recognize that the event is over and gone and that what is left are just memories that aren't real; they are incomplete and untrue, no matter what it feels like in the body. Heal them, reframe them, and let them go. The problem is, we believe our meta stories are real and will have found proof that they are real; proof will be all about how the stories feel in our bodies and be based on our perceptions, which are internal creations. Once we can accept and know they are our creation, we can begin the process of changing and creating new and different perceptions. Think of reframing our stories and negative memories in positive ways. *(You can change any perceptions. Why not? They aren't real and are all made up anyway. And you made them. Take control of your life. Don't keep giving control to your ego. Kill your ego and create a new and better one.)*

Since we are the creator of our world, we are the primal cause; and therefore, it is always us doing it to us. Purpose and means have been reversed. The tool of choice to bring us back into alignment and health is forgiveness. We should forgive ourselves for holding on to unreal memories and letting them run our lives. Forgive others because they are doing the best they can with what they have to work with, and change what we hold inside that causes us to create what we don't want.

MOST MEMORIES AREN'T META MEMORIES

Most of our memories of events and past experiences have little to no emotional intensity attached to them, and they just are what they are, the neutral past. It is how life is and the "isness" of being in our world. The event, as it is happening is neutral and without meaning. It is our perception that puts meaning and intensity into our interpretation of the event and then on into the memory of the interpretation of the event. The vast majority of all our memories have no emotional intensity. From that lower energy state, the memory won't go to the meta level; and while we still can remember them, they won't take on a life of their own. Why is that so? Because their emotional attachment level is neutral or zero. *(You might think about it this way. Do you remember what you had for dinner seven weeks ago from today? You probably won't because it has little emotional energy attached to it, and it isn't important to the mind. You know you ate something that day, but because it's not important to the mind, the memory is given a low priority. That's the way almost all your memories are; you live your life just fine by not remembering your dinner and not remembering most of your memories.)*

With little intensity in the memory, it will have little or no effect on mind or brain/body systems or on the subconscious mind filtering system. At this point the thought may arise: *Won't I need these strong feelings of meta memories to protect me? Who will I be without them?* Meta memories are just embellished stories we tell ourselves for entertainment. They are the body's reaction to those meta memories, as interpreted by the active mind, that causes the body to respond and feel such intensity. It is the wisdom in the body that protects us and responds long before memories can be organized and recalled consciously. If anything, the meta memories distort our inner mind or brain/body wisdom, and we become oversensitive to our current perceptions of present events. We are always "us," but we could be a much happier us by neutralizing our negative meta memories. Remember, they aren't true, complete, or real anyway. So the lessons we think we are getting from them are also untrue, incomplete, and unreal; they are distortions.

It is the egoic self that needs that intensity in our lives of conflict and trauma. Without that stress in our lives, we would be at peace and happy. If that happens, what is the ego's purpose? Without our being on edge and worried, what is the ego to do? It is useless and will fade away and be no more; and if that happens, the body may become aware of its true purpose. So the egoic self needs to keep us in problems, turmoil, and trauma for its survival. *(You do know your ego has a hidden agenda in everything it does, don't you? And it is to save its ego ass.)*

Don't worry about the ego disappearing anytime soon; it has more than enough resources in its warehouse to keep us on our toes, and anxious or depressed until our life force leaves. When the life force leaves the body, the game is over, and we all go home; and the ego dissolves just like the body does because the ego and the body were creations in the illusion. But the life force— now that's another story.

BACK TO THE BODY AS A FRAME

The body is the frame that holds and supports the life force in this three-dimensional, space/time universe. It is the means to the end purpose of the life force in being here now. Therefore, when we look at ourselves or others, we are observing only the frame that holds the picture. The frame is what our culture and society, friends, and relatives have told us is the most important part of us.

It is the life force that animates and gives life to our bodies. Since everything is energy and life force is the animating energy, life force energy is in all things. While bodies or frames may be different, the life force that animates all of us is the same. Why? Because infinite source can give or create only from what it has, which is itself. Behind all the different frames is the same life force. How crazy is that? *(Notice the sleight of hand here? How good can we get at seeing that oneness in the many? You have a different body than anyone else, right? However, that life force that keeps the body moving is the same as everyone else's. Do you see how you are separate and still one? In the world of separate things and yet in oneness at the same time? It is really tricky to be at the fractal edge of expansion and at the same time the oneness the fractal collapses into.)*

How can we understand that at the original self level we are all connected to and part of the same life force, the same subtle field?

All ancient religions and philosophies have always asserted that *we are all one*; however, the ego advocates separateness and specialness. Specialness is another way of making the body the most important purpose of life, and it fragments the oneness even more. There again we must acknowledge the ego's great storehouse of resources and how deeply ingrained the ego is in our belief system. With the ego deep inside our belief system, it is difficult to see, touch, feel, and experience the world in any way other than how the egoic lens has directed us to experience our world.

A METAPHOR: "LIKE A FISH IN WATER"

Water is like the subtle field to a fish. The water penetrates and supports the fish at all levels of its existence. It is through the medium of water that the fish lives and its life is organized. Does a fish know it is in the water and that its whole life revolves around water? Or does it just go about its life as if the water wasn't there?

There is an old Eastern saying that goes something like this: "Sitting on the water buffalo, searching for the water buffalo." Isn't the water to the fish so subtle a medium in its nature and so integrated into its environment that it isn't aware that it's there in any form? Think of a fish swimming in the ocean. How would it know the ocean was there?

Might not we also be in an endless sea of subtle energy or life force that penetrates and supports us in ways we will never know? What might that endless substance be? It gives us pause to wonder, doesn't it?

When all our physicalness disappears, what is left; and what does our physicalness rest on or in? We may be thinking, *But I'm smarter than a fish. I would know because my senses are honed to the greatest perfection, and I would know because I am so aware of the environment I am living in.* When we think of the universe and all we know about it, we should begin to realize that our knowledge and understanding are miniscule compared to the wisdom of the universe. It is the difference between the infinite and the finite. No matter how much we know and understand about the infinite, it is always infinite; and with all our knowledge, we are always finite.

It is the ego's plan for us to believe we are special, the smartest specimen in the universe, and that we can figure out how the infinite works. We may indeed agree that our species is smart; however, our smartness doesn't hold a candle to universal wisdom. What is the universe except part of the unmanifested infinite source energy of everything? Understand that our frame is only a means for the deeper purpose of the universal unfoldment and that life force is beyond our smartness and is opening us up to a brave new world of wisdom and truth. Rather than struggling to discover some new things about the universe, maybe we should gently uncover what has been there all the time. Maybe we shouldn't struggle to discover but pause to uncover what is here already and has always been here. To discover isn't finding something brand new; it is uncovering what has always been there since the beginning of time.

We spend a lot of time and energy remembering the past and discovering the who, what, and why of the past. It is call "history." We all want to get into the history books so we can be remembered. When we come up with a new idea, we want to be known for it and maybe make some money. Different ideas from different people are all surface structure, and they foster separation in the illusion. It is an ego game, and we all play it in this illusion. However, at deep structure there is only oneness, and we are that oneness. So who is uncovering all these new ideas? We are. But who specifically should get credit for uncovering the idea? *(Can you feel how the ego pushes you to be special and separate within the illusion? How can you understand oneness with all that pressure on you to be separate and special? It is "You" who uncovers the new ideas; notice the large "You," which means all of us. Everything needs to be in place for the uncovering of new ideas to take place. With that in mind, you, everyone else, and I are part of the uncovering of all new ideas. The present moment of the unfoldment of a new idea must be the way it is throughout the cosmos, or it couldn't happen, which means you were and had to be part of its unfoldment, or it couldn't happen. Oh now, listen to the ego jump up and tell you that can't be true; and you can almost hear it say, "The discovery of the new idea is special, and we must honor that specialness." Specialness keeps us in the illusion. You may think of the "butterfly effect" in the chaos theory here. Many small uncovering's from different places throughout the world are put together to create a large "new idea." There is never anything completely new under the sun. I said that before, didn't I?)*

The uncovering of something new to us cannot have happened except in the present moment. Which means the whole universe has to be the way it is in that moment for the uncovering to take place; therefore, all of us had to be exactly where we were for it to happen the way it happened. We are one organism, and when we praise the finger for its ability, we forget that the finger operates with the consent of the whole mind and body. Since we are one organism, in the infinitely thin and eternal present moment, everything is perfect and exactly the way it has to be, given the universe is the way it is and therefore there are no accidents. What we think of as accidents are synchronicities of the way things must be in the present moment. *(I know, you want to be special because your ego will feel good, and other egos closely connected to you will feel good and praise you, and that will cause you to feel even better. Can you see why it is so tough to be in oneness within the gross energy system? I'm putting this book together to bring new ideas forward, of which none are completely mine, and to be recognized and make a little money. "Oh, vanity, thy name is Ego." Can you see how easily and seamlessly you can move between being in the world and not being in the world?)*

THE SECRET OF LIFE

Like most things we encounter in our lives, this little discussion will have something almost all of us may agree with, something only a few may agree with, and something no one except maybe me might agree with. However, for some, it may be a gateway into a different understanding of life, and for others it's just trash. And it points to an answer of a couple of old interesting questions: How can we be in the world but not of the world? And under, around, and through this ever-changing world, where is that ever-constant, never-changing reality? And maybe we should ask ourselves the deep question: "Who are we really?"

The secret of life is in knowing life has purpose and in recognizing that the means that life force uses to accomplish its end is the body.

If you don't confuse the two and get it upside down and backward, life becomes a much happier and peaceful place to be. Here we might quote Einstein again *(see how special he is?)*. "I am not interested in this phenomenon or that phenomenon," Einstein said. "I want to know God's thoughts—the rest are mere details." Discoveries are just details; they are interesting but just details. Who are we really? Now there is a question worthy of the smartest specimen in the universe.

CHAPTER 15

Outside Energy, Inside Creation

SERIOUS ABOUT ENERGY

The outside energy system is the realm of the unmanifested, in which everything exists as potential and possibilities within the subtle field. What we experience as the manifested universe of separate objects is the gross energy system of our everyday lives; and that is what we create inside, within the interpreted universe or the gross energy system. We traverse both the unmanifested and the manifested realms at the same time. The gross energy system is inside the subtle field because the subtle field supports, embraces, and permeates everything. Why? Because it is omnipresent and infinite. We have stated this before.

All our discussion so far has brought us to this point. The ever-changing manifested gross energy system is an illusory universe of the ever-shifting sands of perceptions and dichotomies that change with each new manifestation, discovery, unfolding of scientific discovery, and the unmanifested subtle field of everything. What about it? It's the never-changing infinity of everything. No matter how much we take from or understand about the unmanifested everything and make it manifested, the gross will always be finite, and the subtle will always be infinite. In the process of manifesting, the infinite isn't diminished and is undisturbed as we take from it. The gross is always finite and dualistic, and the infinite is forever infinite. To appreciate and glimpse who we are, we may need to approach the subtle field more directly. Why? Because the answer is there. Why would the answer be there? Because everything is there. *(You see where I'm coming from? Since everything is in the subtle field of everything, the answer to any question you have is now there also. Just because you haven't uncovered it yet doesn't mean it's not there.)*

We can wonder, *Would the fish in the last chapter be happier knowing it is in an ocean of water that supports it?* Maybe it would get anxious or paranoid thinking about this, and maybe it would think, *Where does the ocean end? Is there an edge? Will I fall off? What was there before the ocean?* These questions could keep it preoccupied for years while trying to figure things out and maybe keep it up late at night; and in the end, its frame dissolves, and it becomes the answer.

For all our smartness, we may have a lot in common with that fish; and we may wonder, *Would we be happier knowing we are within the subtle field that supports us?* Maybe we would get anxious or paranoid thinking about it; and maybe we think, *Where is the edge of the field? What is beyond it? What was there before the subtle field? Will we fall off? When will it end?* It could keep us preoccupied for years. We may need to do a couple of scientific studies. Maybe we could get a grant to study it or create a career path, trying to figure it out. It could make us anxious or paranoid and maybe keep us up at night; then in the end, our frame will dissolve, and we will rejoin the blob at the bottom of the lamp and become the answer.

IT IS WHAT IT IS

The present moment has to be and must be the way life is for each of us. There can be no other way for us, given the interpreted universe in which we each have constructed it. Again, we need to emphasize that the interpreted universe is a personal construction. This present moment we are experiencing through our interpretation isn't real. Now the present moment is real, but the way we construct it inside through our interpretation, our perception of it, is the part that isn't real. We are experiencing a creation of our interpretive minds; and each of us has a different interpretation of the present moment. Each of our creations will be slightly different or maybe a lot different given the uniqueness of our experiences and belief systems.

Remember, individuals aren't the only ones who have interpreted universes. Families, cultures, nations, and religions have them, too. The differences between all those interpreted universes could cause arguments, maybe hurt feelings, and perhaps wars because each believer within their own interpreted universe believes they are seeing the truth when in fact they are reflecting on their own unique interpretation or construction created through the lens of their deeply held beliefs and prejudices. These believers believe they are seeing, experiencing, and possessing the inside track on absolute truth, which, of course, they are not. But beliefs are powerful drivers of illusions.

Our individual interpreted universe is entwined and entangled with the interpreted universes of family, culture, religion, country, and more. This is because our belief systems are entwined and entangled with those other belief systems, which are all egoically driven.

If we aren't happy with the present moment, which is the world we created to live in, and would like to change it, we can; but here is the interesting thing. It's not the present moment or the outside energy system of everything that must change. We are who must change. Which part must change? Our negative not-so-real memories. Why do we need to change them? Because they drive our filtering system of the incoming data, which determines what data will be used to create the world of objects we live in. We need to reframe them and make peace with our past, which is to say forgive the past, ourselves, and others so we can let go of what isn't real, even though we believe it is; then we can construct and bring to focus a new world for us to be in. *(Later I will develop a model in which you don't need to forgive the other person for his or her offenses against you or wait for someone to forgive you if you are the offender. And yet forgiveness is accomplished. You may or may not find it interesting.)*

What we think the present moment is, it isn't; and what we think our world is, it isn't. What is our world then? It is the interpreted universe created from manipulated and filtered data that has been dragged through our old filtering system of our old not-so-real memories, experiences, references, and prejudices from our past. We should be able to hear our ego come right out of its chair at that, "No! No! You're wrong. I know what the present moment is. I see it the way it is. I don't filter data. You're wrong, I say! Wrong!" Oh, I'm sorry. I did say that before, didn't I?

In the End, It Is All Us

We each created our own world. The world we have is the way it is because we believe the way we do. The end result is our interpreted universe, which is the world we live in; and it doesn't matter whether it's good and we like it or it's not so good, and we don't like it. It's still all a created illusion. If we have pain and suffering, we must change something inside us because the outside energy system isn't going to change. Why doesn't it have to change for us to feel better? Because it's already everything. Since it's already everything, what in the world could we possibly change everything into? How can the infinity of everything change? It can't. All we can do is filter it differently. When we change and reframe our memories, our world will automatically change because we will be using a different filtering system to draw from "the everything" something different. *(I know working with the idea of infinity of everything can seem strange. It may be difficult to imagine being in two places at once—the subtle field and the gross energy system. However, that is where you are. You are in the gross energy system, and you are always in the subtle field. Crazy, right? Crazy or not, that is what you're dealing with. You can never be outside the subtle field. Nevertheless, some have claimed to be outside the gross energy system; these events are called "near-death" experiences.)*

Between the subtle field and the gross energy system is our interpreted universe, and hung between those two horns rests the body. Most of the time, the body is the scapegoat for the mind or brain. If we cannot find someone to blame for our current state of pain and suffering, which is to say our negative interpreted universe, the body is the fallback excuse. When it gets sick, now we have an excuse for not dealing with changing and healing our inner self right now, at least not until we feel better. Remember, the body responds only to the created internal interpreted universe; therefore, to heal the body, the interpreted universe needs to change, which means we must heal our past; and again, the past we think we have isn't the past. It's our manipulated interpretation of events that are gone, and all we have left of the events are only untrue memories. *(Come on now. What proof do you need to begin to accept that your memories aren't the events? If you say, "I want to compare my memories to the event," you can never do that. Why? Because the event is gone and is never coming back. No matter how much physical evidence you can gather, it will never be the event; and the memories you have are constructed of manipulated, filtered, and distorted data. I know you believe your memories are true, but they're not. Get used to it; you live in an illusion.)*

This is difficult to wrap the mind around at first because we have been so programmed to believe memories are real, that our world is outside us and that the outside world controls us; this belief causes us to respond in ways we don't consciously want, but it fits our programming. The world we currently live in is the way it is because of our inside interpretation of that outside energy, which is neutral. The world isn't pushing us around; it is a reflection of our inner state of being. If we put that idea into a series of steps, it may become clearer or make more sense. To do that we must start at the very beginning, which is a very good place to start. We will start in the womb. It is actually before that that our world begins to come into focus, but for our purpose, we will start in the womb. The following steps are general and incomplete, but they may be helpful:

1. We receive our chromosomes, our genetic material for our first cell, from our parents. Half are from our mom, and half are from our dad. The blueprint for all our genes is wrapped within the DNA, which is inside the chromosomes of our first cell. *(Recognized only that some genes are expressed in the first cell. They are the ones our mom and dad were expressing at the time when the first cell came into being.)*

2. At conception some genes are active from both parents, and the rest sleep within the tightly wrapped DNA, which is twisted around the histones inside the chromosomes, waiting for the right signals from the cells to tell the DNA which genes need

to be unwrapped for copying. As we have seen, genes can be "turned on or turned off," expressed or not, depending on the inside environmental signals coming to the cell. We aren't stuck with the operational genes we were conceived with, unless we believe we are. *(Note: To say genes are "turned on or turned off" may not be the correct term scientifically, but understand that genes express themselves based on a dance between environmental signals the cells receive and how the cells interpret those signals. You get the idea that the cells determine and select the genes they need to survive, right? Genes don't make any decisions. It's the cell that determines gene expression based on the environment signals the cell is living in.)*

3. At about the middle of the gestation period in the second trimester, the cells begin to modify their genetic signatures to match the internal environment of the host body, which is the mom's body, where the fetus is living, swimming, and surviving.

4. The fetus's external environment is the mother's internal environment and is determined by the mother's emotional and physical state of health and well-being; her health rests on her relationships with those around her, including the child's father, during the whole gestation period.

5. The fetus's external environment is the mother's internal environment, which determines the internal environment of the fetus; and that is what each cell is trying to survive in. The signals from the cell's environment determine gene expression. *(Can you appreciate that the cells determine gene expression? The DNA is just a collection of plans the cell can use any way it needs to in order to stay alive and survive.)*

6. As the mother's external environment changes, so too does the fetus's internal environment. The mother's internal environment is what the fetus struggles to survive in. During this struggle at the cellular level of the fetus, genes are changed by the cells as they struggle to survive within the fetus.

7. During gestation the fetus and the mother are locked together. The fetus doesn't and cannot distinguish between itself and the mother, and the mother's emotions are the signals that little body is responding to in its survival struggle.

8. The cells modify their genes' expressions and requirements so the newborn child will be genetically positioned to survive in the world it will be born into, as experienced in the womb from the mother's experiences during the gestation period. *(You have heard the saying "As above, so below." In the womb, the saying is "As without, so within" or as in the mother, so within the child. Also notice that the cells aren't doing these gene modifications because they love the fetus and want to help it; they have no concept of the fetus. The cells are quite selfish; they are modifying genes to survive, and that's it. The cells don't give a damn what happens to the fetus. However, they do care what happens to their community, because that is how they survive. The cells are part of a larger community.)*

9. The internal environment the fetus experiences in gestation is the model the cells use to instruct the DNA on how to modify genetic expression to support the child's survival in the external world it will be born into, which is to say the mother's current world. *(Again, notice that this process is all survival driven. The cells don't change because of their concern for the child per se; they are modified to support their own survival. If this helps the child, so be it. It's another symbiotic relationship.)*

10. When the child's brain is electrically turned on in the womb, experiences in the womb are turned into memories. They will be untrue, incomplete, unreal, and very primitive memories indeed, but that's what we start with. They won't be consciously remembered, but they are in the subconscious mind, and they will be part of its filtering system, which will be in place by age six. Since memories in the womb are the oldest memories in the mind, they will have the highest priority in the subconscious mind's filtering system. *(Are you beginning to appreciate the importance of this short time in the womb is as it relates to the life the person experiences?)*

11. The mechanism through which the genes are modified is called "epigenetics" or control above the gene. This mechanism states how genes express, turn off and on, as determined by the cells' external environmental signals, which start in the external environment of the mother and work their way down into the

cells and finally into the genetic expression of the cell as it tries to survive.

12. After the birth of the child, the body responds only to the interpreted universe created inside it, which is quite small in the beginning because it lacks experiences and reference material; beliefs haven't developed yet. Understand this: when the body responds, it responds right down to the cellular level, which will change gene expression throughout our lives through this process of epigenetics.

13. The beliefs, experiences, and reference material the child receives are mostly from within his or her family of origin. In this family system, the child develops his or her fundamental interpreted universe, unique self-identity, and basic core belief system. *(These are all critical programs of how you will experience your life. The more positive the experience of early childhood, the happier your life will be; and the more negative the experience, the more problematic your life will be.)*

14. By age six or seven the child's core beliefs of how his or her world operates, what the child knows and believes, are locked in place in the subconscious mind; and through those beliefs and knowing, he or she will filter and interpret his or her world into existence.

15. Beliefs can be changed, and experiences can be reframed, changing what genes are expressed; however, the person must first recognize a need to change and believe he or she can change or can't and won't.

There is nothing as powerful as our beliefs. Beliefs cause our world to be the way it is; and by changing them, they will create a new world for us. Anything is possible. The only world we have is the interpreted universe we create, and that interpreted universe is the birthplace of all our pain and suffering as well as our joy and happiness. The outside energy system is neutral, meaningless, and unmanifested; and it doesn't have to change or do anything for us to have a heaven or hell right here, right now. We are the ones who must change. Even if the outside energy system did change, without us changing inside we would filter and manipulate the incoming data to create an interpreted universe much like the one we had before; and the world we live in wouldn't change much. Think about it for a moment. We see what we have been programmed to see, which is the world we have from the inside out; and our subconscious mind will work as hard as hell to filter the outside input data into an interpreted world to match our beliefs. *(Again, notice that it is your inside filtering system that determines your created world. Imagine that the external everything could change. You won't know it consciously because your subconscious filtering system will mine through all the changed data and select only what data it is familiar with, which will be the same old stuff you had before. At the interpreted universe level, you wouldn't see any difference.)*

ANOTHER WAY OF LOOKING AT IT

The only world we have is the one our minds create, the interpreted universe, and it is created from filtered and manipulated current and past data. As we create it, we project it onto the outside energy system, and that projected world is reflected back to us, and we believe the outside world is where we live. However, what we think of as outside is still where it was created, inside us. The creation doesn't leave the creator.

To say the interpreted universe is projected onto the outside energy system doesn't mean to imply the outside energy system or subtle field changes in any way. The interpreted universe is always an inside perception that appears to be outside, only because of the slow way the conscious mind processes the information and its method of reporting to us, but it is never outside the way we consciously think it is. It is through our individual interpreted universes that we interact with the outside energy system and each other.

What is that outside energy system anyway? Nothing and everything. It is *nothing* because it is neutral and meaningless, and it is *everything* because it is the unmanifested possibility waves of anything and everything. By changing our filtering system, we also change the energy signature we radiate out into the unmanifested subtle field. That change in our filtering system will bring into focus a new world that matches our new signature or frequency, based on our new filtering system, which is what we are now asking for; and that is what we must get. We, through our internal processes, bring the meaningless everything into the meaningful something. A bold and crazy statement, is it not?

We are radiating an energy frequency right now, and we are getting the reality of what matches that radiating frequency. We are pulling, drawing, and attracting from the subtle field; and we are creating from our current energy signature the reality and world we have now.

It may be that we haven't been bold enough in moving into this brave new world of recognizing our creative abilities. This process brought the world we have now into focus, using our dominant thoughts. We are radiating a certain frequency right now that is generating the world we think we have around us. We are drawing and pulling to us those things that match our radiated frequency; it is called the "law of attraction." What radiates that attracting signature frequency? Our minds. *You're crazy*, we may be thinking. *I didn't ask for the world I have. Why would I ask for this stuff? Just one more stupid statement after another you keep making.*

If we think our most dominant thoughts are the ones we are thinking right now, we're right. However, our dominant thoughts aren't coming from the conscious mind; they are coming from the subconscious part of the mind, from the black box, and that is what is creating the greater part of our frequency signature. Our most dominant thoughts come from the subconscious mind, and they are out of our conscious awareness and are unavailable to be changed directly because we don't know what they are; also, they aren't in words. Keep in mind how much bigger and faster the subconscious mind is than the conscious mind. *(You do know a picture is worth a thousand words, right? Since the subconscious mind radiates a thousand pictures before the conscious mind can generate one word, whom do you think the universe is going to listen to?)*

THE SUBCONSCIOUS MIND'S SIGNATURE FREQUENCY

It's the subconscious mind that is attracting and pulling from the universe. Why would that be? Because it operates so fast, is so big, has all our memories, and operates 24-7; and attached to all those negative memories is a lot stronger negative energy. To find out what kind of energy is being radiated out by the subconscious mind, we need to look for clues. The clues are all around us. A lot will be embedded in our behavior. Smart detectives like us should be able to figure them out. For example, are you angry a lot? Do you play the victim role? Are you always trying to get even for some perceived slight against you? Are you an abusive? Do you always agree with others because you are afraid people won't like you if you don't? Do you always need to be right? Are you always on guard and scanning the environment for danger? Are you sick a lot? What role, what family script, have you taken on from your family of origin or in this life you keep living? Now, where are all our stuff and current energy signature coming from? Our ego-soaked memories of the past.

Cause and its effects are always connected. What we have in our life now is an effect of what we have been asking for. If we consciously don't like what we have, we shouldn't look for the cause in the conscious mind or point a finger at the universe. We should look to the energy being generated by the habitual self, which is the constantly running programming in the subconscious mind. That is where our "frequency signature" is being radiated from, and it's always turned on. *(Anything you have in your life now is an effect. Your life is only an effect, and effects must have a cause. And your past is the cause of your present life. Don't look outside you for the cause because you are the subtle cause of all you have.)*

The subconscious mind is where all our learned, ingrained behaviors, beliefs, and habitual programming are operating from. What kind of dominant thoughts are we thinking at that deeper and more powerful level of mind without words, because that is what is being radiated out? What have we attracted into our lives? The law of attraction doesn't start working when you start thinking a few positive, happy thoughts in your conscious mind. It is always working—24-7, day in and day out, year in and year out. Whatever we have in our lives right now is because of what we have been asking for and working hard to get from the universe for such a long time. What we have right now must match the energy we have been radiating because that's what we have and because that's the way the law of attraction works. *(There is no magic here. It's a process, and you can change it.)*

If we don't like what we are receiving, we will need to change our total energy signature. Just thinking a few little, happy positive thoughts now and then won't do it. Healing at a much deeper level may be indicated. Maybe changes are needed that go clear down to the bone. If our subconscious minds continue to ask for more of what we already have, do we really think that thinking a few happy positive thoughts now and then, without changing anything else in our lives, will really excite the universe to give us our conscious minds our hearts' desires?

Rather than sending out requests for the stuff we think we want from our conscious minds, it might be more helpful to ask the universe, "What am I doing right now that's preventing my desires from manifesting?" As we heal and change from our old paradigm, our desires must begin flowing into our lives. When our frequency signature matches the energy signature in the subtle field of the reality we want, we cannot help but get that reality. We, not the universe, are the ones who need to change. *(So what needs to change is you? You may notice that it always gets back to you. Eventually you will understand that you are the subtle cause of your world as it is. And the neat thing is, you can change it. How good at changing are you?)*

A METAPHOR

The law of attraction is a metaphor. We don't need to send out energy frequencies into the universe to get what we want because everything is already here. The gross energy field, which is our inside interpreted universe, is itself within the infinite subtle field because the subtle field is infinite; therefore, it is everywhere and everything. It is the Tao, the sandbox, out of which everything is manifested, including us.

All we need to do is change our filtering system, and then what is already there will present itself to us, and the active mind will manifest it. It isn't in sending any energy signature outside that changes our world but in healing our inside past memories and reframing our beliefs, experiences, and references that will bring into focus a new and different world. *(Where did you get all or most of your beliefs, experiences, and references? From others. You don't have independent thoughts. Your thoughts are built on what others have poured into your ear, mainly before you were six years old. The good news is, you can change by getting new and different information in your ears and passed the defenses of your subconscious mind. Maybe right here? You don't need to understand how it all works to use it.)*

Refer to the diagram in Chapter 13, "Everything Is in the Mind." Notice that the two individuals create two different interpreted universes from the same input information. We need to be clear on this point. It is never the outside data and information that determines the world we live in; it is always our creative interpretation of the filtered and manipulated data and information the active mind receives that determines our world.

In the diagram, two different interpreted universes are created from the same input data. Look closely. It isn't the outside-everything energy that creates the different interpreted universes. The two individuals are right next to each other. The senses from each individual capture about the same input data from the outside energy field and move the similar data into the two different filtering systems. *(Can you begin to notice that different beliefs create different worlds? Your beliefs are formed from past memories. By reframing your memories, it's like you become the second person in the diagram. When you change and reframe past memories, your world must change. And why not? The memories aren't real anyway. You are the powerful creator of the world you have. And since you now know you can change your world, how exciting is that for you?)*

As we keep stating, it's the filtering system we have, as determined by our beliefs, experiences, and references from the past, which are memories, that guarantees we will continue getting the world we have. Again, are the memories real, complete, and true? No. Do we believe they are true? Yes.

The two filtering systems here in the diagram need to be different because each individual has different memories and past histories; therefore, the outputs from the two filter systems must be different. Each of us has a different history and therefore different memories; consequently, each of us has different filtering systems. Therefore, each of us has a different world to live in. Even if we're twins, triplets, quadruplets, or conjoined twins with the same genetic material, our lives will be different because we each will have different beliefs, experiences, and references, which is to say our objective and subjective worlds will be different because of our different historical memories.

From the diagram in Chapter 13, notice that the subtle field of everything doesn't have to change or do anything for us to have a different universe to live in. All that needs to happen for us to create a different world is to change our filtering system. What is our filtering system? Our beliefs, experiences, and references from the past, which are our memories. Also notice that each interpreted universe will send different signals to the different bodies; therefore, each body will "feel differently." *(I know I'm repeating a lot of the same things, but we are so locked into our old paradigm that even as I repeat this new approach, you may slip back into the old habitual self, and this includes me. I can hold this understanding in my conscious mind for only short periods of time, but it's not the conscious mind that needs the change; it is the subconscious mind. When that happens, the conscious mind will automatically report each little step toward a new world. So wake up.)*

Since the outputs of the two filtering systems are different, the interpreted universe they create will be different. How different will be the two interpreted universes? That will depend on how close or apart their beliefs, experiences, and references are from their past memories.

We are the creators of our world. If we don't like the world we have now, we can change it. Changes won't occur in the subtle field of everything, because outside us is the meaningless, unmanifested everything, and "the everything" is constant and never changing. The only place where anything can change is inside us. It's all about changing internal programming, and the programs are in our subconscious mind; and what are the programs in the subconscious mind developed around? Memories. What are memories? They are our beliefs, experiences, and references of past events that are over and gone. Are the memories real, complete, and true? Now we are back to our first thought experiment. The short answer is no. The ego's answer is yes.

CHAPTER 16

The Body Speaks

CONSTANT COMMUNICATION

All we know is what is inside us, and that's it. Some people know more than we do, and some people know less than we do; but that's not the point. The point is that individually all we know about our world is what is inside us, and we carry all we know around with us. Much of it isn't consciously available to us, but it is always working in the background, in the subconscious mind. And that knowing inside is constantly seeking balance and homeostasis with its environment outside us, in a place of normal and natural balance based on our beliefs, experiences, references, and memories. To reach that sweet spot of balance, the mind and body have to operate as one whole and complete system, including all their underlying subsystems. It needs to work like a finely tuned symphony orchestra, where the uniqueness of each section and subsection is integrated into the whole musical landscape, creating a harmonious response to our inside life and outside world. *(If you can't find or reach that sweet balanced spot, you can get anxious or maybe become depressed. Your outside environment needs to match your inside beliefs about yourself, or you won't feel like you; you will keep moving pieces of your world around, trying to find it. You might even sabotage your current relationships to meet that goal.)*

There is the kicker. The mind, body, or brain must balance all those beliefs, experiences, references, and memories in concert in such a way that what we believe about ourselves inside matches the world we project outside. *(Remember, your world really isn't outside. It's always inside and just seems outside due to the conscious mind's slow processing.)* So what we believe about ourselves is critical, because that is what we will come into balance with as we create our world. The completeness of our self-identity or egoic self isn't always known to us consciously, and we may need to individually discover it for ourselves. If we sing a high note, a low note would balance it. If we believe we are victims, we will need to make a world that will victimize us. If we are bullies, we will work hard to create a world where we can bully. *(Do you see how it works? What you believe about yourself must have a complementary balance point, or you can't have those beliefs about yourself. If you believe you are a victim, you need and must have victimizers and persecutors in your life; or you can't be a victim. It's all so simple, don't you think? So do you see why you are fighting so hard to keep your dysfunctional beliefs about yourself? They aren't real, you know.)*

Who we believe we are must be balanced in the world we create. It does little good to change the outside world we have because it's just an effect of our causal-created internal-interpreted universe. And the causal-created interpreted universe is the way it is because of our beliefs. If we try to change the world without changing the cause, it won't last, at least not for long. The same is true of behavior. Changing outside behavior without changing inside causal programming, which is to say our beliefs, won't last.

If we aren't sure what our egoic identity is, we should look at the world we have. The clues, again, are there. If people seem to take advantage of us, this is a clue; if we are always in arguments with those around us, this is a clue. The sad thing is that we will probably blame others for their behavior and not recognize we are dancing with them, trying to find balance. Here is a little secret: we can't change them, whoever they are. However, if we change and learn new dance steps, they will need to begin dancing differently or leave the dance floor. Recognize that we need to change in some way. Here again, blaming others is a way to save our egos from being bruised and making us feel bad; it also keeps us from changing what we know we need to.

While we have emphasized the communication signals the active mind sends to the body, we need to acknowledge that the body also communicates and feeds back information to the active mind. When the body is thirsty, hungry, or tired—or needs to relieve itself—all that information is fed back into the active mind for a proper response. Again, the feedback from the body is input data to the active mind, and it will create an interpretation; and signals from that new perception will be sent out throughout the mind and body. Responses will be as determined by memories and experiences of how we responded in the past to those signals, and those utilitarian responses will go back to our earliest memories of learned behavior in childhood (for example, the feelings in the body when we needed to go potty and the subconscious mind filtering the environment for a way to do that). *(Can you see the dance that is going on inside you all the time in a way to support your whole being?)*

While the conscious mind is resting, sleeping, or being distracted, the subconscious mind, the body, and the active mind are always up, aware, and communicating at lightning speed. At no time are the active mind and body not communicating. We don't hear this communication consciously because it's not in words, and it is very fast; and it is way outside our conscious awareness.

THE DANCE OF THE ACTIVE MIND AND BODY

For a short time, I practiced tai chi. One of the exercises we did in class was called, "Touching Hands." In this exercise, two partners touched the backs of their hands, with either right or left hands; and as one partner slowly in the beginning moved his or her hand, the other partner followed without breaking contact. This was a way of staying in contact and connected to his or her partner and learning his or her rhythms and feedback, and in so doing learn something about ourselves. It was a very interesting exercise, and I was amazed after a while of how fast we could move and still be in contact and harmony with each other. To accomplish this there was constant feedback between the two partners. When the lead partner felt his or her partner was straining to keep up, he or she would change to support his or her partner's improvement by slowing down a little, and then the speed would again slowly increase. This is a great metaphor for understanding relationships. However, most relationships aren't connected enough to sense the feedback of their partner, or one or the other partner is unwilling to share his or her rhythms and feedback feelings because of hidden agendas. This type of behavior is usually caused by old programs from childhood.

This is the process of feedback that goes on between the mind and body. Sometimes the active mind is leading, and at times the body leads. Whichever is leading, each partner's feedback information is necessary for the continued support of his or her dance within the relationship; whether it is in response to the active mind or in support of the body's needs, it is a supportive partnership. They both must be involved to enjoy the dance, or it will be difficult on them both but mainly on the body because the body is always the scapegoat for the mind. In the musical *Man of La Mancha*, the manservant of Don Quixote, Sancho Panza, visits the dying knight in the last scene of the play. To cheer him up, he sings a song, "A Little Gossip." In the lyrics is the phrase "Whether the stone hits the pitcher or the pitcher hits the stone, it's going to be bad for the pitcher."

This is a perfect metaphor for the relationship between the mind and the body. Whatever we do in the mind, the body will and must respond with an effect. This is a cause-and-effect relationship between the mind and body, and the body is only the effect of the causal mind. When the mind is gentle, all is well for both. When the mind is like a rock, it's going to be bad news for the body.

This partnership of mind and body is always somewhere on a line of continuum between the perception of being under attack and the perception of being at peace and comfortable. What determines where we are on that line is the interpreted universe and the feedback of the body as these two dance together. In this dance, whoever is the leading partner can change as new or different feedback information is entered into the dance, which is to say that new dance steps must be learned. Again, this dance is continuous and very fast in millions to billions of bits of data per second. The slow, conscious mind can only sit on the sidelines and report on what has already happened.

For our purpose we will be concerned only with the fight-or-flight survival part of the dance on that line of continuum. The same process holds for peace and comfort, but our concern is with pain and suffering in this read, which are the downside of the continuum.

WHEN EVENTS HAPPEN

We will need to look deep into this process to see negative events differently than we have been programmed to do. A selective review of some of the things we have discussed may be helpful at this point to set the stage for our next adventure.

REVIEW OF WHAT WE HAVE ALREADY SHARED

- We never experience an event the way it is. We view it only through the lens of our egoic past.
- What we think of as emotions are only the conscious mind's reporting of what has already happened in the active mind and body. Emotions are only word descriptions by the conscious mind of what has already happened in the mind and the body's response to those signals. Emotional words don't cause anything; they are just descriptors to explain to us what has happened. *(This is a different understanding as to what emotions are. In this model, the mind doesn't create emotions. The body responds to the active mind, and the conscious mind describes the feelings in the body in emotional words. Remember, the communication in the mind and body is wordless. It is only the conscious mind that uses words. Again, when the conscious mind is talking to you, whom is it talking to?)*
- Memories aren't real, complete, or true. They are stories we tell ourselves about what is over and gone, and true events never existed the way we think they did.

As we think we are experiencing an event happening outside, it is really being processed and taking place inside us. The process occurs too quickly for the conscious mind to catch everything, and that is why it appears to be happening outside us. To understand what is happening when an event is going on more clearly, the next diagram may be helpful. We will follow the process step-by-step.

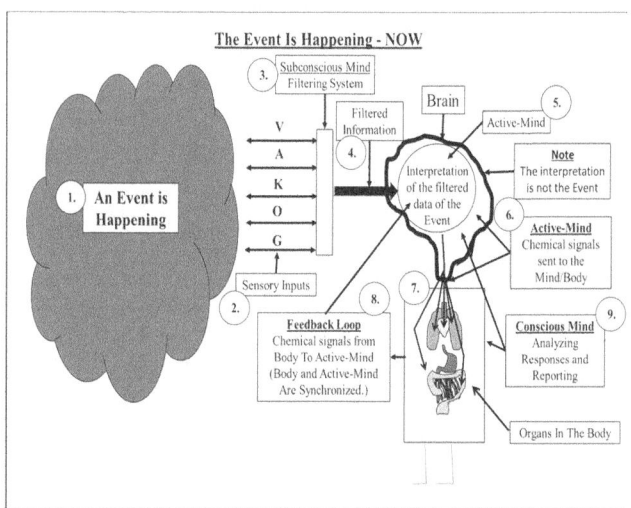

Diagram 19 - An Event Is Happening Now

The sequence begins:

1. An event happens.
2. The senses transmit information about the event to the subconscious mind.
3. The transmitted data is filtered and manipulated by the subconscious mind as it sorts through the data, looking for what it is familiar with based on our beliefs, experiences, and references from past memories.
4. The filtered and manipulated data is sent to the active mind.
5. The active mind creates an interpretation of the event based on the filtered data, which is our interpreted universe. *(Notice again that the interpretation of the event isn't the event and is created from filtered and manipulated data.)*
6. From the interpretation in the active mind, electromagnetic and chemical signals and messages are sent throughout the mind and body.

7. The body receives the messages and responds as is appropriate to the signals communicated.

8. The body feeds back data to the active mind as to the body's response to the messages received. The released feedback signals in the body go back to the active mind as data inputs. The active mind takes the data and creates another perception, and it should match or be in sync with the signals sent out by the active mind. *(Notice that this all happens at millions to billions of bits of data per second. Superman couldn't keep up with this processing, and neither can the conscious mind.)*

9. Then the conscious mind reports on what has happened. We need to know the end result, but the details are lost to the conscious mind and therefore are lost to us. All we know is what the conscious mind tells us.

Remember, this is a model. The active mind isn't a location we can put our finger on. It is a combination of the mind, central nervous system, and brain. When the event is over and gone, which is to say the outside event energy has dissipated and gone up in smoke, what happens to all that inside energy of the perception, the body responses, and all those generated feelings? It all becomes a memory of our interpretation of the event, which is over. It all gets stored in the subconscious mind, and it is stored with all its attached feelings or emotional energy as data. The more negative the interpretation and the energy around the interpretation are, the more difficult it will be to keep them from invading our conscious awareness. The more we try to bury them, the more they become a pebble in our shoe. However, sooner or later, it will all get consolidated into the subconscious mind and become part of its filtering system, and it will also be out of conscious awareness. When I say, "stored memory," that doesn't mean inactive. Depending on the energy it carried with it into the subconscious mind, it may be highly active in the filtering system.

When that memory is triggered or remembered for any reason, it will come into awareness in the active mind with all the energetic data it was stored with. And the active mind will again create a perception from the data and send out signals and messages to the whole mind and body, because that's what the active mind does with data it receives; and the active mind doesn't know or care where the data comes from. The next diagram explores that process of remembering a memory. *(Recall the active mind doesn't know where the data is coming from and doesn't care. To the active mind, data is just data, and it will just process it. Is this beginning to look like a pattern you have seen before?)*

WHEN WE RECALL A MEMORY

When a memory is recalled, a lot of things are different from experiencing an event that happens in the present moment. The first big difference is that there is no sensory input data because it is all happening in our heads, in our imaginations, from stored information. Since there is no event going on, there is nothing for the senses to transmit; therefore, there is nothing for the subconscious mind to filter. The memory is created from already-filtered and manipulated data of our interpretation of the original event, which is over and gone. Thus, the memory is already in a form the active mind can use directly as received. The following diagram depicts this process.

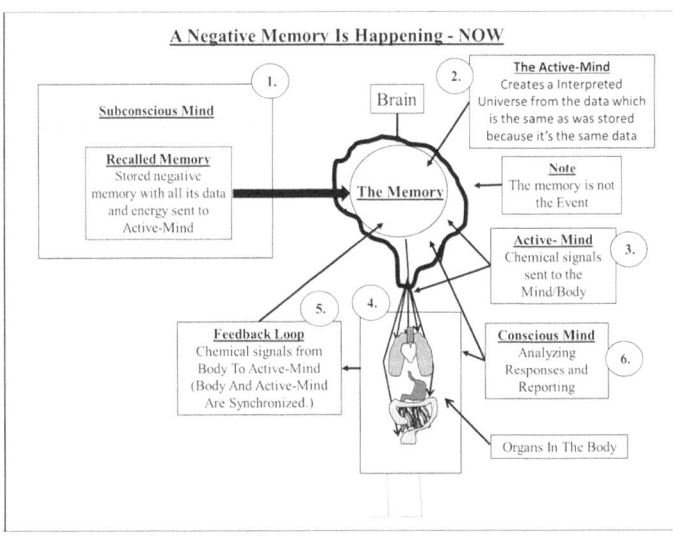

Diagram 20 - A Memory Is Recalled

We will again follow this process in a step-by-step sequence:

1. The memory is triggered or recalled from the subconscious mind into awareness in the active mind. *(Notice, there is no input data or filtering of the data and no event. All that stuff was done when the original interpretation was made. All we have now is an unreal memory. It isn't a copy. The whole memory with all its data is taken out of the subconscious and put in the active mind.)*

2. The active mind will create an interpreted universe from the data it receives, because that is what the active mind does with any data it receives; and the interpretation will be much like the interpreted universe created from the original event, because it is the same data by which the active mind created the original interpretation. Remember, we stated before that the active mind cannot tell the difference between data received from an outside event or data received from a vividly remembered memory or data it receives from the body. The active mind just processes whatever data it receives.

3. From the interpretation of the memory, signals and messages are sent throughout the mind and body.

4. The body receives the messages and responds as is appropriate based on them. *(Here again the body has no idea whether the signals are coming from a memory or from information about an outside event; and it doesn't care. All it knows is what the active mind signals, and the body responds as is appropriate based on the signals received.)*

5. The body feeds back information to the active mind as to how it is responding to the messages it receives in the form of nonverbal data. *(Notice again that this is happening at billions of bits of data per second. To the active mind, the feedback data from the body is just data, and it just processes the data as it receives it. The body is just responding as is appropriate to the signals it receives. Can you see that there is the ongoing dance between these two and how fast it is? At a certain point, balance or homeostasis is reached, and that is where you stay until new data is received by the active mind; and because of the high processing speeds involved, this process takes only nanoseconds.)*

6. When the dust settles, the conscious mind reports on what has happened. It has no idea that the active mind and body dance thousands of dances before they reach balance and agreement, and that isn't its concern. It is just reporting on what has happened in the mind and body as best it can. And it is also unaware that the body cannot respond without the active mind telling it how.

Since the body responds in much the same way it did to the original interpretation of the event, it consciously feels to us as if the event is happening all over again, and that is how the conscious mind reports it to us. That's why we think the memories are real, not because they are real but because of how they feel in the body. We think the memory is real because of the power it has to create pain and suffering or joy and pleasure responses in the body. Now look again and notice; there is no event happening, and there is no input data. There is only a memory that isn't real, complete, or true. It is the great trickster, the egoic mind that keeps us in bondage to our past and our memories. It keeps us locked into the past as prisoners of our old, negative memories, and we are afraid to leave. Notice, the door isn't locked, and our hands aren't tied. We can change our memories and choose to see things differently; yet we can't leave who we have habitually been programmed to be, which is to say our egoic-created self-identity.

How to Change the Dance

The linchpin that holds us captive and in prison to our past is how our old negative memories feel in the body when we remember them. Intellectually we can appreciate that memories aren't real and that the events are over and gone; maybe we did manipulate some of the data in our haste to create an interpretation, and we may not have exactly remembered them accurately. They may be only remnants of an unreal past, but oh, how they feel in the body. Oh, that awful feeling in our stomachs and that angst in our minds; we are convinced the memories are alive and must be real because they feel so real in the body. When the body responds to the interpreted signals of the memory in the active mind and they feel so real and alive, that's all the proof we need to believe the memories are real. If the memory is very vivid, the remembrance of the event through the memory feels like the event is happening all over again in our heads and bodies right now. How can we not believe the reality we are feelings? Know that our bodies' feelings will always override our intellect because as we become lost in our feelings, intellect goes right out the window. It is a form of self-talk and self-hypnosis, and if we can't trust ourselves and our own feelings, who can we trust? The unreal memory has got to be real. Doesn't it? *(Psst—hey you. Wake up. Memories aren't real. They are creations in your head. They are stories you keep telling yourself, and then your body reacts to the signals in the mind. It's like watching a scary movie, and your body jumps when the door slams or the gun goes off. There is no event, no door slamming, no gun going off. Memories are all head games you play on yourself.)*

We will need to spend some time here. The active mind is the cauldron where our interpretations and perceptions are created. They are created from the data received into the active mind from the black box, which is the subconscious mind. The active mind receives data from two places: the subconscious mind and the body. The next diagram shows a model of that. In Chapter 2, we defined the term "active mind" as that unique interface between the mind, brain, and the central nervous system, where perceptions and interpretations are made. Can we reach out and touch the active mind with our finger? No. The active mind is a metaphor for that unique place were perceptions and interpretations spring forth.

There are two sources of input data and information in the active mind, the subconscious mind and the body, as stated above. However, the interaction of the two may not be clear, and the following diagram may be helpful. Recognize that the data from both sources are flowing into the active mind in a constant stream. Body and mind, even with all the subconscious mind's many functions and even with all the body's many internal systems and responsibilities, are always in constant communication; and they have to be, or they would both be in trouble. What a magnificent partnership they have.

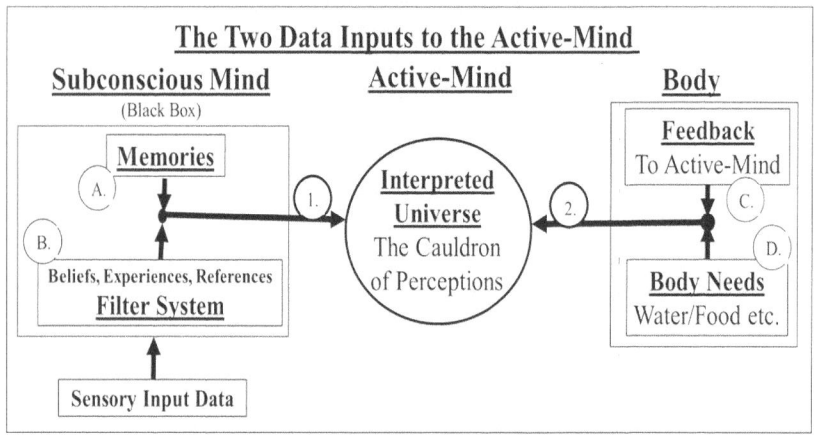

Diagram 21 - Two Inputs into the Active Mind

Input number one is a combination of two data inputs from the subconscious mind: memories, marked "A," and from the filtering system of incoming data, marked "B." Input number two is from the body, which also has two sources of data: feedback data as the body makes changes due to signals the active mind sends out, marked "C"; and data sent to the active mind due to the body's needs (for example, water, food, and rest), marked "D."

There is a constant flow of data into the active mind from these two input sources, and there is a constant flow of signals out of the active mind. When triggered by any means, data from memories are sent to the active mind; and awake or asleep, the senses pick up information, and the subconscious mind is processing it. Also dreams, both during the day or at night, are being created. At the same time, the body is sending data to the active mind as to what its needs and wants are (for example, the sun is too hot on the skin; or I'm tired, hungry, or thirsty; or I need to relieve myself; and so forth). Also there is feedback data as the body responds to signals received from the active mind. *(Can you appreciate why the mind and body has to operate at such a high rate of speed? There is just so much going on inside you at every second. And now your conscious mind has the function of telling you what has happened in that grander system.)*

From this continuous stream of data, the active mind creates perceptions and all our interpreted universes. These aren't snapshot pictures we put in a picture album. They are more like high- speed motion picture camera outputs, with universes coming into focus and morphing into one another so smoothly that we don't even notice the change; and they are all going at billions of bits per second. As each universe comes into focus, electromagnetic signals and chemical messages are sent out to the mind and body, and it responds as is appropriate for the created interpreted universes (for example, friend or foe, danger or relaxation). From those signals and messages, the body changes internal systems in response. As internal systems change, data is fed back to the active mind, which it uses to create new universes. And like Dorothy in *The Wizard of Oz*, we never know what's going on behind the curtain, where the wizard is. We know only what the conscious mind tells us, which is never the whole story. What we get from the conscious mind are just snapshots and headlines of what has happened.

Notice that the conscious mind isn't an active player in the above diagram; it reports to us only on what has already happened. Even though the conscious mind is the least informed and the last to know what is happening, it's all we know—which is to say we are the least informed and the last to know what the subconscious mind and body are doing. Since all the other active players in this operation are operating at lightning-fast processing speeds, out of conscious awareness, it is so hard to even imagine everything that is going on behind the curtain of the subconscious mind and in the body at every moment and every second.

When a memory is triggered and its data is brought back into the active mind, we know intellectually the event isn't happening now. So why does the body respond the way it does to the unreal memory? It isn't responding to the memory; it is responding to the active mind's created interpretation of the memory and the signals and messages sent out. The body knows only what the active mind tells it through its communication system. The body has no connection with the outside energy system or inside memories, so it relies only and completely on the active mind to tell it what is happening through the signals the active mind releases.

This cannot be said too often enough; our bodies aren't connected to the outside energy system in any way, and our active minds cannot tell the difference between data from the outside and data from an old memory. Look closely at the above diagram and notice that out of the subconscious mind is only one stream of data going to the active mind. In that stream is data from both the outside and our old memories. That data is always a combination of both, sometimes more outside data and sometimes more inside memory information and data; and the active mind doesn't know the difference. To the active mind, it's just data. *(What a system! Your body has no facilities to use the sensory data directly and must rely on your active mind through its signals, and the active mind must rely on the black box for its information. And in that stream of information from the black box is both new and old memory data, and the active mind can't tell which is which. What a kettle of fish. The body has no idea of what is happening until the active mind tells it. Again, everything must first be in your mind.)*

Now we may be thinking, *What is he talking about? I can see what's outside. I know what is happening around me. Man, you drive me crazy.* If that is our understanding, we haven't let go of our programming from our egoic selves, our habitual selves. The senses don't speak to the body. The body has no facility to capture or process the raw sensory input data and information. The senses communicate only with the subconscious mind, and the senses don't communicate in spoken words. The body has no way to use the data from the senses. *(I know it is counterintuitive to your conventional understanding, but that's the way it is—from sensory input directly to the subconscious mind to determine relevant data, then from the subconscious mind to the active mind for creations of interpretations and perceptions. From the interpretations and perceptions, signals are released to the body, and from the signals, your body responds. As the body responds, it feeds data back to your active mind, and now you "feel" what is happening in your body. All you know is what is in your mind. Remember, this event is happening at billions of bits per second, in nanoseconds of time. Your conscious mind reports to you the old news of what has happened, and then you think your pain and suffering are in your body. Notice that all pain and suffering are always a perception in the mind, not in the body, but you will consciously believe they are in the body. Crazy, right?)*

The conscious mind reports on what has happened in the body, but because of its slow speed, it has no way of knowing the body is responding to the active mind. It appears to the conscious mind that the body is responding to outside sensory input. Pay attention here because this is the tricky part. The conscious mind isn't connected to the outside environment either. It too is observing the active mind's interpretation and projects it into the outside energy system, so that through the conscious mind's reporting, we believe the body is responding to the outside environment when, in fact, the response is all happening in the mind. Everything is in the mind first and then in the body. Everything is in the mind.

If we could modify those signals and messages sent to the body in some way, the body's response to the memory's interpretation would be changed and modified. Keep in mind that the body isn't responding to the memory; it is responding to signals sent to it based on the interpretation of the memory by the active mind, and that is all happening in our heads. *(Whose head? Your head! It's all you doing it to yourself.)*

There are three ways of changing the signals the body responds to. The first is to change the filtering system of the subconscious mind, which will change the data sent to the active mind and used to create the interpretation and its memory of the event in the first place. The second is to heal and reframe past memories through forgiveness, self-awareness, and self-love. This will also change the filtering system. So basically, the first and second do the same thing; they change memories. The third way is to directly modify the signals and messages the active mind sends to the body. All these methods are interconnected, and in changing one, we affect the others. The ultimate goal is to change the negative memories we hold within us. Our world is the way it is because of what we hold within. We are the problem, but we are also the answer and the solution.

THE THIRD WAY

We have already shared ways of using the first two methods of working with memories in this read but not the third method, and that is because it is more esoteric and may seem strange to many. It is related to a much older understanding of how the body and mind

251

function together, along with their interactions and connections. To begin this journey, we must restate our earlier premise that "everything is energy," both outside and inside us. In the outside is the unmanifested raw material of everything energy, and inside are all the objects we have manifested through our imaginations, beliefs, experiences, and references, which are now memories in the subconscious mind. Everything in the subconscious mind is a memory. *(You may not have recognized it yet, but everything you know is a memory you created at some time in your life. And of course, you believe these memories are true. Then I come along and tell you, "They aren't real, true, or complete." That makes me a saboteur to your belief system, and your ego will fight hard to convince you I'm wrong and that memories are real. Well, that is because the ego has a hidden agenda to try to stay alive.)*

The two main paths for understanding the body's energy system is through the ancient Indian path of Ayurvedic medicine, which uses natural diet, herbs, and the body's energy system of chakras and nadis. These centers of energy in the body support the flow of prana energy or life force. The other path is through the ancient Chinese path of traditional Chinese medicine (TCM) of natural diet and herbs, the meridian system of rivers of energy that supports the flow of chi energy or life force. We aren't going into these systems in any detail. *(If you are interested in more detail, there is much information on the Internet about these two paths.)*

Our concern here is to acknowledge that it has been recognized for a long time, thousands of years, that the body is an energy system; and that there are laws and concepts as to how and why that energy operates and moves the way it does within the energy field in the body. In both of these approaches of Ayurvedic medicine and traditional Chinese medicine, balance is the goal for using them. What needs to be balanced? The energy systems in the body's whole energy field need to be in balance for us to be in health. When the energy in the body's field is out of balance, the body isn't at ease or is in disease; and when the body's whole energy field is balanced, the body is at ease and healthy. *(You may remember here that the reason the body gets out of balance is because it's responding to signals from the active mind. Whatever system is used to balance the energy in the body, it must include changing the signals from the active mind.)*

The two energy systems of Ayurvedic system, chakras and nadis, and of TCM and meridian and acupuncture points are interrelated. But again, our goal is to change how the body responds to negative memories and to heal our pain and suffering; therefore, we won't go into the interrelationship of these two systems. We only lightly touch on these systems to understand and heal from our pain and suffering. It is like driving a car; we don't need to know all the details of how a car is made, including its inner workings, to drive a car; and we don't need to know all the details of these systems to use them to develop an output response in the body.

When the body is under stress, it isn't at ease; therefore, it's out of balance. While there are many reasons for the body being in stress, our concern here is the out-of-balance condition caused by the body's response to negative, unreal memories; therefore, that is the direction of our quest and the direction we will be moving.

When the body begins responding to the signals and messages the active mind's negative interpretation of a memory sends, the body's energy system is thrown out of balance as it attempts to survive based on those signals; therefore, it will express an imbalance in the meridian and chakra systems in the body's energy field. For our purposes, we will use the meridian system in developing our model of healing.

When negative interpretations of the active mind cause the body to respond by moving into survival mode, it is out of balance, and negative energy is expressed in the meridian system. This out-of-balance condition can be cleared by many different methods, including neuro-linguistic programming (NLP), hypnosis, tapping, and more. *(Notice that there are several recognized tapping techniques. All have been shown to be effective, but we all develop a preference as to what works for us.)* Many times these modalities are used in combination. Talk therapy appears less affective and takes longer to cause permanent change because we are working at changes and reframing memories, and memories are the subconscious mind's programming. Talk therapy takes longer to approach these deeper realms of understanding in the subconscious mind and to cause effective change. "All meaningful and lasting change starts first in your imagination, then works its way out." Per Albert Einstein (Posted on June 30, 2013 by Barry, The Quotable Coach http://www. thequotablecoach.com/all-meaningful-and-lasting-change-starts-first-in-your-imagination-then-works-its-way-out/)

Using willpower, which is a conscious mind technique, can change external behavior, but most of the time we stop using it, because we run out of willpower long before we have ingrained the wanted behavior into the subconscious programming. Why would that be? Because as relationships in our world start getting better, the pressure to change is reduced, and we stop using willpower, believing we are healed. Why would that be? Because we believe we are cured and stop using our willpower; and of course, within a short time the old programming, which was just waiting in the shadows of the subconscious, starts right back up again. And out of the old programming will flow the old behavior. When it comes to a tug-of-war between the subconscious mind and the willpower in the conscious mind, the subconscious mind will win in the long run every time.

Our goal is to understand our pain and suffering, and to recognize that how the body feels is the source of our happiness and joy, and the source of our pain and suffering. Begin to appreciate the idea that how the body feels is the result of how the body responds to the mind; therefore, it is ultimately the mind that determines our pain and suffering, our joy and happiness. The body feels the way it does because of what the inner mind is doing. When we manifest pain and suffering, look to the mind for the cause. It's in changing our minds' perceptions that we change our lives, and by changing perceptions, we change our pain and suffering.

As we listen to our conscious mind, with its slow operating speed, telling us what has happened, we need to recognize and appreciate the fantastic processing ability of our subconscious minds, senses, and bodies; and it's all happening without the conscious mind being involved and without words. There is so much going on at so many different levels at such incredible speeds; we must acknowledge that what we think consciously is happening isn't happening the way we think it is happening. It's the conscious mind that tells us when we are sick and well. It's also the voice of the ego in our ear, and it can speak loudly and be quite compelling in convincing us that "it's the body's fault" we are sick. Poor body. Again, it's the scapegoat for the mind, but we've said that before, right? What does the body respond to? Only the mind.

ONE EXAMPLE

As indicated in the diagram earlier in this chapter, in the section "When We Recall a Memory" by changing its internal systems, the body comes into synchronousness with the active mind's interpretation of the memory based on the signals and messages the active mind sends it. The feedback loop from the body to the active mind affirms the synchronicity of active mind and body. The following diagram depicts the steps in the process.

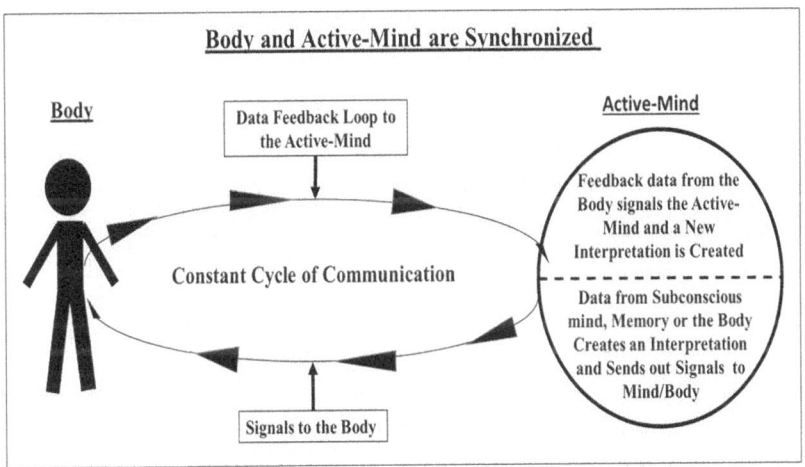

Diagram 22 - Body and Active Mind Coming into Balance

In that circular dance between the signals going to the body and the feedback data from the body going back to the active mind, the body changes its systems; and with the feedback from the body, the active mind changes its interpretation. At a certain point, signals going out and feedback going in will reach a balance and therefore agreement between active mind interpretation and the body's response. *(Notice again that this agreement takes only nanoseconds to be reached, and the conscious mind never knows this high-speed dance is going on.)*

However, if the feedback doesn't match the active mind's interpretation of the memory, what would the active mind do? An interesting question, is it not? We might have thought it would be impossible to have a conflict between body and active mind, with the body not following the signals sent to it and not doing what the mind tells it to do. This is the conundrum the active mind faces when we use techniques that change the feedback loop to the active mind.

One of the techniques to change the feedback loop is tapping. By tapping on selective acupuncture points in the meridian system, physiological changes happen in the body. The body's systems don't respond quite as intently, and the feedback to the active mind isn't synchronized with the active mind's signaling. If the corrective protocol of tapping is used, the body will feel better, and its internal systems won't change as much as they would have if we didn't tap. This positive change in the body will greatly affect the feedback data to the active mind, cause a shift in the active mind's interpretation, and therefore change the signals it sends back to the body. If we continue tapping, the feedback will again change to the active mind, and again the active mind will change its interpretation and signaling to the body. This can go on until an interpretation of the memory in the active mind is positive.

The egoic mind, the great trickster, must question its action and its interpretation of data it created from the memory; and it changes its interpretation based on the feedback information from the body. The body speaks back to the mind through the feedback loop, causing a reaction in the mind based on the new data entering the active mind, because when new data enters the active mind, it creates new interpretations, and new signals will be sent to the mind and body. This new changed interpretation is what will be consolidated back into the subconscious mind as a memory. We might think, *What happened to that old memory with all that negative energy?* It is gone and no longer exists. It has been changed out of existence. *(I know this seems like a dog chasing it tail, but look at it is way: when a memory moves into the active mind, the whole and complete memory is in the active mind; it's not a copy. While the memory is in the active mind, you changed it. It is now different; it is now a new memory. There is nothing of the old memory to restore. All you need to store and consolidate into the subconscious mind now is a new and different memory. You have no old memory. You aren't changing the event because it isn't there to change, and it is gone. All you are doing is changing your interpretation of the event, which wasn't real, true, and complete anyway. So you have exchanged a not-real negative memory for a not-real positive memory. That's not a bad trade-off.)*

When we reach a positive interpretation of the memory in the active mind and stop tapping, that positive memory is what gets stored in the subconscious mind. The old, negative memory doesn't exist anymore. A new memory is now in its place with that positive interpretation. *(You can still remember your memory; however, the negative intensity just won't be there. What else will happen? The memory will have a much lower status in the subconscious mind's filtering system. This will change the world you live in. I will introduce a different model later as to all the interactive changes one memory can have on the matrix of memories in the subconscious mind.)*

FOLLOWING THE TAPPING

Tapping on the body is one method of using the third way of changing the data presented to the active mind and thereby causing a different interpretation of memories, which will change the signals sent back to the mind and body. When the intensity in the body is raised by signals from the active mind, the energy in the body is out of balance; and this will be reflected in the meridian system.

By tapping on certain acupuncture points (acupressure points), the intensity in the body will lessen as the body's energy system begins to move back into balance; and the body won't be as tense, changing the body's systems. The feedback data to the active mind will be out of sync with the signals sent out by the active mind. Now by tapping, new data at a lesser intensity has entered the active mind through the body's feedback data, thereby causing a new interpretation with less intensity to be created. And again, signals are sent out to the mind and body but this time with lesser intensity.

If the intensity of the new interpretation isn't zero, tapping should continue in this back-and-forth process until the negative intensity is gone from the memory and the memory becomes positive. When this new memory, with zero negative intensity that is now positive, is consolidated into the permanent memory, it won't be used in the filtering process of the subconscious mind, which means the data sent to the active mind through the subconscious mind's filtering system will be different; therefore, our interpreted universe will be different and more positive, and the world we live in will also be more positive.

Tapping on the meridian system at selected acupressure points on the body will change the body's energy systems. This is a physiological change response in the body, and we don't even have to believe consciously it will work, because it's a normal and natural response of the body. It operates on the same level of response that all body work operates on. As an example, no matter how stressed or overwhelmed we are, when we get a massage, pedicure, or facial, we feel better; and we don't need to believe we'll feel better. We just feel better because there is a physiological response in the body, and the mind just relaxes into the feedback of the body.

When negative signals are sent to the body, tapping changes the feedback loop data sent back to the active mind from the body. Now we have a dichotomy in the active mind; we have the data from memory, and we have different data that doesn't match from the body's feedback loop after tapping. The feedback isn't in sync with the original signals the active mind sent.

What does the active mind do with its new accumulation of data from the body? It does what it does with all data it receives; it makes an interpretation and sends out new signals to the mind and body. The new interpretation will be less intense than the original memory because of the body's more positive feedback data. This will cause more positive signals to be sent to the mind and body, which will cause the body to change its systems again. In essence, what we have done is take a negative input of the memory to the active mind and a positive output feedback data, and collapse them together into a new interpretation.

The body responds only to the active mind, no matter what it appears like to the conscious mind. When we tap on the body, the body isn't aware of this act until the nervous system sends the information to the active mind and an interpretation is made; then signals are sent to the body. When we tap on the body, the physiological response takes place first in the mind. The body will respond to tapping through the active mind. Some ways of tapping may make it easier to respond to than others, but if we tap on the body, changes will happen.

While we have laid this process out in a discrete step-by-step process, the whole process affects the internal communication dance between mind and body; and it is happening at lightning speeds with much interplay between all the components of body, mind, central nervous system, and the active mind. Back and forth, back and forth, interpretations, new interpretations, new signals, more tapping, new feedback, new interpretations, different signals. Finally a neutral or positive intense memory is consolidated into the subconscious mind. Our world has changed, the subconscious filtering system has changed, and a new world will come into focus for us. How different that world will be depends on how intense and high on the filtering priority list the original memory was and on how many other negative memories were connected to it.

EXAMPLE OF TAPPING IN A GENERAL WAY

We will use a general format, a generic form of tapping, in our following example. While each different tapping method has its own protocol, they all use tapping on selected acupuncture points to break up negative energies trapped in the body that are attached to the memories. Here we have a method that clears trapped negative energy from the body in a short time. Do we need to know exactly how it works to use it? No.

For thousands of years all ships where made of wood because wood floats, and we traveled the world in our wooden ships. Then we discovered the laws of buoyancy. Now few ships are made of wood. Did we need to know the law of buoyancy for Captain Cook to sail around the world? Do we need to know all the details of how a car is made to use a car? Do we need to know exactly how tapping works to take advantage of its benefits? No, of course not. We have several good and sound theories as to how it works, but the reason why tapping is used is because it works. Statistically, its success rate is well above statistically significant evidence and above the placebo effect. And yes, there are over fifty scientific studies with peer reviews and evidence of its effectiveness. The concern isn't with its scientific evidence of how and why it works but with its success rate of use over time.

THE ORIGINAL MEMORY

Recall in Chapter 10, "Memory Coding System," that the coding system of a memory is by the modalities of Visual—Vx, Auditory—Ax, Kinesthetic—Kx, Olfactory—Ox, and Gustatory—Gx components. The x indicates a location in the storage matrix, where the specific memory is stored. By tapping on the body, the kinesthetic component of the memory is changed. By saying an affirmation as we tap, the auditory component is changed. By asking the person being tapped on to visualize the memory, the visual component is changed. The x of each modality is changed, and this changes the whole memory. The x of the modality represents the submodalities within the modality. As we change the submodalities, the memory changes. Therefore, the memory's stored location in the subconscious mind's storage matrix will be different. So when the changed memory is stored, it will be in a new location, because it's a new memory. And the old memory with its higher intensity? It is no more.

Anytime any one or combinations of the submodalities of a memory are changed, the original memory is gone, and a new memory is in its place. While details of the old memory are still there, the intensity and its pain and suffering will now be gone. Recall in Chapter 14, "Switching of Purpose and Means," that we discussed meta memories and how we change memories to a higher intensity by moving them in and out of permanent memory. As we bring the memory into the active mind, its interpretation is altered to fit our current belief system. What we are doing is changing one or more of the submodalities and making the memories more intense or less intense, or they remain the same.

Here again we must be clear: the changes are all made out of conscious awareness. It isn't something we are doing consciously, and it is happening very fast. The stories we tell in the conscious mind are after the memory has been changed. When the memory is stored in the subconscious mind, it will carry the new intensity energy signature. Tapping is a way of controlling the process of change by positively changing the memory to a lower intensity level, and it changes how the subconscious mind uses the memory in its filtering system.

The tapping protocol changes or breaks up the submodalities referenced in the memory. This changes how the active mind interprets the memory and therefore how the body responds, and the feedback data goes to the active mind. When the submodalities change, the original memory is no more. As the body feeds back new data to the active mind with less intensity, the active mind just does what the active mind does and creates a new interpreted universe, which will send new signals with less intensity of instructions to the mind and body. Now, if we continue tapping on the body from that lower intensity starting point, the V-, A-, K-, O-, and G-coded submodalities are changed. The signals from the active mind to the body are different because the interpretation of the data is different; then, of course, the new feedback data is less intense. This is a cool process.

Since this is all happening at billions of bits of data per second, it takes only a few rounds of tapping for changes to occur. This process can be quite confusing for the conscious mind, but not to worry; a new homeostasis and balance point will be reached with less intensity, and the conscious mind will feel better. And now here's a disclaimer: If the person has a secondary gain in keeping his or her pain and suffering, there will be a problem because basically his or her need to keep the perceived secondary gain will prevent him or her from changing and healing. *(If you have a gain in keeping a memory, choose another less intense memory to work with. As you begin changing and healing yourself, maybe that secondary gain will become less important as you resolve other issues; and when you are in a healthier place, then it may be time to change it.)*

EXAMPLE

When working with yourself or someone else, the steps of the process are something like the following. Keep in mind that each tapping protocol is different.

1. Pick a memory that causes discomfort when he or she thinks about it or when it is triggered. Use the SUD scale (subjective units of discomfort) from 0 to 10, with 0 being no discomfort and 10 being maximum stress; then select the level of discomfort felt as the memory is reexperienced. *A number must be given.* Don't accept the comment "It's high" or "It is way up there." Have the person commit to a number.
2. Now, with the selected memory in mind, make the intensity as high as he or she can take it by visualizing, hearing, and feeling by all the memory's aspects. State the highest SUD number reached. The higher the intensity, the quicker it will dissipate.
3. Tap using the tapping protocol of your particular process.
4. Then, after a round of tapping, test. What is the SUD number after tapping? What is the number now? Get him or her to state a number. If it's not zero, keep tapping, following your particular protocol.
5. Repeat tapping and testing until the SUD value is zero and has flipped positive (smiling).

Each time the SUD value changes, different feedback data and information is moving between the body and the active mind. The dichotomy of differences between the body's feedback and the active mind's interpretation will cause the active mind to develop a different interpretation of the information, based on the new feedback data from the body. Remember, the active mind just processes whatever data comes to it, and it doesn't care where the data comes from, because it really doesn't know. When the feedback matches the active mind's interpretation at a positive intensity, we have reached our goal. When the feedback doesn't match perception, change happens in the active mind's interpretation. The interpretation can actually be moved to the positive side of the SUD scale. Again, remember how fast this is all happening. The testing part of the process is the conscious mind reporting to us that the memory is no longer what it was.

So when we test the memory as it is now and the feedback is still zero or has flipped to positive, we can stop tapping. Break the trance state between the mind and body; for example, open the eyes, move the shoulders, stand up, move around, and so forth. The interpretation, with its new zero or positive intensity and emotional submodality changes, will be stored in permanent memory when the eyes open. After the memory is stored, one more test needs to be made. Have the client, or you if you are working on yourself, close his or her eyes and bring the now newly stored memory back into the active mind and try to bring back the negative intensity that was in the original memory again. If the intensity is still zero or positive, we are complete; and the memory will never have any intensity when recalling it into the active mind in the future. If any intensity is detected, go back to step number two in the process and start tapping until it has moved to 0 or positive intensity. Store it, break the state, and retest again. *(You, working with yourself or someone else, are creating a positive change to the remembered memory of an event. Again, it isn't the event you are changing because the event is gone. You are changing the unreal memory of your interpretation of the event. You are changing an unreal negative memory of an interpretation of an event to an unreal positive memory of an event that is never coming back. Don't listen to your ego. It will tell you, "It's against the law to change your interpretation of the past by changing your memories." They are your memories, and no one else has your memories. The memories aren't real, true, or complete; and they are all yours. You can change them. You aren't breaking any cosmic laws of the universe by changing them.)*

Memories are sometimes in clusters that are connected or entangled together. As one memory is changed and healed, another memory may be connected to it and supporting it. Then we will need to go through the process again for that newly identified energy trapped in the body. We need to "chase all of the pain" connected with the target memory to clear it completely. The subconscious mind is the metaphoric mind and will understand the metaphoric processes we have used to quickly and easily change, which is to say change its programming in its operating system.

As the high-intensity memories are changed, the subconscious mind's filtering system changes, and different data will get through the filtering process. When that happens, different data is sent to the active mind, and a different world will be brought into focus. Healing our negative past memories will create a new world for us; a new future will be possible, and a new present world will be there for us to live in.

CONSOLIDATION AND RECONSOLIDATION OF MEMORIES

There are several theories that are developed around how memories are stored, retrieved, and then restored. Again, we must stress and be clear on this point; they are theories, and no one knows for sure what is going on in the subconscious mind, that unknown black box. This will be just a thumbnail sketch of one of those theoretical approaches. The target theoretical approach is called "Memory Consolidation and Reconsolidation."

In this model, when the memory of an event is moved into permanent memory, it isn't put in one spot. Its modalities, submodalities, or aspects are separated and spread throughout the brain based on sensory input. For example, visual data is stored in the visual cortex (and so forth). There is a "memory trace" maintained in the brain or address as to where all those separate aspects of the memory are stored. In this theory, storing a memory may take hours, days, or even longer for all its different aspects to be completely separated and stored or consolidated into all its locations within the brain. The brain maintains the memory trace as a way that allows the brain to retrieve the separate parts; and by using the memory trace, the whole memory can be reclaimed and reconstructed. When the memory is retrieved, there it is in the brain as a complete memory. The theory isn't too clear as to how the memory trace works and how it gets triggered or activated, but there is a hologram in the brain of the retrieved memory.

In studies, when the subject person is stimulated by a request from an operator into remembering a memory, certain clusters of neurons are activated or excited in the brain and can be observed; and when a different memory is requested, different neurons are activated. This leads to an acceptance that memories are stored and retrieved from within the brain.

We need to look closely at some of the assumptions of this theoretical approach. How is the memory stimulated from the outside into presenting itself inside for investigation? It must be stimulated through sensory inputs because that is the only way any outside information can get inside us. In the studies the operator tells the subject to recall a memory. In this theory, the request for the memory goes directly to the brain; the memory is activated, and certain clusters of neurons are excited in the brain. However, the brain doesn't communicate in word language, which means the request needs to be translated from word language outside into the brain's non-word language inside. The programs that do that are in the subconscious mind and are all memories in the misty past of childhood learning. Input data never goes directly anywhere but to the black box. I have used the term "active mind" as the interface between the mind, the brain, and the central nervous system. It's the signaling from the active mind that causes the brain to "light up." And it seems to happen in the following way maybe:

1. The verbal request is given for a memory from the outside in word language. *(Notice that the request can be for anything, and the same process would be applied. Most of the time, the conscious mind has no idea what triggers memory.)*

2. Senses send the data to the subconscious mind, which must translate and filter the data because it is meaningless as received; then it sends the filtered data to the active mind.

3. The active mind interprets the data and sends out signals to the mind and body based on its interpretation.

4. The subconscious mind retrieves the memory as is appropriate for the signals received from the active mind. *(I need to repeat this again because we so easily slip back into the egoic mind-set. This is all happening at billions of bits per second. To the conscious mind, which is all we know, that looks for all the world as if the outside is talking directly to the brain and the brain is responding directly to the outside request from inside the brain. This isn't true and looks*

that way only because of the slow operating speed of the conscious mind. The subconscious mind operates faster than the instruments being used to read the clusters of neurons being excited in the brain can operate. You need to get this; the subconscious mind does things so fast. You or I will never understand, but we will think we do because of our egoic-soaked belief system and the slow conscious mind.)

In the study, the active mind is using the filtered input data from the black box of the subconscious mind to give meaning to the request for a memory. Will clusters of neurons be activated and excited in the brain? Yes, because the brain is part of the active mind. Does that mean memories must be stored in the brain? No. Do we really need to know exactly where memories are stored to create a working model for the black box of the subconscious mind? No. *(I am not the person to go deep into this theory, Consolidation and Reconsolidation, of memories. It's not the model I am using. If you want to know more about the model of consolidation and reconsolidation, there is much information on YouTube and the Internet. What is the point in bringing this example up? To let you know there is much work being done on the topic of memories, the subconscious mind, and where memories are stored; but as of yet, no smoking gun is available. They all have many unanswered questions.)*

BACK TO OUR MODEL

Sensory inputs go directly to the mind. Why would that be? Because they need to be decoded, filtered, and manipulated to fit what is important for us before it can be used. While some of our communication is word language, the mind, brain, central nervous system, and body don't communicate in words. *(Think about it. Even as your eyes follow the words across this page, the information goes to the mind because the words are first input data to the mind; and second, the data must be decoded and converted into another language before the brain and central nervous system can use it. Words are symbols of something else and must be decoded. And the input data must come to the mind in a language for which we have a program to convert it into a language our brain and nervous system can use. If our eyes follow the words across this page and the language on the page is a foreign language we don't know, the information will be meaningless to the subconscious mind and won't get through its filtering system. Language is a secondary learned skill, and the programming for that conversion into body, brain, and central nervous system is in the subconscious mind as memories. The conversion from spoken language into nonverbal language of the mind or brain happens at billions of bits per second, as I have said before. You may still believe that bodies are what communicate. No! No! Only minds communicate. Refer to Chapter 14, "Switching of Purpose and Means," in the section "The Body as a Frame." To stimulate a memory, we must go through the mind. Is your brain part of the process of retrieving and working with memories? Yes. It is part of the active mind. Will clusters of neurons be activated or excited as the brain works within the partnership of the active mind? Yes. Does that mean memories are stored in the brain? No. Here we may be thinking,* Okay, smarty pants, if the memory isn't in the brain, where is it? *I don't know, and I don't care. You don't need to know what is going on in the black box to use its results.)*

Remember that memories can also be stimulated by internal thoughts and outside events. But for the most part, they present themselves because of outside triggers, which again must be decoded. Since memories are stored by information around the modalities of the senses, the triggers will usually stimulate one or more of the modalities (for example, an odor or fragrance, a taste, a touch or feeling, the way the wind blows, shadows on the wall, sounds, or maybe a song on the car radio). The senses send the information to the mind. However, it's how the mind selects and the active mind interprets that information that causes memories to move into our awareness through the active mind's interpretation, signaling the body to respond and finally on to the conscious mind. *(Again, you see in this process that the conscious mind is at the end of what is happening, and it is the least informed.)*

By using the medical model and Newtonian physics as our only tools, we are kind of locked out of developing theories using conscious and subconscious minds and the mind or body connection. However, if we are able to recognize that Newtonian physics is only a special case within quantum physics, we may be able to shift to a different understanding. This will be challenging to some to leave the small known and enter the larger possibilities and maybe the unknown. *(I'm sorry, but critical mass has not reached the point of making this paradigm shift to quantum physics on its own. But as we keep poking at it, trying to get it to shift, suddenly it will shift.)*

> **Remember**: We are using a different model for the storage and retrieval of memories in this read. I have chosen to use a model where memories are being stored and retrieved from the energy field around and within the body by the subconscious mind, the black box. It is when a memory is retrieved from the subconscious mind and enters the active mind that it can be reframed and healed. It is in that realm where the active mind and the body dance together, and it is there that changing the memory is possible.
>
> In the consolidation and reconsolidation model, the subconscious mind isn't part of that theoretical model. Both my model and theirs seem pretty wild, don't you think? Recognize that the excited brain activation is an effect, not the cause. Even in the consolidation and reconsolidation model, brain activation of the memory is an effect of the brain's activating the "memory trace," and the activation of the memory trace is another effect of an even deeper causal process that isn't known for sure at this time.

As the active mind and body dance together around a memory, if any of the aspects of the memory are changed, the original memory is no more. We now have a new memory, and the old one no longer exists. When the new memory is stored, it isn't a reconsolidation process because the old memory doesn't exist. We are consolidating a new memory, and it will carry all the changes in the modalities and submodalities into permanent memory.

With this understanding, in truth rarely is there a reconsolidation of memories because every time a memory is recalled from the subconscious mind, it's changed in some way. Either it goes up or down in intensity as we change aspects of the memory, or it remains the same. When we think about a memory, it gets worse or better in some big or small ways. *(I added the idea that memories are almost always changed in some way when recalled, because that is my experience. But then it's only a theory.)*

Why do recalled memories change, no matter what theory we are using? It is because of us. We will be physically and mentally in a different space than when the memory was first created from its original interpretation of the now-gone and never-coming-back event. Depending on our current state of mind, the recalled memory may get worst or better or remain the same based on us at the time of recall. However, if we have memories that are extremely negative emotionally and stressful, when recalled, we may need help to heal them, changing the energy around them and letting them go. Or maybe we just avoid dealing with them or thinking about them. If this is the strategy, we get used to pushing our pain and suffering away from us, and burying them out of our conscious awareness; they will still work deep in the subconscious mind and affect how we see our world. The true answer or solution is to heal them, changing the energy around them and letting them go.

Begin to appreciate the healing power of reframing and changing negative memories we have been dragging around. If we change a memory, what are we changing? Something that was never real, complete, or true. It is only in our heads, and no one else has our memories the way they do but us. If we reframe our painful memories and forgive ourselves, whom are we hurting? But beware our egoic self; it will fight hard to stay alive, which means keeping the past real and imprisoning us in the past we created.

Think about this: we are all flesh, blood, and bone. Those parts of us are made of particles, and they are all entangled particles. When we heal and reframe any one memory, to some degree we change all our memories. *(Oh no, I hope I'm not saying too much about the mind or body connection. I don't want you to get confused and get the ego whispering in your ear again that you are your body.)*

CHAPTER 17

Changing Vision

DEFINING VISION

To change our understanding of vision, we will need to redefine it. We think of vision as related to the eyes and what the eyes see. However, we now recognize that the eyes collect only wavelengths of energy data with no color and transmit the data to the mind. (Review Chapter 3, "Sensing Differently.") There are no objects to see in the outside energy field, only energy, which the eyes convert into electromagnetic informational data and then transmit it to the mind. It is the active mind that creates the objects with color as perceptions it has made from the data received from the subconscious mind. The eyes as such have little to do with what we see. The subconscious mind has more to do with what we think we see than the eyes do, because of the way it filters the data from the eyes and what it sends to the active mind. It is the active mind that creates all the objects and color we think we see through its interpretation of the data received. So seeing is an inside creative act and has little to do with any outside seeing with the eyes.

Here is an interesting thought. Since the eyes only transmit data and it is the mind that decodes the data to create the objects the way we think we see them, what creates the light that illuminates the objects in our inside world? I mean, in the optic nerve are only electromagnetic signals, no objects, just data like Morse code (on and off tones and clicks), and no illumination, only signals. Where does the illumination in our active mind's interpretation come from? Somehow the eyes must send some code within the data the active mind is decoding to create illumination, right? *(I mean, you don't have light going down your optic nerve into the mind, do you? If there was light going down the optic nerve, science would surely have uncovered that by now, right? So since there isn't light in the optic nerve, what is really being transmitted down the optic nerve, and why do you experience light in the hologram you have created in your head?)*

Here is another interesting question. When we recall the memory of a sunset over a sandy ocean beach, with a clear blue sky above, how is it illuminated? Where do the colors and light come from? Since it is only the active mind's construction in our heads and since there is no input data from the outside, where do the color and light come from in the recalled memory? There is only data from the stored memory in the subconscious mind, and the active mind is now interpreting the data into color, light, and action. Recall that the active mind cannot tell the difference between data coming from input-filtered data by the subconscious mind of an outside event, data coming from a stored memory in the subconscious mind, or data coming from the body's feedback system. To the active mind, it's all just data, and it will create an interpretation of any data received. The color we think we see outside is an inside interpretation, and the color and light we see in a memory are also the same kind of data. The code for the color may be in the data, but the color isn't. Color is an interpretation of data; that's it in a nutshell. Everything must be in the mind first, and then there is color. *(Are you getting this? Now don't just think,* I wish he would stop asking, "Are you getting this?" He's starting to piss me off. *These questions are foreign and outside your normal way of looking at and understanding your world. Here again, the goal is to understand your pain and suffering differently. This is challenging, because to understand your pain and suffering differently, we need to call into question what your world is, how is it created, and how it is maintained the way it is with all your pain and suffering.)*

It is our created inside interpretations that manifest all the objects we believe are outside us. It is the unmanifested energy information and data the senses transmit to the mind, which the subconscious mind picks over and through, looking for relevant data to send to the active mind, that creates the inside manifestation of our world. Our filtering system is the cause of our world being manifested the way it is; therefore, the world we live in is an effect of what we are doing inside our minds. And our memories determine what we are doing in that inner mind. To have a different effect or world, as we have said before, we must change our past memories. Trying to change the outside perceived effect won't change the inside created cause; besides, it is impossible to change the outside subtle field of everything.

When we try to change the outside world. We are trying to change an effect, not its cause, and this won't last long. *(By the way, what you think of as an outside effect is really only an inside creation. We just said, "You cannot change the outside subtle field of everything." Since you cannot change the outside subtle field of everything, the only thing left to change is you.)* As stated before, if we want to have a different world, we must change what we hold inside, which is to say our memories. And to change a memory, we must change what we hold within the memory, which are its modalities; and submodalities, which are the data in those memories.

What we think of as seeing is all done inside, where there is no light; and it is only a product of our interpretation of the data from the eyes after the subconscious mind has filtered and manipulated that data. Therefore, to change our vision, we need to change our perception of the data received. We have spent a lot of time on how to change perception, and it all comes down to healing the past, which will change the subconscious mind's filtering system. This will cause different data to be mined from the incoming information, and with different data sent to the active mind, a different world will come into focus inside us. *(I know I've said this before, but it is so counterintuitive to your programming that it needs to be recognized and understood from many different vantage points.)*

The method for healing the past is forgiveness, and that is all about forgiving ourselves. Forgiving another person or being forgiven by the other person isn't that important. Forgiveness has nothing to do with the other person. Whether we forgive has nothing to do with the other person and what we may think about the other person and the situation. We need to change our view of things and to realize forgiveness has only to do with us. All we are doing as we forgive ourselves is reframing and letting go of unreal, untrue, and incomplete, old negative memories that are inside us around an interpretation of an event that is gone. Oh, but how we believe we can't change them and that they are fixed forever inside us and that those other people involved in the event must forgive us. And of course that is what our egoic-created self-identity would like us to believe. *(Can you see that whatever you think you need to forgive or be forgiven from is about an event that is over and gone and never coming back? The only person you need to forgive is you. Why? Because all you have left of the event is your memory. By forgiving yourself, you are changing and reframing your memory; and as you do, a different world will come into focus for you. Whose memory are you changing? Only yours and no one else's. Later I will add a different and larger understanding of self-forgiveness.)*

Forgiveness is an inner practice; we might even call it a spiritual practice, because it is beyond the body and the conscious mind. And it is beyond the other person in the event that is gone, and it is also beyond the illusion of this life. To the ego, forgiving others is foolish and without gain; unless there are guilt and sin we have attached to the other person, then we can feel benevolent and saintly when we forgive him or her. As for forgiving ourselves, we can't do that, can we?

To forgive guilt and sin, we must first make them real by recognizing and acknowledging that there is some guilt or sin to be forgiven, which means we must first make them real for us so we can, or maybe not, forgive ourselves and others. This brings us back to seeing the sinner and ourselves as bodies, which is also what the ego would like us to believe. When we know and accept that we aren't bodies, forgiveness becomes a completely different process. It becomes an internal healing path; and as we will see later, our forgiving of ourselves changes the perceptions of all involved in the memory of the event we are forgiving.

We and they have made errors. Whatever we think we need to forgive and heal from, they are only errors in perception on the part of both ourselves and the other people. We need to see forgiveness differently, and to see it differently is to change our vision. We need to change and let go; in other words, we need to change our inner perception of the situation, which is now a memory; and again, it is an unreal, untrue, and incomplete memory we are changing. *(I know, the memory seems and feels real in the body, like the event is happening again when you vividly remember it; but come on, it's not real. The event is gone and over. Or you may be thinking,* They did it to me on purpose. How can I just let it go? *You may feel that some compensation is needed, and that may be so. However, forgiving yourself is about giving yourself permission to heal and find peace of mind. If compensation is needed, then pursue it with an open mind and a peaceful heart. As for forgiving the other person, I will address that later.)*

If we are in error, we need to change our vision and forgive ourselves and the other person. If we believe we have been erred against, we need to change our vision and forgive ourselves for being so offended and sensitive at the time, and we need to forgive the other person for his or her error in perception. If we have erred or are the one erred against by another, it is still an error in our vision because the memory we created of the event, which is now gone, would have been completely different if our vision had been different in the first place. Forgiveness is an opportunity to choose again and to choose peace of mind instead of what we did in that moment. *(Please don't try to see this through the worst memory you can remember. At this point in changing your vision, you should be working only with small offenses and irritations, not the major conflicts that have ever happened to you.)*

The error is now a memory; and like all memories, it isn't real, complete, or true. The event the memory depicts is gone and over, and yet we hang on to the memory as if it were real and true and happening right now in our bodies when we think of it. We have an inside scale of our errors from bad to worse and from worse to worst and to the worst of the very worst. In learning how to forgive ourselves, we should start by picking errors that have a SUD scale number of 2 or 3. Gain some success. We need to work our way up to the worst of the worst.

We may feel, "Well, if I forgive them, it makes what they did all right, and it's not." We need to forgive so we can heal. Holding on to our wounds by picking at our scabs keeps us in pain and suffering. It doesn't affect the other person; it affects only us, because the other person will have completely different memories about the situation than we do. Withholding forgiveness, thinking it will cause the other person pain and suffering, keeps us in pain and suffering, and it has no effect on them. Forgiving gives us a great gift because it offers ourselves peace of mind. Retain the lessons learned within the experience and let go of the rest. Holding on to our pain and suffering by not forgiving simply doesn't help and can only be the cause of more pain and suffering for us.

A note here: in some dances of pain and suffering, both dancers, because of their guilt and self-loathing, want to keep this macabre dance of pain and suffering going as a penance for something they believe is beyond forgiveness; and so they continue flogging and beating themselves and the other dancer as punishment. This dance can be emotional and sometimes physical. It is healing that is needed here, not punishment, and an understanding that the events are long gone and over. They are only the memories the two dancers are reacting to, and they can be changed, because they aren't real. They are living deep in their own personal, desperate illusion and cannot see that all they need to do is to change by forgiving themselves. *(How do you do that? By clicking the heels of your ruby-red shoes together and saying, "Even though I have made errors in my perceptions, I deeply and completely love and forgive myself." This may have to be said many times before it sinks in. It might also help for you to tap on yourself as you say it.)*

When we get serious about changing and restoring our peace of mind, which is the say changing our vision, we need to state many times, "I am determine to see this differently and heal!" To heal is to change and let go of the negative memories of events that are long gone and over anyway. How can we do that? By acknowledging that what we think of as our past isn't real, complete, or true; it's a created illusion. When we are determined to change our vision and see things differently, the whole universe comes to our aid, and illusions dissolve. And how great that would be!

WHAT IS OUT THERE?

As the senses capture data from the outside subtle field of everything, it is just information; therefore, it has no meaning at all to the senses. It's just raw data and meaningless, at least to the senses. However, once it's filtered and sent to the active mind, it is perceived into meaningfulness.

The meaning is coming from our inside perception of the outside data, not from the outside data. Since meaning is an inside perception, all that "everything" out there in the subtle field is meaningless until we bring it inside and think about it through the lens of our past. The meaning of any and all objects in our world isn't coming from the energy outside us. Nor is it in the data our senses transmit to us from the outside subtle field, because what is in the outside energy field is neutral and meaningless until the active mind interprets it and gives it meaning. This has all been said and gone over previously, but our egoic-soaked belief system will quickly snap us back into the old paradigm unless we keep repeating it. *(For you, to appreciate that you put the meaning into all the objects in your life is difficult to see, because of your programming. As you look at this book in your hand or at your iPod with this read in it, it is meaningless. Look around the space you are in. All the objects in your space are meaningless, including your lovers, children, friends, car, home, and shoes. You must interpret meaning into each of them every time you observe them. And it happens so fast that your conscious mind – you know how slow it is – will project and report to you that their meaning is in the outside object or person. Think about it for a moment. When you are happy with your lover, you give them a certain meaning. If, however, you are unhappy with your lover, you give them a different meaning. What made the difference was not your lover but your interpretation of them in the moment that determined their meaning to you. Everything in your world is your interpretation, and the meaning of those things change because your attitude about those things change.)*

With that understanding, everything outside us is neutral and meaningless until we think about it. When we are offended, it isn't something that happens to us from the outside that offends us; it is what we have created inside us that is offending us. Yet how quickly and easily our egoic self blames the person outside us for our inside creation of being offended and for the discomfort we feel. Why are we offended? Because we have a button on us that has been pushed. We believe the other person has personally attacked us. In most instances, we aren't physically under attack from them, but the beliefs we hold inside us are being attacked. Since our beliefs are who we think we are, we interpret an attack on our beliefs as a physical attack on us; and since our ego is integrated into our belief system, which is who we think we are, it gets bruised. Hence, we personally feel we are under attack and must counterattack to save our egoic selves.

Being offended could cause us to be sad and depressed or angry and hurt. It could affect our health or maybe cause some pain and suffering. Maybe we might stop talking to the other person. When we are offended, we never know what direction that energy will go. One thing is for sure: wherever thoughts go, energy flows.

How can we protect our health? Forgive ourselves and reframe the memories of our offenses from the past. Stop and think, *Is it worth my peace of mind to hold on to this offense? Can I change my vision and reframe this old memory?* We know that in the heat of the moment, we may overreact because we were caught off guard. It is the ego that convinces us to hold on to the offense. Most of the things we get offended over aren't big things. They are small comments, little slights, and things that happen at family gathering, at work, with neighbors, at church, and so forth. Let them go and save our health and peace of mind. Forgive them, even if we may not feel they should be forgiven. Forgive them, because we deserve the peace of mind that comes with true forgiveness. The event is over, and all that's left is an incomplete memory, a residue of what is over and gone; and it was never the way we thought it was anyway. *(Get your ego out of the process. It will always blame others, because it doesn't want you to change. Change is death to your ego.)*

Some may think, *Well, the hell with them. I'll just stay away from them. I just won't talk to them.* Here's the thing. We get offended because of what is inside us, not because of them. Hiding from them won't heal us or disconnect our buttons. Again, if we get offended once a year, we will work the offense out and get over it. However, if we get angry, upset, and offended two or three or more times a week or a month, we have issues from the past that haven't been dealt with, reframed, and healed. They will affect our health, well-being, relationships, and peace of mind as we carry that energy around. Being constantly offended has effects on our health; and to gain peace of mind, the causal memories must be healed. When we are determined to see things differently, we open up a wormhole, a pathway into the subconscious mind where the cause will be found. It's all in the mind. *(When you isolate from other people or a person, you are limiting your life as to where you can go, what you can do,*

277

and who you can see. I know you will think, It's the solution for me. *But here is the thing. Deep inside you the memory is still at work and affecting how you see your present world. Whether you ever see or deal with that other person again, by forgiving yourself and them, you are healing yourself. You remove the poison from your wounded self.)*

BEING UPSET

Regardless of whatever we think we are upset about, the issue is never what we're really upset about, because what we think we are upset about is all conscious mind chatter, an effect, and a reflection of a button that was pushed and connected to a past memory or cluster of memories. What we are really upset about rests in our deep programming in the subconscious mind. We know only what the conscious mind tells us, and part of the conscious mind's function is to come up with reasons why we behave and do the things we do, so we and others won't think we're crazy. Oh yes, and again, the conscious mind is the least informed and the last to know anything about what is happening in the mind and body. The reason we are upset is because of what is going on inside us at the subconscious level, and its interpretation in the active mind; and the matter has little to do with the other person or situation outside us because they are neutral until we think about them. The person or situation in front of us is a reflection of the original causal memories lost from conscious awareness and deep in the past; and those causal memories may go all the way back to childhood. *(What is needed is to find a different understanding and to heal the causal problem, which isn't what is happening now that makes you offended. However, what is offending you now can be a door that leads to a path that will bring you to your causal problem for healing.)*

At this point, someone might be thinking of all the worst-case scenarios and might say, "Okay, Mr. Smarty Know-It-All, what would you do in this situation? How would you handle that situation, ah? Tell me!" We are changing how we create our vision. We are retraining our understanding of how we operate. We start with small upsets. After playing with little things first, we gain some success and understanding in healing and changing little things first. As we gain experience in how to resolve little concerns, more complicated issues will work themselves out. We are powerful creators of our world. *(This is a repeat of what I stated before. Start small and work your way up to more embedded and chronic issues.)*

I SEE LONDON, I SEE FRANCE, I SEE SOMETHING THAT ISN'T HERE

Seeing something that isn't there is why we are offended and upset in the first place. Here we are right now in the present moment, and with us is something that isn't here. Now that's an oxymoron to have something that isn't here. But we easily forget we are living in an illusion, and it is all around us all the time. It's why we can't experience the present moment as it truly is.

If we were to see anything as it is in the present moment, we would have to become as little children with eyes full of wonder, innocence, and excitement at experiencing this present moment in all its splendor as it is. To do that, we would have to let go of our interpretations and judgments we use to distort what is here now. What isn't here but is our past, our filtering system, our lens, through which we distort the present. And what is the past? Memories. Just memories.

We know the past distorts the present, don't we? We should know that by now because we've mentioned it throughout this whole read. But it is so counterintuitive to our belief system that without constantly bringing it into our awareness, we slip back into unconsciousness and the ego's realm; we slide into the realm of believing the past and its memories are real. The past is over, but the unreal interpretative memories of the past linger on in our subconscious minds.

Not all memories distort the present. Most memories are neutral or have very little emotional charge and won't be used to filter and obscure the present moment. Even good and happy memories distort the present, but their effect isn't as damaging. However, negative memories can keep us imprisoned and locked in the past. This causes the future to look much like the past and may cause depression or anxiety to enter our lives. What is between the past and the future? The infinitely thin and always here, the present moment where we live; and the now moment will be negatively distorted or not, depending on our filtering system, which is the lens of the past through which we see the present.

REVERSE MAGIC

A "stage magician" presents us with magic tricks, which they hide from us on the stage, in their pockets, and up their sleeves. Things appear and disappear, as if they came from nowhere all by themselves; it's a magic show, you know. The magician's sleight of hand manipulates us, and our minds are overwhelmed and distracted. How exciting is that. Things appear out of thin air and then disappear again. It's all fun and exciting.

We also make magic but in a reverse kind of way. Our senses bring the outside data to our minds, inside us, in great quantities of information from the outside subtle field of everything; and nothing is hidden. It's all there in that incoming information, and it's all out in the open. Then our subconscious minds mine the data, pick over and filter the information, and use only those parts of the data that match our past experiences, expectations, and what we are familiar with. We take the new, exciting, and different out of the information and keep only the old and familiar parts that fit into our history, our paradigm, and through the lens of our egos. Looking at the information through our lenses of the past creates our present interpreted universe, which will be much like yesterday. In fact, 95 percent of what got through our filtering system yesterday will be about the same 95 percent that will get through our filtering system today; so today will look much like yesterday.

We start with everything from the subtle field; and then by filtering the subtle everything through our past beliefs and memories, we create tricks of perception, which we play on ourselves. By filtering the present through our past, we create what we believe is the present moment, which it isn't, but we believe it is; and we do that all the time in this illusory world. Therefore, by using something that isn't here in the present, our past, we create something that isn't here in the present either, at least not the way we think it is, and that is our interpreted universe, which is never the complete present moment.

Now for the real magic. We believe the present moment we created by our perceptions is really here and is real, complete, and true. How is that for real magic? Look closely and don't miss the magic; we absolutely believe our created perceptions are absolutely true and real events; and we will fight to the death to save our egoic-self, the great trickster that tells us it's all true. What great and powerful magicians we are. *(Even now you may be thinking,* That's just dumb. I know exactly what is going on and what's happening right now. I have my senses and my wits about me. *That's the point; you don't. You don't see the magic. You are listening to your conscious mind because that's all you know, and it is the least informed and the last to know anything that is happening in the present moment. But oh, my God, don't you and I believe we know what is happening in the present? It's so easy to slip seamlessly into the illusion of the egoic realm. Once you accept and know you are in an illusion, your vision begins to shift, and your world will change.)*

NOTHING IS AS IT SEEMS

It's a rare occasion to be completely in the present moment without the past, because what we think of as present is filtered and manipulated data; and then that distorted data is interpreted into what we think is the present. As mention before, only innocent, small children can accept and be in the wonderment of the present moment the way it is, because of how little past they have. They can reference and filter the present moment; and their minds are open. Think of the joy a small child before age six has at Christmas; it gives us joy just to watch them. That is because they are living in the moment. However, we who are more learned than a child are obsessed with our unreal past. If we don't have some reference in our past for the incoming information of what is in the present, we throw it out; therefore, we don't and can't see the present as it is. "Unless I know the mechanism for how it works, it's not real," we might say. To "know" indicate past experiences, which is to say, "I'm not going to see what is there. I'm only going to see what is familiar to me." That is to say, "I'm going to see only what I want to see and hear only what I want to hear." Working with the past so preoccupies our internal processing that the present moment is lost.

As we move through our world, we keep bumping into things. We look at the object we bumped into through our internal-created perception of the object inside us, which isn't with our eyes, because the eyes only transmit data to the mind, but then we knew that, didn't we? The eyes don't "see" anything but energy. What we bumped into is energy, and it is the active mind that decodes the data sent by the eyes through the subconscious mind's filtering system. Then the active mind makes a perception of that energy based on our past to determine what the object is we bumped into; and all that happens in a nanosecond, so fast that our conscious minds believe the object is outside us and is what it tells us. This all happens at millions of bits of data per second. Then, after the perception is made, the conscious mind, operating at its slower processing speed, reports to us on what we think the object is we bumped into; and of course, that all depends on our past experiences, and the object we think is outside will be an internal creation.

Since our mind's eye, which is to say the active mind, makes interpretations only from filtered and manipulated data, we never completely see what is there. What we see is through our perception, not through the eyes at all; and it is always something different from the reality of what is out there. *(I know, I have said this before; what you bumped into feels so real in the body that it must really be there, outside you. But it is only a perception of that energy in the active mind, which then sends signals to your body. It's not the object your body feels but the mind's interpretation of what is there. What we think of as being out there is a creation inside the active mind.)*

IS THAT A CUP I SEE BEFORE ME?

It's all energy; that's all that's there. So why is it that what we aim our eyes at looks like a chair, a door, a rock, or a car if all there is energy? An interesting question, right? Imagine I'm holding a cup in my hand; and as we look at it, I ask, "Do you see this cup in my hand?" We might think, *What a silly question. Yes, I see the cup in your hand! These questions are getting dumber and dumber.* But what makes this cup, the cup you see in my hand, the way it is for you? "Another not-so-smart question," we may say, until we think about it.

We look at the energy with our senses. The data and information go through our inside filtering system, where the data is compared with all our past beliefs, experiences, references, and memories of all the cups and all the things that perform the same function as cups (for example, things holding liquids to drink out of, such as glasses, paper cups, our hands, sippy cups as children, and so forth). Then there are all kinds of past memories about cups and how we drink from them. They are all used to match and compare the incoming data to *this cup*; and information is added, generalized, subtracted, and manipulated. Then that data is pushed on to the active mind. where we rationalize, generalize, delete, and combine data to make our interpretation. If I drop *this cup* and you have some idea of whether it will break, you don't know from *this cup* in my hand. That information can come only from your experiences with other cups from the past. Can we see why we can experience the present moment only through the past and why you can't know or see *this cup* in my hand the way it is, but must know it only through the lens of your past? *(At this point, don't think about whether it's a good or bad thing you know whether the cup will break. Look at the model I'm presenting. You never see the present moment the way it is. You can see it only through the lens of your past. Do you get that, and does it make sense to you yet?)*

I know, we absolutely believe we are seeing this cup, but we are not. It is our perception of the cup we are seeing. We are seeing through the lens of our past and can't see this cup as it is. We don't experience this cup that is there. What we are experiencing is a creation or a conglomerate of all the cups we have ever experienced. Every object and situation we experience in the present moment is like this cup, and it is never seen the way it is; and the cup I hold is unseen as itself even by me. Once you define an object and name it, it slips into your subconscious mind, and you never see it the way it is again. It was the Danish philosopher, mystic, and theologian Kierkegaard who made the observation, "Once you label me, you negate me." Once you name me, you never see me again; you only hear my name and know me from your past, but you never know me. I'm always filtered through your lens of the past, just like this cup.

The name we give an object is a symbol, a metaphor, for something beyond the name. Yet when an object is named and defined, we no longer have to look at the object. We just say or think the name, and now we know all we need to know about the object, the person, or a people; and we don't need to deal with them directly again. Language becomes part of our filtering system. Language becomes the brush with which we color our world. Language alone can cause others to do wonderful or terrible things. The power of language to affect the world we live in, which is our internal created world, was demonstrated on Sunday, October 30, 1938, when a radio drama *The War of the Worlds* was aired.

It was Halloween Eve, and the radio station wanted to have a scary program, so they reworked H. G. Wells 1898 novel *The War of the Worlds* to fit our modern language news broadcasting methods. The director was Orson Welles, who went on to become a filmmaker and actor. He was the narrator in the radio drama that Halloween night. The program ran with no commercials. At the start of the program, they made it very clear that it was just a scary story. However, some people tuned in after the program had started and had no idea it was only a reenactment of an old novel. Through the power of language used in the drama to create perception, people believed the fake news broadcast. They called friends and family members, who turned the program on, and called more people. And like a virus infection, panic broke out. People grew scared, and the police were called. The fake news broadcast kept running, because in the broadcast studio, they had no idea anything was wrong. The radio station's phone switchboards were overwhelmed, and no calls could get in. Telling people one at a time over the phone that it was a fake news show didn't stop the panic. At the end of the show, all was made clear. However, there was a big investigation after the event, and broadcast rules changed (Wikipedia, "The War of the Worlds [radio drama]").

Different languages create different worlds from the same outside energy system. Think of how Shakespeare used language in *Julius Caesar*. Marc Antony turned the crowd of funeral mourners into a weapon of mass destruction, starting with the famous phrase, "Friends, Romans, countrymen, lend me your ears" (*Julius Caesar*, Act III, Scene II). Words are symbols for something else.

Once we have made a perception of the filtered information through our past, the reality of the object is really unimportant to us. Our perception becomes the only reality we have or care about. So when we look at a cup, are we really seeing that cup that's in front of us? No. We are seeing a facsimile based on our experience with similar and familiar information from our past. We aren't seeing this cup in front of us. Now some may become anxious by that thought and think, *No, no. That's not true! I know I'm really seeing that cup. Look, it holds water. Look, I feel it on my lips. I can test it scientifically. You're wrong, you're wrong. I see that cup. I see this cup right in front of me as it is.* Oh, how we struggle to keep our perceptions and make them real, which is to say our beliefs, experiences, references, and memories from the past. They are all created out of whole cloth and kept deep inside us in that black box. We know that, don't we? Which is why we experience nothing as it really is. Remember what we stated before. "The observer affects the observed." To say we, as the observer, affect the observed is to say, "I change what I observe to fit my past and the lens of my ego." Since we each do the same thing and since we have consensus agreements, the reality of the same thing is never seen as the same thing by both of us, but we will agree that it is.

A scientific fact is that "we find what we look for or die trying." So if we know what we want to find, the black box will keep sorting through the input data until it finds it and in the process throw out all the things we don't want to find; and the conscious mind will never know it. Why? Because it never knows what goes on in the subconscious mind, for what we want to prove we keep looking and testing for until we find it. This is how most "scientific studies" are made. I have a concept of what I want to prove, and I develop a study to prove it; and I will keep tweaking my study until I find it. *(You probably know that some scientists get paid big bucks to prove very scientifically that something is true, and they will. In some cases, it will be true for just a very small sliver of the experimental data. But when you add the right language, it becomes the gospel truth and becomes the unquestionable scientific gospel truth. Who would question the findings? Not me. I'm not a scientist. The white coat of the scientist, along with his or her credentials and pedigree, is very hypnotic. There is an old saying: "If you want to know the truth, follow the money." Money can create new truths right in front of our eyes out of thin air. You know that, don't you?)*

We aren't objective in our researching; we are subjective. There may be many new things uncovered as we look and test for what we want to find, but if those new things aren't what we are looking for, we won't see them and will disregard them as we continue looking for what we want to find. And we will do that until we find what we are looking for. Other people may even point out the new things to us, and we will still "negate them," because that's not what we want to find.

This is as true with physical cups and relationships as well. We see what we want to see and hear what we want to hear, and we all do that. To change and see things differently, we may need an emotional slap alongside the head with a two-by-four of a significant emotional event. Many times illness, the end of a relationship, or the death of a loved one is that emotional event of awakening.

Every object and event we encounter is seen and experienced the same way, through our past. We don't see the object in front of us; we can see only a facsimile or likeness of what is there based on our past; and it appears to be so real, complete, and true, doesn't it? We can never encounter any object the way it is; we can only experience it the way we are, as defined by our individual past. Here is an interesting understanding. The next cup we experience will have within it the experience of the interpretation of the last cup that was in front of us; and we still won't see the cup in front of us as it is, but we will believe we do. The process is seamless to the conscious mind, and we will always believe we are seeing the object in front of us as it is, because of the slow conscious mind's reporting system. Illusions work that way, you know.

RELATIONSHIPS AND CUPS

Relationships are like cups. We may not want to think so, but our relationships are the way they are because they can be the way they are as seen only through the lens of our past, which includes all our past relationships going back to our very first relationship. A relationship isn't experienced uniquely as it is. Like everything else in our lives, it can be experienced only uniquely the way we are. *(A disclaimer statement: You will experience the relationship the way you are, after the honeymoon phase, because during that phase you are operating on a chemical high and aren't your true habitual self, and neither is the other person. You override your habitual self during the honeymoon to impress the new partner; and for the most part, it is unconscious to you, and you will think you are being you, but you're not. This phase can go on for years or only months.)*

Unless we heal our past negative relationships, our current relationship may be much like our past relationships after the honeymoon is over. Maybe not in the beginning because of the chemical high of the honeymoon effect we are in at first; nevertheless, each partner's normal habitual personality will emerge from the chemical high in a short time, and the personality of the habitual self will step out of the shadows and into the light. This may take weeks, months, or years.

While relationships are more complicated than cups, underneath them is the same process. The external form of the person or situation may be different, but the content underneath, our programming beneath, will be the same. Why might that be? Because underneath in our deeper structure, we operate on the programming of our habitual selves. It makes no difference whether it is a business relationship or a love relationship. How we experience relationships is driven by forces deep within each separate partner's programming.

Those driving forces for the most part are unconscious and unknown consciously to us or our partner. Consciously, we know why we would like to partner with the other person, but the real reasons are beyond conscious awareness in deep structure. Conscious mind awareness is surface structure of the relationship, which is all we know, because the conscious mind does all the talking; and it operates so very slowly and is the least informed and the last to know anything.

The underneath driving forces are programs in deeper structure from older memories, are operating at lightning speeds, and are far outside our conscious awareness and understanding. Where might those older memories of relationships come from? They will be from our first models of how relationships work, our "family of origin." Will we know we are modeling our current relationships from our parents' interaction with each other and with us? No, not usually. And when relationships end, they will end first in our deep structure, at the energetic level; and after a while, our conscious mind catches on and tells us about it. Then we take action and end the relationship or change it or not, depending on our fears and experiences from the past and how those other deep drivers are being met.

If we have low self-esteem or a victim belief about ourselves, we will stay in a dysfunctional relationship longer; or if our deeper drivers, which we aren't aware of consciously, are being met, even though the surface structure of the relationship is dysfunctional, we will stay in the relationship. This is true in part because we believe what the slow processing conscious mind tells us, and we may think, *This is the best I can do, or this is what I deserve?* And we may view the relationship as a punishment for past "bad deeds" from this life or past lives or because of religious beliefs, which are deep learned drivers and structures.

If we have a less-than-happy relationship, we need to change, which is to say both partners must change. Why must they both change? Because it is a symbiotic relationship, and it depends on both partners being in balance with each other the way they are. In a nutshell both partners are contributing to the way each partner is experiencing the relationship; therefore, both partners need to change.

Many unhappy relationships can go on for a very long time, years and years, and maybe to death they do part. And why would that be? Because the driving forces in deeper structure, out of conscious awareness, are being met until they are not; and when deep structure drivers aren't met, change will happen. If one partner changes his or her deep structure and the other remains the same, an imbalance is created, and that imbalance will tend to dissolve the relationship rapidly.

What must change? The past. And what is the past? Memories. Past relationships must be healed—not necessarily the current relationship but past relationships, which are only memories now. The current relationship is a reflection of the past ones. Can we learn from past relationships and do things differently? Yes. If our current relationship is in trouble, did we learn from past relationships, change, and forgive ourselves? No, at least not enough. And of course that means both partners haven't learned, changed, and forgiven themselves enough. *(A relationship is a dance, you know. And each partner is using the dance steps he or she knows. If you keep using the dance steps you have always used, you are going to keep selecting the same dysfunctional dance partners to dance with. In troubled relationships, if one partner learns new dance steps and the other uses only the old dance steps he or she knows, the old steps, the imbalance may cause the dance to end. Both partners must change, or they may both need to leave the dance floor, because they keep kicking each other in the shins and stepping on each other's toes.)*

If only one partner changes, the imbalance that occurs will cause a change in perception of his or her partner. Recall what we stated before: "The observer affects the observed." As one partner changes, there will be a paradigm shift in that partner, and they will experience the relationship radically different than the other partner. Their subconscious filtering system will present to them new options, self-esteem will improve, and what was before will no longer be true.

When we quoted Dr. Wayne Dyer before, we may not have grasped the statement fully. "When you change the way you look at things, the things you look at change!" This isn't a metaphor. The "things" we see change will physically change. What we saw physically before won't be there to see again. Something else will be there. It works like this: what we saw before was because of the filtering system we were using. When we change the filtering system, we will physically see something different right in front of us, because that is what we are now filtering out of the milieu around us. Remember, everything is there, and what we take from the "everything" depends on how we filter that everything. We exchange one reality for another by the way we filter it; and it will be in a very physical way. *(Do not get confused here. You see what you see because of your filtering system. If you change your filtering system, you will see and must see something else. You will see something that has always been there but is out of focus, something that has been there but at a different frequency. It's like you are listening to a radio station, and then you tune to a different frequency. There it is, a new station; and the other station isn't heard anymore. Both stations were always there. However, the one you are tuned in to is the one you heard. When you change your filter or tune to a different frequency, you will physically hear different music. The other station is no longer in your awareness, but it is still there. You just won't hear it. When your filter system changes, the subconscious mind will filter every one of your sensory inputs differently; and you will bring a new world into focus.)*

If we hold up a red piece of plastic in front of a television screen, we will see a lot of red people. If we change the plastic and hold up a blue piece, we will see a lot of blue people. Did the television picture change? No. Did what we observe change for us as we changed the color of the plastic filter we held up? Yes. The outside energy of everything doesn't have to change or do anything for us to physically experience a new world right in front of us, because "the observer affects the observed." *(You are the observer; therefore, you are the subtle cause of the effects you observe as your world.)*

Appreciate why changing the balance in a relationship could make it more difficult to hold it together; and it may end because of the weight of the imbalance. How far back into the past do we need to go to heal past relationships? As we just said, we may need to go all the way back to our first relationships, which is to say our family of origin and our initial programming around how relationships were modeled during our childhood. That can be a scary thought for some. However, when both partners have healed their past, they are in a position to work together on their current relationship. Will the relationship then hold together and improve? I don't know. But both partners have an opportunity to be happier.

We need to be clear on this point and state again that if a relationship is in trouble, both partners need to change, because both contributed to the way it is. Many times one or the other partner will feel all the fault lies with his or her partner, and feel it is the other partner who must do all the of change; and if the other partner changes, everything will be fine. A relationship is a very complicated dance; and the reasons why we picked the partner we did, for the most part, are out of conscious awareness. However, we picked the partner we did because of the way we are, not because of the way they are. *(Your deep drivers picked the partner you picked, and they fit your needs.)*

If we were different, we would have picked a different partner. In troubled relationships, both partners will have made errors, and both need to change; also in troubled relationships, each partner will have personal issues from their past that they need to identify and heal. Those personal issues won't show up or be seen at first because of the chemical honeymoon high. And now that there is a troubled relationship, the couple will be so absorbed in wanting to heal their current relationship that they won't recognize that the relationship issues are made up of two individuals with past unresolved issues. Just working on the perceived issues of the current relationship won't address the causal issues of their current problems. In the heat and struggle of working on their current relationship problems, the underlying causal individual issues will be hidden from view and from being healed; and the relationship will continue to be in pain and suffering for both partners. Sometimes relationships must end for the health and healing of all concerned.

It's never about the current relationship. At root will be the individual issues of both partners. Since the current relationship is only a reflection and an effect of past relationships and their individual past memories, trying to change the effects the current relationship is expressing, without healing the causes in past relationships, may be problematic and too scary to confront. So blaming our current partner is how the egoic self usually deals with this, and then we don't have to look at, resolve, or heal our own issues.

Remember what we are changing. We are changing memories of past events that are over and gone. We are changing only the unreal, incomplete, and untrue memories that are uniquely and only in our heads. We are healing ourselves, and wouldn't that be nice? Each partner will have his or her own memories of past relationships. Different memories will produce different filtering systems, and different filters create different worlds they are both living in. And each world will have different rules of engagement. Different rules of engagement imply that what is acceptable behavior for one partner's world may not be acceptable to the other partner.

EVERYTHING IN YOU IS YOU

When we recall a memory, we bring the memory into our mind's eye, into our active minds. It comes with all the stored data of the memory. As mentioned in Chapter 10, "Memory Coding System," we don't

291

bring a copy of the memory into the active mind. The whole memory is pulled into the active mind. At this point, the active mind doesn't know whether the data is memory, outside data, or feedback from the body. From all that data received, the active mind forms interpretations, and from the interpretations signals are sent out to the mind and body. The body responds to the signals by changing its systems of operation to match the signals. Then later, the conscious mind reports to us on the holographic movie playing in our heads about what happened and on the feeling response in our bodies, because the body must respond to the signals generated in the active mind around the interpretations. We have gone over this before, and that's not the point. The point is, memories through the active mind generated responses in the body, and all those other people who populate the holographic movie of the memories we play in our heads are all us, because there is only us inside us. Where do all those people come from? We created them the way they are based on our interpretation of them, and we are those who give life to them and give them room in our heads. Those other people in our memories are us disguised as our interpretation of them. *(Be aware that you can never know other people completely. All you can know of them is your perception of them based on your beliefs, experiences, and references of them. They are like the cups in front of you. They act and behave the way they do because you are the way you are. If you change, they will change. How exciting is that to know? But as you are now, you may still believe they have to change for you to be happy. Silly person, it's all you inside you.)*

Here's the thing. Those other people exist the way they do inside us only because that's the way we have interpreted them. We never "know" the totality of other people because they are the most complex organisms in the universe, just like we are. All we can know of them are aspects of them after we have filtered the information through the lens of our past. *(You see why you don't know other people the way they are and why you know them only by the way you are? This was said before, but do you see how easily you can slip back into blaming them? However, it may also be true that you may have to separate from them to heal yourself. You can't change other people; you can only change yourself. You know that, right? And for you to heal, you may have to block them from your life until you are healed enough to appreciate you, which may be forever. Will the other person understand why you need to do that? No, probably not.)*

In the holographic movie in our heads, we are the directors. We build the scenery for the movie, and we are all the actors. There is no one inside us but us. It can only be us because they, whoever we think they are, just won't fit in our heads; and for us to know the totality of them, they would have to be completely in our heads, and that isn't possible. So it is all us in there. *(You need to get this. And it may not be easy at first because of how you were programmed. We have covered this before. You and you are alone are in your head. But again, you have been programmed to believe memories are real; therefore, if there are people in our memories, the people must also be real, or the memories can't be real. Can you see it's all smoke and mirrors? And again, are you getting this? Do you understand you are creating it all from what you hold on the inside?)*

We know that if the memory is vivid enough, strong enough, feelings come up in our bodies, and we feel as if we are interacting with all those other people just as we did in the original event, but we're not. We are interacting with them in our heads only by talking to them or yelling at them, but it is all us in there. The event is over and won't happen again. As we stated before, when our feelings are strongly engaged, our logical and rational minds go out the window. In that moment it is difficult to remember and understand that it's all us inside. We are directing and acting out all the parts in that movie of the old memory in our heads.

THE ORIGINAL INTERPRETATION OF THE EVENT

Let's step back a bit and look at the original interpretation of the event, which was stored as a memory. When the interpretation of the event was created, how did all those people get into that interspace in our heads of that first holographic movie? We created them the way they are based on our interpretation of the event and our past experiences with them or people we think were like them that we carry in the black box, the subconscious mind. We created them out of all our memories of similar events, situations, and people from memories already stored in the subconscious mind and our interactive memories with those types of people from the past. None of those people were ever inside us, only our perceptions of them in our heads. *(Again, think of the cup. Do you see this cup in front of you? No, you can see only a facsimile based on your past. Quit thinking the past is real. The people you think are inside you aren't. You're in an illusion, or did you forget? As Einstein observed, "Reality is merely an illusion, albeit a very persistent one." Although it's a very persistent illusion, it's still an illusion and not reality.)*

We know other people based on only who we are, which is to say through our lens of the past. Whether it's a stranger, a friend, our mom, a sister, or a brother or father, we know them only the way we are. They can be experienced only through the lens of our past; and like this cup in front of us, we create an interpretation of them based on the way we think of them from our past. What we have in our memory is us disguised as them through our interpretation of what we think about them. They can be for us only what we think about them; therefore, we thought them into being the way they are for us. Everyone and everything in all our memories are us disguised as what we think they are; and using that palette and the paintbrush of our past, we disguise ourselves to be them. We do such a good job at disguising ourselves as them and acting perfectly to fit our beliefs about them that we fool ourselves into believing it is them inside us. But—and this is a big but—there is no one inside us but us.

Since we are alone in our memories, why is it so difficult to change them? Because we have been taught; we have been programmed. We believe from ancient times as a species, a culture, and a family that we can't change events in the past; and that's correct because they are over and gone. But by default we have been programmed into believing as a species, a culture, and a family that the memories of events are also real, but memories are not. What is left of events when the events are over? Nothing. But there will be old, unreal, incomplete, and untrue memories, which are only in our heads; and only everything in our heads and inside us can be us. *(It's true: you can't change the past. But you don't live in the past. You live your life in your memories about past events that are gone. They won't come back, and your memories of the events aren't real, true, or complete. I know, your ego will tell you that your memories are real. You need to stop listening to that little devil in your ear.)*

Also, there may be bits and pieces of undissolved physical stuff from the event still here in the present moment. There may be pieces of carved stone and clay tablets, old tools, bits and pieces of bone, and parts of buildings; and there may be more modern pieces and bits of the past, such as videotapes, photographs, blogs, and copies of tweets. All kinds of physical stuff. Some people may even have woven some of those bits and pieces together into an interpretive story and proclaimed, "The past is real. Look at my evidence." Notwithstanding the evidence, events don't happen in the past. Events can happen only in the present moment, and then they are over and gone. We can think of the physical stuff as old hardware. However, what makes the event an event isn't the physical stuff but the programming that operated that hardware, the energy behind the hardware. And the best we can do now is play "let's make-believe or pretend" with the old hardware. *(Can you see that again you are creating stories or listening to stories someone else has created using the physical pieces of hardware? It is just like the unreal, untrue, and incomplete memories we make of your current events; and it can be fun, but it's not real. How can old hardware from the past tell you a more real, true, or complete story than your current perceptions? All your interpretations are creations of what never happened the way you think they did. Perceptions are always stories you tell yourself; you create them, and they are unreal memories. There is no place where you can step in this three-dimensional universe that isn't an illusion. But oh, don't you believe it's real?)*

Part of our problem here is language. Events occur, and then they are gone. They can occur only in the present moment. When events occur, they are neutral and meaningless, as we discussed before; and then they are gone. There are unimaginable numbers of events occurring in this present moment, and they are all neutral and meaningless. Do you care? Probably not. In Chapter 3, "Sensing Differently," we asked, "When a tree falls in the forest, does it make a sound if there is no one there?" And the answer was no. Why not? Because sound is an interpreted construction in the mind. Did a tree fall in the forest? That's an unimportant and meaningless question. What is the importance of any event? The interpretation we give it. *(Can you see that if an event happens and you don't know about it, it is meaningless to you? Now, if you do know an event happened, it may or may not be important to you, depending*

295

on how you interpret it. Notice again that it isn't the fact that an event happened but your interpretation of it that is important. Your interpretation is an inside activity, not the outside event.)

Is the interpretation of the event the event? No. Did an event happen? Again, that's an unimportant and meaningless question. Is the interpretation of an event the event? No. If the interpretation of the event isn't the event itself, then the memory of our interpretation of an event we carry in that big black box isn't the event either; therefore, the memories we carry in the subconscious mind aren't real. They are faulty memories of something that didn't happen, at least not the way we think it did. When the event is over and gone, and our memory of the event is faulty, did the event happen? Again, that's another unimportant and meaningless question, because the event is gone and cannot be verified. All the physical evidence we can come up with will never be the event. But does it make an interesting story we tell ourselves? Maybe we could make a movie, write a book, and sell a few books about the event, which means we now have a vested interest in keeping the past real. But it will never be the event. It can be only a story we are telling ourselves. *(Now, don't let your ego get upset. It needs the past to be real to stay alive. What is the only importance of any event? Your interpretation of the event, which is to say how your past memories filter the information of the event. When you use your past memories, you get your interpretation of the event. If you could use my past memories to filter the information of an event, you would get a different interpretation of the event. Can you see that? Which memory of the interpretation of the event would be the real, true, and complete memory—you using my past or you using your own? Neither. Why? Memories aren't real. But don't you believe yours are real? Yes, of course.)*

All we have inside us are memories of interpretations of events and no actual events, and the memories aren't real either. Memories aren't events. They are interpretations of something that is over and gone. So we have only memories. We never have events; even when they are happening in the present moment, we never have events. So what are all those bits and pieces of physical stuff? They are evidence of something that isn't here now, something that is over and gone. Well, there we have it. We might say, "The event happened. You just said it is evidence that something happened." Yes, but what happened? No one knows for sure, and we will never know because the event is over and gone.

What do we have left over of the event now? Only an interpretation, a perception of what is no more and never was the way we interpreted it to be. No matter how much and how many bits and pieces of physical stuff we have, we will have only a memory of an interpretation of something that is long gone and will never, ever come again; and the memory of an interpretation of an event will never be the event. *(I know you are probably thinking,* This is just BS. I know what is real. He is talking just to hear himself talk. *Here is the point. When you absolutely believe the past is real, which it isn't, you can't change it, and you can't grow. Your pain and suffering are because of your past beliefs, experiences, and references; and they are all memories. I am bringing you to a new understanding that memories aren't real. Since memories aren't real, they can be changed, and you can heal. But oh, how strong is your belief that the past is real and cannot be changed; and it is supported by so many stakeholders in the illusion. Even to suggest the past isn't real will label me a heretic. Heretics get burned at the stake, you know.)*

Now again, memories aren't real, complete, and true. Did the events happen that the memories are depicting? Well, maybe, yes. Are the remembered memories that something happened real? No. We don't have the events in our memories; we have *interpretations* of the events in our unreal memories. Did the events happen the way our memories remember the events happening? No. The event never happened the way we remember it, because it is an interpretation of filtered and manipulated data that is only in our heads. *(You need to stop listening to your ego. The ego has a reason and a hidden agenda in keeping the past real. Keeping the past alive keeps your ego alive. Your past is only unreal memories. Keep the good ones you like, and reframe and let go of the negative ones that cause you pain and suffering. The ego lives only through your old memories, and to change your memories is to kill your current ego.)*

What we think of as history is only memories. Whether it's ancient history of decades ago or yesterday's news, it's all just memories now. Who we think we are is based on our memories. For us to be who we think we are, we need our memories and our history to be real. The more we believe the past is real the way we think it is, which is to say our interpreted memories, the more real we think "who we think we are" is real. The more real we think we are, the more in control the ego is in all its forms as a culture, as a family; and of course, that is what egos need us to do, so they can all stay alive.

Are our memories of the past real, complete, and true? No. Do we believe they are real, complete, and true? Yes. What do we call something we believe is real, complete, and true but isn't? An illusion. Can we ever experience an illusion as real, complete, and true? Only in our imaginations with the help of the great trickster, our egoic self.

Can we change memories? Why not? They aren't real, complete, or true anyway. Changing negative and painful memories will change the world we live in for the better, and we will be happier. Why wouldn't we want better and happier lives? Why wouldn't we want to change negative memories? Because we believe what the ego tells us through our conscious minds that "my memories must be real, or who would I be?" *(Wake up! You're in an illusion, and you can change.)*

Baby Steps to Successful Change

At this point, some may think, *Well, okay, I'll give change a try.* They start thinking about the worst memories of events that ever happened to them and how they might change them. Don't start with the worst of the worst negative memories and attempt change. On that SUD scale of 0 to 10, pick a memory around a 2 intensity. Use one of the techniques we have discussed in this read. Go on the Internet and read more about it, look it up on YouTube, or find a practitioner to work with and change it. From successes, move on to a slightly higher intensity on the SUD scale. *(Be brave and heal your past. Let go of what isn't real anyway. Know you have value in yourself and that under all your pain and suffering is a cause, and that cause will be in your past, no matter what your egoic self tells you through your conscious mind. Be determined to see things differently and to change your vision.)*

CHAPTER 18

Dissolving Illusions

EVERYTHING IS OUTSIDE! EVERYTHING IS INSIDE!

We have suggested that what is outside us is the subtle field of everything in an unmanifested state; and since that field is infinite, it is also inside us. We exist in that uniqueness of being like a fish in the ocean, except we are in the subtle field of everything. And like a fish, we aren't aware of what is supporting us.

As we use our new vision, we may begin to view a small crack in the cosmos, as science is also beginning to change its vision but quite slowly. Quantum physics is the opening of science into a larger, more profound, and—for some—scarier appreciation of this subtle field, this everything, out of which everything comes and into which everything returns.

As we change the way we filter data transmitted by our senses from the outside everything, new worlds will come into focus for us. When science says they have discovered something new, it's not new. It has been there all the time, waiting in the unmanifested everything for someone to come along with the right mental filtering system and imagination to uncover what has always been there. There is nothing new under the sun or in the cosmos. Everything is there unmanifested, waiting to be uncovered. When we uncover something, we can almost hear the subtle field saying, "Well, it's about time you finally got it.

Welcome to your new paradigm!" And of course, it will take fifty or more years for the new paradigm to reach critical mass and become accepted and change all those egos that need to hang on to the old paradigm, because of who they think they are.

We have stated that what is inside us, in the gross energy system, is everything we know. It is what we have manifested. It is the world of objects, and it is created from our interpretation of the incoming information of the senses after being filtered through our past, which is to say our memories in the subconscious mind. Our everyday lives are lived in this interspace, and each of us will have our own objective world to live in. However, by mutual consent and consensus agreements, our individual world of objects will be much the same as those other objective worlds around us, because of how the brain processes and how society and culture direct us to interpret into being the world we have. It is in the subjective part of our manifested world that we wander into separate worlds.

THE TRUTH AND HAFT-TRUTHS

We have said before that our interpretation of an event isn't complete, real, or true; therefore, it isn't and can't be the event. The memory of an interpretation of an event isn't complete, real, or true, because the interpretation from which the memory comes isn't complete, real, or true. It is a distortion of the event and therefore an illusion, which is to say it is untrue. However, there may be bits, pieces, and fragments within the memory that are true. Because it's our interpretation and because we believe the whole perception and its memory are true as created, we believe the memory we carry in the subconscious mind is real, true, and complete. If we didn't believe the memory was true, we would have perceived something different in our active mind in the first place. *(You see why you hold your memories in such high regard? Do you see why your current egoic self needs you to believe they are real? And the ego will fight hard by whispering in your ear all the reasons why your memories are real. Oh, how that great trickster will so logically work on you.)*

When questioned about our memories based on interpretations

of events that are over and gone, we may think, *Well, maybe I did overexaggerate here or there, and maybe I did generalize a little bit there or here, and maybe I did leave out a part here or there*, but we will say very forthrightly and self-righteously, "The rest is true." We might think of another question. "Is she pregnant or not?" "Well," we might answer, "she is just a little bit pregnant." Our interpretations and memories of those interpretations are either the truth or lies? They cannot be true and haft true at the same time. You are either pregnant, or you aren't; and your memories are either completely true or untrue. If untrue, which they are, why do you want to hang on to them? Why don't you just change them into the whole truth by taking out the distortions? It's because of your ego.

We view events through the lens of our egoic selves, which are who we believe we are. And so we change our interpretation of the event to match who we think we are, and to help us feel better about who we think we are. Here our egos might jump up and say, "You can't do that! Parts of the memories are real. There are lessons to learn in those memories. You can't just go changing or throwing memories away hither and yon or willy-nilly. They are important!"

Since memories aren't complete, real, or true, we believe they are at least partially true, but which part is true, and which is false? If we know which part is true and which isn't, why wouldn't we put into our memories only the truth? Another very interesting question, is it not? It's like lying to ourselves and then believing the lie we know was a lie. *(You are in an illusion, you know. You can tell yourself lies and believe them at the same time.)* It's all about our egoic self. To save our egos from being bruised and causing us to feel worst then we do, we create memories that favor who we believe we are, which is to say our egoic self. See how manipulative we can be to save our egoic self, because it is through the lens of our egos that we see the world we see. *(Your conscious mind never seems to catch on to this self-deception until it is forced into a corner, which I am trying to do for you.)*

In Chapter 13, "Everything Is in the Mind," we stated that the egoic self, our identity of who we think we are, becomes the lens through which we "see" the outside world. The ego is an integral part of the subconscious filtering system and is integrated into our belief system. It is part of the reason why memories aren't complete, real, or true. We see what we want to see and hear what we want to hear based on our beliefs, experiences, and references, which are now our memories and our ego identity of who we think we are. Guess what lens we were using to select the data to create those untrue memories? Yes. It was the ego. And the conscious mind never knows it; therefore, it reports only on the flawed interpretation and the body's response to that unreal interpretation. But then it does seem real, and some parts of it may be true. *(Oh well, what the hell. Let's just say it's close enough for who it's for and accept the illusion as reality. What do you say?)*

With that understanding and knowledge, we know how bad it causes us to feel when we bruise our egoic selves, because when our egos are attacked, our self-identity of who we think we are is attacked. Is it any wonder why we manipulate, delete, and generalize our input data the way we do to save our egos? And is it any wonder why we see and live in the world we do? Our goal isn't to see the truth and reality or even to be happy. Our goal is to save our egoic asses, our identity of who we think we are from being hurt. *(I bet you thought your goal was to find and follow the true path of knowledge and walk it. No. That was never your goal. Your goal is to save your egoic ass of who you think you are. You see why your world is the way it is?)*

To save our egos, we have a tendency to take disjointed bits and pieces of data that are true for us and to sew and stitch them together with other unrelated bits of cloth to make a collage that satisfies our personal identity of who we think we are. Then we call the collage our truth. It's not important what the memory is or whether it is complete, real, true, or untrue. What is our goal? Our goal is to save our egoic selves. This is done behind the curtain and out of sight of our conscious awareness. However, when the slow conscious mind catches up and reports on it, we will believe its interpretation of the event and the memory of the interpretation, because it will seem so rational and logical to the conscious mind that we just accept it; and because we so want to see what we want to see and hear what we want to hear that we make it happen. The conscious mind has been called "the rational lying mind," and it is. It justifies to us what we do and why we do it in a very logical manner.

As we begin using our new vision and change who we think we are, our old ego will die to be replaced by another. This will happen quite naturally. There will be no remorse, only a sense of lightness as our original self begins to come more into focus. It is like taking off the protection of a winter coat when springtime comes and feeling the excitement of what has changed and the anticipation of what is coming. We will go through the death of many egos as we become aware of our original self.

Each time we change and heal some aspect of who we think we are, the current ego dies to be replaced by yet another different egoic self, another different identity. This process can be positive or negative. We would like to think we are moving forward from positive to positive, but the same process can move us backward as well. There are so many things going on at our deeper internal levels and behind the curtain of our conscious awareness that it boggles the mind; and then little bubbles of change start floating up into conscious awareness. Then, just like with a paradigm shift, a critical mass is reached in us, and change happens; and when it does, it will seem so natural and logical that we won't even remember why we ever believed it would be difficult.

If we move in a positive direction, the illusory world we live in will get lighter and brighter, and we will like ourselves more. If we move in a negative direction, the illusions we live in will get darker and heavier, and we will blame others outside us for our discomfort, which will compound our distress. Whichever direction we move, we will find or create the proof we need to rationalize that we made the right choice for us; and our rational, lying conscious mind will logically tell us a story as to why we are where we are and doing what we are doing.

Memories are just memories. They aren't events. They are just stories we tell ourselves about what is gone and never were the way we think they were. Memories aren't real and are made up of haft-truths and in some cases out-and-out lies. The only way to change and let go of negative memories that are the causal issues of our problems is through forgiveness. True self-forgiveness dissolves illusions.

CHAPTER 19

Forgiveness

In Chapter 17, "Changing Vision," we discussed forgiveness, but now we will look deeper into this method of changing negative memories, recognizing it will change our lives. Forgiveness is an ancient path of healing and restoring our peace of mind. We will play with forgiveness a little and see how we can use it to reframe memories. All we are, comes from our memories, and everything inside us comes from stories of how we have interpreted events in our lives; therefore, we are the memories we hold within. Events always and must happen in the present moment; and when they are over, they're gone and are no longer here. They have dissolved and disappeared; and since they are over and gone, they can't be changed because they're not here and don't exist.

What is left when the events are over? Nothing of the events. All we have are unreal memories we think are real, but as we now know, they're not. So when we change past memories, we aren't changing events. What we are changing are unreal memories of interpretations we made of events. Changing what we think of as the past by changing memories won't change the past, because the event isn't there to be changed; it is over and gone, and it will never come back again. All that is left to change are the memories. Will changing the memories change the past? No. What will changing memories do? It will change our interpretation of what we thought was the event but really never was. The past always controls the present, so by reframing memories, we change the present, which is the world we live in. When we release the past, we are opening to a new present moment.

To appreciate forgiveness differently, we will need to develop a new metaphor. We will refresh some of the things we have discussed before and reframe some of the models we have used up to this point. We stated that the body is like a shell around the mind or brain, intended to protect it. So how we view the body in our new model will be depicting the body metaphorical and differently. Keep in mind that the body functions in the same way it does; we are just showing it in a different metaphorical model.

We need to be clear about this, since the sense organs are housed in the body, but their input data goes directly to the mind; and the data has no effect on the body whatsoever. In the mind, the subconscious picks over, mines, and selects input data using our past memories and looking for things it is familiar with. Again, recognize that the body isn't connected to the outside environment in any way and that it knows only how to respond because of signals sent to it by the active mind. The sense organs transmit data only in the form of electromagnetic and chemical signals. The senses make no judgments or decisions based on the data they are transmitting. This is so difficult to get at first because of the way we have been programmed and use language. When we say, "I see you," we think the eyes are seeing some object that is you and that the eyes are interpreting what they are looking at. The eyes don't do that. The ears don't hear sounds either. Everything we think the senses are telling us is wrong; they are not doing that. Everything we attribute to the senses is interpreted in the mind. *(This is important for you to understand; everything is first in the mind. Your body is an instrument of the mind. While your body speaks to the mind, it is the active mind that interprets what the body is saying.)*

The active mind is the cauldron in which our constantly flowing interpretations are generated. Each thought or interpretation causes electromagnetic and chemical signals to be produced and sent throughout the mind or body. And these signals stimulate responses in the mind and body. As the mind and body respond to the signals, they send feedback data to the active mind. This feedback verifies to the active mind that the mind and body systems are synchronized to the active mind's interpretations.

There is a dance between the mind and body. The interface of this dance is the active mind. Data flows into the active mind, and it makes interpretations of the data and sends out signals. The mind and body responds to the signals and sends feedback data from the mind and body. The active mind accepts the feedback data as new data, makes another interpretation based on the new data, and sends out different signals, which will affect the response in the mind and body. Then more feedback of data is sent to the active mind, and then different signals are sent out. This dance reaches balance and homeostasis in nanoseconds because of the processing speeds involved, and then the conscious mind tells us what happened.

The following diagram depicts a metaphoric model of this process. Input data from the outside goes straight through the body, into the subconscious mind, and through its filter to the active mind. The filtered data sent to the active mind will be used to create our interpretations. The active mind then signals the mind and body as to its interpretation; and the mind and body sends feedback to the active mind as to its response. As stated before, it's like a checks-and-balance system. Notice the conscious mind's function in the diagram.

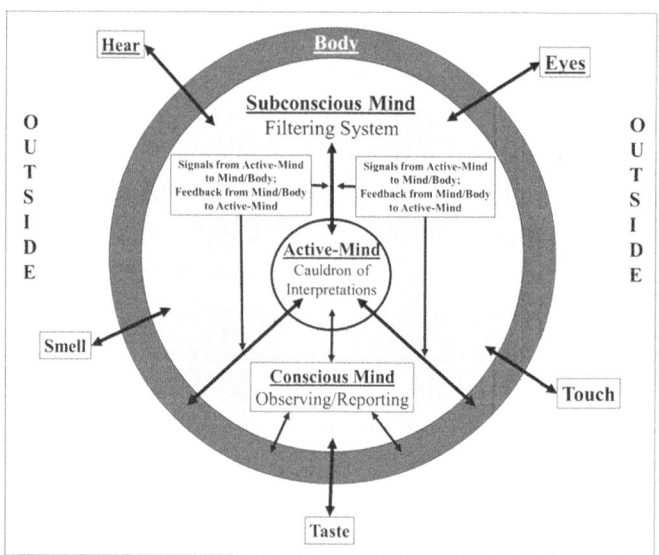

Diagram 23 - The Body as a Shell to Protect the
Mind, Brain, and Central Nervous System

Notice in the diagram that all sensory information goes directly to the subconscious mind, not to the body. The first thing the subconscious mind does is filter the data and send it to the active mind. The active mind interprets the data and sends signals to the mind and body; and the process is all over before the conscious mind has any idea something has happened. Then the conscious mind tells us what it knows about what has happened. *(Who is your conscious mind talking to when it is talking to you? That's another interesting question.)*

When a memory held in the subconscious mind is triggered, it is pulled directly from the subconscious mind, where it is stored, and put into the active mind. This isn't a copy because there is no facility in the subconscious mind for copying memories. It is the whole memory with all the data stored of the interpretation of the original event. While the memory data is in the active mind, no part of it remains in the subconscious mind. The active mind takes the data and does what it does with all data it receives; it makes an interpretation with it. The interpretation will be much like the original interpretation because it's the same data. Then signals are sent out to the mind and body, and they will be much like the signals sent out by the original interpretation because they are created from a similar interpretation based on the same data. The more vivid the memory and its data, the more intense will be the feeling in the body. Notice again that the memory isn't the event; it is a memory of our interpretation of an event.

Whether information comes to the active mind from the subconscious mind as filtered outside information, stored memories, or feedback from the body, the active mind takes the data and makes interpretations of it; and the interpretations, as we have stated many times, aren't real because the data is filtered and manipulated before the active mind gets it. The data in our memories is already filtered and manipulated from the original interpretation of the event that formed the memory; therefore, it goes directly from being a stored memory to being data for the active mind to interpret.

A disclaimer: There may be fragmented and disjointed bits and pieces of data from a memory left in the subconscious mind when the memory is pulled into the active mind. These are much like free radicals moving and floating around in the body. Since they aren't connected to anything, the mind disregards them.

Using this metaphoric model of the body surrounding the mind, we will incorporate it into a more conventional model than we have used before, but we will use it a little differently. We have said before that the interpretation of an event isn't the event. Since it isn't the event, what is it? The interpretation is a creation, a construct. Who created the interpretation? Our active mind. What did the active mind create it from? Filtered and manipulated data. What causes the data to be filtered and manipulated the way it was? Our beliefs, experiences, and references, which are our memories. We should be together up to this point, right?

We need to look closely and understand that everything inside us is us; we have made this point before. There is nobody inside us but us. We are it. We're the whole megillah. We're the full Monty, and we're the whole thing. To imagine other people are inside us is an illusion, but then we are good at living in illusions.

This is an important understanding. Our interpretations are our handiwork, our craftsmanship; therefore, our interpretations are uniquely and only ours. Interpretations are turned into memories, and memories are stored in the subconscious mind for later retrieval and are used in the filtering system of incoming information. Why we are learning new skills and seeing things differently, our craftsmanship improves, and we create different interpretations and can reframe our older memories into more positive ones or worse ones. We have a choice, you know.

We cannot reframe old memories while they are locked and stored in the subconscious mind. We need to get them out and into the active mind. As stated before, when a memory is triggered and recalled, the whole memory with all its data is pulled out of the subconscious mind and into the active mind. It is then that the recalled memory in the active mind can be reframed and changed. Again, we are reframing and changing something that isn't real in the first place, and the memory isn't the event. Remember that.

The next diagram depicts the senses transmitting data about a person. The input data goes directly to the subconscious filtering system; then the output data, which is different from the input data, is sent to the active mind. From that data, the active mind creates an interpretation and sends out signals of its interpretation of the person to the mind or body. Within less than thirty seconds, the interpretation moves into permanent memory in the subconscious mind. In the diagram, the memory of the interpretation of the person isn't the person; and as we may have heard before, "The map isn't the territory." The map is what we have inside. The real territory is outside, and we never experience it the way it is. We have created an artistic masterpiece, much like the artist Salvador Dali did, from our imagination. It is a depiction of life, but it isn't life. It is our own "reality show," and it looks and feels so real, doesn't it?

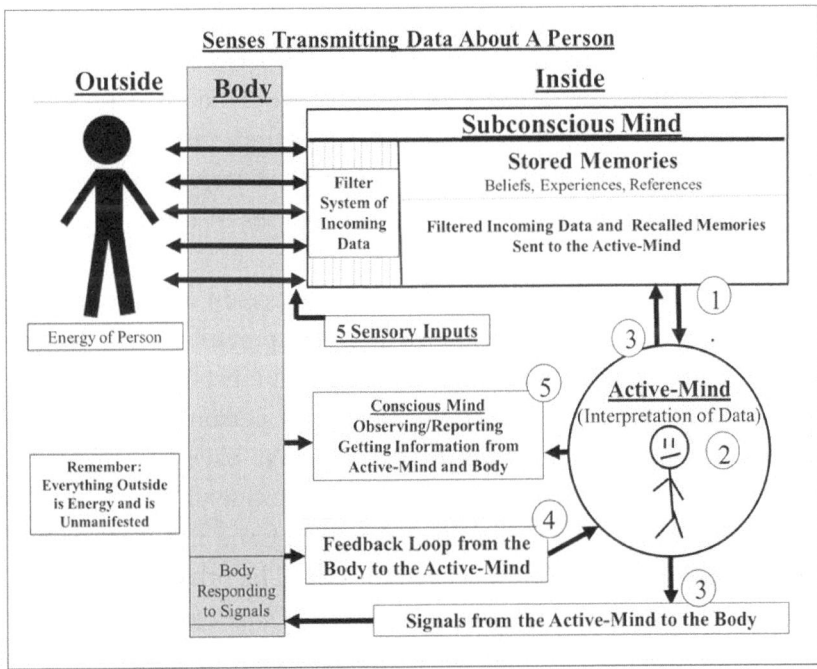

Diagram 24 - Outside Energy, Inside Interpretation

The diagram depicts what happens when sensory-transmitted data from the outside enters the mind. We will again go through this diagram step-by-step to understand the internal process starting after the data has entered the subconscious mind and is filtered.

1. The filtered and manipulated data is sent to the active mind.
2. The active mind makes an interpretation of the filtered and manipulated data.
3. Signals are sent to the mind and body.
4. The body responds to the signals and sends feedback data to the active mind. *(Notice that up to this point, everything is happening at lightning speeds of billions to millions of bits of data per second. Information is just flying around, but no language is used.)*
5. Now the conscious mind reports on what has happened in the mind and body at its slow speed and in word language.

There are only two inputs to the active mind: (1) The subconscious mind sends data to the active mind in two ways. As filtered input data is triggered, data of stored memories moves to the active mind, and it gives feedback based on the signals sent by the active mind's interpretations. (2) The second input to the active mind comes from the body informing the active mind of its needs (for example, food, water, rest, and so forth) and also feedback based on the body's responses to the active mind's interpretations.

From the above diagram, we see that the person we have inside us isn't the person outside. It is our created interpretation of the filtered and manipulated data; and since it is inside us, it must be all of us inside, wearing our interpreted disguise of that other person. Think about it a moment. There is no one inside us but us. We have said that before many times; therefore, what we have created inside us has to be all us too. We have created a facsimile of the person and not "that person"; we can create only from what we have inside. The other person cannot and won't fit inside us. It's all us inside us. *(Think about this cup I had in front of me that you were looking at. You didn't end up with a cup inside you, did you? When you look at someone—your mother, a friend, or an ex-lover—you don't end up with him or her inside you. But it might feel like the person is inside you. But no, they aren't. It's all you inside you. Therefore, you can change and reframe the memories around the person, because it is not them; it's only you disguised as them. Isn't that great?)*

We never know another person by the way they are. We know the person only the way we are. In our memories, we are the director of the play and all the actors. And like a good actor, we completely fool the audience into believing the play is real. Who is our audience? It is us, of course, because there can be only us inside us. This is so far away from our current understanding; we may have to catch our breath for a moment. The illusion is so compelling that it's difficult to believe it's not real. *(I know it feels like all the other people in your memories are inside you and taunting you, yelling at you, or telling you things you don't want to hear; but they aren't and cannot be there. This is how it feels in your body in a physical way and how you imagine it in your head in an emotional way that convinces you they are in there, inside you. But—and this is a big but—they're not. I said before that when you are lost in your feelings physically and emotionally, your intellect goes out the window.)*

When our bodies are responding to the signals sent out by the active mind's interpretation of a memory, the conscious mind reports much like it did for the original event's interpretation, because the whole memory is playing back the same recorded data just like the original remembered happening; and that's why it feels like it is happening all over again, because we are using the same playbook and script as the original interpretation. We are directing the replaying of the same play from the same playbook and the same memory. We are fooling ourselves into believing the event is happening again. Even if the body is responding as if the event is happening again, there is no event. It is all magic. It's all smoke and mirrors in our head; and boy, can we create a great magic show to entertain ourselves. *(You do know you are living in an illusion, right? Oh, okay then.)*

Forgiving the Other Person

When we recognize we need to forgive someone, it isn't because of the event, because the event is gone; it is because we have a memory of something we think we need to make peace with. If we had no memory of a past painful interpretation of an event, we wouldn't know, remember, and therefore care that there is something to be forgiven. Without the memory, nothing happened, or it is neutral, at least as far as we consciously would know.

Memories with positive emotional energy attached or with zero emotional energy won't cause any need for forgiveness on our part. Whether a memory is positive or negative may change over time as we gain more understanding, wisdom, and enlightenment. Even so, it's only us in our memories; therefore, we alone are in need of forgiveness. This is an important point and needs to be said again: we alone need to forgive us. *(Be aware that only you are in your memories in various created forms, and only you in your memories are in need of forgiveness. Again, because this is so counter to your cultural belief system to forgive yourself, it may seem absurd. As you begin to see things differently, the things you look at will change.*

Whether you think you should seek forgiveness or offer it, there is always a memory, and in that memory there is only you. Who is the other person in your memory, the person you are forgiving or seeking forgiveness from? It is only you because there is no one but you inside you. It is you disguised as the other person because there is no one inside you but you. But doesn't it feel to you like they are in there with you? When you see them on the street or at a family party, don't you play those old feelings through your head? Later, we will look deeper into the effects of forgiving ourselves. For now, recognize that your memories are not their memories; they have different memories than you do and lives in a different world than you do. But the different worlds are entangled.)

If we withhold our forgiveness, thinking that our withholding will cause that other person to suffer, we are right. But who is the other person in our memory? Who is really suffering? Only us. Why? Because there is only us in our memories, and therefore we are the only ones in our memories who can suffer.

What about the other person? Get this: there is no other person in our memories; we alone are in there. The other person who was in the original event have their own memories, and they will be different from our memories. That person has their own interpretation of the event and therefore their own memories, and how they do that won't be like we have done it. The person will need to reframe and heal their own negatively energized memories by healing their past. We really cannot do that for them; well, maybe we can in a way *(to be discussed later)*. Since we are only forgiving ourselves, the other person isn't involved in our process of forgiveness and doesn't even need to know we are healing our memories and forgiving ourselves.

We sometimes become addicted to the drama of the illusion in all its various forms. To step outside the illusion is almost impossible because of the withdrawal process of our addiction and how it causes us to feel; and of course, we won't know or believe we were even in an addiction because that's just life for us and the way life is. To us the emotional highs and lows of our world and their feelings seem so normal. If the thought of changing arises in our trauma-addicted world, it may create more trauma; and we will blame those who suggest we need to change. But then this is an illusion, and that's what we do in an illusion, right? *(Can you appreciate that you can't see what is right in front of you except through the chaotic and traumatic lens of your past? Therefore, you may need a new path that leads to your healing and peace of mind. I did ask you to stop listening to your egoic self, didn't I?)*

BEWARE OF THE EGO

As mentioned before, we have egoic selves that are our created identities; and so do our family, culture, nation, religion, and any other grouping of people that will have unique egos. All those egos strengthen each other and set the norms for what is acceptable and unacceptable behavior, and of course, how to forgive and accept forgiveness is part of our egoic cultural norms. All those norms are based on the belief that memories are real. Therefore, forgiveness is basically a sham state, or a "Let's pretend" state. *(When you forgive others for what they did, you are saying, "I know you really did this bad thing, and I'll pretend you didn't do it. But when I see you, we will both know you did it, because I have a real memory of you doing it." When you believe memories are real, how can you change them? The secret of change is to know memories aren't real, true, or complete; and when you know that for sure, then memories can be changed.*

Once the memory is changed, what is there to forgive? Oh, how the ego will jump up at that.)

Now, with the belief that the memories are real, true forgiveness is impossible. How can what is real and true ever be changed by forgiveness? If we have what is true, the memory, and now wave the magic wand of forgiveness over it, does it become a new and different truth? How can that happen? It can't. Although the ego wants memories to be real, that keeps us stuck and imprisoned in the past with no way out; therefore, there is no way of changing, and our current ego will live until we die; and of course that is what it wants. If we change by forgiving ourselves, our current ego must die.

When we come to the understanding and recognition that memories aren't real, true, or complete, forgiving ourselves becomes a real and true response to healing our pain and suffering. By forgiving ourselves, we move out of the illusion of the gross energy system. When we move out of the gross energy system, the only place we can be is in the subtle field. We move closer to oneness and our original self.

To change our belief that memories are real and move to the belief that they aren't real may take a little time. It is the great trickster, the ego in all its forms, that will work hard to convince us they are real. We need to have a different insight here, a deeper insight, and begin to appreciate for ourselves that memories aren't real. But oh, how strongly we have been programmed to believe without question that they are so real and that, that belief goes right down to the marrow of our bones. To try to think differently may cause us to have a headache as our egoic selves and all the other egos around us step forward to explain to us exactly why memories are real and must remain real, that forgiveness is foolish and especially self-forgiveness, that self-forgiveness is an abomination in the sight of God and all the other egoic states. *(Oh, you will really hear your ego light up at this. Be gentle with yourself, pay no attention to the ego and love yourself, and let go of what you don't need.)*

When we forgive ourselves, we change what we believe about ourselves. When we change our beliefs about ourselves, we change our identity. When we change our identity, our current ego must die and be replaced by a new ego identity that reflects our new beliefs. *(Can you see why our ego will fight to keep the belief that memories are real? Can you see that when you change your memories, you are changing who you think you are, and who you think you are is your identity? And to change your current identity kills the current ego and creates a new one that reflects your new beliefs? So your current ego will literally fight to the death to keep memories real, to stay alive and stay in control. Can you see why any change of any kind that you may want will be difficult to achieve? Memories are the programs that keep you where you are, which is your habitual self. When you change, this effects not only you but also all those around you. They may not want to change and might consciously and subconsciously sabotage your process of self-forgiveness.)*

All those other egos of family, culture, nation, religion, and groups won't want us to change either, not really, no matter what they may say, because if we change, we threaten who they believe themselves to be. It weakens their control and brings into question their belief that their memories are real. If we forgive ourselves and change, they may stop talking to us. They may run us out of town or kick us out of church. And in some egoic states, they may hurt, maim, imprison, or kill us for what we now believe. It can be dangerous forgiving ourselves and changing. Why? Because forgiving ourselves exposes the illusion of the whole system we live in. *(You do remember that you are living in an illusion, don't you? I know I've said that a lot, haven't I?)*

All ego states will have rituals around the act of forgiveness; and they will be around guilt, shame, sin, and punishment. They won't be around error, correction, and true forgiveness. They may tell us what we can forgive and can't forgive, and how we must approach the act of forgiveness. This keeps the current ego states of family, culture and religion in control. It is amazing how much egoic energy in the illusion is around the simple act of forgiving ourselves for something that is over and long gone. We might even feel that if I don't do it the right way, it's not real forgiveness. And of course, the right way is their way; and that is what keeps you in the illusion because it must be done their way. The event is over and never coming back; the memory of the interpretation we gave to the event isn't real, complete, or true. If it is a painful memory, heal it by self-forgiveness and just let it go, like smoke through a chimney.

As we begin working with self-forgiveness, it may seem strange at first because we are doing something we didn't know we could do or had the right to do for ourselves; or maybe we thought we needed permission to do so. Now the thought may come up. *That's silly. I know I can let go of old memories. I've done that a lot.* What we normally do with painful memories is sweep them under the rug or push them so deeply into the subconscious mind that the body can't feel them, and the conscious mind can't report on them and then think, *There, that solves that problem,* and go on with our lives.

While those memories may be out of conscious awareness, they are still active in the subconscious mind. Since they are still active in the subconscious mind, they are still part of its filtering system. And since they are part of the filtering system, they still affect the data that is sent to the active mind and affects our interpretations that we use to create the life we live. They may affect our health and our pain and suffering, but because they are out of sight of the conscious mind and out of touch with the body directly, we think they're gone. No, no, they are still there, active and deep in the subconscious mind. They still influence our present moment, which means they are part of how we bring the world we have into focus.

Another thing. Just because we know what our problem is, which is to say we know the memory of the event that is causing our pain and suffering and that it happened a long time ago—and just because we know what it is, and it's out of conscious awareness, and just because we have forgiven the other person or were forgiven by the other person, all that has little effect on us in healing our own wounds and correcting our errors. Our memories, with all our errors, are our memories, and only we can reframe and heal them. Self-forgiveness is still the key to healing. *(Just because someone else forgave you or you forgave him or her, this has no effect on the memories you carry within. You need to reframe and heal your memories to change your pain and suffering. Can you both forgive the other person and forgive yourself? Of course. However, the most important forgiveness is the forgiveness of yourself and the reframing and healing of your memories. The rest will happen in due course.)*

Knowing what the unhealed problem is, means we can feel its effects at some level; however, knowing the problem doesn't mean the causal problem has been healed and released. Time is distorted in the subconscious mind, and old negative memories of childhood that haven't been addressed and healed will feel like they have just happened, when they are reawakened after a long sleep of hiding in the subconscious. Forgiving the other person has little to do with forgiving and healing ourselves. And being forgiven by the other person won't forgive us or help us in the process of forgiving and healing ourselves, as we stated. The negative errors we have made are now only memories. Since they are our memories, we are the only ones who can heal them. The act of another person forgiving us won't change our internal programming, and our forgiving another person, because we became offended, won't disconnect our buttons or change our internal programming in anyway. Our ego may feel better, but this won't change our programming. Sorry, we must do our own forgiving work and heal ourselves.

If we are holding a helium balloon in our hand and we open our hand, the balloon floats away and is gone; that is how self-forgiving works, and we feel the freedom it offers us. If we push the balloon under our shirt or down our pants, we may not see the balloon, but we will surely see and feel its effect. So maybe burying memories alive inside us might not be the solution the mind or body is looking for. The buried memories might cause physical conditions in the way the mind or body has to deal with the memory's effects. Maybe the memories cause some discomfort, maybe some pain and suffering, maybe some illness. Not knowing or remembering where we pushed or buried the causal memory, we are left to deal with the effects and wonder where it came from; and we will usually blame other people or our bodies. We did say the body is the scapegoat for the mind, didn't we?

As we said before, when beginning to work with self-forgiveness, don't start with the worst thing that has ever happened. Start small. On that SUD scale of 0 to 10, start with negative memories that have an intensity of about 2 or 3. Begin with a small, uncomfortable memory. Bring a small irritation up into your active mind to work with. Feel how the body responds to it. *(Then remind yourself that the event that created the interpretation and its memory is over and gone. Remind yourself that the memory of how you interpreted the event at that time wasn't real, complete, or true. Therefore, it is okay to change and reframe the memory, because you are the playwright, the director, and all the actors in your memory. Your memories*

317

are all created from what you hold inside you, which is to say other older and unreal memories. Reframe them, tap on them, change their submodalities, and let them go. Your world will be different and more positive.)

THE WORST OF THE WORST

What can we do with the worst memories in our past? Notice that what is the worst memories depends on each individual. One person's worst memory may not seem as bad to someone else. Whatever the worst memory is for us, the event is over and gone; and the only reminder we have of the event is our created memory. What we are discussing and are concerned about here isn't an event but a memory of an interpretation of the event that isn't here. Whatever is left of the event is only a memory, and that memory is only inside us; and since no one else has our memory, what is the big deal if we change it by forgiving ourselves?

If we feel we are the injured person, that judgment is an interpretation and will create an inaccurate memory of what we think happened and what we believe others did; and of course, we will believe it is real. The event is over, but the memory lingers on. We may have some physical pain, emotional pain, or both due to the memory. Look closely now and recognize that the memory will have a physical component in the body that we interpret as our pain and emotional suffering. If there is no feeling in the body, there is no pain and suffering; and there is no problem. All physical and emotional pain we feel is an interpretation in the active mind and feedback from the body.

So here we have the whole thing. If we want to change our pain and suffering, we need to change the feedback from the body. To change this feedback, we need to change our interpretation of it. To change our interpretation, we need to change our filtering system in the subconscious mind. And to change our filtering system, we need to heal our past. This isn't brain surgery or rocket science, but it is counterintuitive to our cultural norms. The mind is the subtle causal source of all our pain and suffering being the way they are; and only the mind needs to be healed for our pain and suffering to be different.

While medication may moderate effects in the body, to heal the causal problem, the source of our pain and suffering, the mind needs to change; and to change the mind, the past must be addressed and healed.

Since the event is over and the memory isn't real, what can we do? Whether it is physical pain or emotional suffering, there will be a feeling component in the body. If there is no negative feeling component in the body, we don't have a problem. Who tells us whether we have a problem? The conscious mind reports it to us. If there is nothing to report, there is no problem. Well, if there is nothing to report and we like the trauma and excitement of having something to report, we may need to create something to report. This could be problematic because the subtle field has anything we want in it; and if we want something to report, the subconscious mind can always find some trauma to report from the input data from "the everything" outside us.

Using the above model, when the body receives signals from the active mind, it will change its systems in response to the signals and send feedback signals as to its response to the active mind. Since now the active mind has new data from the body, it will create a new interpretation, and new signals will be sent back to the body. They will affect how the body responds, and then new feedback data is sent to the active mind, with a new interpretation created. This back-and-forth communication will continue until there is a balance and an agreement between the two is reached. Keep in mind that this is happening at billions of bits of data per second; therefore, within fractions of a second, balance is reached. When the interpretation and feedback are in balance, the active mind receives no new data; no new interpretation is created, and homeostasis is reached. Think of ongoing chronic pain, depression, anxiety, panic, PTSD, guilt, and grief as a homeostasis negative state that is at a negative balance point of interpretations and feedback loops of the body. To change the negative balance point, either the interpretation or the feedback from the body must change.

Since we are talking about the worst of the worst memories, the body will be involved. Feeling good or bad is determined by how the body responds to the interpretation in the active mind; and if we feel the worst, that feeling of "worstness" must be coming from the body as feedback; and that bad feeling feedback data will affect the interpretation in the active mind. *(Can you imagine and visualize the lightning-fast dance going on inside you between the mind and body, until homeostasis is reached? It is so fast and integrated within your belief system that your conscious mind can never keep up; therefore, you conclude from your conscious mind's reporting that the body is the source of all your pain and suffering. Yes, yes, you may appreciate that you are thinking negative thoughts or that a negative emotional event happened (for example, your partner left you). But if there were no negative feelings in your body, you would rationalize the event away, and the ego has fooled you again into blaming the body and not changing the mind, which is the ego's realm. Taking medications doesn't change the body; it changes the chemical messages sent to the body. Changing the signals sent to the body changes the body's response. If you heal the mind, you also change the signals. You see, it's never the body; it's the mind that tells the body how to respond. However, taking medication is surely easier than changing and healing your mind, at least in the short run. If it wasn't so sad, you could laugh at the comedy relief the ego offers in convincing you the body is your only problem.)*

Here again, from the data in the feedback loop, the active mind creates yet another interpretation because it is receiving new data and signals from the body, affirming its response; and a new memory will be created and put into the subconscious mind. We may ask, "What happened to the memory we recalled into the active mind that started this whole process?" It is gone and replaced by a newer memory. The new memory may be worse, it may be better, or it may be the same. *(Every time you bring a memory into the active mind, it gets changed to some degree, sometimes a little up and sometimes a little down; or it could remain the same. The way it is done is a little haphazard and depends on your frame of mind at the time. But by forgiving yourself at that time, you have the most positive effect on the memory; and then the memory is stored in your subconscious mind with all those positive changes. Your old memory is no more.)*

If the new memory is more negative, it will consolidate into the subconscious mind and be used in the filtering system of new input data; and since it is painful, it will get a higher priority in the filtering system. So now we have a self-propagating and self-fulfilling negative memory. The conscious mind reports all this and brings it into our awareness. *(Are you beginning to see how your pain and suffering are locked into this repeatable pattern and your memories?)*

As the dust clears around the interpretation of the event and the feedback loop, we will have a cluster of memories. The event will be no more and not here. It is over and gone, and it may have been over and gone for years, maybe for generations, maybe for thousands of years; but the memory cluster will still determine our current interpretation and feelings in our bodies or maybe in the corporate body of a nation. It may affect what is taught in schools or churches so the next generation can carry on the negative memories. *(The history you learn in school and the history in other educational institutions is designed to keep you aligned with their belief system and for you to take on their egoic identity. Can you see why currently people hate each other for events that happened thousands of years ago? Can you see why they are looking at the present moment through the lens of the past and see the world they do today? Can you understand why you hate the people your parents hate and love the people your parents love? It has nothing to do with the other people. It has to do with your formal, systematic cultural programming. Can you see that history is just another way of saying memories? Are the memories real, true, and complete? Is the history real, true, and complete? No. But are you obsoletely taught and believe they are and can't be changed? Yes. Here's a disclaimer. If you can make money off the people you were taught to hate, is it all right to work with them, make money and change? Well, of course, this is an illusion you are in, you know. And nothing is as it seems.)*

It is our filtering system, whether as individuals or as the corporate body of family, country, or religion, that determines the world we see and respond to. Before we consolidated the memories into the subconscious mind, all the memories within the cluster will be interconnected, influence each other, and behave as one interactive memory. The body will do the best job possible to heal itself based on the information it is given from the active mind and its own inner wisdom. However, the secret to supporting healing in the body is to change the information the body is receiving. How would we do that? By healing and reframing negative memories in the mind. *(You see how easy it is to have a different world to live in. Forgiving oneself is the answer. Ah, but how good are you at that?)*

Where does the body get its information? From the active mind. Where does the active mind get its data? It gets its data from only two places, the subconscious mind and the body. One of those sources must change to support the body in healing. Understand that as one of those components changes, the other will change in response. As we then create a positive self-propagating feedback loop, the body's systems change in response to those positive signals; and therein lies the path of healing.

Realize the subconscious mind and body are entangled systems. As one changes, the other will and must change. The connecting point of the two systems is the active mind. They are operating and processing information at millions and billions of bits of data per second, and all we know is what the slow conscious mind lets us know. How can we not have a distorted understanding of the processes going on behind the curtain of our awareness?

If we want to heal that cluster of memories around our interpretation of the event, which is over and gone, we need to reframe the cluster in the best positive way possible. We need to realize the memories aren't real and not think, *I know what I feel, and I'm just being realistic about this*, because what we think we are being realistic about is an illusion due to the memory not being real; so we need to stop this thinking.

If we have physical injuries resulting from an event and are holding onto guilt or blame about the event and aren't forgiving, our healing process will be slow. It may stop altogether or get worst. We may need to look deep into our old memories because of our current situation. Older memories we thought we buried and put out of our mind may come to light and float into our awareness; and we will need to make peace with them. The subconscious mind connects and clusters memories of events together in ways the conscious mind will never know or understand. The path of healing major physical and emotional injures is an opportunity to change our whole life by changing old memories. We now know that just because we don't consciously remember a causal negative memory doesn't mean it isn't affecting us.

We are our memories, and that's all we are. By reframing and changing the negative outlying memories, we create a new interpretation of who we think we are, and a new identity for us will come into focus.

A new world will be right in front of us. If we do change our memories, forgive ourselves, and make peace with our past, will we heal completely from our pain and suffering? I don't know. However, if we don't change, tomorrow will look much like today, because if nothing changes, then nothing changes. The more positive interpretations we create in any situation, the more positive will be the signals we send to the body and the more positive will be the body's feedback. As we have said before, "What the mind perceives, the body must respond to; and it cannot not respond." Our memories in the subconscious mind determine what the mind perceives. The more positive we reframe our negative memories, the more positive will be the body's response, and the more enjoyable will be our lives.

Whatever our pain and suffering are, they won't get better by name-calling and blaming ourselves or others for the way we are feeling or for what our unreal memories remember of what happened in the past. For the body and mind to use their natural healing systems to their fullest potential, we need to reframe our negative memories and forgive ourselves. If we make peace with ourselves, which is to say make peace with our past, whatever medical interventions may be appropriate and used, the more effective they will be as we forgive ourselves.

CHAPTER 20

First the Thought and Then the Act

EVERY THOUGHT CREATES CHEMISTRY

Communication within the mind and body isn't in words. It is through electromagnetic and chemical messages. Every thought we think in the mind, brain, and central nervous system creates nonverbal signals throughout the mind and body. They aren't in any word language we would understand directly. Interpretations and perceptions in the active mind aren't in words either. The heart doesn't use words in communicating with the brain, nor does the brain use words in any of its communication with the body. There is no one in the subconscious mind or body to hear the words. Thoughts are perceptions, and every thought produces electromagnetic and chemical signals in the mind and body, because consciously we can't communicate to ourselves and other people without words; we need to use words, but the mind and body has no use for them. Words are added later as the conscious mind reports on the responses in the mind and body. But inside us, there is no one in there to talk to in word language. Again, here's the question. When the conscious mind is reporting on what has happened in the mind and body, who is it talking to? And who is listening to our self-talk?

Memories are thought forms stored in the subconscious mind. They are energy beings that have location somewhere because they can be recalled and remembered. They can't be physically held in our hands, but they can be felt in the body as the body responds to the active mind's interpretations. When memories are recalled in a very vivid way in the active mind, perceptions are made, chemistry is produced, and signals are sent to the body; we feel the changes in our bodies as they respond to signals; then they are reported by the conscious mind. We believe the memories are real and have power because of the way the body is forced to respond. We've gone over this before. The secret to changing memories is to realize they aren't real; and while the responses in the body are predictable, based on the signals received, the event is over and isn't happening again.

Memories are just creations made in the active mind, then stored in the subconscious mind. And it's okay to change them. Oh, be careful of how you feel when you read those words: "It's okay to change memories." Our egoic self may just jump right up in your face and proclaim, "That's wrong! That's wrong! Memories are real!" Silly ego! Don't listen to it; it is just trying to stay alive. *(If you go to a workshop or lecture and weigh yourself beforehand, then go into the workshop and get all kinds of new information and concepts, making a lot of new memories. Then if you weigh yourself later, you will weigh the same. Memories don't weigh anything. Since your memories don't weigh anything physically, you don't know where they are stored, you aren't sure how they are recalled; and no one really knows, how they are reconsolidated back into your subconscious for storage. So maybe your memories, which are who you think you are, aren't stored in the body. Maybe memories are stored outside the body. Oh now, that thought may have caught you off guard. If your memories are stored outside the body and are stored in the subconscious mind, that would mean the subconscious mind isn't in the body either. No wonder science can't find where memories are stored. They keep looking in the body. But if they are stored outside the body, the only place the subconscious mind could be is in the subtle field. What a thought. Your body and conscious mind in the gross energy system and the subconscious mind, with your memories and creations, are in the subtle field. That is just too much to think about now.)*

When we observe a person or an object, we create a perception in our active minds, and this is through the process we have already gone over several times; it is our perceptions that give meaning to the people or objects in our lives. Again, the person or object has no meaning in and of itself for us because it is neutral and meaningless in the outside everything. Why is it meaningless? Because everything is meaningless until we think about it. The meaning we have for it comes from our internal perceptions. What we think of them isn't them; it is us pretending to be them based on our past memories of them or similar people and objects. Remember, there is only us inside us. The people and objects are never inside us; only what we think about them is inside us as weightless thought forms, and those aren't the people or objects.

The internal nonverbal message from the body of, "I'm cold," will cause an interpretation in the active mind, and signals will be sent out to the mind and body for appropriate responses; then actions take place throughout the mind and body, with feedback being sent back and forth between the mind and body and active mind. Our primal drives move us away from discomfort and pain, and toward comfort and pleasure; and we will seek warmth. This again is happening at billions of data bits per second except of course in the conscious mind, and then the conscious mind reports on what has happened. So much is happening outside our conscious awareness.

The total mind/ body system is always moving to reach balance and homeostasis. To do that, constant communication and feedback loops of responses are constantly going on. They are touching hands in each moment. It is a moment-to-moment communication system, and it is faster than a speeding bullet, except for the conscious mind. Each thought creates a new interpretative universe and different chemistry and signals; and each universe creates signals requiring responses from the mind and body.

As we mentioned before, 95 percent of today will be like yesterday. To conserve resources for the whole system, we develop many ingrained behaviors that happen automatically; and out of conscious awareness, we call them habits. So if we are cold a lot, we will have automatic behaviors that will be ingrained to resolve that condition. We develop habitual ways of responding to life. They make it difficult to change, even if we want to change at a conscious level. Why would that be? Because our habitual self is out of conscious awareness in the subconscious mind, where all our programming is. And every habitual thought creates similar chemical signals that tell the mind and body how to respond;

they respond in much the same way every time they occur. It's not by accident that we keep acting and feeling the way we do. And it won't be by accident that we change.

Perception and Its Cause

Everything starts with a thought, which is to say a perception. First, there is a thought, a movement in the mind, brain, and central nervous system of the active mind; and then things happen. The perception is the result of the constant flow of data from the subconscious mind and the body. It is the interpretation of that data in the active mind that causes signals to be sent out to the mind and body, which in turn produces responses; and from the responses come more input to the active mind as feedback from the mind and body. And from that feedback data are more perceptions. *(You see, it is a well-orchestrated process, and it is so fast. Within nanoseconds balance within the whole complex is reached, and then the conscious mind gets involved.)*

Again, by looking closely, we will see that perceptions in the active mind aren't the cause of the mind or body's responses. Perceptions are the by-products of interpretations in the active mind; and interpretations are the natural outflow of the data received from the subconscious mind and feedback from the body that determines our perceptions. Therefore, our past memories cause the world we have and our responses to it. Our past determines our current world, our response to that world, and by default the life we are living right now.

Response, Behavior, and Effects

The mind and body are only responding to the interpretation of the active mind as is appropriate based on the signals they receive, and their response to the perception is an effect. If the body feels sick, it is an effect. If the mind is confused, it is an effect. What is the cause? Our past and the way we are using it to interpret the current filtered data. Where is the first place we look for the cause as to why we have any feelings of discomfort, which is to say pain and suffering? The body. And it is only an effect. It may be appropriate as a first response to support the body. However, after the first response, the cause needs to be addressed, which is to say our past. The causal problem is in the mind, and the answer is also in the mind. Again, if two aspirins take care of a problem headache, great. But if the problem cannot be healed that easily, the underlying cause needs to be uncovered and resolved so healing can occur. *(Can you appreciate that if the cause is resolved, its effects disappear? However, while moderating the effects will mask the cause and the body may feel better, without healing the cause, you are back in the same kettle of fish when you stop moderating the effects. Which means you are enslaved and in bondage to your system of modifying the effects. Whatever the method is, prescription medications or self-medications, they are all intended to conceal the unhealed cause. Heal the cause, and you are out of bondage and free.)*

At this point, the ego may again jump up, saying, "No! No! I have a virus, a bacterial infection, an accident. My genes or something else. The past and my thoughts aren't the cause of my illness. This is real. It isn't just in my head. I feel it." The truth will out. We all have viruses and bacteria in the body all the time. When the immune system is healthy, the body is getting positive signaling, and the body is in a healthy and balanced condition, which is to say its inner environment is in a loving, caring, and peaceful state, it can easily take care of protecting the internal body from viruses, bacteria, and rogue cells. With genetic diseases, we have earlier shared some thoughts and understandings on epigenetics, and our biology can change that gene expression. Our interpretations in the active mind change our biology, which is determined by the subconscious mind's filtering system or our past memories. We aren't stuck with our genes unless we think we are.

As for accidents, we may not be able to follow the cause-and-effect relationships back to the "first cause"; however, nothing comes from nothing, and accidents aren't acausal. They are effects; so there is a cause, but we might have to go through the math of chaos theory to find it. A moment or few seconds' difference in our behavior and our actions, either slowing down or speeding up, and there would have been no accident. The healing process after the incident will be enhanced and improved or diminished and slowed by how the active mind interprets it. A more positive interpretation will result in a speeder recovery, and a negative interpretation will result in a longer recovery period. Perception is everything, and it is changeable.

We cannot have a cause without some effect; therefore, if there is an effect in the body or in our world, there must be a cause in the mind. Cause and effect rise together. Problems occur when the response in the body is negative; notice this is an interpretation. When the signals the active mind send out are negative, the response in the body is negative, and the body goes into self-protection. When the fight-or-flight response is activated, the sympathetic nervous system is turned on as the body prepares to survive. The survival response changes many systems in the body as it protects itself, including shutting down the internal immune systems as a survival technique. Why would the body do that? Because when there is an interpretation that the greatest threat is from external attacks, we don't need to protect ourselves from internal threats until the external attacks are resolved and cleared; then the immune system is compromised, reduced, or shut off completely as determined by the external perceived threat. If the cause that produces our perception, our past memories, isn't addressed and healed, our immune system may be operating at minimal effectiveness for a long time; and this will reduce our ability to eliminate viruses, bacteria, and rogue cells.

This ongoing, negative inside environment is what the cells are trying to live and survive in. Depending on the chemical messages and how negatively contaminated the blood gets, we could begin to feel some discomfort in our bodies. The cells receive signals from their environment or our blood, and they must respond to survive. Which genes will be ordered up and expressed within the cells as they work hard to survive in their environment? They aren't changing their genetics to support the body. They don't give a damn about the body. They don't even know they are in a body. All they want to do is survive. They are like a fish in the sea, and their sea is toxic, because of the chemical-contaminated messages sent out by the active mind's interpretation chemical and electromagnetic feedback responses of mind and body.

Cells are the building blocks of the body. For them to be healthy and therefore for the body to be healthy, they need a friendly, caring, and loving environment, which is also what we need in our environment. If we are operating in less than that kind of caring and loving external environment, the body will be in stress and disease. Those will cause an unhealthy internal environment, which will affect how cells respond and how the body feels. It may affect what genes are expressed in our cells. It may express itself in pain and suffering in the body, which is caused by an interpretation of the mind, brain, and central nervous system or active mind.

Habitually, 95 percent of what we did yesterday is what we will do today. If the immune system was operating at minimal effectiveness yesterday and nothing changes, it will operate at minimal effectiveness today, causing a minimal immune system tomorrow and into the future. At some point our bodies will become compromised to the point of sickness, and pain and suffering may occur. The cells may express different genes to survive, the body may develop symptoms, and we consciously will have no idea where they came from. We will look at and feel that the body is the blame for our pain and suffering, and we will try to change the body, which is only an effect. We did say the body is the scapegoat for the mind, didn't we? Yes, we did, and it is still true.

Just because we aren't able to consciously remember the causal problem isn't proof that there isn't one. What is our proof that we have a causal problem? Effects in the body. If we have symptoms and effects in the body, the presenting problem, we have a causal problem somewhere. It won't be outside us in the current situation or event; it will be inside in our negative memories in the subconscious mind, triggered into the active mind many times by the outside situation or event. It will create negative interpretations and memories of events that are long gone. The causal problem will be around memories had haven't yet been healed, released, cleared, and forgiven.

Don't expect the conscious mind to remember what the causal problem is. It's too small and slow to carry that information; however, it will report on the feelings in our bodies. It has only temporary memory, and that lasts for only half a minute; besides, it can report only on what has already happened. On the other hand, if we could ask the subconscious mind, the answer would be clear because the subconscious mind is where all our memories are stored; and memories are the programs the subconscious mind is operating with. Hence, it knows where the data came from that produced the interpretation that caused the body to respond with stress and disease, pain and suffering; and when known, then it can be changed. If we can feel it in the body, point to it, or put our hand on the location of our pain and suffering in the body, we can change the kinesthetic submodalities of the memory; and those will reframe and change the whole memory.

In Chapter 6, "Making Friends with the Subconscious Mind," we shared two methods of moving into the subconscious mind for the purpose of making changes in our memories, which will change our subconscious mind's programming. In Chapter 7, "The Subconscious Mind," we shared a general tapping system for releasing emotional energy trapped in the body. Tapping on our bodies and using a particular tapping protocol will change the emotional energy in the body, which will change our interpretation of our pain and suffering, and will change how we feel in the body. The tapping changes the feedback loop and data between active mind and body. Notice that this will consciously change the feeling in the body as the kinesthetic submodalities of the memory are changed. By changing kinesthetic submodalities, we change the whole memory.

In Chapter 10, "Memory Coding System," we suggested a model for how memories might be stored in the energy matrix around the mind and body system. In that model, visual—sight, auditory—sound, kinesthetic—touch, olfactory—smell, and gustatory—taste components of the memory's modalities are stored in specific locations within the matrix of the black box. These components of stored modalities are what make up all memories. If a given modality within a memory is changed, the memory is changed, and so is its coded location within the matrix. The old memory is no more, and there is a new memory with different modalities and a newly assigned coded location.

We can use any or all modalities to change memories. However, our concern is with pain and suffering, which is to say the negative feelings in the body; and that is the kinesthetic modality of the memory. It is the one we need to change to shift out of pain and suffering. Since the kinesthetic modality is an integral part of the whole memory, when we work with it, we are affecting the whole memory. If we aren't aware of the memory determining the active mind's negative perception, we can start with the pain in the body. The subconscious mind will do the rest. *(If you can point to where you feel pain in your body, you can change it. The body is the gateway, the wormhole, into your subconscious mind; and into changing your memories.)*

Whatever method is used—tapping, hypnosis, submodality shifting, NLP, or some other method—the memory will change. The response is physiological and is consistent with the normal functioning of the body, and it doesn't require our belief. Our primal drive will move us away from discomfort and pain, and toward comfort, pleasure, and peace of mind. If we are in discomfort in the body, we will want to move to a place of comfort and pleasure. Trying to manipulate external behaviors and external situations through the use of willpower can work; however, most of the time, we run out of willpower long before we ingrain the behavior we want into the subconscious mind.

We can move to a place of comfort, pleasure, and peace in two ways: (1) heal, resolve, and change the negative memories from the past; or (2) escape into addictive behaviors and/or substance use (for example, using alcohol, shopping, exercising, gambling, experiencing dramas and trauma, or others). The first way will have no side effects and will be a permanent solution; and the second, by trying to escape, will have many side effects, won't be permanent, will offer only short-term release, and will cause greater pain and suffering than it will relieve. The problem is in us, and the solution is also in us. Looking outside for a solution and using outside behaviors to escape the inside pain and suffering of our problem will only create and cause more problems; they won't resolve the causal problem. The only solution that really works is to heal, resolve, and change our negative memories.

After the old memory is healed, resolved, and changed, it is no more; and a new memory will be consolidated into the subconscious mind with no trapped emotional energy; and the old memory that had the trapped emotional energy will dissolve and disappear into the new memory. The new memory, with no negative energy, will be consolidated into the subconscious mind; and this will change the subconscious mind's programming in more positive ways, which is to say that its filtering system of the present moment will be different.

The thought forms or memories are all stored in the subconscious mind. When triggered, the whole thought form or memory is moved into the active mind. An interpretation is created, and signals are sent out. Then a response is produced in the body; it will cause an effect, a feeling in our bodies. From the response, our outside behaviors and actions automatically spring. What happens in our perceived outside world is always a reflection of what is going on inside us. *(Notice that this will happen unless you have been trained through family or culture to hide your feelings and emotions. Since you have no reference to what drives your subconscious programs, you will be confused and may blame others, because you aren't connected to yourself, your feelings, or your emotions; you will believe it is them. It is those outside you who have the problem; and if only they would change, you would be okay. Silly person, it's you.)*

Everything flows downhill. Our memories in the subconscious mind cause us to create the perceptions we have in the active mind. The perceptions cause the body to respond the way it does. How the body responds causes the behavior we present to those around us. Therefore, how we are in our current lives is caused ultimately by our past. If there are unhealed memories, we will have one life. If we reframe, heal, and change past memories to a more positive interpretation, we will get a different, more positive life.

CHAPTER 21

The Slippery Slope of Forgiveness

WHAT IS THE OPPOSITE OF FORGIVENESS?

For most, the opposite of forgiving is blaming and holding on to our grievances against other people or situations, and seeing them as offending sinners. We might even think; *How can I pardon them? How can I ever forgive them? Look what they did to me. That hurt me very badly. I'll always remember it.* We blame other people, groups, or situations for the offenses committed against us. This blaming and lack of forgiveness hold us bound and tied to the other person, group, or situation. We are tied to him or her by our resentment, indignation, and anger. In the eye of the offended, the grievous offense demands some kind of punishment, reimbursement, or compensation. *(Notice again that it's only your memories that hold your pain and suffering in place because the events are gone and will never come back; and all you have left of those events are memories, which as we said before aren't real, true, or complete.)*

Now if we are the offending person, we can blame ourselves, but we more likely will manipulate the memory of the event so it's not so bad or maybe convince ourselves it was really the other person's fault in the long run. And we might even think, *Well, if they wouldn't have done "X," I wouldn't have done "Y!"* The ego is only too glad to help in this manipulation of the facts in that process to save its egoic ass. The event

334

is over and gone, and all we are doing is beating a dead horse, because we believe the memory is real and still alive.

In this short read, we won't be addressing major offenses, such as murder, rape, treason, and so forth. We will confine ourselves to the lesser offenses of personal slights and hurts between family members, friends, and lovers. However, the same process will apply to those other deeper offenses too. These lesser slights are those that cause relationships and friendships to collapse; they cause us to stop talking to or seeing the offending other person for weeks, years, or maybe forever. Major offenses are few and far between, but these lesser offenses happen every day, and the pain that follows them can last a long, long time and maybe, as we know, forever.

Since blaming and being unforgiving keep us tied and bound to other people at some level, we are continually dancing with them, even though we may never see or talk to them again. We are dancing with ghosts of our perception of them that isn't there, and we are doing it only in our heads, usually not consciously. Regardless of whether we see them, talk to them, or even have them in our lives, they are there, affecting how we see and live our lives. It's easy to keep them out of our conscious awareness because the conscious mind is so easily distracted and has such a small temporary memory; however, the subconscious mind always remembers. If the offense is very grievous to us, the subconscious mind will put it high on the priority of its filtering system; and the offense will be part of why we see the present moment the way we do. It will be triggered and brought into the active mind a lot, even though we consciously won't be aware of it. *(Just because you have so cleverly hidden your grievous memories from your conscious self doesn't mean they aren't affecting you, because they are still affecting how you create your world.)*

The remembered offense may keep us on high alert and always looking over our shoulder, while keeping our survival systems turned on in various degrees and at various levels of stress. This will affect the responses in the body's systems over time and influence the effectiveness of our immune system. It may cause the body to express symptoms of pain and suffering, and we consciously will have no idea where they are coming from. Holding on to our negatively attached memories of grievances and burying them out of our conscious awareness can affect our physical and mental health and our peace of mind.

WHAT ISN'T BEING FORGIVEN?

We experience an event; following the same system we have already discussed and gone over several times before, we interpret the event, using perceptional filtered data from our past as offensive. The event itself is neutral until we think about it through our interpretation. What makes it offensive to us is something in us and our past memories of being offended. From that interpretation signals are sent to the mind and body, and they respond. Since the signals are, "I'm under attack!" It is our beliefs of who we think we are, that is under attack, and the body will change. Maybe the interpretation is a physical attack. Maybe it's an emotional attack or a combination of both, and we will automatically turn on our survival systems in the body to match the perceived attack. Part of our survival systems is to shut down or lower the immune system; and if the survival system is left on too long, the immune system can be compromised to the point of not being effective enough to protect the body.

Can we now appreciate that if events of childhood where negative, when we had little survival skills, the memories of our interpretations of the events will more deeply affect us? The child's priorities in their filtering system may be set for their whole life by those early experiences. This situation may have a great effect on how the child filters and creates the world they will lives in today. If the offense or attack is repeated over time, the greater and deeper will be the effect on the body's systems; and it will be more difficult to change or even to recognize that change is needed. We may think, *Well, that is just the way I am. It is genetics or something, and besides there is nothing I can do about it now. (When you acknowledge and understand memories aren't real, there is a lot you can do to change and reframe your memories. Are you ready to take that quantum leap yet?)*

Events always end and are over, gone like mist in the morning sun. Is anything left of the events? No, nothing is left of the event, only memories of how we interpreted the event. Are memories real? We must be careful here because we may have a tendency to bring more grievous memories into the mind and feel the energetic responses in our bodies when answering this question. And of course, when we bring deeply negative memories of grievances that are still festering in the active mind, the body will respond negatively, and the conscious mind will report on how awful we feel. We will believe the memories must be real because when we are feeling awful in the body, logic goes out the window.

Memories aren't real; they are created from filtered and manipulated data. When we are offended, all logic goes out the window, because of the feelings in the body, and we are lost within the body's response and our ego's judgment. Our memory may have become a meta memory.

Refer to Chapter 14, "Switching of Purpose and Means," the heading "The Feelings in the Body Are Primary," for a description of meta memories. This is a model of how memories take on a life all their own and why we can't think clearly as our bodies respond to the pain and suffering embedded within the meta memory. Notice, if we have meta memories, we have healing to do. However, we may not think so because we will believe the memory is real and can't be healed or changed; and if that is the belief we have, we will find evidence that it is true. The more we believe anything, the more faith we have in the belief, and the more difficult it will be to see any other possibility. And they will be right, because the subconscious mind will filter only for the proof that matches our beliefs, and the proof will be found; and it will be true for them. *(Oh, by the way, will your subconscious mind find the proof that your belief is true? Of course, it will. Because your egoic self must keep sorting until it finds proof or die trying. Remember, everything is out there in the subtle field of everything, and the ego will find its proof for you.)*

Since the event of why we were offended is over, what are we offended about now? Since the event is over and gone, all that is left is our memory. All that we keep bringing up in our active mind is the unreal memory of our interpretation of the event. When the active mind receives any data, it makes an interpretation; and then the whole routine starts all over again, as we have described. We aren't now offended because of the event, since the event is gone. We are offended because of the unreal memory of the event, and that we don't have to keep, and we can reframe it. We can change memories of offensives like we can change any memory. Memories are energy thought forms inside us. They aren't outside us, and they don't have other people in them. They are inside us, and we alone are inside our energy field. The offending person or situation isn't in us; only the unreal interpretations of the other person and situation, which are now just memories, are inside us.

THE UNDESERVED PARDON

To pardon is to forgive without penalty or punishment. Since we blame ourselves or others for offending us, to pardon them or ourselves may seem like a lie, a false act, and a complete denial of the truth. We may feel like it's too much of a sacrifice or a lie for us to forgive them or ourselves. We might hear our ego, saying, "Where is the fairness in this? To just let them off the hook like that?"—snap fingers—"They need to pay!" We might even think of ourselves, *I must suffer for what I did. (You might even feel or believe you must suffer for your misdeeds to understand that the event is over, gone, and won't come back; and that your memory of the event isn't real, true, or complete; and that your memory is only in your head and that no one else has it. However, that may be a stretch for you at this point in restructuring your vision. Should you make restitution? Maybe. Should you apologize to the other person? Maybe. Should you stay angry at the other person until they apologize? No. Forgiveness has nothing to do with the other person. They have their own problems, and you can't change them. You have your problems, and those you can change. Change and forgive yourself, and the right action will flow out of that act of true self-forgiveness; whether the other person forgives you or you forgive them is really unimportant. Forgiving yourself is the important thing. You made an error in your perception of the event. If you had a different filter system, a different past, you would have had a different response to the event. What is your filter system? Your past memories. Reframe your past, and your present moment will be different; and so will your future.)*

We will need to shift the way we understand what we are doing when we are forgiving or pardoning others or ourselves. Are we pardoning what they did or what we did within an event? No. We can't pardon the event or what they did (and what we did) within the event, because the event is over and gone; it's not here and will never come back again. Just like no two snowflakes are never the same, that event will never come back. Since the event isn't here, what is here? The unreal memory of our interpretation of the event and what we perceive happened within the event. *(Can you see I am repeating the system over in different forms so you can understand that the content underlying all the different forms is the same? Different forms but same content. You are programmed to feel guilty about the past. If you forgive others, you are letting them off the hook, and that will seem like a lie. If you don't forgive them, you are mean and spiteful. If you forgive yourself, you are arrogant and lack understanding. Can you see how your egoic self keeps you under control and in guilt and shame? By forgiving yourself, reframing your negative memory, letting them go, and seeing things differently, you are healing yourself; and your world must become more positive.)*

Is the memory real? Here we go again. No, it's not real. Why isn't it real? Because it's a creation of filtered and manipulated data that has been pushed through our past memories. *(I know the memory seems real to you because of how it feels in your body when you think about it. I know that when those feelings come up, depending on how intense they are, it's hard to realize the event isn't happening all over again inside you, even though logically you know the event isn't happening. But because of the feelings in the body, your logic has a hard time standing up to them. You need to be gentle with yourself at this point. Slowly, step-by-step, changes will occur as your awareness increases. The beliefs you have are driven by your family, culture, and all those other egoic systems; and they are ingrained in your subconscious programming. For you to even consider there may be another way of seeing the world takes courage and challenges what your ego is telling you, even at this moment.)*

Begin to bring into our understanding as a belief the idea that memories aren't real, true, or complete; and that the event they depict will never, ever come back again. The event is over, and what we think about the past is untrue, because our past comprises only memories. This will be difficult at first because there will be bits and pieces within each memory that are true for us. Nonetheless, memories as a whole are unreal, untrue, and incomplete constructions; and while some bits and pieces may be partially true, the wholeness of the memory is unreal, untrue, and incomplete. As stated in Chapter 9, "Memories," we will never know which parts of the memory are completely true and which are completely untrue. If we did, we wouldn't need to put the untrue, filtered, manipulated data into the memory we stored in the subconscious mind in the first place. Or would we?

So we have a past that isn't all true and not all untrue; however, we believe it's all true, or we wouldn't have put the untrue part into the memory. What do we call something that isn't true but we believe is true? An illusion, right? Now we are back to what the ancients called the "reality of this world," an Illusion. It's beginning to feel like that old comedy routine of "Who's on First? What's on Second?"

Now, when we forgive an offense, what are we pardoning? Not the event because it is gone and will never come back. Okay, but what are we pardoning? All that is left to forgive, reframe, and pardon is the unreal, untrue, and incomplete memory. To pardon an unreal memory isn't a lie. To pardon an untrue memory isn't a false act. To pardon an incomplete memory isn't to deny that it's truth, because it's not. We are forgiving and pardoning something that was never completely real, true, or known in the first place. But oh, don't we believe it was and still is real? And oh, how it feels in the body when we think of it. Now, all that will change when we truly forgive ourselves. *(If you are addicted to the feelings of drama, family enmeshment, and/or trauma, if they define your life, self-forgiveness will be more difficult. Whether you are taking a drug from the outside or creating the chemicals in your body by traumatic thoughts, addictions all work the same way. And every thought you think creates chemistry, and you can get addicted to the self-created chemistry of drama just like alcohol; and of course, like all addictions, you will deny you have a problem. You may even say, "I don't like drama. I hate it!" But there you are, always in the middle of it.)*

Whether we are the perpetrator or the offended victim, it is all us inside us now. There is no other person inside us but us. If we grant a pardon, who are we pardoning? Ourselves. If we are asking for forgiveness, who are we asking to forgive us? Ourselves. If we withhold forgiveness, who is suffering? Ourselves. We are the directors. We make the scenery for the memory, and we are all the actors in our memories, and we are the audience of the memory. There is no one inside us but us. The "others" will have their own memories of the over-and-gone event, and their memories won't be like ours. *(Are you getting this? Later, I will bring a different concept of an "entangled memory system" into our understanding of what the past is. But first you need to let go of your prejudices regarding memories and recognize that they aren't real, true, or complete. You need another goal. Recall the goal you had? It was to "save your egoic ass." You need to change your goal to peacefulness, and your new goal should move you to live at the level of "peace of mind.")*

We can live only in the present moment. When we move into our memories or pull them into the present moment, we have moved into a place that doesn't exist. It is an altered state of consciousness, a trance state that is only in our heads. Memories in that state are illusions. That state is also called a "dream state"; and we have talked about the dream state before.

So what are we forgiving? Something that is only inside our heads. And self-forgiveness has nothing to do with the other person. We are always and forever forgiving only ourselves. Even if we go to the other person and forgive or ask for forgiveness, whether they do or don't forgive us has no effect on us until we can change and reframe the memories inside us. It always gets back to us. *(I know it doesn't feel that way inside you. I know you believe the memories are real. It's time to see the world differently and heal from your pain and suffering, which is for the most part self-inflicted. Who is the subtle cause of all your memories? You are. By default, who is the subtle cause of your pain and suffering? Well, let's just leave that unanswered for now.)*

Forgiveness is being compassionate, loving ourselves, and healing errors inside us. And by the process of self-forgiveness, we release other people so they can forgive themselves. If we don't heal the error in us, we may need to experience more pain and suffering for a long time and therefore be the cause of pain and suffering for those around us. *(You may or may not have noticed. I said, "Release the other people," because when you are experiencing an event, you are entangled in the combined energy of all those involved in the event; and when you hold on to the energy of offense, you keep others energetically attached to you and you to them. As you*

341

forgive yourself, you bring your energy to a neutral state, which allows others to change (or not) how they are attached to the memory of the event. As you begin moving from surface structure to deeper structures and toward oneness, begin to appreciate that the entangled energy of those others will change. At the surface, you are separated from others and everything else; and at oneness, separation, time, and space collapse, and you are one.)

THE FRAGILE ILLUSION

It takes a lot of cooperation to maintain an illusion as big as the one we are in. All of us need to do our part. We need a lot of different egos, both as individual and as groups, to keep it going. We need a lot of conflict and trauma to keep the mind engaged and preoccupied in believing we are our bodies and to keep us deep in the gross energy field. A big part of keeping the illusion going is our pain and suffering, and we do so by blaming others or ourselves. Our egoic self will be more than happy to help us do that.

If we start changing the rules of engagement, the whole illusion might just collapse; it might implode, and then behind the illusion there just might be the subtle field of reality. If we begin to understand that we can change our world just by changing our minds, what would happen to all those egos? Think of all the financial institutions that would suffer. This could be the end of the world as we know it. Nah, that won't happen. Not to worry. All those egos in high places won't let that happen; besides, our own egos will fight hard to stay alive and make memories seem real; and this strategy will ensure that the illusion won't collapse.

But maybe, just maybe, a few might break out of their imprisonment of the past. They might lift the curtain and look behind the illusion. They would have to be careful though, because as a few individuals start changing and move out of the illusion, they will weaken the fragile illusion, and a panic might break out. To prevent that from happening, the few rogues who have escaped the illusion may be hunted down and made fun of, maybe ridiculed or arrested. Don't be too surprised by what might happen if a few start opting out of the illusion. Look at what happened when a few individuals first proclaimed the world was round and not the center of the universe. Some were arrested, jailed, imprisoned, and tortured; some were even killed. Right now, in some countries, we could lose our heads if we were to go against the current illusionary state. Belief in the illusion is very strong and powerful. So much fear is generated within the greater whole because of the few breaking from the mainstream illusion. Why? Because it calls into question the whole illusion. So we can't be too overt in what changes we make in our beliefs. Understand that by changing our minds by self-forgiveness, we are changing our memories and healing the body and mind in the process; and this might be beyond the pale for many to accept who are heavily invested in the illusion.

The secret is to learn how to be in the world but not of the world, to be separate and yet in oneness at the same time. To be our "self" (small *s*) and at the same time to be our "Self" (big *S*). The thought of being in two different energy systems or locations or states of being at the same time may seem crazy, especially for those of us in the illusion of the gross energy system. To be a separate individual in the gross energy system and, yet at the same time, be within the oneness in the subtle field of everything—how crazy is that? When we are consciously aware and are observing our "self" with the conscious mind, we are separate individuals in the gross energy system. When we aren't consciously aware of our self, we are open to our deeper "Self." We can slip closer into oneness in the subtle field.

We may think of these as states of being in the world but not of the world in terms of quantum physics. In quantum physics there is a state known as "superposition." Superposition is a place where two states of being exist at the same time. In our case, one state is the "egoic state," and the other is our "Original Self State" or oneness state. *(You might think again of quantum physics. When you consciously observe or are aware of the self, you are a separate being and particles. When you aren't observing or aware of yourself, you are open and move toward oneness and your Self. So like quantum physics, in one state we are separate particles, and in the other state, we are like waves; between those states is the superposition of being in both at the same time.)*

Recall Chapter 11, "Gross and Subtle Energy Systems," in the section titled "The Oneness in the Many." There I stated, "How to display oneness of the many in the three-dimensional space/time universe is a daunting task. It is like making a paradox seem real." We resolve this paradox by imagining switching from one to the other very quickly. We imagine doing that because we believe the gross and subtle are separate states and don't recognize that they are in a special state of entanglement of both, which can be called superposition. *(Look closely at the two states, and you will see that the gross is always inside the subtle.)*

Now, we can't understand this state in Newtonian physics; we can approach this possibility only through quantum mechanics and quantum physics through the little wormhole of superposition. Now superposition doesn't apply to people, as far as we know; it applies only to things like subatomic particles, things we can't see or weigh. But the theoretical idea that speaks to being "in the world but not of the world" and of being "self" and "Self" at the same time comes close to this idea. When we look with a conscious mind, we are the "self" of particles; and when we aren't looking or are unaware, we can be anything. When we become aware, we collapse into one state of self. *(If you were to apply this line of reasoning to you or me, you might recognize that this is what happens in the famous and infamous double-slip experiment of quantum physics. You may have heard the phrase "We are spiritual beings having a physical experience," and that would be a superposition of being the spiritual Self and the physical self at the same time. What determines which state you are in? Your conscious awareness or your consciousness?)*

CHAPTER 22

Unmanifested Everything and the Manifested Everything

Lasers, Information, and Holograms

I know little about lasers, but I want to use the idea of lasers and holograms to understand our pain and suffering from a little different vantage point and how a reference beam or the subtle field is used to create holograms from stored information in the subconscious mind. This will take some redefining of our belief system; therefore, we can look at this approach as a metaphor. Don't look for a lot of detail in this understanding. See it as a model, a metaphor, a thought adventure. The properties of the laser we will be using in its model is the ability to create holograms, a three-dimensional picture, out of energy. What we will be doing conceptually and metaphorically is using components of the laser system in the construction of our holographic world. The components we will be using are an energy source (the laser source), the reference beam (unmanifested everything), the information medium (the film or the subconscious mind), and the resultant hologram. *(Play along with me on this. You might notice that some of these concepts and ideas will resonate with you, and you may also notice that some don't. Your subconscious will select which works for you and which doesn't. Let the rest go and begin to see things differently.)*

This model uses the following components:

- The outside unmanifested everything is our source energy of our make-believe holographic system.
- Our senses represent the parallel, monochromatic, and coherent reference beam, which is to say the constant flow of everything captured by the senses.
- The information medium that interferes or filters the reference beam is the subconscious mind.
- The hologram is the created output in your head. It is the interpretation by the active mind as the output from the interference of the reference beam of everything and the filtering process of the subconscious mind interfere with each other.
- This is the hologram the conscious mind projects into the outside everything; and we believe it is the outside world.

Scientifically (kind of) to create a hologram, the laser light beam source is split. Half of the beam is reflected onto a photographic film or plate using mirrors. The other half is bounced off, mirrored, and hits an object; and then it is reflected onto the same photographic film or plate as the reference beam. And then the photographic film or plate is developed. The film is the storage medium of the information, and the information is stored within the thickness layers of the photographic film or plate. The storage medium carries its patterns of interference between the two halves of the beam.

Now to create a hologram, the same type of reference beam as was used to put the information onto the developed film in the first place is shined onto the developed film. From the interference between the reference beam and the stored information in the film, a hologram of the original object will reflect off the film and appear as a three-dimensional object. It's the interference waves between the reference or source beam and the stored information in the thickness of the film that produces this holographic effect. As the film is moved in relationship to the reference source beam, the hologram shifts and moves. *(This is a thumbnail description of how a hologram is produced, and it isn't complete or scientific, but it may give you an idea of what I want to show. Do you see that the produced hologram is a creation and that there is really nothing there, but it looks, for all the world, like something is really there? As I have said before, when you believe something is there but it's not, that is called an "illusion." You and I live in an unreal world. There is a new concept that is being scientifically considered, and it is this. We live inside a computer simulation in a virtual reality. Is it possible? Maybe.)*

The sensory input, the "source reference beam," moves onto and collides with the information medium or film, which in this model is the stored information in the subconscious mind. From that collision between the input reference source beam of everything, from the senses and the information medium, which is all our memories stored in the subconscious mind, will develop interference patterns. These interference patterns produce the holograms in our heads based on the information stored in the medium storage film or the subconscious mind. As our minds move through different memories and thoughts, different holograms are created in the mind's eye, which is inside our heads. And those holograms move into the mind, become new memories, and add to the stored information. *(Notice that while I have said "mind's eye," all your senses are involved. Each hologram will be rich in detail.)*

Each hologram, which comprises thoughts in the mind, brain, and central nervous system, produces signals that tell the body how to respond to the holographic world inside us. We see again that the body doesn't respond to the outside subtle field of everything; the body responds only to the active mind's signaling. *(You need to get this. You live through your head. You live and function in the inside world, and that world is only an interpretation of the outside world. That is a big difference. Why? Because when you appreciate that you live through your inside construction, you have control of what is inside you; and you can change it.)*

The following diagram is a way of depicting this holographic model. Look closely and notice; it isn't the outside source reference beam that changes to create the holographic world we experience, because the outside is constant and is everything. It is the stored memory information that must change to create different holographic worlds. The holographic world we now live in has nothing to do with the outside constant source reference energy of the "everything," and it has everything to do with what we hold within our minds, which is to say our memories. *(You will need to change your filter to have a new world to experience, because it is your current filter that interferes with the wave function of everything and collapses into the hologram you see in your head now. It is you who determines your world. And that determination is made by what is inside you, not what is outside you. You do remember that "it always gets back to you, doesn't it?" Why? Because you are the creator of your world.)*

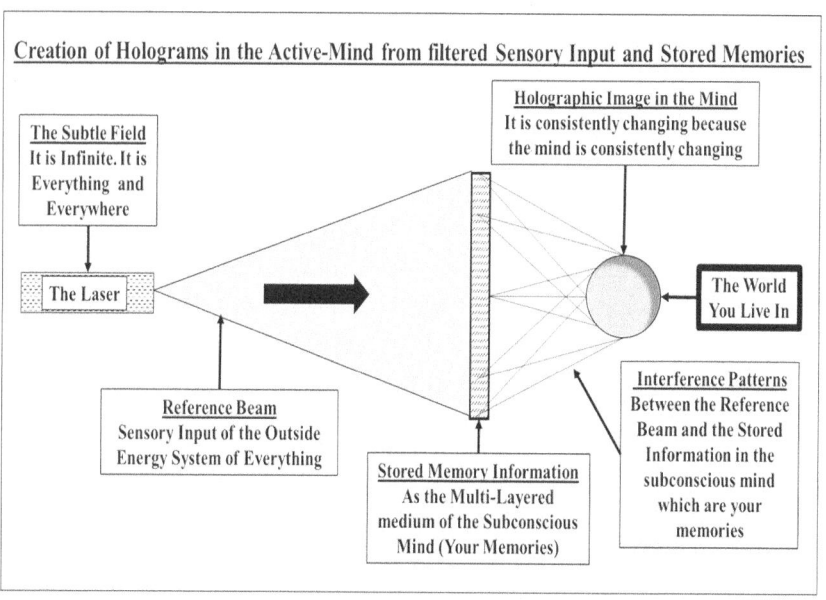

Diagram25 - The Holographic World You Live In

In this model, the laser, the subtle field of everything, is constant because it is infinite; and it is everything and is everywhere. Everything is there, unmanifested within it; and nothing can be added, and nothing can be taken away because it is everything; and again, it is infinite. The reference beam is also constant because the senses are capturing the unchangeable and unchanging subtle field. So what causes the holographic image to change? What causes our world to change and be the way it is? The stored information, which is our memories and who we think we are, changes with each new hologram. We are synchronized with and interconnected to the gross energy field; and that gross energy field undulates under the influence of its attitudes, beliefs, experiences, and interpretations in all its forms of egoic states.

We may be able, with this model, to understand how we can see the inside manifested hologram projected onto the outside subtle field of everything by the conscious mind. The reason we can project the inside world into the outside is because it is already there but unmanifested. It is the way our lens is constructed from our past that brings what is there in the "everything" into focus inside us. We match the frequency of the unmanifested, and we resonate with that frequency, and it comes into focus for us as an internal hologram. We are touching hands with the subtle field; and based on our feedback, the unmanifested is responding to our requests. *(Here again you are getting in your life what you are asking for by dancing with, and giving feedback to, the subtle field.)*

Outside is the constant infinity of everything, and inside shifting layers of information in the mind become a fractionation process that creates the hologram of our world. The oneness of everything is becoming fragmented into the many separate things in our internal world. We now have "the many" inside the infinite oneness of the subtle field. We are always embedded in that infinite field, but of course our egoic self keeps us dancing so fast in the gross energy system of everyday life that we miss it altogether. *(Can you see this as another model that may bring us to the understanding of how we can be "in the world but not of the world"? It is the recognition that the gross, everyday life must be, and always has been, within the subtle field. You are the oneness dreaming of the virtual many; and it is so real, isn't it?)*

EXPERIENCING THE SUBTLE FIELD

How can we experience the subtle field from within the gross energy system? We can't. Why not? If one of us experienced that state of oneness completely, we all would experience it, because at root we are all one; and in the instant of that experiencing oneness, time and space would collapse, and we would be the oneness and be home. Now this has almost happened a few times. But luckily we managed to stop them from reaching that oneness, or we would be there in oneness now and not here now.

Where is the oneness? It is the subtle field. Again, see the paradox here. We are in the gross energy system of everyday life right now, and at the same instant, we are also in the subtle field of everything right now. What prevents us from experiencing this integrated oneness? Fear of the unknown and our past memories. We have experienced only the separation in the illusion. Oneness is scary. *(Who would you be with? Would they be like you? Would your loved ones be there? Or would there just be you in that oneness? Would you be in oneness with all those others (you know the ones), those you don't trust, those you don't like, or those who look a little different from you? Come on, let's get real here. Who needs that? Experiencing oneness may be greatly overrated.)*

I'm sure all these questions and concerns have been worked out by infinite source by now, right?

THE HIDDEN PATH TO ONENESS

While we may not be able to experience this oneness, there is a path that leads us to the gates of oneness, to just a step away. It is a path we have already laid out in some detail; however, it still may be a path that seems too foreign for us to follow, too counterintuitive to be taken seriously. It is strongly opposed by the egoic self in all its forms, and to select this path would appear to be stupid, irrational, and dangerous, at least to the egoic self.

To follow this path is to change who we are. It is to set our feet on a different path and stop traveling the old egoic road. *(I would suggest that if you choose to take this path, don't tell others of your decision, at least not at the beginning. I would do so for two reasons: One, you will need to explain yourself to them, and you may not be able to do that yet; and they won't understand because they won't be where you are on their journey. And second, gain some success and strength in the practice of this path. It is a very personal path and a very personal journey you would have chosen.)*

What is this path? Self-forgiveness. It is the gentle path of self-forgiving, which in truth is self-loving. It is a self-directed path with few signal posts along the way to help us. However, once we have truly started on that path, heaven and earth will move to support us. The past is over and doesn't exist; we know that by now, don't we? It will never come back. The only things we have of the past are unreal, untrue, and incomplete memories. As we move toward oneness, we will realize this is all an illusion. Nothing has ever happened the way we think it did, and nothing is happening now the way we think it is. Why? Because the present is always filtered through and manipulated by the unreal, untrue, and incomplete data of our interpretations of the past, our memories. We can experience only the present through the lens of our past memories, and no one else has those memories but us. Therefore, only we individually experience the world we have no matter what the ego whispers in our ears and no matter what it looks and feels like in the illusion of our created hologram.

We aren't forgiving the event because there is no event here to be forgiven; it is gone. We are forgiving our interpretation, our memory, which is all we have to change and forgive. Know there is no event to change or forgive. This path will bring us out of guilt, pain, and suffering, which are all self-induced and into self-love, which is always a journey of self-unfolding and is also self-induced. Now here is an interesting thought. Once we can completely love ourselves unconditionally, we will be in the state of oneness because we will have collapsed the many into the one; and wouldn't that be perfect? *(You can come so close to oneness by self-forgiveness. It will change your life.)*

LIFE ISN'T PERFECT

While this read addresses forgiveness in a matter-of-fact path and a straightforward approach, we may not be ready for that kind of understanding, which is too bad because self-forgiveness is truly the answer. The following two quotes relating to forgiveness are from *A Course in Miracles*:

- "Forgive, and you will see this differently."
- "I will forgive, and this will disappear."

(https://acim.org/workbook-lessons-overview/
A Course in Miracles: Lesson #193)

As the offended person, we may not see the lesson presented to us through the current experience; or as the offending person, we may not have learned our lesson of seeking forgiveness through honesty, compassion, and loving kindness. Therefore, we keep offending. Whether we are the offended person or the offender, the behavior we exhibit is because of learned behavioral programming from the past, which is our system of beliefs and our memories.

It isn't by accident we behave the way we do. Relationship is the mechanism the universe uses to heal old wounds and maladaptive behaviors of the past, particularly around childhood wounds. Unfortunately, within relationship the partners may not be ready to heal; or maybe only one of the partners is ready to change. This will cause ongoing pain and suffering for both in the relationship, and the partnership will be out of balance.

An impasse may occur in our relationships that will prevent those involved from reaching a successful resolution of their lesson. *(You do know life is a series of ongoing lessons that move us forward into the infinity of oneness, don't you?)*

If an impasse occurs that can't be truly forgiven, it may be more helpful to dissolve the current relationship and seek a new partner or circumstance to complete our life lessons; but know we are destined to learn the lesson presented to us in the current relationship. With that in mind, if we choose another partner or a different situation at another time, we will be presented with much of the same lesson. This will continue to occur again and again until it is successfully completed. *(Life can be a bummer at times, you know.)*

The form of the new partner or situation may not look anything like the old person or situation; however, the underlying content of the lesson will be the same. Life can be a bitch about learning our lessons. So it may be better to resolve our current situation with the partner we are now with. But don't wait too long; if the current partner just isn't ready and you're ready to change and move closer to your original self, change partners. *(But you need to be careful because you are very likely to select a partner much like the one you just had, even though they may seem different.)*

BREAKING UP CAN BE LOVING

Now, if partners cannot reach complete forgiveness, separation may be the only solution. Three choices could be tried:

1. Stay in the relationship and live in the energy of unforgiveness and suspicion.
2. Stay in the relationship, learn our lesson, and change what needs to be changed; then if needed, separate and move on.
3. Separate and find someone else or a different situation to complete your lessons but don't just move because you don't know what to do. *(Heal yourself, love yourself, and forgive yourself; then see what the next step will be. When you have healed and forgiven yourself, you will make the right decision.)*

If separation is the solution of choice, great compassion and love must be brought into dissolving the relationship. When compassion and love are integrated into the process, the life lesson is much closer to being completed. At this point, blaming and finding fault won't resolve the situation; however, using compassion and love will. This may not be an easy thing to do because of our distorted expectations, interpretations, and perceptions around the relationship or the situation, and our egos need to blame the other person and make it their fault to protect our ego from getting emotionally bruised.

HONORING THE DEEPER SELF

Beyond the situation, our current partner, all our concerns, and our bodies is our deeper self. If we are very still, quiet, and at peace with ourselves, we will be able to hear that still, quiet voice of our inner wisdom, our original self, even through all the present turmoil. At root all problems are spiritual. We are energy beings of crystallized light, here within a space/time body; and as such, we exist in a paradox.

The paradox is this. We exist here in a world of space/time, the gross energy system; and yet we are at our essence within the subtle field, far beyond space/time. We are confronted with many challenges here in space/time or lessons we struggle to resolve. As we struggle with all the challenges, it's easy to forget we are much more than physical bodies and our challenges. But as the old saying goes, "When the alligators are biting our ass, it difficult to remember our job is to drain the swamp."

Whether we stay in our current situation with our current partner isn't the important question. Whatever our decision is, the important thing is to do it with forgiveness, compassion, and love. By using compassion for the situation and our partner, and with love for ourselves, we will dissolve any future pain and suffering or resentment around the memories of our interpretation of the event. This allows us to be free to experience a new present moment and a new life with greater peace of mind.

This isn't a process of being passive or just rolling over. It's a process of self-forgiveness, self-love, and compassion. Balance and equanimity are needed in dissolving the situation or the relationship; and it needs to be done without anger or blaming. Remember, anger and blaming are tools of the ego. At its source, all those involved in the relationship or situation contributed to the current condition and its outcome in some way, and we can look to the ancient wisdom that states, "There are no accidents." However, because of our egos' desire to be right and the projection of our own unmet expectations and beliefs around the situation, it will take some effort to let go or dissolve the relationship or situation with true forgiveness, love, and compassion.

Forgiveness is truly the answer to letting go of the past, and gratitude and appreciation for what we have now are the keys to unlocking a healthy and happy future. No matter how physical the situation appears, everything is energy; and at a deeper level, all problems are spiritual lessons.

The first to apologize is the bravest.
The first to forgive is the strongest.
The first to forget is the happiest, and
Happiest is the goodest.

CHAPTER 23

Entangled Connections

ENTANGLEMENT

Throughout this book we have mentioned entanglement within different contexts. Basically, when things are entangled, all mixed up, and enmeshed within each other, boundaries are lost; and we can't tell where one ends and the other begins. There is no clearly defined separation between objects.

Quantum entanglement has a unique quality that can be observed at the subatomic level, and this quality has been scientifically verified many, many times with proof positive that this phenomenon does indeed occur. So, what is this quantum entanglement? Quantum entanglement is the phenomenon that, when two or more subatomic particles are all mixed up and enmeshed within each other's energy systems, they cannot be viewed anymore as separate particles, but they must be viewed as an integrated, interrelated whole system. It is this scientifically proven quality of entanglement we will be using to view events, interpretations, and memories in a much different way.

Entanglement at the quantum level is a unique physical phenomenon Einstein called "spooky action at a distance." Entanglement basically is a phenomenon that scientifically states, "When two particles or groups of particles are entangled in each other's energy systems and then separated, what happens to one particle, instantly effects and changes the other particle or groups of particles. The strange property of this effect is that time and distance have no effect on this process." Therefore, as one particle within the system changes, all the particles in the entangled energy system will change. How much will they change? That's an interesting question that isn't well defined as yet (Wikipedia, s.v. "Stevie Nicks," last modified April 2, 2016, 18:30, http://en.wikipedia.org/wiki/Stevie_Nicks.). "[Entanglement] … essentially involves placing two seemingly separate particles in a correlated state, [entangled in each other's energy systems] such that changes made to one particle will instantaneously also influence changes to the other, even if the two particles are separated by great distances. Theoretically, two entangled particles can remain correlated even if they are on opposite sides of the universe from one another" (Mother Nature Network. July 6, 2018: https://www.mnn.com/green-tech/research-innovations/stories/quantum-entanglement-demonstrated-level-visible-naked-eye).

So here we have this well-proved phenomenon, particle entanglement, that happens in our known universe, and we don't experience it happening in the gross energy system, which is to say the world we live in. And yet the subtle field, the whole cosmos, our universe, went to all the trouble of creating this phenomenon. Why wouldn't it operate throughout the cosmos and universe right down to the gross energy system? I don't know. It works with subatomic particles, and we and everything else in the universe are made of those little particle buggers; therefore, it would seem that this phenomenon must be at work throughout the universe and inside us in some way. However, since we see what we want to see and hear what we want to hear, maybe we have filtered out of our awareness what we have been programmed not to see and hear. Maybe the data that would prove this phenomenon is happening in the gross energy system is manipulated and filtered out of the data sent to the active mind; therefore, we create no beliefs, experiences, references, or memories related to this unique phenomenon. What is the greater part of our filtering system? Our egoic self. *(Makes you wonder (doesn't it?) who is in control here. Science kind of says that the reason this phenomenon isn't seen in the gross energy system at your level of grossness is because there is too much noise. Too much noise or interference in the gross energy system is the reason usually given.*

They don't say, "Because it isn't there" because it is here. They just say because here is too much noise to feel it.)

There have been several experiments conducted to show the mind can affect physical things. The experiments aren't around quantum entanglement but other phenomena. What kind of experiments and what kind of phenomena?

- The effect of prayer groups on healing people who are sick
- The ability of some people to heal others by their intention and sometimes at great distances
- The laying on of hands as a healing modality
- Studies involving large numbers of meditators to change violent crime trends in a target city
- Using the mind with intention to effect random number generators

All the phenomena studied showed statistical improvements. But then how statistical can we get when we are trying to prove something mainstream science believes doesn't exist? In the experiments and studies, entanglement wasn't studied because it's too noisy to be detected in the gross energy field, and of course there is no current instrumentation for detecting entanglement.

While each of these groups have their own beliefs as to why their particular protocol works, under all of them may be the phenomenon of entanglement. Look here, we have several different approaches to changing outcomes by using the mind with intention, and they are successful to varying degrees. It would seem reasonable to imagine a common underlying cause for all of them, and entanglement fits the bill here. Entanglement has always been here. It didn't start when we stumbled into quantum physics, even though we have been aware of it only since quantum physics entered the picture.

Maybe we have always been entangled with everyone else. Recall that at root we are all one. Being one would be pretty entangled. Think of moving from oneness in the subtle field into separateness in the gross energy system. What if the whole universe was one big entangled system, starting with the "grand poobah" of all entanglement processes, the big bang?

Yes, there is noise in our gross energy system, which is our world; and yes, we can't find evidence of entanglement here in our gross energy system with what we know now. However, we know it's there because it's operating in the very small worlds of particles. And the small worlds of particles are the building blocks of the gross world we live in. We might think of that old saying "As below, so above." And we might also say, "As the small, so the large."

Quantum entanglement happens, and that is for sure. As we begin to reach critical mass of this new paradigm shift, beliefs will change more rapidly; and then, like magic, there it will be, filtered out of the everything in the subtle field, and it will seem as if it were always so. If we look around, even now entanglement is being developed for industrial use in a serious way, and soon we will see it throughout the gross energy system. It may be that some reading this right now may already have some knowledge of its unique phenomenon and its expected uses.

Let's review what our memories are. They have no weight, and that in itself is easy to prove with a bathroom scale, although science may require a more accurate device. We have no idea where memories are stored. Do we have a lot of theories about where memories are stored? Oh, yes, but none have panned out yet. So we have some things that have no weight, and we don't know where they are. When we recall a memory, there it is as a thing in our active minds; and when we aren't thinking about it, it is nowhere we can find or maybe spread out everywhere. *(Look closely here. When you bring a memory into your active mind, there it is like a real thing; and it appears to be made of real stuff, such as particles. It is a hologram in your mind, in your head. It causes your body to respond, and you think it's real. When you aren't thinking of that memory, it is nowhere; therefore, it can be everywhere, just like a wave. Is the memory beginning to take on the characteristics of a subatomic particle? I have no answer to that question. But it's interesting, don't you think? Until something more interesting comes along, let's make believe, "Memories are subatomic particles." Or at least assume they act like subatomic particles, because their coming and going are determined by your awareness.)*

EVERY EVENT HAS AN ENERGY SIGNATURE

When an event happens, energy is released in a chaotic manner; and the energy released will have an underlying structure or signature; and it doesn't matter whether the event is taking a trip to the supermarket, buying a new house, or having a wedding. All events have an energy signature, and all those involved in and participating in the event consciously or subconsciously are entangled within the event's energy structure. And they will absorb varying degrees of the event's energy based on their sensory input and their different unique filtering systems. Each of those participants will have a different interpretation of the event and different stored memories of their interpretation of the event. Therefore, each memory, each thought form created and stored will also have an energy signature memory stored with it for each participant. *(Can you appreciate the underlying entanglement of the energy structure or its signature? With that in mind, you must see the structure as one entangled and enmeshed system.)*

We might think for a moment that our bodies are made up of particles, and each of those particles, each of our cells that make up who we are, is entangled with all the rest of the cells in our bodies, which also make up who we are. Therefore, we cannot view who we are as separate particles or separate systems, but we must be viewed as a wholly integrated system, which is to say viewed holistically.

When we move into an event, we are entangled within the energy structure and the energy signature of the event; therefore, the entangled structure, with us in it, must be viewed as a holistic whole. We will receive information of the event through our senses, and that information will go through the process we have already discussed for creating memories from our interpretations of our part in the event. All participants in the event will go through the same process. Begin to appreciate that all who participated in the event in any way are entangled in each other's energy systems to varying degrees around the event. *(Here again your conscious mind, with the help of your ego, will present to you a view of separateness with the event; and at the slow-moving conscious level, you won't recognize or understand your entanglement with the event's energy signature. However, behind the curtain of the conscious mind, systems are being entangled at lightning speeds. The conscious mind can never tell you or show to you in any way how fast everything is really happening, how integrated this dance of reality is, how entangled you are with everything, and how interconnected we all are. What it will tell you and show you is separateness, because that is all you know from listening to the ego.)*

How much or how little each participant is energetically engaged in the event isn't the point. What is important is noticing that they, like us, are made up of particles; therefore, each of those participants within the event's structure is entangled within the integrated holistic system of the events. That includes their memories, their energy forms, of their interpretations of the event that is now one system with us. The following diagram depicts that process as the event is happening.

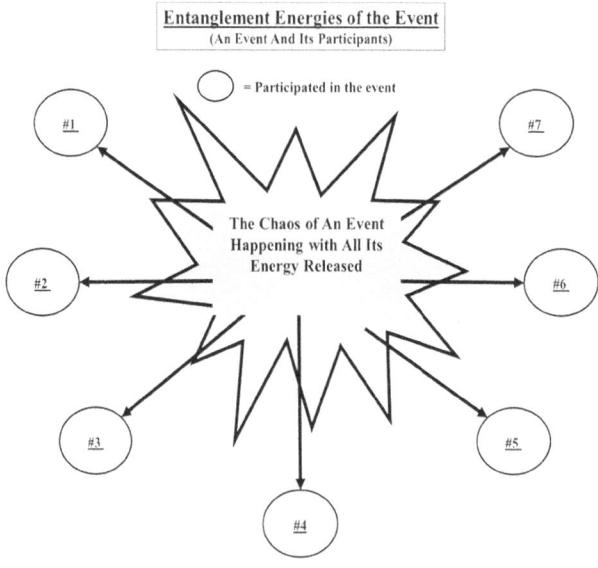

Diagram 26 - Underlying Energy Signature of the Event

ENTANGLED ENERGY, ENTANGLED MEMORIES

In the above diagram, the event releases its energy signature. The participants in the event filter and interpret that signature as is appropriate for each, given their beliefs, experiences, and references. When the event is over, those individual memories of their unique interpretation of the event will be stored and will be used in their future filtering systems. The more negative the interpretation, the higher it will be in their filtering system. The individual memories of the event are now entangled in one system. As such, as one of the entangled memories is changed, all the memories will be affected to some degree. How wild is that?

Since now, each participant's energy systems are entangled, and ultimately, each participant's memory of the event is entangled into the holographic whole. The event will end, but the memories are still energetic thought forms in the subconscious mind of each individual who participated in the event; as such, they are still entangled within one entangled single energy system, which must be described for the system as a whole. They are no longer independent, individual memories; they are a system. They are a wheel within a wheel, within a wheel, in such a way that as one memory changes, they all change to varying degrees. Now we may be thinking, *This is crazy talk. I have control of what goes on in my mind and in my memories; and no one else, no matter what they do, can get inside my head and affect my memories. (You may have noticed that the model has changed. I stated before, "No one is inside you but you." Think differently for a minute. You have no idea what goes on in your subconscious mind with your memories, because it's a black box. You have no idea whether someone is entangled within your memories; and you have no idea whether he or she has changed something that affected your entangled memories. Besides, it's a dance. You are both touching hands and feeding back information to others within the entangled system in ways far beyond your conscious awareness or its understanding. The feedback is at deep structure as you move toward oneness, and your small, conscious mind is operating at surface structure and clinging to separateness. It has no idea of the dance going on in deep structure.)*

When a memory is changed, two systems are affected. One is the memory matrix of the person who made the change, and the other is the entangled single energy system of the entangled memories of all the participants of the event. *(You may be thinking, What if there are no other participants? Well then, if there are no other participants, it should be easy to forgive yourself, unless you believe you can't, because of old programming.)* Once one memory within the entangled systems changes, everything will be different. This will happen within the group of entangled memories and also within the individual memory matrix of each participant. Why would that be? Because that one changed memory is connected to all other individual memories, which is a single entangled system.

We are dealing here with a matrix of interconnected black boxes and subconscious minds of all participants. We might think of it as a "super black box," "super subconscious mind," or the "subtle field." We have moved outside the gross energy system and into the subtle field of oneness. As such, that one individual changed memory will affect and change all the other memories connected to it; and that will affect the lens each uses to construct its present moment and the world each will experience. *(You may have noticed the correlation between how each individual black box works and how the super black box works. All memories in your subconscious mind are interconnected through that three-dimensional spiderweb referred to in Chapter 10, "Memory Coding System," in the section "Memory Storage Model." You may even recall the saying "As above so below." You might also think about its corollary or reciprocal aspect: "As below so above." And from this you may be able to connect the dots to the understanding you are in, connected to and part of a holographically entangled universe, because in a hologram each individual peace reflects the whole.)*

Since when one memory changes in the entangled system, all memories connected in the system will change in varying degrees. Now because a memory has changed in each participant's black box, all his or her memories will shift. Recall that all our memories are interconnected, and if one changes, all shift in varying degrees within each individual, to reach a new balance, a new homeostasis point. Each participant's lens, through which they experience their individual world, will change. *(Now you can begin to appreciate that when one memory is changed in your matrix of memories, all the memories shift in varying degrees to support the change. Therefore, the memories of anyone entangled with you will also change. If you can imagine this dance, this undulating rhythm and this flow of information within the super matrix of interconnectedness of all those black boxes and the speed at which it is happening, you can understand how the paradigms of each participant, when critical mass is reached, will shift. And you can learn how new inventions can happen at the same time in different parts of the world. And with just a slight tweaking of your awareness, you can appreciate the oneness in the many. Maybe you can begin to appreciate why meditation and prayer can be so effective.)*

(Warning! You may have spotted the concern here. This process happens whether the change is positive or negative. The entangled memories can be positively and negatively entangled, and the process doesn't care, because it's just a process. However, if your entangled memory is negative and negative-entangled change happens, the two will add to each other, and dark magic will happen, moving you deeper into the illusion and separation. Consciously you won't have any idea why. It could cause some pain and suffering. But don't worry, your ego will have an answer for your pain and suffering, "It's the body's fault!" Again, believing that answer will take you deeper into the gross energy system and away from wholeness and oneness.)

All our memories are interconnected and entangled inside the black box of our subconscious mind. As one memory within our subconscious mind is healed and reframed, all the other memories built on it, attached to it, and interconnected with it will change in response to that one reframed memory. There is a ripple effect throughout the matrix of our stored memories. All our memories, to be consistent with the change of the one memory and as we constantly reach for homeostasis, will shift and change. The subconscious mind does all its processing and makes all the required changes automatically in the blink of an eye, out of conscious awareness and without its involvement in any way; and we consciously will have no idea that anything has changed because all our beliefs, experiences, and references will have been updated to support the new changed memory. Our old ego dies, and a new ego with the new changes will be installed; this will all happen outside our conscious awareness.

Entanglement moves us out of a surface structure of separateness and into a deeper structure, which will bring us closer to our Original Self and to oneness. The entangled memories, whether around an entangled event or within our own subconscious minds, are one system where time and space collapse. Don't look to Newtonian physics for the answers and proof of the entangled process; they won't be found there. We must look deep into quantum physics. All is one, is it not? Beyond the illusion of separateness, all is one. Trying to experience entanglement in the gross energy system or at surface structure is impossible, because of all the interference from the competing energy systems and egoic defenses in all its many forms.

Entanglement is another gap or crack in the ego's fortress of separation. Entanglement collapses time, space, and distance; and this quality brings the process into the realm of the subtle field and out of conscious awareness. We must be clear here; deep structure isn't down or below something. Deep structure and the move toward oneness is done within the subtle field, which is everywhere because it is infinite. Surface structure is embedded within the subtle field, and deep structure is part of the subtle field.

As we forgive ourselves, we change our energy around that memory of our interpretation of the event we are entangled with, and the event is now gone. Since our memories are who we think we are, by changing our memories of our interpretation of events through self-forgiveness, we have changed our egoic identity and created a new egoic self; and it will be a more positive one.

Since the entangled memories are one system, it should not seem so surprising to appreciate that if one memory is healed, the system must change; and that the other entangled memories of the event will also change. Again, the other participants may not consciously recognize that they have changed, and that isn't our concern. Our concern is to heal our own pain and suffering. It doesn't matter whether we are the offended or the offender; as we forgive ourselves, the whole system of entangled memories around the event shifts more positively.

It's a dance with its own music and its own dance steps that is well beyond conscious awareness, because we are well beyond the egoic self. We are touching hands and entangled with those in our radiating energy field; and as we change, they will change, and as they change. we will change until a balance or homeostasis is met. Wouldn't it be nice to forgive ourselves so they can feel better about themselves? See how, as we forgive ourselves, we radiate a different energy and will draw to us a different world or create a different hologram of our world.

TIME TRAVEL

Events are complicated systems; and once started, we never know for certain how they will end. Complicated systems are governed by mathematic structure called "chaos theory." We aren't going into chaos theory except to state two of its premises used in the theory: the outcome of the system is sensitive to and dependent on the initial conditions, and the "Butterfly Effect," which states a small change in one place will cause major changes in another. As a general statement, we could say, "The starting conditions greatly affect the end result."

Through entanglement, as stated before, when we change one aspect of an entangled system, the whole system automatically changes in some way. We may not know how it will change, but it must change because it's one entangled system. When we forgive ourselves, we change our energy around the memory of our interpretation of the event, which is now gone. This change in the memory of our interpretation of the event will create a new and different memory for us, and an energy shift will occur in our individual memory matrix. We have stated this before. *(You change a memory, and that change will shift all your memories around that changed memory to support the newly changed memory. So far, so good. The interesting things will follow.)*

If we are entangled with other systems, which we are, those other entangled systems must also shift and change in some way. Why? Because each entangled system must operate and be viewed and described as a whole complete system, right down to the individual memory entangled within the event, which is now gone. When one of the memories within the entangled system changes, all others instantly change to some degree. *(Are you beginning to see that how healing yourself will affect those around you? You are a very powerful creator of the world you have. But again, if you change negatively, that will also affect your world. Guess which way your ego wants you to move and why?)*

So if one of our memories changed in our individual memory matrix for any reason, the memories around that changed memory will shift to support it; and from that shift a ripple will move through all our stored memories, shifting and changing them until balance and homeostasis are again reestablished. *(You may still think memories are hard physical objects, such as baseballs or stone tablets, on which the memory is written. They aren't. They are like Silly Putty or a will-o'-the-wisp you can't put your finger on, an ether, that isn't there but is; and you can change and shift them, move them back and forth, or make them bigger and smaller. They can get more intense or less intense, and they are fluid. They have no weight, and you don't know where your memories are when you aren't thinking of them. There is an uncertainty about them. They can disappear for long periods and then reappear within another context. They can come and go in dreams and can be triggered at work or in a movie. A look, a noise, a touch, a smell, a flavor on your tongue—and there they are, as if the event is happening again. And yet your memories are who you think you are. If you look really closely, you will see characteristics of subatomic particles within these descriptions. The thought may come.* Maybe I'm not who I think I am.)

Will all those other participants involved in the event know or consciously feel that their memory of the event has shifted and changed in some way? I don't know because it's not a conscious change; it is a shifting within the individual's black box. *(I said all this earlier but a little differently. You should begin to see how fragile and changeable your matrix of memories is.)*

The following diagram depicts an interconnection of the entangled system memories of the event in Diagram 26. Notice there is no event happening now. There are just entangled memories within the one system, which is changing.

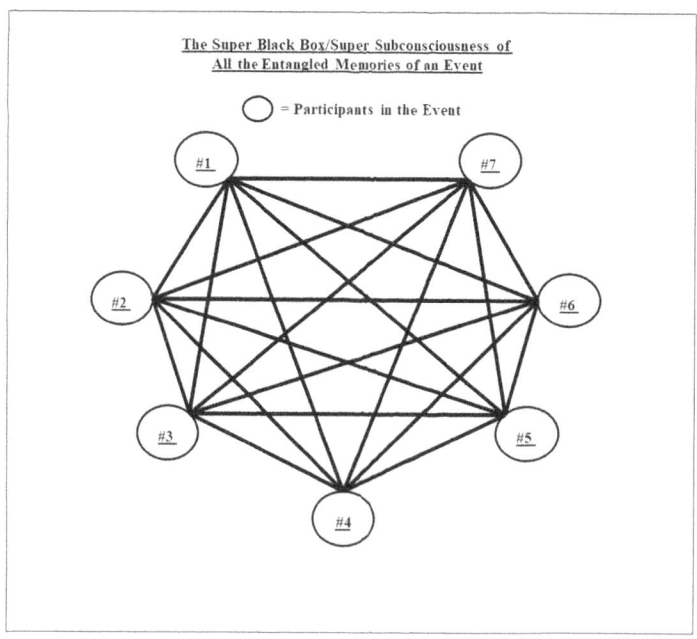

Diagram 27 - The Super Black Box of Entangled Memories

Super Black Box/Super Subconsciousness of Entangled Memories

In the above diagram, the entangled memories embedded within the super black box system aren't separate memories. They can be viewed only as a single interconnected system. As one memory changes, all memories must change to some degree. How much each changes will depend on the intensity of energy attached to the memory from their original interpretation of the event, which is now gone.

Recognize that by forgiving ourselves and changing our old negative memories created around the event, we are changing the "sensitive dependent" initial conditions of the entangled interpretations of the event, held by all those who participated in the event. This will change our memories as well as all other entangled memories to some degree, as we have stated before. *(Notice here that it makes no difference, if the change is positive or negative, your memories and all the other entangled memories with yours will change. How can you be sure that regardless of whatever others do, you will always create positive change? The short answer is, you can't. However, what will help and support you in positive ways is for you to carry a positive attitude on a daily basis and be aware of how you talk to yourself. If those two indicators are positive, you are on firm ground. If not, it is you who needs to change.)*

Now for the "time travel." Since each new present moment is built on our memories, if we remember an old memory, we are going back in time. We are going to the sensitive dependent initial conditions. By reframing ourselves, we are changing every memory interconnected with that old target memory. The older the memory, the more memories will be built on it; therefore, when the target memory is reframed by self-forgiveness, more memories will be automatically changed and reframed by the subconscious mind in support of the changed memory. An example may be helpful here.

A traffic accident occurs. I drive through a stop signal and hit another car. The participants in the event may be those in the other car, observers, police, a tow truck driver, me, and maybe many others. Each of the participants will have a different interpretation of the event, based on many factors—for example, how close or far away were they from the accident, whether it was their car that was damaged, how long did they have to wait in traffic, and of course their beliefs, experiences, and references regarding traffic accidents from their past. And so there are different memories created based on their interpretation of the event; and there will be different memories created for each. *(Do you see how complicated the energy signature of one event can be?)*

People may be hurt and need to go to the hospital, cars must be repaired, and people are inconvenienced and may be late for meetings and events with loved one; their lives are affected. It's like dropping a pebble in a pond. Ripples spread out to the shore and rebound to their source. How do I feel about my part in the event? I feel guilty, ashamed, anxious, sad, and fearful as to what will happen—for example, getting a ticket, discovering insurance rates are going up, fixing my car, and so forth.

Imagine what the ripples on the pond's surface would look like as each participant dropped their pebble into the pond. Some pebbles would be big and some small. Some care a great deal about the accident, and some don't give a rip. That combined effect of all those pebbles represents what the energy signature of the event and its entanglement memories of each interpretation from the event would be like, and the memories of the event that are now entangled into one system. What about the event? It is over and gone. What is left of the event? Nothing of the event, only entangled memories of individual interpretations of the event.

If I forgive myself, I shift my memory; and as I heal from my wounds physically and emotionally, the memory of the event becomes more positive for me. Think again. What am I changing? An unreal, untrue, and incomplete construction of something that was never the way I thought it was. *(Use your new vision here to recognize that you can't know the whole event. You can know it only through the lens of your past, and you aren't seeing this event the way it is. Think again. Do you see this cup in my hand? Can you see any event as it is? No, and you can't see the accident the way it is either.)*

Within the entangled memory system of the interpretations of the participants of the event, the system must shift as I forgive myself. Why, again, would that be? Because it is now one entangled system. So who might notice a change? Those who are major stakeholders in the original event may. What about those who don't give a rip? They still won't give a rip.

Here again, we cannot look in our gross energy system and Newtonian physics to explain this concept of entangled memories, because it won't make sense. Entanglement cannot be observed there. Understanding, accepting, and appreciating that entanglement moves us closer to oneness and our original self, we will need to use the lens of quantum physics. Since entanglement happens instantly, which means faster than the speed of light, maybe the only state that can happen is in the subtle field, where space and time collapse.

Since all those other memories entangled within an event, that is now over and gone, are now one system, they will also shift when we forgive ourselves. We have a new entangled system, and since older memories are the ground on which other memories are build, all our individual memories from the point of our self-forgiven forward will shift and change right up to today; and also our memories going deeper into our past, those that supported the old interpretation, must also change. *(I said this before in slightly different ways, you know, your memories are inter-connected and influence each other; and entangled memories are the same way. Can you see the domino effect here, as you change your entangled memory, you are effecting all those other memories entangled with you. Can you see the possibility that one positive act can have on changing your world?)*

Our world will change, and a new world will come into focus for us. Why will that be? Because our memories have changed, and our memory matrix is the programming that determines our present world. Will we like it? I don't know, but we will be happier in this world than in the one we were living in. *(Look closely again. The memory of the interpretation, which you changed through self-forgiveness, was the way it was because of the memories in place before it. Since that is what determined the interpretation given to the event in the first place, by reframing that one memory, all the old memories that were in place before you changed that memory must also change, or you wouldn't be able to reframe it the way you did. It is a very convoluted process and makes little sense in the gross energy system and your ego. However, it is a piece of cake in the subtle field. Are you beginning to see why your ego wants to keep the past real? And right now, you may be thinking the same thing. Not to worry. You are much more than you think you are. You are the oneness inside the many. You are the dreamer, dreaming of the many.)*

Don't worry about the "what and how" of the shifting memories because the black box, which is the subconscious mind, will automatically shift, change, refile, and consolidate all the memories behind the screen of the conscious mind. The effect, which is our now new world, will seem quite natural and normal. Why? Because all our beliefs, experiences, and reference materials, which are our memories, will now all support our new sense of self and a new egoic self-identity. They will be in place. Our new ego identity and our new world and its effects will seem quite normal; and what is the cause of these new effects? Changing our memories. *(I did say changing your negative memories would create a new and happier world for you, didn't I? Surely I did. Remember this is all happening faster than your conscious mind will ever know, and your conscious mind will just accept the new world as if that's the way it has always been.)*

In astronomy looking deeper into space is said to be like time traveling and seeing what happened millions of years ago, and looking back tells us why things are the way they are now. In a sense, going back into our memories is also like time travel; and it starts with the phrase "I can remember _____." When we hear that phrase, we move on the magic carpet of our imagination back in time to memories of the events that are long gone.

To change a memory, we must go into the memory, which means we need to bring it into the active mind. When we change a memory, we are changing our perception of the past; and in doing so, we have changed the sensitive, dependent, initial conditions. All the causes and effects that flowed out of that target memory, the original memory we changed through self-forgiveness, must also change. This will shift and change everything and all memories that happen after our self-forgiveness in some way; and as we just went through, it will change what went before it. A new world will come into focus for us. The old has passed away, and the new is here to stay.

So when we forgive ourselves, we are changing but not only our memories; we are also causing all those other memories systems entangled with us to shift as well, and that shift will flow through our memories from beginning to the end and flow through all the memories of those who participated and are now entangled with us from the event. *(Now don't listen to your ego. This is a completely new way of seeing and understanding your world and universe. The physicalness of your world and its separateness are at surface structure, and the reality of you and your oneness is at deeper structure. And you are in both at the same time. You know the surface structure pretty well. How well do you know deep structure? Oh, I forgot. It is too noisy in the gross energy system to hear the still sounds of the entangled oneness.)*

Look at this as a cause-and-effect process, where each memory is an effect of what went before it. As we said before, the present moment can be the way it is only because of the memories of what happen before; therefore, the present is the effect of the causal past. How crazy is that? *(Can you appreciate how your small act of self-forgiveness can have a major positive effect on the lives of so many others? Everything is interrelated and entangled together in some way and at some level. You know that, right? I did say we are all one at deep structure, didn't I? I know you believe you are an independent individual and that you make up your own mind and make your own decisions, but it only looks that way from the chaotic surface structure in the gross energy system. At deep structure, you are moving into oneness. You are entangled with the subtle field and touching hands as you dance together.)*

371

CONDEMNATION

Now the question may come up. What if an entangled participant, rather than forgiving them self, condemns and blames them self, or condemns and blames the other participants in the entangled memory system of an event that is over? Will the entangled memories still change but in a negative way as well? They will. In such a case, the entangled system will move further away from oneness and go deeper into illusions and also higher into surface structures of chaos and drama. Energy flows where thoughts go. The highest energy intension, positive or negative, will determine whether we move into oneness or into a more egoic illusion. *(You see why it is important for you to forgive yourself and start the whole process moving in a positive direction? At the end of Chapter 22, I made Four statements:*

> *The first to apologize is the bravest.*
> *The first to forgive is the strongest.*
> *The first to forget is the happiest and*
> *Happiest is the goodest!*

That is your shield against the dark side.)

From the last diagram we may be able to appreciate the interplay of all the different intensions that can be brought to bear on an entangled memory system. Think of systems within systems. Think of families, communities, and nations. The more self-forgiving energy intensions are, the closer to oneness and peace of mind the whole system moves. The more condemnation there is, the deeper into the chaos of illusions we move, and deeper into the angst of feeling more separated.

Can we begin to appreciate that we have a tool for changing the world and our lives? We have always had this tool; it is forgiving ourselves. We don't need to join a movement, organization, or cult; and we don't need to follow any rigid protocol or teaching. All we need to do is decide to love and forgive ourselves. *(If you do join a movement, organization, or cult, remember, it will develop an egoic identity, and the ego will take over because that is what egos do. It will proclaim that your group is the true group and that it's on the true path. What about the other groups? They aren't on the true path, because you are on the only true path, and so they can't be on the true path. Oh, the ego is very crafty and sneaky. I shared that before.)*

REACHING HOMEOSTASIS

Recall in Chapter 1, "Energy, Energy Everywhere, and Not an Electron Do I See," we discussed the interaction of all the systems of the body and the mind, and their effect on the total radiant energy signature of mind and body. This is because of all the different interference patterns of energy frequencies from all the interdependent systems within the whole of the mind and body system. When all systems are operating normally and healthily, one type of energy signature is sent out to the universe, but if some systems become unhealthy or diseased, a different signature is sent out, depending on which systems are diseased and distressed. The interplay of all participants within an event affect the radiant energy and the entangled memory system in the same way. Since time and space collapse into one entangled memory system, all individual memories are like the different systems in the body, in that they interfere with each other, causing there to be one radiant energy signature for the entangled memory system.

Homeostasis is a balance point of equilibrium between forces within a system or an organism. It is the system or organism as a whole that determines where that balance point will be. We are cells within the organism of humanity; and the homeostasis balance point of humanity changes as the forces shift within this organism. As was stated before, for most of us our goal is to save our egoic selves, our egoic asses. Forgiving ourselves doesn't fit with the ego's goal and therefore won't be high on the agenda of most people because that isn't their ego's goal. *(You have seen that in others, right? They are bound and determined to be right, no matter what because not to be right causes their ego to feel bad; and their ego is who they think they are. You may be one of those people. How would you know? I mean, given you are always right, you will never see when you are not. If you come close to being wrong, you will see it as someone else's fault and blame him or her so you can be right. You see the game you play with yourself and your ego? Your balance point will keep you deep in the illusion.)*

What is the ego's goal? To stay alive and in control. How does it do that? By keeping us individually and collectively distracted. By keeping us deep in conflict, confusion, and disease at all levels of our lives; by so doing, the ego is alive, healthy, and in control. It has done this for a long time, and that is the direction the ego will continue to push us because it works for our ego. *(Don't forget, your ego is ingrained and integrated throughout your belief system. It knows all your logical arguments and how to counter them. The ego whispers in your ear, and it sounds so logical, right, sweet, and seductive. Why would you ever want to forgive yourself and reclaim your health and peace of mind? What is your ego's goal? To stay alive by keeping you in conflict, confusion, and disease. How does the ego do that? By getting you to listen to its guidance and then following it. Remember, each country, culture, organization, and family also has an ego that is doing the same thing. You will need to use your new vision and see things differently, then see beyond and pass the ego's lair, because that is where dark magic is brewed. And then you drink the lemonade.)*

The ego's lair is the cauldron in which the dark magic is brewed. Where is it kept? It is the past. And what are the ingredients used in this dark brew? Negative and hurtful memories of the past. Are the memories real? No, but that doesn't matter, because we believe they're real. We need to remember what the ego's goal is. It is to distract us through conflict, confusion, and disease in our lives. How is the ego doing in all its forms in meeting its goal? If we listen to the news in all its forms, at all its different levels, it seems pretty clear; the egoic world is here to stay. *(If you want to find peace of mind, you will need to escape out of the ego's lair, which you are now in. You need to learn and practice the art of "being in the world but not of the world." You must be a clandestine rebel and a peaceful warrior. I said before that as you start down this path of self-enfoldment, keep it a secret. Start by breaking your habitual habit of listening to the news. You really know it is designed to increase your anxiety, conflict and keep you confused, don't you? Become aware of how it intrudes in your daily life and blocks your peace of mind. It's a small act for you but a big step toward gaining control of your life and peace of mind. And don't listen to what the ego is now whispering in your ear as you consider not listening to the news.)*

Whatever the homeostasis balance point is for a system or organism, all its interdependent systems will tend to attune to its dominant energy frequency. Would we expect this to be at a conscious level? No, it happens out of conscious awareness. It happens through the individual memories within the entangled memory systems and the overall energy signature of the individuals and the system. We call is "normal daily stress." Recognize there is no normal stress. We create the whole thing from inside of us and call it normal because we don't know what to do with it.

I wonder what would happen if one of the brave participants in an entangled memory system became aware that self-forgiveness is the path to self-healing and self-compassion, to true self-love and peace of mind, and practiced it. On a deep level, we already know and realize that without the ego's influence, sooner or later we will move toward forgiveness and oneness, and away from condemning and blaming, which is the realm of illusions, chaos, and the hidden lair of the ego.

Begin to appreciate that the past is as fluid as the future, because both are unreal memories and neither is here now; both can change by the caprices and whims of the mind. Ancient wisdom has known that for thousands of years. The following quote was written in the fifth century BC during the classical Sanskrit era in India. It is attributed to Kaladana, widely regarded as the greatest poet and dramatist in the Sanskrit language. It is still commonly quoted today. "Yesterday is but a dream, tomorrow but a vision. But today well lived makes every yesterday a dream of happiness, and every tomorrow a vision of hope. Look well, therefore, to this day. Such is the salutation to the dawn" (attributed to Kaladana, "A Sanskrit Proverb," https://www.goodreads.com/author/show/186034.K__lid__sa).

By forgiving ourselves, we are added to the critical mass of a paradigm shift toward oneness and closer to our original selves. The past is a dream, and the dream is a succession of images, ideas, emotions, and sensations that occur involuntarily or as triggered in the mind during certain altered states and sleep. The future is also a dream, because it's our memory of our interpretations of speculations of what isn't here yet.

(You may recall in Chapter 6, "Making Friends with the Subconscious Mind," that when you move your mind from the present moment, either into the past or into the future, you are in an altered trance state. This is a state that exists only in your head, which means it isn't real and is a whim of the mind. You might not even notice when you do this, because it seems so real, and you do it so often that it's seamless to your conscious mind. You believe the past is as real as the present moment, don't you? It's not.)

When we awaken from our dream, we will be where we started in the blob at the bottom of the lamp in the oneness and know it for the first time. "We shall not cease from exploration, and the end of all our exploring will be to arrive where we started and know the place for the first time" (excerpt from T. S. Eliot, "Four Quartets," https://www.goodreads.com/work/quotes/2886568-four-quartets).

CHAPTER 24

Expanding Memories and Entanglement

In Chapter 9, "Memories," we discussed that memories aren't real, true, or complete; and why we believe they are based on how we feel in our bodies when we recall them. We are going to expand on memories in relation to our understanding of entanglement. We don't know much about entanglement because it is so far away from what we have been programmed to believe that it can seem scary. *(You're brave, right? You don't mind moving into the unknown, do you? And as such, you don't have any answers. So this will be an adventure for both of us.)*

MEMORIES ARE UNIQUE CREATIONS

A memory is a uniquely created structure. If we look at a newly formed memory, we will notice that it's the way it is because of all the other memories stored in the subconscious mind before it. It is the active mind that interprets the filtered data the subconscious mind sends it. And the sent data is the way it is because the filtering system in the subconscious mind is the way it is. And the filtering system is the way it is because of the past memories that make up the filtering system. It's important to appreciate that past memories determine the interpretation of our present moment. And the current interpretation determines what the next memory will be. Therefore, the newest memory must be the way it is because the memories created before it are the way they are. *(Can you recognize the entanglement of all the memories stored in the subconscious mind? How they support and hold each other in place where they are? If you change one memory, the whole structure quakes and ripples to rebalance and reach a new homeostasis.)*

We may have noticed that the fragile illusion of the gross energy system has a similar structure and is just as sensitive to change. Each ego state of individual, family, country, religion, and so forth holds the whole illusion, where it is at any given time frame. Here again we can hear the echo of that holographic phrase "As above, so below." *(You may recall that in a hologram, each fragment reflects the whole. You may begin to notice that the holographic whole is embedded in the subtle field of everything.)*

THE NEW UPON THE OLD

New memories are built on our older memories. Old painful memories will have greater influence in the black box filtering system, because they were there first and are the oldest; therefore, they are the most familiar to the subconscious mind. As a result, data selected through them will go to the active mind before neutral and benign memories' selected data. From this understanding, if our painful memories were to be reframed into more neutral, benign, or positive memories, we would experience a more positive world. This will be, because as our filtering system shifts and sends more positive memories to the active mind, more positive interpretations will be created.

The following diagram is an attempt to depict this understanding that a new memory is the way it is because of the old memories.

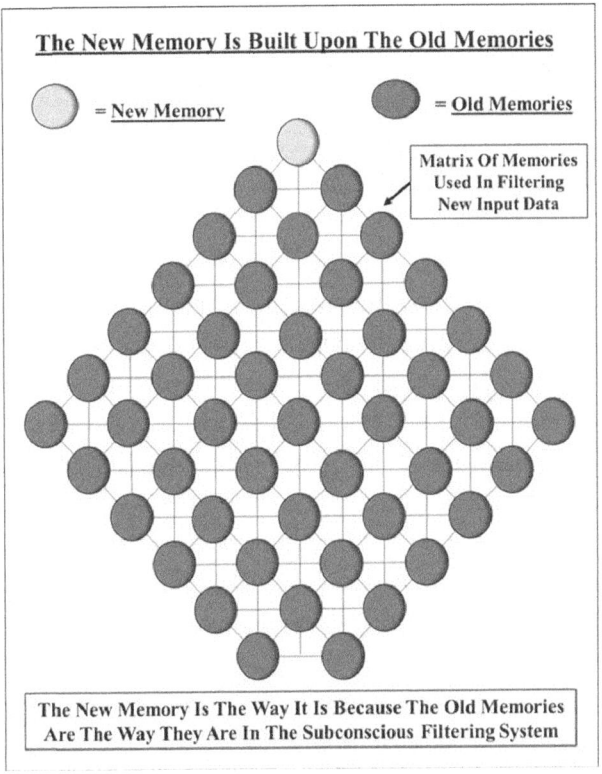

The New Memory Is Built Upon The Old Memories

= New Memory   = Old Memories

Matrix Of Memories
Used In Filtering
New Input Data

The New Memory Is The Way It Is Because The Old Memories
Are The Way They Are In The Subconscious Filtering System

Diagram 28 - The New Memory Is Built on the Old

The new memory must be the way it is because the old memories are the way they are in the subconscious filtering system. As soon as a new memory is integrated into the memory matrix of the subconscious mind, it is now an old memory within the matrix. This happens so fast that we are consciously unaware of it and believe each memory is a unique and independent, real, true, and completely accurate recall of the event. We will have a difficult time at the conscious level understanding or believing it is made from filtered and manipulated data that is dependent on our past memories. That new unreal memory is now part of the matrix. It appears to the conscious mind to be a natural response to the outside energy system, which is always an inside hologram and is never outside. *(Can you appreciate the very rapid dance of manipulating data creating interpretations and the body's responses to signals from the active mind's interpretations? It all goes on long before the slow conscious mind gets involved. Oh, but don't you believe what your slow conscious mind tells you is the truth? So now you have a paradox. You now know that what really is happening out of conscious awareness and what the slow conscious mind tells you. And the event! Is the memory of the event the event? No, and it can never be. But don't you believe it is the event? Silly person, you have been living under the ego's spell and believing it is the real reality. No, no, you are in an illusion.)*

If we have a negative, painful memory and decide to reframe and heal it, we must move into the realm of alchemy, of changing the base and pain into the pure gold of self-forgiveness, self-loving, and peace of mind. The target memory, the one targeted for change, is an old memory with many entangled and interconnected memories attached to it. Some of the attached memories may be in other entangled memory systems with many other participants. *(Are you coming to an understanding of how extensive the web of interconnected memories may be, both inside and outside you? As you heal, changes may simultaneously occur on many different levels by your reframing one of your memories. Your changing one memory may change worlds. Each of those entangled worlds will quake and ripple as each shifts to find a new homeostasis point of balance. And how cool is that? However, only you will know it because when change happens, all the beliefs, experiences, and referenced memories in each of those entangled systems from the past, which supported the old memory, will also change to reflect and support the new change. It will appear that that's the way the memories have always been. Think of memories as Silly Putty that can be moved into any shape. Begin to appreciate that the past is as fluid as the future; neither the past nor the future is real because they are nowhere but in your mind.)*

Again, recognize that the target memory was created the way it was because of all the memories in place before it. If we change the target memory, all the memories in place before the target memory, the ones that caused the target memory to be the way it was, must also change to some degree to support the changes in the target memory, or the target memory can't remain changed; and it will move back into its old state. All past memories must change to support the changed memory. *(This is important to understand; all your memories in the black box of the subconscious mind are entangled. When you change one memory, when you forgive yourself, you affect all those entangled with it. Do you see how extensive the healing process is in you? Notice, you don't need to change every negative and painful memory you are carrying around with you; you only need to heal and forgive the oldest and more intense memories. The entangled system will take care of all the details. It's not magic; it is how the subtle field and the subconscious mind function. And it happens so fast that the conscious mind will never even know it.)*

Notice also that if all the memories in place before the target memory must change to support the target memory's changes, all the memories put in place after the target memory must also change because what holds them in place the way they are is the target memory. The memory matrix is an entangled single energy system, and it cannot be viewed as separate parts. *(As you change one memory within an entangled matrix, you are changing everything within the system to some degree. Here again notice that you don't need to reframe every negative memory you ever had. You just need to change a few big ones, and then an internal shift will occur for you. Here again, your conscious mind won't even know it.)*

We need to stop and remember what we are changing. We are changing memories. Are they real, true, and complete? No, they're not. They are Silly Putty. They are fluid and can change with our desire to change. What causes them to seem so solid? Our belief that they are real and true and written in stone. Whatever the event was that was interpreted and remembered is gone now and will never come back. Ah now, the memory lingers on, and that is all that is left of the event, and it's only a story we made up.

The following diagram may give some structure to this concept. When we honestly change a memory in a positive way, everything in the universe moves to support us. Notice that it works the same way for negative memories, except it's the ego that rushes in to support the separation it creates. *(Begin to appreciate your importance in this process and for everyone who is participating with you in finding oneness. As you change and heal by forgiving yourself, you are the subtle cause of changes throughout the universe and with those who are entangled with you, which is all of us.)*

See the target memory in the next diagram as entangled within a larger matrix of memories. As we change the target memory in positive and healing ways, there is a ripple effect throughout the whole matrix. *(Do you see what a great creator you are? You can change your world and influence many others just by reframing your past memories.)*

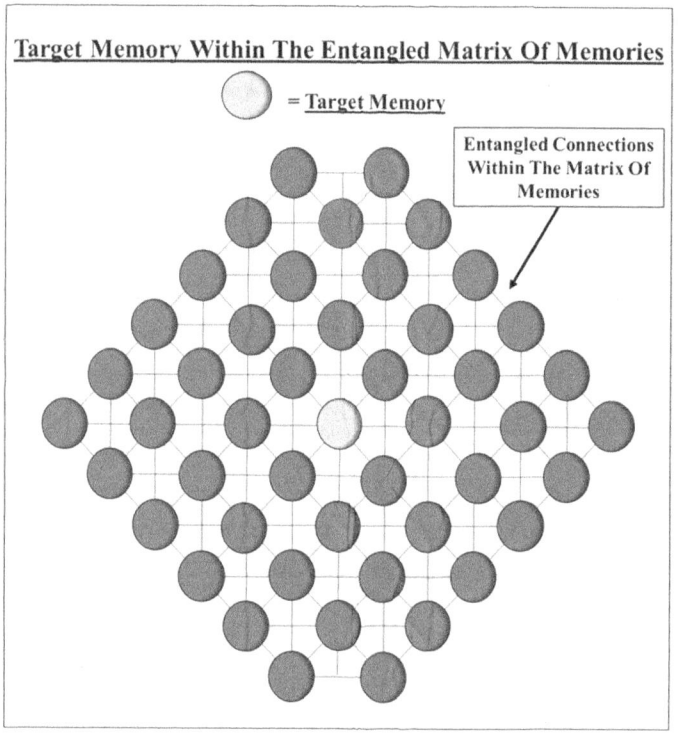

Diagram 29 - Changing the Target Memory Changes Everything

When the target memory changes, all memories must change to some degree to support its new changed state because all the memories are interconnected and entangled. It might seem that if one brave person would just step forward, change, and heal them self through self-forgiveness, in a short time we would all be feeling happier and healthier. Well, of course, there is a problem here. The ego in all its forms wants to stay alive. It whispers sweet nothings in our ears as to why we can't let go of our past, why it is real, why it is important to keep our grudges and condemnations, why we shouldn't let others off the hook by forgiveness, why it shows weakness to forgive, and why we must keep our guilt. And so we keep our negative memories real and alive, or we make them worse or hide them deep in the subconscious mind and out of conscious awareness so they aren't felt consciously, but know this—they are still active.

Therefore, entangled memories never get changed, at least not for the better, and we are stuck with another old saying. "If nothing changes, then nothing changes." And we are locked into the separateness inside the gross energy system with our egos and egoic matrix with everyone else. *(Do you see why, if you choose the path of self-forgiveness and healing, you should keep it secret? All those other egos in very clever ways will go out of their way to bring you back into the illusion and away from oneness and peace of mind. You're not playing with amateurs here. They are trying to save their egoic asses, and you're the saboteur and a real pain to them in their world, which is an illusion.)*

THOUGHT FORMS OF THE MIND

We have used the phrase "thought forms" to describe memories throughout this read. We have no idea where or how memories are stored. They don't seem to have any weight. If we weigh ourselves before we go to a class, attend a workshop, or see a movie and weigh ourselves afterward, we won't gain any weight, unless we eat a lot of popcorn during the movie.

If we bring a memory into our active minds, we don't seem to change our weight. In the active mind, memories cause the brain to light up; and we can see the effects of remembering on the brain as it lights up by using certain instrumentation and then seeing how the body responds. Memories cannot be physically touched, but they can be felt in the body. So memories as thought-forms are basically just information and have no physical attributes until our bodies respond to the signal sent out by the active mind, based on the interpretation of the remembered thought form.

When we aren't thinking about them, memories are nowhere; and when we think of them, they are somewhere in the active mind. Really, we don't know where those nowhere and somewhere spaces are. We can think of the results of remembering a memory as the created hologram we are within. Just because the brain lights up when we think of a memory doesn't mean the brain is where the memory is stored; nor does it mean the hologram is in our brains, because the brains' behavior is only an effect of a primal cause. What is the primal cause? The thought form. Where is the thought form kept? We don't know.

Here again we so want badly for the memory to be in the physical brain because then we can use Newtonian physics to play with it. However, that just doesn't seem to be the case. We must look to quantum physics and the subtle field for answers.

So now we have thought forms that, when we aren't thinking about them, are nowhere we know of; and when we think about them, they are somewhere. These two characteristics are somewhat familiar, are they not? The characteristics of being nowhere and yet having the potential of being somewhere is very familiar. With that in mind, consider this. When we think about a memory or it is triggered into remembrance, there it is right there in front of us with all its data and information; and that is also a familiar characteristic. *(Recall the double-slit experiment of quantum physics. When you don't observe or look at the experiment, you get one result. When you do observe or look at the experiment, you get a different result. When you don't look at the experiment, the information is nowhere and is just a potential or probability wave. When you look at it, the information is right there in front of you, and it's now somewhere. When you look at something, you first must have a thought in your mind because input from the eyes must go to the mind and then to your active mind to have an interpretation made. So you don't see any experiment; you can only think about the filtered information and then make an interpretation about the experiment. And then at that point, you see the untrue response and feel it in the body.)*

The memory thought form is floating between nowhere and somewhere. When we aren't thinking about a memory, it is in the state of nowhere; and when we think about the memory, it is in the state of somewhere, which is right there in our minds. We may be able to relate memories to the double-slit experiment conclusion. The memory, when not observed, is in the state of nowhere and is only probability waves of information. When the memory is in the state of somewhere, we are aware of it and observe how it is behaving; and it is like a consolidated entity of particles, and we feel it in our bodies.

If we can't find where memories are stored in the brain or body system, maybe that is because they aren't stored there. The reason why we haven't been able to find where those elusive memories are stored, and how they are retrieved and restored, may be because the place they are stored isn't in the gross energy system, where we have been looking. Maybe memories are stored in the quantum field, the subtle field, in which the mind or body system is embedded. A crazy idea, right? But it is no crazier than what is currently proposed. *(Begin to appreciate you are not your body. Begin to appreciate that your memories aren't real, true, or complete. Begin to appreciate you are entangled in a deeper system far beyond your conscious mind's awareness. Begin to appreciate you are entangled within the subtle field.)*

CHAPTER 25

The Observer and the Observed

OBSERVING IS AN INSIDE ACTIVITY

When we observe anything, we assume we are observing something outside us. Using all the sensory data, we form an interpretation. However, we know now that we don't use all the sensory data. We use only what is important to us in that brief moment. We really don't care about the event. What we care about is what is important to us. We believe we consciously care about the event, but in truth the subconscious mind filters only what is important to us. Remember, the event is meaningless and neutral until it is interpreted through our filter of the past, and the conscious mind won't even know the data was filtered. In truth, what we think of as the event is a story we made up out of disjointed bits and pieces of data that got through the filtering process; and the conscious mind makes it sound so perfect and logical that we won't know it's just a story. *(I have said all this before. But it is so easy to slip back into the ego's mind-set. Even though you heard it before, it still doesn't sound quite right to say, "Memories aren't real!")*

We now should be able to appreciate that what we are observing is our perception of what we think we are observing and not what is being observed. *(It may seem to you that this is a convoluted statement, but that is what you are doing. Just like "This cup in front of you," you can see only a facsimile of what is there.)*

When we move our awareness from the object of our attention, what happens to the object? It goes away. What does that even mean—"It goes away"? Ah, now we have a problem. The problem is the "measurement problem" of quantum physics, and the double-slit experiment will raise its ugly head. We aren't going into this sticky wicket. People have spent their whole careers working and thinking about the "measurement problem." *(If you haven't heard of the double-slit experiment, just google it. In short, you have a gun that fires small particles like light photons at a screen. But between the gun and the screen, a barrier is placed with two slits in it. The gun kind of automatically sprays the photons toward the screen, and some go through the slits. As you fire the gun, you get a pattern on the screen. If you just fire the gun and don't look or observe the experiment, observe only the pattern; after you pulled the trigger, you get one pattern. If you observe which slit the particles go through, you get a different pattern. Do you see the problem? Why does your observing the experimental process or not observing it change the pattern? Observing is measuring the process.)*

The outcome of the double-slit experiment is this: When we don't observe the experiment, we get a wavy pattern, as if there is no particle as such, and it is a spread-out energy or potential wave. But when we observe what is happening, the pattern observed is that of particles. The conclusion appears to be this: When we observe our world, it is a world of particles and things; and it seems solid. When we aren't looking at or observing the world as we know it, it becomes spread-out energy or potential waves. Crazy, right? So observing affects the world we observe. In Chapter 7, we stated, "The observer affects the observed." Maybe this will add some strength to that understanding.

In Chapter 3, "Sensing Differently," see the section "Senses and the Environment." We discussed meaning in the outside environment and also throughout this read. We can do a little experiment right now on meaning.

Lesson 1

1.   Whatever space you are in, look around and pick out two items or objects that seem interesting to you. It doesn't matter what they are. They can be people or objects.

2. Look at the first object and say aloud, "This (name the object) has no meaning."
3. Notice how you feel in your body as you say the statement and name the feelings.
4. Do the same thing with the second object and notice how you feel in your body and name the feelings.

Depending on the objects selected and our memories around the object and similar objects, feelings may be felt. Here is where we need to be careful. The body responds only to the mind. If we are feeling something in the body, the body responds to signals coming from the mind; and it has nothing to do with the body's feelings about the object. The body isn't responding to the object but to signals only from the mind.

Lesson 2

1. Look at the first object again and say aloud, "The only meaning this (name the object) has for me is the meaning I give it."
2. Notice how you feel in your body as you say the statement and name the feelings.
3. Do the same thing with the second object and notice how you feel in your body and name the feelings.

What is the conclusion of these two tests? Look closely and notice that nothing outside us has any meaning and is neutral until we think about it. Nothing in our world has any meaning in and of itself, and it is neutral until we bring the data inside and make an interpretation of it. Nothing outside us has any meaning except through our past memories. When we step into an environment (room, store, new school, and so forth.), we put the meaning on everything, every object, in that space. *(I have said that several times in different ways.)* We must observe it in our minds before the object can have any meaning for us at all. The only meaning the object can ever have for us is the meaning we individually give it based on our past memories, and we will each have our own meaning because we each have different memories. *(Can you imagine a universe where the world you live in is completely different from everyone else? Well, that is exactly the world you live in, but it doesn't seem that way, because of the conscious and subconscious "consensus agreements" we have all agreed to; and the fact that your brain and my brain operate a lot alike. Can you see that what is outside you is neutral and meaningless until you create the meaning? Can you appreciate that before you observe the object, it is like spread-out energy and isn't an object, because the energy is meaningless to your senses, and it might as well be only a potential wave? When you bring the information into the mind and think about it, it consolidates into a hologram in your mind, and your body responds to the signals sent out. Now when meaning is given to it, it becomes a "real object." You are the one who creates the meaning of everything in your world; therefore, you create the objects in your world the way they are. You as the observer and the giver of meanings determine the effects of what the objects have for you as you are observing them; therefore, the observer affects the observed.)*

What is outside us, being meaningless and neutral, is just energy. It isn't good or bad. Through our unique interpretation, we determine the goodness or badness of every object in our world. We have no idea what is outside us, and it might as well be nothing or everything in an unmanifested energy form. There is no way the outside energy means anything until we bring it in through our senses, filter and decode it, and think about it. *(Nothing outside you can be understood at all because it is neutral and meaningless. The only thing you know is what is inside you. How fast is your subconscious mind presenting filtered information to your active mind and your active mind sending signals to your body? Faster than a speeding bullet. By the time your slow conscious mind gets around to telling you about it, you will believe there is an outside object and that the meaning comes from the outside object; but it doesn't.)*

Lesson 3

- You cannot know or understand anything outside you because it is meaningless.
- Whatever you think you know about what you think is outside of you, you don't because what is outside of you is only energy.

- What you think is outside is a projection of what you have formed inside the way it is, because of your past, which is to say your memories.
- The outside is unknowable and therefore not understandable until it is perceived inside.

There may be a tendency to say, "That sounds like you're just splitting hairs here." We said before that everything is outside us and everything is inside us. What is outside is everything unmanifested and unknowable, and what is inside is everything we have manifested, which we have given meaning to and is knowable to us. These are two completely different universes. We create the knowable from the unknowable. The unknowable is always unknowable and is always the infinite and always outside us in the subtle field. The knowable is always our creation from what we hold inside us.

What is outside us? Unmanifested information. What is inside us? Manifested information. The three lessons we have gone through here are the first three lessons, more or less, of *A Course in Miracles Workbook for Students* Lessons 1, 2 and 3. (https://acim.org/workbook/lesson-1/) (https://acim.org/workbook/lesson-2/) (https://acim.org/workbook/lesson-3/)

CHAPTER 26

Over and Over

We have gone over a few topics several times from different vantage points in this read. It may have seemed overly repetitious at times, but because some of the concepts and ideas may be new and perhaps strange to some, I felt that sharing different viewpoints would be helpful; or maybe they were repeated because the writer got confused, cannot remember whether the subject was completely covered, and couldn't find their way out of the word maze and jungle they found them self in. Be that as it may, the mind or brain learns by repetition and by shock and awe. New thoughts and ideas need to be heard many times before they can penetrate the defenses of our current mind-set of the ego and the subconscious mind's filtering system.

The concepts we have shared aren't new and have been around for a long time in one form or another, eons of time in some cases. They are like perennial flowers. The seeds of these perennials are always there just underneath the surface of the ever-changing and never-complete current cultural and scientific belief system. However, because those within the illusion may have seen these flowers as dangerous, they have been categorized as pseudo knowledge and sham information based on what we thought we knew at the time; yet when we compare our gross energy system, which is finite, with the subtle field we are embedded in, and infinite, we know so little. We are so confident in the little we think we know from philosophy, logic, religion, and the scientific mind-set that it's scary to imagine from the viewpoint of our inflated ego that there may be other ways of understanding our world that may be more valid. *(Your ego should stand right up and yell at you, "This guy is crazy. You can't trust him. He doesn't even use the scientific method. He's not a scientist, doctor, or full-blown psychologist. How can you believe a word he says?" I'm telling you, stop listening to that little bugger and letting it run your life. You need to just step aside and go beyond your ego. The ego in all its forms will fight tooth and nail to maintain the old paradigm and the old power structure. It's trying to stay alive. It isn't your friend, and it has its own goals and agenda to save its egoic ass; and it cares nothing for you or your health, well-being, and peace of mind.)*

Science fiction and what is unbelievable of today is the scientific fact, which is believable tomorrow. What we believe as the absolute truth in our scientific world of today changes even from day to day, year to year, and discovery to discovery; yet we believe science is so right, real, and very trustworthy and fixed. In the magic of our shared illusion, we never seem to catch on to the fact that the trusted science of yesterday, which was obsoletely true then, is untrue today. Which means it was never completely true, even when we believed it was true and were living in an illusion of that belief. But no one jumps up and stouts, "How dare they tell us all those scientific facts that aren't true today. They were practicing pseudoscience and pseudo knowledge, and giving us sham information. Put them in jail!" And yet the poor perennial flowers are treated so badly. But such is the arrogance of the egoic self in the illusion and the power structure of today's paradigms. And what is the ego's goal? To keep us distracted and deep in the illusion, and keep us from remembering who we really are and what the body's purpose is.

We traveled throughout the world, using a piece of rock hung on a bit of string that for some strange unknown reason happened to always move and point in the same direction. Maxwell didn't discover the equations for how magnetism worked until well into the nineteenth century. If we would have waited for scientific proof before using magnetism, we would be hundreds of years and more behind where we are now.

Since 600 BC the mystical powers of lodestones were known and used by ancient man. The lodestone defied the scientific knowledge of their day. The stones gave a constant effect but without any known cause. They knew there must be a cause; however, they had no idea what it was. So without a cause for how they worked, did that stop them from using them? No. They did the only thing a civilized, rational society could do; they gave the cause away as a "gift from the gods;" and traveled over the horizon and around the world, using a stone on a string and the sun by day and the stone on a string and stars at night.

We don't need lodestones anymore; we have GPS. Its scientific cause is rooted in quantum physics. The little quantize particles run our world now. And we don't know how these subatomic quantize really work either, but that doesn't stop us from using them?

The effects in the body, our pain and suffering, have underlying causes; and many of those causes aren't known yet. However, the effects will happen regardless of whether the cause is known. For many of the effects, we have only theoretical causes experts have put forward in the field of the body. In most of these theories, the overriding power of the mind isn't mentioned because it lies beyond the body. It lies in the quantum state; it lies in the subtle field, which is unknowable through the Newtonian scientific method. However, this is changing—not because of the experts but because of the rebels within the scientific community of experts. And in the beginning, they will suffer for their new views, just like all those who first claimed the earth is round. (Do you see? Underneath we haven't advanced that far since the dawn of science.)

There are many theories about what goes on in the subconscious mind by these well-positioned and intellectually accredited experts, but the subconscious mind is still a black box. We know some of its input and output effects, so we use the effects and guess at the causes. If the causal guesses put forward by one accredited expert, which we just accept because of the weight of their accredited expertise, are proved wrong by newer accredited experts, we just change our minds and say, "Oh, we have new information now." But again, no one jumps up and says, "Oh, my God! We have been living in an illusion all this time and didn't realize it. Thank God, we now know the absolute truth." Can we appreciate just a little bit of why we are like fish in the infinite ocean and don't realize it? Can we see that while we may be smart, we are still fishlike in many ways?

See how elusive this ongoing illusory process is? Every time we find out how a trick is done in the subtle field; another mystery comes into being. So even though we are smart, we are still embedded in the infinite unknown and will never get out until we change the rules that keep us imprisoned, which is the whole egoic mind-set. If we knew the cause of the effects we are using, might we be able to get better results and make better choices? Yes, probably. Do we need to wait until we know the cause before we can use the effects? No, and that's a good thing.

EVERYTHING IS ENERGY

This has been our starting point, and it is also our ending point. "Everything is energy." It has always been that way. Everything has been and is energy and has always been energy. All we think we touch, see, hear, smell, and taste with our senses are just crystalized energy. Remember now, the senses only transmit data. The senses don't transmit good or bad data to the mind; they transmit only neutral data. The good, the bad, the ugly, the beautiful, and the not so beautiful are all interpretations from within the mind and have little to do with the senses. We now know that, don't we? *(You never know what's behind the curtain and out of sight of the conscious mind. But you now know there is a lot of everything going on behind that curtain, and it is happening at millions to billions of bits of information per second, and the conscious mind is grabbing only what it can get of the headlines at its snail's pace. Don't forget that! The ego will do its best to have you fall back into its realm. Be alert!)*

As we look deeper and deeper into any physical object, its physicalness begins to give way and disappear into empty space with a few unrecognizable specks of energy whizzing around. It makes no difference whether we are looking at our hand or a rock. The deeper and closer we look at anything, the more its physicalness disappears; and then it is absorbed into the subtle field of everything that supports it.

If we stop looking so closely, the more solid and identifiable the energy becomes until its objectiveness reappears, and we again have a hand or a rock again. It is almost as if there is a consciousness within the subtle energy field that is interacting with us. It's almost as if our energy frequencies in the gross energy system of the visible world and the subtle field of the invisible were dancing together, touching hands as it were; and the subtle field is responding to our needs based on our feedback with it. Sometimes it is slowing down so we can catch up, and sometimes it is moving faster as if there is a goal we are trying to reach. Here we might relate this dance and feedback to the law of attraction.

A WHEEL WITHIN A WHEEL

Just above, we said again that everything is energy, and it has been said many times in this read. In science, energy is the ability to do work. Whether it is energy of motion (kinetic energy), stored energy of position (potential energy), or energy in its mass, the energy has to move, or nothing happens. We have suggested two energy systems: the gross energy system of everyday life and the subtle field, of which our minds are unable to penetrate directly through our senses. Or maybe our senses transmit the data, but the subconscious mind just filters it out. Either way, the gross energy system is embedded within the infinite subtle field of everything.

As we think of those two systems of the gross energy system and the subtle field, does either system have a head or feet? No. Does either have an anus or a nose? No. However, metaphorically we may have assigned body parts to both systems because that is what we know an entity has, body parts; and then we project metaphorically what we know and assign it onto those systems. How we relate to these two systems is through metaphors of what we know from within the gross energy system. However, those energy systems have no individual organs or parts.

On the other hand, there is a cultural, historical, and religious tendency to believe the gross and subtle systems have body parts, such as feet and hands, heart and head; and we view those systems not metaphorically but as if they really do have human individual parts.

We believe there really is a big gluteus maximus sitting on a throne in space, with its feet on a footstool of stars, or dragons in caves that breathe fire and are ready to devour sinners, bad people, or people who do bad things. As we think of the all mighty source energy, or the subtle field, it has a heart and puts its hands on our shoulders, and it makes footprints in the sand, walks with us, and talks to us; however, none of those body parts exist in those energy systems. We are the fish in the subtle ocean, and the ocean has no head, heart, anus, or nose. *(You might think those metaphors have guilt-inspired stores of the ego to keep us under its control. Again, don't just think of your ego. Think of the ego as an interactive community of egos, your family, your society, your country, your religion, and all-controlling groups of people as keeping you imprisoned in a web of interactive egos. For you to think outside the web of egos can be a dangerous thing, as I mentioned before.)*

These descriptions of body parts for the energy systems are all metaphors, of course; the subtle field is everywhere in all of time/space and beyond time and space. As a metaphor, it may be helpful to gain perspective by using body parts to understand it; however, when the metaphor is believed to be the truth and we believe the infinite subtle field has parts, we distort the infinity of the whole into something it isn't, and we live in that illusion. That belief keeps us in the illusion of what never was and what can never be. *(You may even know some people who are so invested in believing that their metaphors are real that they would burn you at the stake for suggesting there are no footprints in the sand and no one sitting on a throne in space.)*

When we believe the metaphor is true, our perception is distorted, and we are lost in the illusion; and the reality of oneness is unavailable to be experienced. The gross is always within and supported by the subtle. The "seen and manifested" rests within the "unseen and unmanifested." The small is within the large, the finite is always within the infinite, and the fish is always within the ocean.

By believing the subtle field has body parts like us, we can also attribute other human characteristics to the infinite subtle field that, of course, the infinite field doesn't have. Why would we do that? Because it lets us justify our more negative human characteristics by assigning them to the infinite—in other words, wars, revenge, murder, and all manner of abuses. These are all ego driven, and as we know, the ego has many forms. We may not know how to resolve these issues, but that is no reason to attribute them to the infinite, so we can do them to each other with impunity and say from our high moral perch, "I'm only doing what God does, what God has directed me to do for him." Again they are ego driven, and we are marching to the egoic drumbeat and believing we are following the infinite subtle field, the Almighty's divine command. *(Even as you read this, some egos may jump right up in your head and quote ancient laws, old stone tablets, and older books to justify you doing unloving things; and call them loving because you attribute them to the almighty, infinite subtle field. They cry all those old, ancient books and stones as proof, and like a witch doctor right in front of you, they shake their beads, roll their bones, and rattle their sabers in your head. All this will happen inside you from your ancient programming to drive you back into the illusion. Take a chance. See through your new vision and see things differently.)*

Come on, all those things that were written and chipped out of stone were all done by other humans. They all had egos, and they were egoically or divinely driven but with an agenda. We have two choices here; they either wrote or chipped from being deep in the gross energy system of separation and illusions, or they wrote and chipped them from within the oneness, inspired by the infinite subtle field. If their writing and chipping promoted wars, revenge, murder, sacrifice, and all manner of abuses, from which system, do you think, they were operating? From within the system of separation and illusions or from oneness and the infinite subtle field? We have to give the ego its due here, because it is so clever in taking unloving things and calling them loving in such a way that we believe it's so.

WHO WE ARE

In this space/time universe, "who we think we are" is only what we can remember about us, which are all memories. To think of us in any other way, we must use abstract thinking. Abstract thinking moves us beyond the physical and into the imagined. But even to go into that realm, our starting point is still our experiences, which are our memories. To think of an object, principle, or idea is to think of a memory we have created and then move the memory or combined memories around.

Abstract thinking is the ability to think about objects, principles, and ideas that aren't physically present. It is related to symbolic thinking, which uses the substitution of a symbol for an object or idea.

A variety of everyday behaviors constitute abstract thinking. These include the following:

- Using metaphors and analogies
- Understanding relationships between verbal and nonverbal ideas
- Spatial reasoning and mentally manipulating and rotating objects
- Complex reasoning, such as using critical thinking, the scientific method, and other approaches to reasoning through problems

(Abstract Thinking—GoodTherapy.org, https://www.goodtherapy.org/blog/psychpedia/abstract-thinking)

We know who we think we are only through our past, and our past is only memories. And those memories are our beliefs, experiences, and references of our interpretations of events that are long gone. For all our memories, we have little conscious awareness of who we are. Not really, because all our memories and programming built from them are in the subconscious mind and that's a closed black box. The conscious mind has no access to what is going on in that black box.

We are consciously aware of who we are because of our behavior, as reported by the conscious mind and observed by others in the gross energy system. That is why when we change our old memories about the past, we change who we think we are, which is to say our ego identity. The old ego self must die so a new one can be created and integrated into our new belief system, which has incorporated our new changes. This is the separateness of ourselves within the gross. Our oneness in the subtle field is different from who we think we are, because it is our original self. And we dance between our self (small *s*) and our Self (big *S*) all the time.

Let us be clear here. The past cannot be changed because it's over and gone. However, the residue of our interpretation of the events, our distorted memories, can be reframed and healed because they aren't real, true, or complete. *(Remember, your memories are entangled within your own subconscious black box and within entangled memory systems with others, which now must be viewed as a single system. If you look closely, you may or may not see that even if you are sitting in the middle of a forest all by yourself, you are still entangled. Why? Because at root, you and I are one; and in that state, time and space collapse, and we are touching hands. Changing your memories and reframing them will not only change you but also affect all who are entangled with you. You won't experience this at surface structure. You will know it only at deep structure, which is out of conscious awareness; however, you may feel the body's response.)*

How does the above paragraph fit with Chapter 23, "Entangled Connections"? Even at the smallest level of the butterfly effect, we affect our world in ways we will never understand. Can we begin to accept that at each and every moment we make decisions that are the sensitive-dependent initial conditions for changing our world positively, keeping it the same or moving it in a negative direction? Those decisions will either move us deeper into illusions and separation or move us closer to oneness and our original self. Currently most of our decisions are automatic and for the most part programmed responses because of our memories in the subconscious mind. To have a different world, we will need to awaken from the trance of our programming and our habitual self, and develop more positive programming, which is to say reframe our negative memories.

THE EVENT ENERGY SIGNATURE

When an event happens, energy is released in a chaotic manner, and the energy release will have an underlying structure or signature; and it doesn't matter whether it's taking a trip to the supermarket, buying a new house, or having a wedding. We went over this in Chapter 23, "Entangled Connections." We are always entangled within what we are engaged in. Even if we are sitting in a cabin deep in the woods with our dogs *(I did say that before, didn't I?)*, we affect our surrounding systems, and they affect us. However, nature has a high resonant frequency; as we attune to nature's energy, we move closer to oneness. There is chaos in nature, but like all chaotic events, there is a structure under it in ways we won't understand, but we can appreciate and use the healing effects of Mother Nature.

Since we are always entangled within the energy fields of others and our environment, when we forgive ourselves, our world changes, and so does theirs to varying degrees. So we may have to revise our thinking about the statement we made earlier that "changing our memories affects only us." We have a new understanding now that we are always dancing with those whom we are closely connected with and with our environment in ways beyond our conscious awareness. Dancing is responding to the feedback of those we are touching hands with, both in physical and subtle ways, and at emotional and energetic levels, both consciously and subconsciously. Sometimes as we dance, we get our toes stepped on, and the healing response to that is always self-forgiveness. The other person will have to do his or her own healing and forgiving processes. *(Remember, you can't change other people directly. However, if you change your dance steps, they will change. Or they won't be able to dance with you without getting their toes stepped on, and they may have to leave the dance floor.)*

QUICK RESULTS

Since negative memories, when triggered in the active mind, override all other activities in the mind because of our minds' or bodies' primal drives of survival, they signal the body to respond by turning on its survival systems. By changing and reframing our oldest and most negative memories, we will have the greatest and most immediate positive effect on our lives. This is important to get, not just intellectually but right down to the marrow of our bones. Memories aren't real, and the oldest, unreal memories will have the greatest negative effect on us. With that in mind, negative childhood memories will have a more devastating effect on us right now than today's negative experiences.

Memories are our created thought forms; and because they aren't real, it's okay to change them. *(Now, don't fall back into your old belief that memories are real because of how they make you feel in your body. Your memories are distorted interpretations of events that never happened the way you thought they did. Come on now; we are getting close to the end of this read. Maybe you will need to go back over some of this information. Memories aren't real.)*

Our strong, negative emotional memories feel real in our bodies when we think about them, don't they? We all have experienced events that were hurtful, embarrassing, or frightening. But the events are over and aren't coming back. We can't live in the past, not even for one moment. We can live only in the present moment. However, if we keep dragging the past into the present by holding on to old distorted memories, our tomorrows will be a lot like our yesterdays; and our todays will be distorted by our clinging to what isn't here now. It isn't the event we are dragging into the present; it is only our old, distorted memories of the event, which aren't real. We are only dragging around our created, inaccurate interpreted thought forms of what are gone, over, and never-coming-back events. Heal it. Release your pain and suffering and let go of the negative memories of your past. This is called "healing yourself." Everything starts in the mind; therefore—now this is important—*only the mind needs to be healed.* When our pasts are healed and reframed, our presents will reflect them as new and different worlds.

THE MIND

By convention we have two realms to the mind or maybe two minds: the conscious mind and the subconscious (unconscious) mind. We have shared a lot about the two realms of the mind—their separate functions, their different processing speeds, how they appear to operate, and their different communication systems. Again, there are a lot of theories about the mind, the brain, the central nervous system, and their interactions; but there's not much we can take to the bank and cash in.

In this read, we have used the term "active mind" to suggest the interaction among the mind, brain, and central nervous system. The combination is basically a black box, because the subconscious mind within this combination of the active mind is a black box. Maybe we can solve what the subconscious mind is by using mathematics. Since the subconscious mind is the unknown, it can be equal to X. And since we know the other components—the conscious mind, brain, and central nervous system in a more finite form—we can solve for X. And since we are concerned about our pain and suffering, we will let Y represent our pain and suffering.

Now, since our pain and suffering are our bodies' responses to the active mind's interpretation of data from the subconscious mind or X, we can put some things together here.

Total mind + brain activity + central nervous
system = active mind's interpretation
Active mind's interpretation signals = the body's response
Y = pain and suffering = body's response to the active mind
X = subconscious mind
C = conscious mind
X + C = total mind
(X + C) + brain + central nervous system = Y
Since C + brain active + central nervous
system are all known, let them = Z
Therefore: X + Z = Y
Or X = Y/Z
Solution: subconscious mind = pain and suffering/Z
What is in the subconscious mind? Only memories from the past.
So we can rewrite the solution.
Memories = pain and suffering/C + brain
active + central nervous system
Therefore, memories = pain and suffering/conscious
mind + brain active + central nervous system

Now, we know what our pain and suffering are, right? Now this journey down the mathematical garden path may feel like being on a snipe hunt, finding the snipe in our pillowcase, and not knowing what to do with it. Actually, the conclusion is accurate, even if the math isn't. Memories are causal issues of the pain and suffering we feel in our bodies, and the memories that cause our pain and suffering are the negative ones. *(I know you may not consciously remember what the causal memories are. I know you are thinking that viruses, bacteria, genetics, the plague, wars, and accidents from the outside environment, not memories from the inside, are the cause of your pain and suffering. This has all been gone over before, except for plagues and wars. Negative memories in the black box of the mind, which are distortions of interpretations of events long gone, are the underlying cause of pain and suffering. This is tough to get because of our cultural bias, prejudice, and programming; and our desire to protect our ego's self-identity and our family and cultural history. This approach is counterintuitive to current cultural and social understandings and beliefs. But there it is.)*

ONLY MINDS COMMUNICATE

We believe that when we are communicating with someone, we are talking to some body. When we are communicating with a body, we think we are communicating with somebody. We are not. We are communicating with some mind. It is that old trickster, the ego, that convinces us we are communicating with bodies. Why would the ego do that? To have us believe we are our bodies. Refer to Chapter 14, "Switching of Purpose and Means." *(You believe you are your egoic self-identity. If you can understand and appreciate just for a moment that you aren't a body and that you are beyond your ego, the ego would be no more, and you would be your original self. So the ego needs to keep you distracted with the body. But know for sure that you are always communicating with your mind. It is the mind that moves the body to appear happy or sad, angry or joyous. Stop blaming your body for what the mind and ego are doing.)*

The body does only what the mind tells it to do. It is like this: if we went shopping and forgot what we were shopping for, we may be able to call our significant other to remind us of what we forgot. So we take out our cell phones and call them. The cell phone represents the body in our example of communicating with others. It is the mind holding the phone that is communicating. The phone is responding only to the mind's causal voice. The phone isn't communicating; it is responding to the mind. The body isn't communicating; it is responding to the mind. It is the mind, speaking through the body, that is communicating. And again, we see the body getting blamed for what the mind is doing. Rarely, if ever, do we recognize that the mind causes our problems with communication, not the body. Mind and body, software and hardware, just aren't connected in our thought process. *(Changing how you hold your phone, which is your behavior or hardware, doesn't change your communication, although you will think it does. The only way to change your communication is to change your mind, which means you need to kill your current ego and create another ego, which incorporates your change. You see why the ego wants you to believe you are your body? When you believe you are your body, you are operating through the illusion. When you believe you are your body, you won't heal as easily. When you believe you are your body, you can hide from your wounded self. When you believe you are your body, you don't need to reframe and heal your stuff from the past. When you believe you are your body, being sick is a great ego defense, because you can blame the body and tell all others with great sadness in your voice, "I'll change as soon as I feel better." And that remark will keep you sick longer. Your ego hopes you will be sick long enough to forget your need to change. And, of course, you can still blame the body.)*

Many times in couple and family therapy, the couple or family will say, "We can't communicate with each other." They will tell me all the things their partner has said and the behaviors they have done that was hurtful and painful. And they want their partner "fixed." The tricky part of working with them is working with them in ways that will change each of their minds because both have contributed to the problem, and both must change. Couples and families dance together. They learn the dance well. If they want to dance differently, they all must learn new dance steps. Remember, it is the mind that is communicating, so don't blame the physical responses of the body. Refer to Chapter 17, "Changing Vision," in the section "Relationships and Cups." *(This is so hard to do because your ego will go crazy trying to convince you that the other person must change and not you. There is always one in the relationship who feels morally superior, and it's the other person's fault that the relationship is in trouble; therefore, they don't have to change in any way. This is especially true between children and parents. Remember, all have contributed to the problem, and all must change. If you feel you are the morally superior one, oh, how your ego will jump to your defense and make it clear that it's not you who needs to change; it will rationalize why only the partner must change and not you.)*

SENSES

In Chapter 3, "Sensing Differently," we shared the fact that senses don't sense; nor do they select. They neither interpret nor judge anything. They just transmit energy data and information. None of the senses do anything we believe they do. We don't see any objects with the eye, because the eye transmits only energy data. What we think we see with the eye is an interpretation in the active mind. Again, because of the conscious mind's slow processing speed, it projects our inner-created interpretation onto the outside energy system, and we believe what we see is outside us, but we never catch on to the fact that everything is an inside creation and that the outside projection is an inside-created hologram.

The ear doesn't hear music. Music is an interpretation of the active mind. Everything we think is outside us is an inside interpretation of the active mind. This is true for all our senses. Everything we think we experience from the outside is inside because outside is only neutral and meaningless energy until we think about it. *(You have read what I wrote a little bit ago, right? "There is no meaning in the outside energy system." Whether you believe it or not, within seconds you will slip back into the egoic state, and you won't remember it. Your programming is very strong, and you will quickly slip back into listening to the ego and believing that objects, including people, have meaning and that meaning is out there in the outside world. Silly person, you are creating the whole thing, and there is nothing out there but energy. But don't you believe the meaning is out there in the great outdoors? You see how the great trickster, the ego, turns everything around so you believe you're a body, which you aren't?)*

If everything outside us is only energy in its unmanifested state and if everything we have inside us is a manifestation of an interpretation by the active mind, what can we do with that understanding? Use it. The senses are sending us everything—the good and beautiful, the bad and not so beautiful, and the ugly. The holographic world we have created inside us is our manifestation. It has nothing to do with the senses, but it has everything to do with the data, the information that gets into the active mind from the subconscious mind. How that data input we receive is mined through the black box of the subconscious mind determines our world. By using our distorted negative memories, which the filtering system used, we manifest something different inside us. To have something new and maybe something better, all we need to do is heal, reframe, and change our distorted memories of events that are gone. The senses send us all the data and information they can of the outside energy of everything; then we filter, mine, and select the data using our memories into something less than what is there, into something else. That less-than-distorted data sent to the active mind results in the creation of a less-than-accurate interpretation, and the residue of that less-than-accurate interpretation will be another distorted memory we have of the event, which is gone and of course isn't the event and isn't real. *(Can you appreciate that the memory of an event isn't the event itself? The memory of an event is never the event, no matter what your ego tells you. I know; it will have bits and pieces of truth held together by your imagination and older memories, but memories are never real, true, or complete. And they are never the event.)*

Look closely and notice. Since memories are distortions and we use those distorted memories to filter and mine new and current incoming sensory data, won't we create more distorted memories? It seems highly likely. *(I know your memories seem accurate, real, and true to you; or you wouldn't have them. But they are creations and constructions based on filtered, manipulated, and distorted data. How distorted they are isn't important, because the events they depict are gone and cannot be used as a reference. Might there be lessons in the events you may need at some point? Perhaps. Do you need to keep the painful memories to have the gifts of the lessons? No. When you get a gift of a shirt or blouse, must you keep the bag it came in to enjoy the gift of wearing the shirt or blouse? No, you throw the bag it came in away but keep the gift. And you don't need to keep your painful memories to keep and use the gift of the lessons that came inside the now-gone event. You can separate the painful experiences from their lessons. The separation happens naturally in the healing, reframing, and changing process of self-forgiveness.)*

The Body

Refer to Chapter 14, "Switching of Purpose and Means." We aren't our bodies; and that's it, a simple statement. We are beyond the body; however, we need a body to be here now. Because we have gotten confused as to who and what we are, we have defaulted to the lowest common denominator, which is to say the body. We have switched means with purpose. In this egoic place, we have exchanged means for purpose; and it's so easy to do, given the social pressures of marketing and public relations around the importance of the body. It is part of what makes the illusion work, and it keeps the egoic self in its many forms in control.

Look closely and notice. It isn't the body that has done this, because the body doesn't care. The body responds only to the interpretation in the active mind. It is our internal active mind that has switched means and purpose. Everything is first a thought in the mind and then a response in the body. Here again we see that the body is the scapegoat for our mind.

Where does the data come from that drives the interpretation in the active mind? The manipulated and filtered data from the subconscious mind, our black box. *(How you experience your body is through your conscious mind. Why your body responds the way it does is because of the signals it gets from the active mind. Your body has no direct connection to the outside energy field or to the marketing and public relations; it doesn't care about social media marketing and public relations. Those are concerns of your egoic self-identity, which is integrated into your belief system in your subconscious mind. So don't blame your body for why you feel the way you do about your body, because the body has nothing to do with the body. It is all about your inside distorted memories and how you have chosen to use those memories to interpret your life. What you attract into your life is based on what you hold within you. If you don't like what you are attracting, change what you hold inside, because that is the cause of the effect you think you see outside. It's all you and what you hold within. The outside world is neutral and meaningless. Your thoughts about the data in your active mind are what give life and meaning to data you hold and not what is outside and neutral until you think about it.)*

As Within, So Without

Everything outside us is in the unmanifested state of the subtle field. We have stated that several times. Refer to Chapter 22, "Unmanifested Everything and the Manifested Everything." Since what is outside us is unmanifested and what is inside us is manifested, we are the ones who project the inside onto the outside and consciously believe what is inside us is outside, when it's always inside us. The conscious mind does that automatically because of its slow processing speed. (Refer to Chapter 2, "Two Minds," and the section titled "Backup Information Transmission and Processing Speeds").

Therefore, what we experience as the outside world is because of what is being interpreted and manifested in the active mind. The world we experience is always because of what we hold inside us, which are our beliefs, experiences, and references, which is to say our memories.

To say, "What you hold within you determines what you will experience outside you" is to make an accurate statement. But of course the ego will always blame what is happening outside us for the life we are experiencing inside, and it's only a projection. That is what we do in this illusion. Notice how convincing the egoic self can be when its thought process is being challenged?

The Law of Attraction and the Subtle Field

Throughout this read we have discussed the law of attraction in its more conventional understanding. We radiate an energy frequency into the universe and attract from the universe what matches our energy frequency. If we look closely, we might notice that the process may not work quite that way.

Just above we stated, "Everything is outside us in the unmanifested everything of the subtle field." Think about that statement. If everything is in the subtle field because the subtle field is infinite and is everywhere, then everything must already be here. We don't need to send out a radiant frequency from our energy system into the universe and wait for a response. Why? Because what we want is already here, waiting for us to manifest it.

Recall that in Chapter 22, "Unmanifested Everything and the Manifested Everything," there is a diagram that metaphorically depicts using the components of a laser system to create a hologram in the mind. The hologram is our created interpreted universe in which we live. In that model, the reference beam of everything hits the stored data of our memories, and the interference patterns based on our past create a holographic universe inside the mind. It is that holographic universe we live in. If we want a different universe to live in, we need to change only the medium through which the beam of everything passes; and that medium comprises the memories of what we hold inside. *(Now don't let your ego start whispering to you again. This is just a different way of understanding how you are always getting what you are asking for and that you can change what you are getting simply by changing what you hold inside about your past, which is always your constructed memories. These are models I'm presenting to you to stimulate new ideas for you to chew on.)*

THE FINAL STEP

Forgiveness is the final step. This is difficult to understand because we have been programmed to believe memories and the past, which comprises only memories, are real. And if memories are real, how can what is real and true be changed into something that's not? How can real memories and the truth be denied? How can we really forgive ourselves or others? Won't that just be lying to ourselves or playing "Let's pretend" in our minds? *(The way you have been programmed, you can't. How can we make something real and true into something it isn't? So the egoic conclusion of this is, we can't; so from the ego's thinking system, for you to forgive yourself, you must move deeper into the illusion. That is why, with our current culture belief system, forgiveness seems to be a lie or a make-believe act. You may also call forgiveness "a state of grace," which is another way of saying, "You can't do it for yourself"; and for you to forgive, you need permission from the egoic authorities. Did you hear your ego jump right up and say, "That's not true. I can forgive whoever I want, and I will if they deserve it"? You see, deserving has nothing to do with forgiving. Both have made errors, and both need to make peace with themselves. Do you want to know the real secret of forgiveness? The event, for which all you now have is a memory, was never real, true, or complete in the first place. You aren't forgiving a "truth." You are letting go of an "untruth.")*

From the ego's point, to forgive or be forgiven, we need to feel we are getting something in return. Our egoic self will tell us that. We might think in terms of the old statement "Forgive me for what I have done to you as I forgive others for what they have done to me." If we can strike a bargain, then it's okay to forgive, because it becomes a bartering system; and it make sense to the ego and helps us feel better about forgiving others or being forgiven. It is commerce and a trade agreement. "I'll do for you if you do for me." Why? Because of the belief that memories and the past are real and that they fit within our programming and the ego's plan for continued control. *(Have you noticed how much I used the term* programming? *You might begin to wonder and relate it to computer language and think about software and hardware, and the mind and the body. If you aren't writing your programming code, who is?)*

The whole egoic plan begins falling apart with the understanding that memories aren't real. The whole illusionary structure quakes as just one of us forgives them self; and demons are released in the forms of family, cultural, and religious egos that shriek at us, "You can't forgive yourself. It's against the law. This is a dangerous practice, this idea and process of self-forgiveness."

How frightened the illusion becomes when someone puts his or her foot on the path to oneness and starts moving outside the illusion and dream state. *(You may have noticed that all those egos are interconnected and form a virtual structure, supporting each other; and your ego is part of that structure. Your unreal memories also form a structure in you, and your ego is part of that virtual egoic structure; and your ego is connected to the gross energy system. You might now be able to recognize the connecting element that holds the structure together; it is your ego. Your ego, memories, and the larger egoic structures are interrelated, supporting each other and this virtual structure. For you to choose a different path could be dangerous. You would be pushing against the whole weight of the illusionary structure, and it will push back.)*

So again, as we start working with self-forgiveness, keep it a secret and don't go to the worst of the worst to try to shoot holes in this approach. Start with small personal offenses or irritations. We haven't yet completely integrated into our own individual belief systems the understanding that memories aren't real. How can we expect society and the larger world to understand memories and that the past isn't real and can be changed? We as a society have built empires, power structures, and personal wealth around the world on the belief of memories being real; and we have also created personal hells around the belief that memories must be real. We have started wars and taken revenge on other people and nations based on the belief that memories are real. We have caused centuries of strife between peoples and nations because of the belief that memories are real. We have developed religions around the belief that memories are real. The fact that memories aren't real isn't going to change the world anytime soon, because the negative egoic energy states and their power structures are just too great. *(Here is the thing. You can change you. You can slowly begin to move from illusion toward oneness and peace of mind. However, you must be careful because you will become the saboteur within the system, the ghost within the works. You will be viewed as a terrorist, even though that's not your goal. You are just forgiving yourself and letting go of the unreal past.)*

True forgiveness is about personal transformation, and that is where it needs to start, with you. Take any negative memory of 2 or 3 intensity on the SUD scale. Make the memory into a still picture in the active mind. Bring all the modalities of the memory into the picture (visual, auditory, kinesthetic, olfactory, and gustatory) in the active mind, picture where it took place and the time of day, the time of year, what was around you, who you were with, and especially how you feel. Make it as clear, detailed, and complete as possible. *(Notice that some people have difficulty visualizing; if that's you, use any of the other modalities and represent the memory anyway that works for you. Know you are the director*

411

of your memory story and creator of your holographic picture or representation inside you. Recognize that all the actors and actresses in this play are you, disguised as your interpretation of the other people. You made the scenery and all the stage props. They are your creation, based on the data you stored as an interpretation of an event that is no more. All you have now of the event is an old, distorted script of the play, the memory. As you look at the stage, understand the event you are trying to recreate on stage is gone and never was the way you have set the stage, and it will never come back.

If you see one of the players in the scene as the cause of your pain and suffering, know the person is you disguised as them. If you see yourself as being at fault and in need of forgiveness from another character in the play, know you are the other character. In all cases, you are only forgiving you in this play, because it is only you in the play and only you inside you. There is no one inside you but you, and you are such a perfect creator of the play. You know all the parts, and you play them all so perfectly that you have fooled the audience completely; and you have been fooling them for a long time into believing the play is real. At the sad parts of the play, the audience cried, and at the funny parts, the audience laughed. What a great playwright, what great directing, and what great actors and actresses. The play is perfect. Guess who the audience is?

It's you; it is all you. You are the only audience of the play. You wrote the play as it is, and you direct the play the way you do. You act out all the parts, and you are also the audience. Oh yes! You are the audience. You have entertained yourself for a long time with this play. You have told yourself and others how it makes you feel as you watch it in your mind. It is now time to let it go. It is now time to realize the event is gone and can never come back. It is time to forgive yourself for something that was never real, was never complete, and was never true or the way you think it was. It is only a created play you made up and keep playing in your mind. Let it go or rewrite the play into a comedy. It is all you, and it is all make believe in your mind. There is no reality of the play outside your mind. It is only you, and it's not real. The memory is only you, and it's not real; and all the plays you create from your unreal memories are only you and unreal. Listen, there is only you. Notice there is only you tormenting you, only you entertaining you, and only you giving you an excuse for staying stuck where you are. Sickness is always a great excuse for staying stuck where you are. Move your body, heal, change, and move on. Moving your body is a quick feedback system for changing and healing the mind.)

Those other people who were with us during the event that's now gone have their own memories, and their memories won't be like ours. They will have to go through their own forgiveness process—or not. However, because of entangled connections, your self-forgiveness and whatever they do within the entangled single memory system will affect each other. Why is that? Because it isn't the event or what happened in the event we are forgiving. All we have left is the memory, and we are reframing the memory; we are changing our interpretation of the event that is never, ever going to come back. We aren't able to change the event because it is gone, and that isn't the point or the problem. The problem is, we believe the unreal memory is real; and we so want the memory to be real, but it's not and never was. *(Listen as you read that in your mind. Listen for your ego to jump in your head and tell you, "Your memories are real. That's crazy talk. Throw that book in the trash!")*

COMPENSATION

Again, we must be clear. We are playing only with small emotional slights and irritations in our learning and practicing of self-forgiveness in the beginning; therefore, compensation for a slight or an irritation shouldn't be an issue in our discussion here. However, compensation may be a concern in some of the worst or the worst of our worst-problem memories. We are in the world, and while here, the world will impinge on us. Some forms of interactions in the gross energy system may require us to ask for compensation or give compensation. This is built into the structure of the illusion.

Compensation has no effect on our forgiving ourselves or others for errors in perceptions. They are all distorted perceptions from within the illusion. There is a dance between egos that have been negatively entangled through misperceptions, and we may be stuck and can't move beyond our ego states; and oh, how we fear for our egos' safety, which is to say our own self-created identity.

FORGIVENESS, A GATEWAY INTO DEEP STRUCTURE

Forgiveness is an act within the gross energy system. Through true forgiveness, vision changes, and the surface structure of the gross energy system shifts. With a clear vision, our distorted perception is corrected. With a new clearer perception, a portal, an opening, or a wormhole is opened from the illusion into a deeper structure beyond gross awareness.

We can never change the event because it doesn't exist anymore to change, and it never existed the way we thought it existed anyway. Something did happen, and it will never happen again; it's gone. What we have now is a memory of the distorted interpretation of the event. Whatever actually happened doesn't matter, because no one has the complete, real, and true knowledge of the event the way it happened; and it doesn't exist now, so it can never be verified. All the players in the event can have only distorted memories of the event based on their distorted memories from their past.

As was mentioned before in this chapter and the last one, there is an energy signature around the entangled memories. As we rewrite our own script of the play, which comes from our memories, on a subtle level all the entangled memory scripts are being rewritten to some degree as well. *(I know you are struggling against your own programming and belief system here. Your ego is probably whispering in your ear right now, "This is crazy talk. The past doesn't exist? Come on now! This can't be right. Memories are real. You surely know that." And then your ego tells you from its standpoint why memories are real and must be real. And there is a high probability you will believe your ego because your ego is very persuasive. Unless you have moved beyond your egoic self, unless you move beyond surface structure into deep structure, you may fall back into the dragon's lair.)*

With the understanding that memories aren't real, forgiving ourselves is a natural step in the healing process for ourselves and all those who are entangled with us in the event. Since during the event all those who were engaged in the event where energetically entangled, as we forgive ourselves, the energy signature of the event, which is now only the entanglement of individual memories, will shift. Our forgiving ourselves will cause changes in the vibrational energy through the deep structure of oneness. We are reaching down through forgiveness into the subtle field and changing the entangled, energetic structure of the memory energy signature.

We stated before in Chapter 4, "No energy, no matter. Energy is the matrix on which the physical matter is hung and grown." By the act of self-forgiveness, we move the entire entangled memory matrix closer toward oneness and into deeper structure. The system is locked in place by all the individual unreal memories. By changing our energy signature through self-forgiveness, we cause the whole structure to shift, and as it shifts in a positive direction, each individual vibrational memory formed within the structure will also change. On that shifting energy structure is hung the physical gross energy system.

We are reaching up from the deep structure into the gross energy system by changing and shifting the combined energy forms and total energy signature of the event as it is reflected in the entangled memory system; as a result, the changing underlying energy signature will cause physical changes in the gross energy system to occur as well.

Refer to Chapter 11, "Gross and Subtle Energy Systems." In the section "Reaching Down, Reaching Up," we are beginning to peek behind the curtain and see that we are the creators of our world; and we are the ones who can change what we have created. The greatest elements of change are our awareness and self-forgiveness. Out of those acts will come positive changes and release for all. The greatest element of disagreement between us and our egoic selves is our self-forgiveness and of course the arguments from all those egos of family, culture, religion, country, and more that need to keep memories real and unchangeable to maintain control.

Refer to Chapter 7, "The Subconscious Mind." In the section "Seeing Things Differently," events are complete chaotic explosions with many levels of information; and we can take in only what will fit through the lens of our past. Whether the event is a massive event, like being in a war, or a very small one, like an interaction with a loved one, the subtleties and internal nuances of all the interactions with the event are filtered through our past and won't be known by our conscious awareness; therefore, the memory of the interpretation of the encountered event can never hold the whole event. And no one involved will ever know the completeness of the event. *(Are you beginning to understand why your forgiving yourself supports creating a new world for all? By your healing, all are changed. Look again. You are the one asleep and dreaming of the many; as you heal, all will heal, because at that deep level, you are the oneness.)*

Do we need to make amends for our errors in perception and for our behavior, which flows from those perceptions? Maybe. Will the ego tell us, "You must"? Yes. What are we forgiving? A misperception in our interpretation of an event, which is gone and will never come back; and all we have left is an unreal memory. The first step in changing the energy signature around the memory is to heal ourselves, and the first step in that process of self-healing is to forgive ourselves; this act will lead to self-love.

What is real, and what is unreal? We will never know on the conscious level and from within the gross energy system. Since we are here and it is now, what can we say about the here and now?

Nothing real can be threatened. Nothing unreal exists.
Herein lies the peace of God.

—*A Course in Miracles*

GLOSSARY OF TERMS

The terms in the glossary are only for those terms not used the way they are commonly used in this book. If there are some missing, you are free to guess at what in the world I was thinking.

Active Mind: This is where all our interpretations and perceptions are created. They are created from data received from the subconscious mind and the body. Interpretations are produced in a stream and are not like individual snapshots or pictures. They are more like an ongoing movie that never stops. From the interpretation, electromagnetic and chemical signals are sent out to the mind and body. The active mind is the interface and combination of mind, brain, and central nervous system acting together. The signals sent out by the active mind, based on its interpretations, are the only way mind and body know how to respond because mind and body aren't connected to the outside environment directly. They are aware only of anything through the active mind's interpretation and messaging and the signaling it sends out. We must be clear here. The body, the conscious and subconscious minds, and the active mind aren't directly connected in any way to the outside environment. The outside environment comes to us only through the senses. Refer to Chapter 3, "Sensing Differently."

Body: As it is used in this book, the body is a metaphor. It represents a shell or membrane of protection around the interworking's of the mind and brain; and it also interacts with the active mind. This is important to understand; the body has no connection or interaction with the outside environment. All the body is aware of are the signals from the active mind. The body and the active mind are in constant communication.

But the body and the outside environment never communicate directly. Everything that ever happens to us is first in the mind and then in the body. The body has its own wisdom and automatic systems. However, it is designed to respond to and give feedback information back to the active mind's signaling. They operate in partnership with each other. We aren't our bodies. The body is our servant, unless the egoic self hijacks it.

Conscious Mind: See "Mind"

Critical Factor: In the model we are using in this read, the critical factor is a subconscious mind activity, and it has the function of testing and filtering all information and data that come to the mind through sensory input. In other models, the critical factor is a conscious mind activity. However, as we know, the conscious mind is too slow to perform this activity. (Refer to Chapter 2, "Two Minds.") All the filters are called "perceptual filters" and are created from our memories of the past. They compare incoming data to what we are familiar with from our past memories stored in the subconscious mind. If we have no reference to incoming information, we will test and criticize the new data; and if it doesn't meet our beliefs, experiences, or references, it is disregarded or quarantine for later investigation.

Gross Energy System: This is the energy system we call our world. It is where we think we live. It is our manifested objective universe and our interpreted universe. It is the output and creative action of the active mind. When created, we perform a neat trick with this internal system through the conscious mind; we project the gross energy system onto the outside subtle energy system. While we consciously believe the world is outside us, it is always inside us.

Interpretations: Interpretations are created from the constant stream of data sent to the active mind from the subconscious mind and the body. Interpretations are actively in constant fluctuation and change like an active volcano, constantly spitting out molten lava or interpretations. Interpretations are changing at billions of bits of data per second.

Electromagnetic signals and chemical messages from the active mind are sent out to the mind and body. These signals and messages inform the mind and body of how to respond to their world and environment. Every thought we have creates chemistry and electromagnetic signals, and the interpretations are in nonverbal thoughts (not in words).

Interpreted Universe: The active mind creates interpretations in a constant stream from the data received from the mind and body. From this constant stream of interpretations, an internal universe is created. This is the universe and the world we live and function in. Since it is created from filtered and manipulated data from the subconscious mind and feedback from the body, it is only an interpretation and isn't real, true, or complete. Outside us is the unmanifested, subtle energy system; inside us is the manifested, interpreted universe of the objective universe of the gross energy system.

Mind: There is no universal agreement for the definition of what a mind is and what its distinguishing properties are, although there is a lengthy tradition of inquiries in philosophy, religion, psychology, and the cognitive sciences (Mind- Wikipedia https://en.wikipedia.org/wiki/Mind). In a nutshell, there is no definition for *mind*. There are many theories, but those are all theories. One point on which there is some agreement is that the mind as such isn't the brain. By convention there are two minds: the conscious mind and the subconscious (or unconscious) mind but this is not known for sure. These two minds don't appear to be connected. Since there is no agreed-on definition, the following will be used in this read:

Conscious Mind: It is the state or quality of awareness. When we talk to ourselves, it is the conscious mind that is talking. It operates and processes data and information at a very slow rate of speed, compared to everything else that is happening in the mind and body. The conscious mind fills the function of the reporter of what is happening in the mind and body, and it doesn't appear to be an active player in what is happening. It tells us some of the things that are going on in the mind and body but not everything, because what is happening in the mind and body is much too fast for the conscious mind to understand. The conscious mind is the least informed and the last to know what is happening. However, because it fills our awareness, we tend to believe it knows all; but it doesn't. The conscious mind processes data at the rate of forty to one hundred bits of data per second, while all other components in the mind and body operate at millions to billions of bits of data per second.

Subconscious Mind (Unconscious Mind): Nothing is known directly about the subconscious mind. It is a "black box." All we know about the subconscious mind has been gained through observation, empirical experimental data, and guesswork, but it's great guesswork by experts in the field of the mind and body, at least sometimes. From that experimental work, there is the theory that the processing capability of the subconscious mind operates between forty billion to four hundred billion bits of data per second, depending on the study referenced. Notwithstanding all the studies, the subconscious mind is still a "black box."

The subconscious mind operates outside our conscious awareness. All our memories, beliefs, experiences, and reference information are stored there. All our programming and habitual behaviors are in and operate out of the subconscious mind. It processes data at least four thousand faster than the information transmitted by the senses, and maybe much faster. Nonetheless, the subconscious mind is basically still a "black box."

Perceptions: This is like a snapshot or screenshot of the constantly changing interpretations in the active mind. Perceptions are what the conscious mind reports to us. We never see or understand all that is happening in the mind and body, and we know only what the conscious mind tells us, which is only a snapshot in time or a perception. By the time the conscious mind presents us with a perception, it has changed.

Senses: Senses are instruments. They transmit information in the form of electromagnetic and chemical data to the subconscious mind. They make no judgments or decisions. They just transmit data. The body houses the sense organs, but the data from the organs goes straight through the body to the subconscious mind. Sense organs themselves are moved by signals from the active mind as commands, based on the active mind's interpretations of data sent to it by the subconscious mind. The body has no idea how to direct and move the sense organs without signals from the active mind. All the senses together transmit data at the rate of about 11 million bits of data per second. Most of our input data comes from the eyes.

Subconscious Mind's Filtering System: The subconscious mind has a hierarchy of memories of importance. What was accepted as true in the mind first has greater value and importance to the subconscious mind than what follows. Memories accepted as true from early childhood are more familiar to the mind; therefore, they are more important to the subconscious mind than current memories. Consequently, data that matches higher-priority memories will be selected easily and first; and then other data we have references for from later in our life.

Data that isn't familiar to the subconscious mind or for which we have no reference information will be modified or filtered out of the stream of data going to the active mind. Negative memories are more important to the subconscious mind than positive memories, because they carry survival signals.

Subtle Energy System: This is the energy system of the unmanifested everything that is just outside us. Since there is nothing new under the sun, everything is there, waiting to be revealed by someone with the right filtering system, set of circumstances, and mind-set. This energy system is called "subtle" because it's just beyond the mind's ability to detect it in the data received from the senses. Out of this system come the eureka moments of opening our imaginations to uncover the unmanifested and make it manifested. It is infinite; and what we take from it and manifest doesn't diminish or disturb it in any way at all, because it will still be infinite. And infinite is always infinite.

Subtle Field: As our senses encounter the outside subtle energy system of everything, we can imagine the subtle energy system as a field we move through with our senses and the interface between body and what we encounter. However, this subtle energy is infinite and goes beyond our awareness and understanding. We may imagine patterns in it, and out of those patterns, we may see systems of order within the infinite; however, the infinite subtle field is beyond patterns and imagined systems of order. Since it's infinite, it isn't just in the outside energy system; it is inside us right now and right down to and beyond our cellular level. It is a field, and as such, it is much like being inside a magnetic energy field that completely engulfs us; and we move in this field like a fish swims in water, except we are embedded and move within the subtle field. The subtle energy system is in this field; the gross energy system is in this field as well. The mind and the body are in it, too. Wherever you look, whatever you touch, smell, hear, or taste, is in the subtle field. It is the Tao of everything and is the unconditional and unknowable source and guiding principle of all and everything.

We may think of the subtle energy system and the subtle field as subatomic particles. Sometimes they're a wave of potential energy, and sometimes they're a particle. The subtle energy system is the particle aspect of the infinite, and the subtle field is the wavy aspect of the infinite.

Thoughts: Most thoughts aren't in words. While we are aware of the conscious mind communicating in word language, most communication in the rest of the mind or body is nonverbal. Thoughts are primarily electromagnetic or chemical forms that continually stream throughout the mind and body at millions to billions of bits of data per second. Language isn't needed to form thoughts and communication in the mind and body. Language is a learned secondary skill and the communication we are aware of consciously.

Unconscious Mind: See "Mind," then "Subconscious Mind."

AFTERWORD

I am left with the conclusion that our pain and suffering rest in the mind and then are felt as a response in the body. Notwithstanding there may be some outliers or anomalies to the following statement, however. The mind determines what goes on in the body. Outside events or situations are neutral and meaningless in and of themselves. Not until the event or situation is thought about in the active mind is meaning given to it by the mind's interpretation; and that is an inside job. It is done inside the mind. With that understanding, everything outside us is meaningless and unmanifested until we think about it.

This isn't meant to infer that pain and suffering aren't real for the individual experiencing them, because the body is giving feedback that it's in trouble. However, the effect in the body is the result of what is happening in the causal mind; therefore, the body isn't the primary cause of how it feels or why. It's responding the way it is because of the mind's interpretation. *(Now, don't get hung up because the conscious mind tells you the feeling is in the body. You now know that your conscious mind is too damn slow to know where your pain and suffering are really coming from.)*

I know it isn't a popular understanding that all our pain and suffering come from the mind, because we like the old paradigm that basically says, "You aren't accountable for your pain and suffering." We would like to believe that our problems are outside us; or they are the body's fault. How popular that belief is. However, we need to call a spade a spade and quit hiding the truth under conventional social correctness of not wanting to offend the offender. I'm saying it plainly here; those who are ill, aren't blameless of their own illness. We always get what we ask for. We should be aware that our pain and suffering is related to personal lifestyle choices. This is especially true with chronic illness.

Oh, now don't let your ego get bruised. This has been known for a long time, but we usually don't say it aloud. However, we know by many studies that 80 to 90 percent of all doctor's office calls are because of "stress." *Stress* is an engineering term doctors and psychologists have borrowed. From an engineering perspective, stress is an external force, acting on a system or organism. But when applied to the body, the body doesn't respond to the outside. It responds only to the mind. It is the mind's interpretations that signal the body on how to respond, and those signals force the body to respond with what we call "my pain and suffering." I know when you go to the doctor that you believe you are in the 10 percent group that has a real illness, not just self-created stress. But statistically, you're not. You have some self-induced stressful condition in your lifestyle. If you change your lifestyle, the condition will disappear or at least moderate to a lower state of pain and suffering. If you don't change your lifestyle, you will be in bondage to the medical system and medications for a long time.

Generally, 5 percent or less of all illness is genetic. Genes express themselves through the process of epigenetics or control above the gene. Basically, all new studies indicate that it's the cells that determine what genes will be expressed. This is because of the cell's interpretation of its external environment or signals sent by the active mind through the toxicity of the blood. The cell's external environment is the blood, which is the medium the active mind uses to signal the body of its stressful interpretations, and the body uses that to give feedback to the active mind of all the systems it has changed to deal with the stressful situation to survive. The blood can get pretty toxic and muddy. It might cause the cells to call up genes that, while not good for the body, make perfect sense to the struggling cells trying to survive.

Why is the blood toxic? It's because of what is going on in the mind. We all have wild and crazy genes wrapped around histones in our DNA inside our chromosomes in each of our cells. However, it's what is going on in the mind that determines their expression in the cells. And the poor body will again take the fall for what the mind is doing. Your egoic self, which is integrated into your belief system of who you think you are, will tell you all kinds of things to stay alive. If you change—change your lifestyle, change your beliefs, and heal your negative memories—the current ego must die. So your ego can be very persuasive, and you will more than likely believe your ego and continue to point your bony finger at your poor body as the cause of your pain and suffering. The body is trying its damnedest to stay alive and healthy, and it is doing what it's told to do. And who tells it what to do? The active mind. It always gets back to the mind. Whose mind? Your mind.

I know I'm being hard on you here at the end of this read in hinting quite openly that your pain and suffering are self-induced in most cases. Why do you think I would do that? Perhaps you think, *He is probably trying to bring to my new awareness and my attention that I'm doing it to myself so I can wake up and change the way I look at things, and this will change the things I look at. And maybe I can change the lens of the past and see a new and better world.* Eventually everything comes to pass. Eventually what you want will come to you. However, to have that happen as quickly as possible, you need to do something. You need to change your mind.

There is a little-known booklet published by the Foundation for Inner Peace in 1976. This is the same foundation that publishes *A Course in Miracles*. The booklet is titled *Psychotherapy: Purpose, Process and Practice*. The first three sentences in the booklet state, "Psychotherapy is the only form of therapy there is. Since only the mind can be sick, only the mind can be healed. Only the mind is in need of healing."

Be gentle with yourself on your journey of uncovering who you are. Peace.

Conversation with a Stranger
(How True)

"Walk with me awhile. For we seem to be moving in the same direction. Your stride and rhythm are much like mine. So walk with me awhile?"

"But," I said, "you have no legs with which to walk."

"How true," he said.

"Well then, stay with me awhile for we look much alike. I see you have a questioning air in your appearance, a look that questions all."

"But," I said, "you have not eyes with which to see."

"How true," he said.

"Then will you not talk with me awhile, that we may share our thoughts and grow in wisdom by our sharing?"

"But," I said, "you have not lips or mouth to form the words, and no sound do I hear."

"How true," he said.

"Then let us break bread and drink together and let the fragrant breeze bring the world to us, for the slightest breeze can stir understanding."

"But," I said, "you haven't nose with which to capture the scent on the wind."

"How true," he said.

"At least hold me in your arms that I may touch your heart and you may know me?"

And as I opened my arms I said, "I know you, friend. You are my own true self that waits behind the walls of my illusions."

"How true, how true," he said.

Michael Faff, January 14, 1995